Demography, State and Society

*In loving memory of my mother
and with love to Kathryn*

Demography, State and Society

Irish Migration to Britain, 1921–1971

Enda Delaney

LIVERPOOL UNIVERSITY PRESS

First published 2000 by
Liverpool University Press
4 Cambridge Street
Liverpool
L69 7ZU

Copyright © Enda Delaney 2000

All rights reserved. No part of this book may be reproduced, stored in a retrieval
system, or transmitted, in any form or by any means, electronic, mechanical,
photocopying, recording or otherwise without the prior written permission of the
publishers.

British Library Cataloguing-in-Publication Data
A British Library CIP record is available

ISBN 0 85323 735 2 *cased*
     0 85323 745 X *paperback*

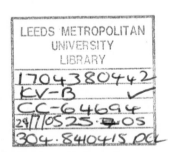

LEEDS METROPOLITAN
UNIVERSITY
LIBRARY

1704380442
KV-B
CC-64694
29/7/05 25.2.05
304.840415 DEL

Typeset by Northern Phototypesetting Co. Ltd, Bolton, UK
Printed and bound in the European Union by Bell and Bain Ltd, Glasgow

Contents

Tables

Figures

Acknowledgements

During the course of the preparation of this book many debts have been incurred. First and foremost, my sincere thanks are due to Professor Liam Kennedy, who supervised the original PhD thesis on which this book is based, for his intellectual stimulation, support, enthusiasm and gentle guidance. Dr Alun Davies, head of the Department of Economic and Social History at The Queen's University of Belfast until 1996, placed much faith in my ability, as did the late Mr David S. Johnson, who was equally supportive at all times.

The Institute of Irish Studies at The Queen's University of Belfast elected me to a fellowship in 1998–99 which enabled me to complete the typescript in a congenial and friendly environment. My thanks go to the Director, Professor Brian M. Walker, and all the staff and fellows, especially Catherine Boone and Catherine McColgan. In recent times, colleagues in the School of Modern History at Queen's, especially Professor Bruce Campbell and the Head of School, Professor Ian Green, have created an atmosphere in which the value of scholarship is recognised in the face of increasing other demands on limited time and energy.

At the National University of Ireland, Maynooth, where I completed my earlier historical training and was, more recently, a member of the academic staff, I should like to acknowledge the assistance of Dr Denise Dunne who supervised my MA thesis, and Dr Colm Lennon who carefully nurtured my interest in history as an undergraduate and who has since remained a source of inspiration. Professor Vincent Comerford, my mentor for nearly ten years, has been at all times a valuable fount of wise counsel and support, and he has retained a close interest in my development as a historian.

The research on which this book is based was funded by a postgraduate award from the School of Social Sciences at The Queen's

University of Belfast, and my particular thanks go to Professor John E. Spencer, formerly School Director, who has taken a close personal interest in my research. Research in London was funded by a Sir Michael Postan Award from the London School of Economics and a very generous gift from my aunt, Una Buggy.

Scholars who have provided advice on my research include Professors D. H. Akenson, L. A. Clarkson, Colin Holmes and Russell King, and Dr Michel Peillon. Dudley Baines provoked many original and intriguing lines of inquiry in relation to the historical study of migration. The completion of this book owes much to the influence and infectious enthusiasm of Dr Donald MacRaild. Dr Carla King read parts of the original PhD thesis as did Dr Kevin Conway and both made useful comments and suggestions. Dr Mary Ann Lyons and Dr Adrian Kelly read most of the original thesis in draft and provided detailed criticisms which improved the work greatly. Other scholars and friends provided crucial support at different times over the years and I should like to mention in particular Dr Fergus Campbell, Katrina Goldstone, Dr Gerard Keown, Dr Fearghal McGarry, Dr Breandán MacSuibhne, Pauline Mooney, Matthew O'Brien and Dr Seán O'Connell. Robin Bloxsidge of Liverpool University Press has been a model publisher at all times.

Some of the material in this book was previously published in *Irish Political Studies*, vol. 13, 1998, pp. 25–49, *Archivium Hibernicum*, vol. 52, 1998, pp. 98–114 and *Immigrants and Minorities*, vol. 18, nos 2 and 3, July/November 1999, pp. 240–65. I thank the editors for giving me permission to reuse this material here.

Finally, this work is dedicated to two powerful influences on my life. My late mother, Marie Delaney, fostered in me a precocious curiosity about history and public affairs. It is a source of deep regret that she did not live to see all of her efforts come to fruition in this book. Kathryn Doyle, with whom I have found true happiness, has deeply influenced the way in which I see many things, not least being the value of love and friendship.

Enda Delaney
Belfast

Glossary of Irish terms

Term	Literal translation	
An Foras Talúntais	Agricultural Institute	
Clann na Poblachta	the republican family	a republican/ socialist political party
Cumann na nGaedheal	society of the Irish	a political party of the period 1922–33
Dáil	assembly	lower house of the Irish parliament
Éire	Ireland	
Fianna Fáil	soldiers of destiny	Ireland's largest political party
Fine Gael	family of the Irish	Ireland's second largest political party
Muintir na Tíre	people of the land	a rural development organisation
Tánaiste	second, heir, successor	deputy prime minister
Taoiseach	chief, leader	prime minister

This glossary is based on J. H. Whyte, *Church and state in modern Ireland, 1923–1970*, 1st edn, Dublin, 1971, pp. xi–xii.

Abbreviations

Agric. Hist. Rev.	*Agricultural History Review*
Commission on Emigration, *Reports*	Commission on Emigration and Other Population Problems, 1948–54, *Reports* [1955], Pr. 2541
Comp. Stud. Soc. & Hist.	*Comparative Studies in Society and History*
Econ. Hist. Rev.	*Economic History Review*
Econ. Soc. Rev.	*Economic and Social Review*
ESRI	Economic and Social Research Institute
Geog. J.	*Geographical Journal*
Hist. J.	*Historical Journal*
IHS	*Irish Historical Studies*
IMR	*International Migration Review*
Ir. Econ. & Soc. Hist.	*Irish Economic and Social History*
Ir. Geog.	*Irish Geography*
Ir. J. Agr. Econ. Rur. Soc.	*Irish Journal of Agricultural Economics and Rural Sociology*
J. Econ. Hist.	*Journal of Economic History*
J. Eur. Econ. Hist.	*Journal of European Economic History*
J. Hist. Geog.	*Journal of Historical Geography*
JRSS	*Journal of the Royal Statistical Society*
JSSISI	*Journal of the Statistical and Social Inquiry Society of Ireland*
NESC	National Economic and Social Council
Scan. Econ. Hist. Rev.	*Scandinavian Economic History Review*
Trans. Inst. Brit. Geog.	*Transactions of the Institute of British Geographers*

Archives

NAI	National Archives of Ireland
NLI	National Library of Ireland
PRO	Public Record Office, Kew
TCD	Manuscripts Department, Trinity College, Dublin
UCDA	Archives Department, University College, Dublin

Records

AVIA	Ministry of Aircraft Production
CAB	Cabinet Office
DFA	Department of External Affairs
D. Ind. & Comm.	Department of Industry and Commerce
DO	Dominions Office
DT	Department of the Taoiseach
HO	Home Office
ICTU	Irish Congress of Trade Unions
LAB	Ministry of Labour

Introduction

The distinguished Irish statistician, R. C. Geary, once recounted a story that told of when an eighth-century Irish poet, Sedulius, arrived at a monastery on the continent. The abbot, Strabo, musing as to why Sedulius had left Ireland, asked 'whether it was due to the unsettled state of the country or the Irish habit of going away'.[1] This 'Irish habit of going away' perceptively identified by Strabo is a central feature of modern Irish demographic history until the present day, and this is particularly the case for the period after the Great Irish Famine (1845–50). The sheer volume of scholarly literature on Irish migration since the early eighteenth century is a testament to the enduring interest in the subject. However, one lacuna in the current state of knowledge relates to Irish migration to Britain between 1921 and 1971, one of the most significant flows of migrants in twentieth-century Europe.

The aim of this book is to remedy this deficiency. The principal objectives of the study are threefold: firstly, to examine the patterns in Irish migration to Britain from 1921 until 1971; secondly, to investigate the factors which account for this migration; and finally, to assess the policy of both the British and Irish states in relation to large-scale movement between the two countries. While the structure is basically chronological, within each chapter a thematic approach is adopted. Certain themes recur throughout, such as the role of the state in facilitating or hindering migration, the relationship between population movement and the standard of living (broadly defined) in Ireland and Britain, and factors that contributed to high levels of migration from particular regions. However, the examination of these main themes is complemented by a discussion of a range of secondary themes, such as the gender dimension to Irish migration, the relationship between religious denomination and patterns of Irish migration, and the reaction of the various churches in Ireland to the large-scale movement of members of their flocks to Britain. Aspects of the migrant experience are also explored, drawing heavily on oral testimony. While the focus is undoubtedly national, regional patterns of migration are necessarily examined in some detail.

A comment on some of the terms used throughout this book may be helpful at this point. Demography is the scientific study of population, a discipline which developed over the course of the twentieth century. The term 'migration' refers to the 'movement of individuals or groups which involves a permanent or semi-permanent change of usual residence', normally for a specified period of time and across an administrative boundary.[2] Our principal concern in this study is with migration from the Irish state rather than with internal migration. 'Emigration', the 'process of international migration viewed from the standpoint of the nation from which the movement occurs', was the term used extensively by contemporaries in Ireland and on occasions this designation is employed.[3] In political and popular discourse 'emigration' was associated with negative connotations and it was more often than not viewed as a pernicious feature of Irish society. It should also be noted that our concern here is with the 26 counties that from 1921 constituted the Irish Free State (Éire from 1937) and later the Irish Republic (from 1949 onwards). The term 'Ireland' is used in the text as a convenient shorthand for this political unit and thus does not refer to Northern Ireland. Migration from Northern Ireland, it may well be argued, is best examined within the wider context of the history of the United Kingdom labour market. There is clearly plenty of scope for a specific study grounded firmly in primary sources of migration patterns between Northern Ireland and the rest of the United Kingdom. Of especial interest would be the period of the Second World War when workers from Northern Ireland were transferred to Britain.[4] Some assessment of the movement of population from Northern Ireland to Britain is contained in Isles and Cuthbert's massive economic survey first published in 1957.[5] Research findings based on data for the 1970s and 1980s demonstrate the persistence of this trend and it is surely desirable that a comprehensive study of this movement of population should be undertaken.[6] In addition, whilst migration from the Irish Free State to Northern Ireland is referred to in the course of this study, the main focus will be on the destination of the majority of Irish migrants throughout this period, that is, Britain rather than the United Kingdom in general.

The long time range of this study is a result of a number of considerations. In the first instance, demographic patterns unlike political events are not discernible or easily categorised within short time spans. Whereas it may be possible to analyse the phenomenon in meticulous detail for an intercensal decade, inevitably this perspective is far too narrow. Secondly, Irish migration in the twentieth century is more usually associated with the postwar period, although it will demonstrated later that the genesis of the large-scale movement after 1945 can be found in the earlier patterns of migration, particularly the outflow during the Second World War. Finally, whilst periods of high rates of net migration are without doubt of interest to the historian, it is equally important to examine the years when the migration flow was but a trickle compared with earlier and later time periods.

The book is founded upon a wide range of sources, both published and unpublished. The statistical data are for the most part derived from the censuses of population. For the period prior to 1952, a vast amount of statistical information is available in the *Reports* of the Commission on Emigration and Other Population Problems, 1948–54.[7] Equally valuable sources of statistical information are the files of government departments that are available on both sides of the Irish Sea. In terms of quantitative demographic history, even though some relatively simple methods of population analysis are employed, such as cohort depletion, this book does not claim to be breaking new ground in advancing sophisticated technical models or developing innovative methods of tracing migration histories, such as those associated with the present generation of demographic historians.[8] Rather, what is relatively unusual about this book is the synthesis of diverse forms and spheres of historical investigation with demographic, social, political and cultural history all being represented to a significant degree. Clearly much of the analysis of the patterns of Irish migration has to be statistical in nature and it is also instructive to evaluate the different types of statistical data available. Quantitative findings in isolation can be quite revealing, but it is an integral feature of this study that statistical data are aligned with the documentary sources in order to construct a rounded assessment of migration from independent Ireland.

In terms of manuscript material, one of the most novel aspects of this study is the synthesis of findings from a corpus of unpublished official records generated by both the Irish and British states. This body of archival documents relating to Irish migration has not been exploited to date by researchers. Drawing on this evidence, this study outlines in some detail for the first time the policies adopted by the state in both Ireland and Britain to the flow of migrants between the two countries. During the Second World War, the development of policy *vis-à-vis* migration is of particular interest as a degree of co-operation existed which facilitated Irish citizens wishing to travel to Britain to take up employment in wartime industries. Other collections of little used manuscript material, such as the papers of a member of the Commission on Emigration, Arnold Marsh, deposited in the library of Trinity College, Dublin, shed much new light on aspects of the history of twentieth-century Irish migration.[9]

Migration does not occur within a vacuum and it is therefore crucial that the responses of a broad spectrum of public opinion are outlined. Population decline was associated with 'emigration', and in the postwar period this was the subject of much public debate – and political rancour – in Ireland. Many non-official printed sources such as newspapers, journals and periodicals are employed in order to assess the reaction across a diverse range of interested parties including the clergy of the Roman Catholic church in Ireland, members of the intellectual élite and political leaders to the phenomenon of large-scale Irish migration to Britain. Taken together with reports of government-appointed commissions and committees of inquiry, it has been possible to attempt a nuanced and balanced assessment of Irish public opinion. Recent published work such as that undertaken by Quine and others has illustrated the complex relationship between population issues and politics throughout Europe.[10] The present study adds to that expanding area of historical interest by examining the role of migration in Irish political discourse. The Irish state was called upon on numerous occasions to put in place policies that would 'stem the flow'. Of course, it was relatively straightforward to condemn the 'evils of emigration'; outlining concrete policies that might reduce the level of migration from independent Ireland was an altogether different and much more complex matter.

The reaction in Britain to the flow of Irish migrants is a particularly interesting element of this study. A difficulty exists, in that, apart from a fleeting time during the interwar period, Irish migration attracted relatively little public interest and Irish migrants in twentieth-century Britain were to a certain degree 'invisible' in the minds of contemporaries.[11] Notwithstanding this obstacle, some assessment is made of the reaction to Irish migration to Britain, dealing in particular with official attitudes. In the postwar period, the policy of the

British government in relation to Irish migrants is contrasted with the reaction to immigrants from the 'New Commonwealth'. Undoubtedly a comprehensive account of the Irish in Britain between 1921 and 1971 would involve another complete study. However, some effort is made here to outline the principal characteristics of the Irish-born population in Britain in terms of settlement patterns, occupational profile and, to a lesser extent, experiences of life in Britain. In the post-war period in particular, numerous contemporary studies touch on the Irish in Britain and it is possible to identify a number of the problems faced by Irish migrants.

Throughout this book, a wide range of sources relating to Irish migration and broader theories of international migration are used to contextualise and substantiate conclusions made in the course of the analysis presented here. The discussion is also underpinned by a knowledge of global migration patterns and especially migration within postwar Europe. Often, Ireland's exceptionalism in demographic matters is argued on the basis of ignorance of the conditions that prevailed elsewhere.[12] Throughout this book reference will be made to comparative patterns of migration. In addition, this study makes a contribution, not only to the history of Irish migration, but also to migration studies more generally. The movement of population from underdeveloped economies to industrialised countries is an overarching feature of modern economic development and the migrant flow from Ireland to Britain is a particularly revealing example of this phenomenon. Even though our main concern is with Irish migration, this study raises issues that are of significance for the broad field of migration history.

NOTES

1 This story is taken from Damian Hannan, *Rural exodus: a study of the forces influencing the large-scale migration of Irish youth*, London, 1970, p. 29.

2 Roland Pressat, *Dictionary of demography*, ed. Christopher Wilson, Oxford, 1985, pp. 82–83.

3 Ibid., p. 69.

4 Phylis Inman, *Labour in the munitions industries*, London, 1957, pp. 173–74.

5 K. S. Isles and Norman Cuthbert, *An economic survey of Northern Ireland*, Belfast, 1957, pp. 239–64.

6 Frank Forsythe and Vani K. Borooah, 'The nature of migration between Northern Ireland and Great Britain: a preliminary analysis based on the labour force surveys, 1986–88', *Econ. Soc. Rev.*, vol. 23, 1992, pp. 105–27; Paul Compton, 'Migration trends for Northern Ireland: links with Great Britain', in *Migration processes and patterns, II: population redistribution in the United Kingdom*, ed. John Stillwell, Philip Rees and Peter Boden, London, 1992.

7 Dublin, 1955, Pr. 2541.

8 See, for example, D. S. Reher and Roger Schofield, eds, *New and old methods in historical demography*, Oxford, 1993.

9 TCD, Marsh papers, MS 8297–8401.

10 Maria Sophia Quine, *Population politics in twentieth-century Europe*, London, 1996; Carl Ipsen, *Dictating demography: the problem of population in fascist Italy*, Cambridge, 1996.

11 For the 'invisibility' of the Irish in postwar Britain, see Bronwen Walter, 'Irishness, gender, and place', *Environment and planning, part D: society and space*, Vol. 13, 1995, p. 36.

12 For a more detailed discussion of this issue, see Enda Delaney, 'Placing postwar Irish migration to Britain in a comparative European perspective, 1945–81', in *The Irish diaspora*, ed. Andy Bielenberg, London, pp. 331–56.

1

Perspectives on Irish migration

The historical study of migration from Ireland is striking in that little or no heed is paid to the vast and burgeoning literature on possible theoretical frameworks which attempt to explain and understand this phenomenon in many analyses – both historical and contemporary – of Irish migration. Even though Irish migration would appear on first inspection to conform to general models of migration which view the movement of people as part of the natural process whereby labour is directed to those areas or regions that require large numbers of people to sustain economic growth, this is far from the complete story. Equally Irish migration may well also be interpreted as a flow of people from the periphery to the economic core zones of the United States, Britain and other diverse places, which reinforced the uneven nature of capitalist economic development in the nineteenth and twentieth centuries. Needless to say no one all-encompassing model neatly explains migration from modern Ireland. However, the benefits in reviewing theoretical approaches to the study of migration are twofold. Firstly, migration theory raises many intriguing lines of inquiry, and the principal objective of this chapter is to illustrate briefly the scope and range of migration theory and in doing so to assess the possibilities of its application to the evidence available for twentieth-century Ireland. Secondly, the existence of this body of research underlines the obvious point that migration is a global process that has shaped the evolution of most societies in the modern world, albeit to varying degrees.[1] This universal phenomenon has been the subject of extensive inquiry and research by scholars working in the distinct fields of economics, history, geography, population studies and sociology. In recent years migration theory has developed in a multidisciplinary framework, rather than remaining purely within the strictly demarcated confines of economic and social history, labour economics or demography.[2] Many of the issues which are discussed in this book concern scholars researching migration in other geographical contexts and time periods. In addition, the main patterns and features of Irish migration in the nineteenth and early twentieth centuries are briefly outlined – more detailed studies are numerous and readily available elsewhere – in order to provide the necessary historical background for the following chapters.

I

The starting point for any assessment of migration theory still remains Ravenstein's classic formulation, his 'laws of migration', first postulated in the 1880s.[3] Few studies have displayed such an enduring quality, although this 'classic' genre of a formal rigid model of migration has been superseded by more recent research which draws on a number of disciplinary backgrounds.[4] Nevertheless, Ravenstein's 'laws' merit consideration since they make for a useful starting point for an analysis which ostensibly views migration as being primarily concerned with the migrant as a rational economic actor who 'responded to discernible pressures so as to maximise advantage and minimise discomfort'.[5] Grigg has conveniently summarised Ravenstein's 'laws' (see Figure 1.1).

Even the most cursory perusal of these 'laws' indicates the primacy of economic explanations for migration. Undoubtedly, the applicability of this set of propositions varies over time and space; for instance, the patterns of nineteenth-century Irish migration would seem to conform generally to some of the 'laws' (2, 3, 4, 5, 7 and 10) and deviate from others (1 and 6). The paucity of published research on internal migration in Ireland during the nineteenth century, comparable in range to that of Baines on England and Wales, results in a difficulty when assessing a number of the 'laws'.[6] The data on which Ravenstein bases his hypotheses – birthplace statistics for the second half of the nineteenth century – also circumscribe the applicability of the propositions. Ravenstein's concentration on the economic motives underlying migration is closely associated with 'push-pull' models of migration, the most frequently cited explanation for the decision of an individual to migrate. 'Push' factors are generally regarded as being in essence economic (dearth of employment opportunities, low wages, population pressure), and the 'pull' factors (higher standards of living,

1 The majority of migrants go only a short distance.

2 Migration proceeds step by step.

3 Migrants going long distances generally go by preference to one of the great centres of commerce or industry.

4 Each current of migration produces a compensating counter-current.

5 The natives of towns are less migratory than those of rural areas.

6 Females are more migratory than males within the kingdom of their birth, but males more frequently venture beyond.

7 Most migrants are adults: families rarely migrate out of their country of birth.

8 Large towns grow more by migration than by natural increase.

9 Migration increases in volume as industries and commerce develop and transport improves.

10 The major direction of migration is from the agricultural areas to the centre of industry and commerce.

11 The major causes of migration are economic.

Source: D. B. Grigg, 'E. G. Ravenstein and the "laws of migration"', *J. Hist. Geog.*, Vol. 3, 1977, pp. 42–43.

Fig. 1.1 *Ravenstein's 'laws of migration'*

increased opportunities, lure of urban centres), whilst including some cultural and social aspects, clearly underline the economic considerations in the mind of the migrant. Lee's influential contribution to migration theory is perhaps one of the more sophisticated attempts at the development of a set of hypotheses loosely based on the 'push-pull' model.[7] One of the problems with the 'push-pull' model is the uncertainty relating to the relative importance of 'push' factors *vis-à-vis* 'pull' factors. Baines rightly argues that 'the majority of emigrants would have been unable to make so fine a distinction if asked', and consequently that this model 'is a crude approximation of the actual factors that may have influenced the decision to emigrate'.[8]

Economists and economic historians, drawing on variations of the 'push-pull' model, have elaborated complex and technical models of migration, based on the a priori assumption that the fluctuations and changes in the labour market, in either the sending or receiving society, explain rates of migration. This approach, which has been embraced particularly by economic historians, implicitly assumes that the rationality of the migration decision is, to some extent, beyond doubt. A volume of essays edited by Hatton and Williamson provides detailed evidence of the relationship between migration and wage rates, but also raises a number of hitherto neglected considerations. According to the editors, the data on emigration rates for Europe after 1830 demonstrate that differing rates across countries and through time 'can be explained by a common framework and by reference to a surprisingly small number of economic and demographic variables'.[9] These variables include the ratio of home to receiving country wages, the rate of natural increase lagged 20 years – since differences in natural increase in the population cohort regarded most prone to migration would affect migration rates – and finally, the proportion of the labour force engaged in agriculture. Based on data from Latin countries (Spain, Portugal and Italy), Hatton and Williamson concluded that 'urbanisation and industrialisation tend to raise the rate of emigration after controlling for other factors', but perhaps of more consequence, they found that 'the rate of natural increase two decades earlier has a powerful and significant impact on emigration'.[10] This is a suggestion that obviously requires further testing with data from elsewhere. Unsurprisingly, the contrast in wage rates between the sending and destination societies is also shown to have a significant impact on migration rates.

A key assumption in much of the economic work on migration and the various 'push-pull' models of migration is the flow of information, regarding wage levels or other economic and social conditions, from the receiving country to the sending society. By its very nature, information, as such, is not conveniently quantifiable, and therefore this factor may pose a serious challenge to the validity of explanations of migration chiefly constructed in economic terms. To assume that migrants had detailed information about their prospective destination is, at best, a naïve starting point, yet it was only either a foolhardy migrant or one seeking refuge from distress of some form (famine, religious persecution, etc.) who would have left their home country without at least some information on the conditions in the prospective receiving society. One possible way of measuring the impact of the information flow on migration rates is to examine the 'diffusion' effects of migrants' experiences. Gould has suggested that the higher migration rates experienced by southern and eastern Europe at the beginning of the twentieth century can be attributed to 'the progress of the diffusion of emigration in potentially emigration-prone areas', and he places a strong emphasis on the role of 'feedback' from migrants.[11] However, Faini and Venturini argue that the diffusion effects were in fact quite limited in Italy and, drawing on a detailed analysis of the factors underlying Italian emigration in the period from 1861 until 1913, they posit that the economic conditions 'at home and in the main destination countries were instrumental in favouring the surge of migrations after 1900'.[12] Clearly, the diffusion effect of the experiences of migrants was a factor in the decision to migrate, although the economic conditions in the sending country also played an important part in influencing the deliberations of the prospective migrant.

The information factor is without doubt of great consequence when embarking on an analysis of migration patterns. One possible method of estimating the amount and quality of information percolating back to the sending society is the examination of emigrants' letters, since invariably migrants will convey some detail on the destination society. Collections of letters used by Erickson, Thomas and Znaniecki, amongst many others, point to the fact that observations on the economic situation did form part of the content of the correspondence emanating from the receiving society.[13] However, as has been noted by Baines, these collections relate 'only to a minute proportion of European emigrants'.[14] None the less, content analysis of emigrants' letters does allow an insight into the volume and nature of the information flowing between the receiving and sending societies. For instance, Schrier highlights the effects of letters on the dynamic of Irish migration to the United States in the second half of the nineteenth century.[15] Fitzpatrick's collection of a series of letters sent by nineteenth-century Irish migrants in Australia to relatives and friends at home reveals that emigrants' letters do contain comments on wages, work and opportunities and the all-important news from faraway places.[16] In many cases, emigrants' letters were coloured by the bias of the author and on occasions motivated by a desire to encourage other

LEEDS METROPOLITAN UNIVERSITY LIBRARY

family members to take the plunge, as it were; yet the readers may have obtained sound and useful information which was subsequently a factor in the decision to migrate since the inherent risks involved in such a move were lessened.

Another source of information for prospective migrants was returned emigrants who were able to proffer – solicited or unsolicited – advice and guidance.[17] Return migration is notoriously difficult to investigate since the distinction between temporary and permanently returned emigrants is an arbitrary one. During the second half of the nineteenth century and the early part of the twentieth century, the return migration rates to many European countries increased, although a higher rate of return is evident for southern and eastern Europe.[18] Wyman has documented in some detail this pattern of return movement, and it seems disingenuous to argue that this ready and accessible pool of information regarding wages, experiences and opportunities did not influence migration rates to some extent.[19] Curiously, Irish return migration rates from the United States for the nineteenth century were quite low in comparison with other ethnic groups.[20] Miller and 't Hart have demonstrated the limited effects that these returned emigrants had on nineteenth-century Irish society, although the information offered to prospective migrants remains to be fully investigated.[21] During the twentieth century, and more particularly in the postwar period with increased and cheaper routes of transport across the Irish Sea, the numbers of return migrants exceeded 't Hart's estimate of 10 per cent for the second half of the nineteenth century.[22] Drawing on the country of birth data in the census reports, Garvey found that in the 1960s the substantial net loss of 183,000 Irish-born persons was 'partly offset by a net gain of over 50,000 persons born outside Ireland, about 32,000 of whom were under 15 years of age and born in Great Britain', which demonstrates that Irish migrants were returning with their families.[23] Anecdotal evidence of temporary return visits by migrants in the 1940s and 1950s for holidays is recorded in the well-known autobiographies of Donall Mac Amhlaigh and John O'Donoghue, and the image of the 'successful' migrant in the local community must have been a factor affecting the decision of those considering migrating to Britain in the postwar period.[24] One contemporary in the late 1940s alluded to the impact of migrants at home on holidays: 'The lure of England, emphasised by the "grand" appearance of the returned emigrant when they came home for their holidays, was a main factor [sic] [in influencing] the level of migration'.[25]

A relatively recent development in the myriad theories of international migration is a focus on the decision-making processes of collective groupings such as the family or household, rather than on the decisions taken by individuals to migrate. This body of theory, which is loosely categorised as the 'new economics of migration', underlines the point that migration of some members of a family or household diversifies risk by ensuring that, whilst some family members remain in the local economy, others are dispatched to work in other regions or countries.[26] Should some disaster befall the local agricultural economy, the household or family would thereby have migrant remittances as a source of indirect income.[27] This proposition has important ramifications for migration research in that wage differentials become of far less consequence, since 'households may have strong incentives to diversify risks through transnational movement even in the absence of wage differentials'.[28] An equally important element of the 'new economics of migration' is the use of the concept of 'relative deprivation' in explaining migration. According to this theory, people assess their own 'deprived' position in the economic hierarchy relative to the reference grouping around them, usually the local community. In theory, if a household feels 'deprived' in comparison with their neighbours this will result in a migrant leaving their home area in order to obtain a source of income that will improve the economic status of the household as a whole through remittances.[29] Much of this theory was developed for analyses of contemporary migration patterns from developing countries. Nevertheless, there are some intriguing lines of inquiry in relation to a historical context. For instance, it may well be argued that households in rural Ireland adopted a strategy whereby remittances from family members in Britain or the United States not only enhanced the economic well-being of the household as a whole, but also ensured that even with a downturn in the rather precarious agricultural economy, the family had a source of independent income. In particular, the stress on the behaviour of households rather than individuals offers a useful and innovative framework for analysing migration, counterbalancing the excessive concentration on the individual migration 'decision'.

II

With the notable exception of the 'new economics of migration', the analyses of migration discussed thus far invariably centre on the decision to migrate being an individual choice facing the prospective migrant, whilst also linking the decision to leave a particular area to fluctuations and changes in the labour market in both the sending and destination society. The other body of work completed in the past 30 years or so is that which examines migration within the framework of a sociological phenomenon. The central tenet of this work is that migration is an element of social change since 'the social structure and cultural system both of places of origin and of destination are affected by migration and in turn affect the migrant'.[30] Some historians have implicitly embraced this approach by seeking explanations for the movement of population in the social and economic structure of the sending society and elaborating on the effects of the influx of migrants on the 'host' society. A common feature of recent migration theory emanating from the social sciences is that it tends to be generally historical in approach, 'not in the sense of dealing with the distant past, but rather in paying appropriate attention to the changing specificities of time and space'.[31] Therefore, while the decision to migrate may be the most apparent cause of migration, other more fundamental factors, 'which predetermine the choice situation [and] are specific events which have brought the migrant to the point of the decision', must also be examined.[32] These factors include considerations such as whether a tradition of migration exists in a household, local community or region, or changes in the social or economic structure such as, for instance, agricultural mechanisation which reduces the demand for farm labour. Yet clearly the factors at work on a structural level did not result in every person migrating from a particular area. Hence, the question of differential migration arises: what determines at a societal level who goes and who stays? Age, sex, social class, family and kin structure, migrant networks, educational attainment and level of aspiration both in terms of income and occupation have been suggested as possible explanations for structural differentials in migration rates, although obviously the weighting given to each factor depends on the particular circumstances. This also raises the issue of explaining non-migration, which is a fundamental challenge for historians of migration, and one that is too often neglected in many analyses. In order to understand and explain migration, it is crucial that the reasons why the majority of people did not leave be explored, since this was clearly the case in countries throughout western Europe.

Whilst much of the research completed by sociologists has concentrated on assessing migration within the wider process of socio-cultural change, the effects of large-scale migration on the send-ing society are still the subject of well-informed conjecture. Few schol-ars have risen to the challenge of Scott who argued in 1960 that 'the departure of large numbers of people is not likely to produce sweeping social change', although socio-cultural change will be brought about if contact is 'maintained with the emigrants in their new environment'.[33] To apply this to the situation in postwar Ireland, it is frequently sug-gested that migration to Britain provided a 'safety-value', obviating the consequent social unrest that would occur in theory if large numbers of dissatisfied – and unemployed – persons remained in Ireland.[34] Thus it may be speculated on the basis of the Irish evidence that the continu-ous migration of persons influenced to some degree the prevailing ethos of a society, since rural Ireland in the postwar period was not characterised by radical unrest and it is generally regarded that it was conservative in outlook. The labour militancy that MacDonald noted in areas of rural Italy in his long-range review of possible responses to rural poverty in Italy during the nineteenth and early twentieth cen-turies is not evident to any significant degree in the Irish Republic.[35]

The effects that migrants have had on the destination society are the subject of extensive research by sociologists, with an emphasis on the reception, absorption, assimilation and integration of migrants. However, the traditional interpretation has focused on the issues of assimilation and integration and only in recent times have sociologists turned their attention to the resistance to adaptation, including possi-ble conflict, due to a desire to adopt in a selective manner the cultural and social norms of the 'host' society.[36] This resistance to embracing the norms of the 'host' society is related to ethnicity: 'a way of giving specific meaning to a distinction conferred by membership of an eth-nic background'.[37] The acceptance by the 'host' society of ethnic group formation varies depending on each particular country, and as Castles and Miller argue, the development of an ethnic identity has led to marginalisation and exclusion in some cases, such as that of Turkish migrants in Germany in the postwar period.[38] Questions of ethnic identity have also been linked to those of class and 'race', especially in the work of the group of sociologists associated with the Institute of Race Relations in Britain in the 1960s and 1970s.[39]

The question of immigration policies is an important one since ultimately access to a country, without hindrance from entry controls, is a crucial determinant in migration patterns. Increasingly scholars are recognising that 'it is precisely the control which states exercise over borders that defines international migration as a distinctive social process'.[40] From the 1920s onwards, the United States instituted a policy of restricting entry based on a national quota system, favouring north-western European countries.[41] Throughout the postwar period, immigration policies were instituted by all the major western European industrial states, regulating the entry of migrants.[42] For instance in Britain, legislation appeared on the statute books in 1905 and 1914, although these acts were more concerned with national security and the removal of 'undesirable aliens' rather than with a determined policy to restrict immigration. However, the Aliens Restriction (Amendment) Act, 1919, together with the Aliens Order (1920), a 'temporary' measure, formed the basis of British policy in relation to aliens, under which entry became a discretionary matter for an immigration officer, restrictions were imposed on the employment of aliens, and the home secretary was granted substantial powers in the matter of deportation.[43] This legislation constituted the central bulwark of British government policy towards aliens until the Immigration Act of 1971.[44] In 1962, with the increase in immigration from the 'New Commonwealth' (and some evidence of racial prejudice amongst the populace at large), an act was introduced which 'was the first in a series of legislative measures used to close the door selectively to migrants from former colonial territories that remained in the Commonwealth'.[45] Together with further acts passed by parliament in 1968 and 1971, this body of legislation formed the backbone for British policy towards 'New Commonwealth' immigrants and 'shattered the tradition of free entry'.[46] As the British example clearly illustrates, an evolving trend in restricting entry is the pre-eminent feature of state policy in most western European countries during the postwar period.[47] The specific consequences of state policy that aimed to control the entry of migrants have been explored in a number of contexts and the overarching role of the state in determining migration patterns is clearly evident, although clandestine migration can still, of course, take place.[48]

Recent theories examining migration have stressed the globalist element of migration. A central feature of global migration patterns is the movement of labour from underdeveloped regions to industrial areas, internally within states and across national boundaries. Traditionally, the 'core–periphery' approach, associated for the most part with Marxist or neo-Marxist thinking, argues that the patterns of economic development that have emerged over time result in an international division of labour, with advanced capitalist states on the one hand, and underdeveloped countries on the other. Breathnach and Jackson conveniently summarise the central features of this theory:

> A fundamental feature of this [international economic] system has been the generation of interregional and international economic relationships based on functional complementarity, giving rise in turn to an idea of an international division of labour involving a set of underdeveloped peripheral economies with limited economic functions and orientated, in a dependent fashion, to serving the needs of a set of developed, diversified and dominant core economies. These needs have been served primarily by the global periphery acting as a reservoir of primary materials and (particularly in the late twentieth century) of cheap labour for manufacturing industries based in the global core.[49]

This 'core–periphery' analytical framework was developed initially during the 1960s for the study of the development of Third World economies by theorists examining the effects of imperialism, and a substantial literature has developed around the concepts of 'dependency' and 'underdevelopment'.[50] The application of this theory to the study of migration raises a number of interesting points. In the first instance, even within the nation-state, the 'core–periphery' approach can be applied to rural–urban migration, since industrial areas tend to attract substantial numbers of workers from rural and predominantly agricultural areas. Secondly, the process of inequality both in the export of primary goods and human labour results in the periphery lacking the capital resources to develop an economic structure conducive to growth since the only supplier for manufactured goods will be the core economies, thereby 'emphasising and confirming their dependency'.[51] Lastly, as Petras observes, one of the key factors in determining the movement of labour from the periphery to the core is geographical location. For example, in Sweden the largest numbers of foreign workers are from Finland, and a similar trend can be noted with reference to the numbers of Mexicans and Canadians in the United States, Italians in Switzerland and also in a number of other countries adjacent to each other where an advanced capitalist economy is located in close proximity to an underdeveloped economy.[52] However, by way of sharp contrast, Irish migration to the United States would not neatly fit within this framework which lays stress on geographical proximity.

Historians and social scientists have long recognised the crucial role of kin and personal networks in the migration process. Network theory has been used extensively in order to analyse migration flows and their determinants. The existence of a family member or friend in the prospective destination society lessened the obvious trauma of the move to a new and strange environment. In addition, networks also reduced the element of uncertainty inherent in the decision to travel to a foreign country.[53] It has also been posited that regardless of wage differentials or rates of unemployment, the growth of networks reduces the costs and risks of migration thereby accelerating the flow. But networks also contributed to migration becoming a self-perpetuating phenomenon as each wave of migrants established a range of contacts which were available to subsequent arrivals.[54] There is much of value in network theory, and throughout the following chapters it will be demonstrated that kin and personal networks shaped the history of twentieth-century Irish migration to Britain to a greater extent than is commonly acknowledged, by determining not only who went and who stayed, but also the place of initial settlement in Britain.

The final body of theory that will be discussed is derived from the work of economists and political scientists, and termed the 'exit–voice' polarity, first outlined in the famous work of Hirschman, and later adopted and applied by Rokkan in comparative studies of European state formation and nation-building.[55] In brief, Hirschman's theory can be summarised with relative ease and as Barry argues, it has 'an unlimited range of applications'.[56] Originally, Hirschman argued that decline in firms, organisations and states elicits three possible responses: 'exit', 'voice' and 'loyalty': ' "Exit" simply means leaving; "voice" means trying to get the managers to reverse the decline by complaining, protesting or organising internal opposition. Loyalty affects the individual calculus by making voice, as against exit, more probable than it would otherwise have been, all else remaining the same.'[57] In relation to 'exit' from the modern state, a cautionary note is sounded by Finer who underlines the vital consideration of the power of a state in limiting the number of persons wishing to leave, and perhaps more fundamentally, he points to the fact that the corollary of 'exit' is 'entrance', an option which, as was demonstrated above, became increasingly restricted throughout the western world over the course of the twentieth century.[58] Nevertheless, this model can be applied to the study of migration with a fair degree of plausibility, whilst recognising that over time and space other factors, especially border controls, may have determined the availability or otherwise of the 'exit' option. Hirschman's original formulation was more concerned with demonstrating how economists had 'disregarded the possible contribution of voice', that is, political protest; however, in his later work, he developed the framework to include an analysis of the importance of the exit option in relation to the state.[59] He posits that large-scale emigration may have made it possible for democratisation and liberalisation to proceed in several European countries prior to the First World War without political instability being seriously affected. This was because radical revolutionaries would have taken the exit option due to their dissatisfaction with the *status quo*. According to Hirschman, the political élite in Europe during the nineteenth and early twentieth centuries benefited from emigration since the 'ships carrying the migrants contained many actual or potential anarchists and socialists, reformers and revolutionaries'.[60] This may seem at best a rather speculative assertion as data on the political outlook of migrants are not readily available, and whilst acknowledging that many dissatisfied persons might migrate, to further argue that the political élite therefore believed it was now safer to begin the process of democratisation is a somewhat naïve proposition. Hirschman provides little in the way of hard evidence to support this observation. Kuhnle effectively challenges Hirschman's assertion by examining the available data on migration and enfranchised citizens as a proportion of enfranchised age groups for 12 European countries between 1866 and 1910. Kuhnle concludes that, while he could not 'disprove that exit may have resulted in efforts of democratisation on the part of political leaders in some countries, steps to democratise appear much more dramatic in countries with negligible exit'.[61] In the absence of firm evidence on the rather elusive political outlook of migrants, Hirschman's observation will remain difficult to apply with any degree of certainty, although one possible line of thought would be to examine the involvement of migrants in political organisations in the 'host country', an aspect that is as yet for the most part unexplored. Quite apart from the empirical considerations, it is clear that the 'exit–voice' polarity is not a closely specified model, although it does raise interesting questions with regard to the relationship between migration and social and political change.

The central finding to emerge, apart from noting the diversity of theoretical approaches, is that a general set of hypotheses explaining migration is not discernible. One systematic evaluation of the myriad theories of international migration concluded that 'at present there is no single, coherent theory of international migration, only a fragmented set of theories that has developed largely in isolation from one another, sometimes but not always segmented by disciplinary boundaries'.[62] Studies in economics and economic history almost invariably focus on the migration decision, assuming the rationality of the migrant, whereas sociological approaches emphasise the importance of the social structure, cultural norms and the role of state policy. Clearly, there is much of value in both approaches and some of the most illuminating accounts of migration incorporate elements of individual decision-making and the economic and social processes at work; for instance, Miller's *Emigrants and exiles* is a good example of this holistic genre.[63] The tendency in migration studies in recent years is to view migration as a global process and cognisance needs to be taken of the multiplicity of population movements across the world, rather than merely treating one 'sending' country in isolation. Whether migration is the result of the international division of labour between 'peripheral' and 'core' economies is another question that merits serious reflection. The fact that migration is most evident from countries or regions with an underdeveloped economic structure may add further weight to 'core–periphery' models. Finally, can migration be assessed within the framework of Hirschman's 'exit–voice' polarity? Certainly, 'exit' may have been an option in contrast to voicing political dissent, but while the general theory appears attractive, its application to a particular case study may prove more problematic. In raising these issues related to the study of migration at this juncture, the essential frame of reference in theoretical terms for this account of Irish migration to Britain has been constructed. This body of theory raises many of the questions that will be addressed in the following chapters.

III

International migration was an overarching feature of nineteenth-century European history. Between 1821 and the outbreak of the First World War in 1914, approximately 44 million people emigrated from Europe to North America, South America, Australia, New Zealand and many other diverse places.[64] The size of the Irish contribution relative to the total size of population was unprecedented, but many other countries including Britain, Italy, Spain, Portugal, Norway, Sweden and Germany also experienced large-scale emigration. Ireland was at the top of the league table for the second half of the nineteenth century, which illustrates the profound impact emigration had on Irish society.[65] The movement of people from Europe occurred in peaks and cycles, with different countries occupying the position of suppliers of emigrants at different times; however, Ireland was one of the principal sending regions throughout the nineteenth and early twentieth centuries. The British Isles were the chief source of emigrants in the early nineteenth century; by the 1850s Scandinavia and the German states were providing a significant share of the total number of emigrants; and at the turn of the century, southern Europe, particularly Italy, and eastern Europe, had overtaken other European countries.[66] Within the international context, nineteenth-century Irish migration to Britain, North America, Australia, New Zealand, South Africa and elsewhere remains one of the most significant movements of population in modern European history, both in terms of the total number of people involved and its incidence relative to the size of the population of the island

Migration has been synonymous with Irish history from the eighteenth century until the present day and this subject has generated a large and ever-increasing literature, attracting the attention of many historians, ranging from those scholars who have undertaken studies of Irish migration at the micro-level, such as Scally, to those interested in the broader sweep, as exemplified by Miller's *magnum opus, Emigrants and exiles* or Akenson's *tour de force, The Irish diaspora.*[67] Although approximately eight million people left Ireland between 1801 and 1921, the number of people who left the country over the course of the second half of the nineteenth century and early twentieth century varied widely (see Table 1.1).[68] The rate of Irish emigration was determined by a range of factors such as the economic situation in Ireland, the demand for labour in the United States and Britain, state or landlord financial assistance for emigration, and the prices of fares from Irish ports or other centres of departure, the principal one being Liverpool.

Migration from Ireland was not simply a nineteenth-century phenomenon. Throughout the early modern period and the eighteenth century, large numbers of Irish persons left for the New World, although many also travelled to other destinations, mainly Britain.[69] Between 1815 and 1845 a steady flow of people left Ireland for North America and Britain. It has been estimated that over one million Irish migrants travelled to the United States during the pre-famine period

Table 1.1 Total Irish emigration, 1852–1921[a]

Period	Males	Females	Total
1852–60[b]	518,257	493,101	1,011,358
1861–70	469,817	380,019	849,836
1871–80	342,317	281,616	623,933
1881–90	395,298	375,408	770,706
1891–1900	201,570	231,956	433,526
1901–10	172,297	173,727	346,024
1911–21[c]	81,187	83,204	164,391

Notes: [a]As Ó Gráda has pointed out, these figures should be adjusted upwards yet for the present purpose the patterns rather than the true figures are our chief concern (Cormac Ó Gráda, 'A note on nineteenth-century Irish emigration statistics', Population Studies, Vol. 29, 1975, pp. 143–49)
[b] 9-year period
[c] 11-year period
Source: Commission on Emigration, Reports, table 28, pp. 318–19.

and approximately 500,000 people went to Britain.[70] Within the aggregate figures significant annual differences are evident: for instance, in 1837 more than 47,000 people travelled to North America, yet in the following year only 11,000 people made the same journey.[71] The sharp decrease in 1838 can be explained by reference to the financial crisis in the United States which resulted in a significant slowdown in the rate of Irish emigration. The period between 1839 and 1845, as Miller observes, witnessed large-scale emigration with not less than 30,000 people leaving Ireland annually.[72] Therefore the popular – and enduring – assumption that large-scale Irish migration was initiated by the Great Irish Famine (1845–50) is at odds with the available evidence: what was new about the famine exodus was the sheer enormity of the numbers involved.

During the famine, emigration from Ireland reached unprecedented levels. Between 1846 and 1855 approximately 2.5 million people left Ireland.[73] In 1851 more than 250,000 people emigrated, a level of emigration which, relative to the size of the total population as recorded in the census of the same year (6.5 million), marked the peak of emigrant flow in the nineteenth century. The rate of emigration from post-famine Ireland fluctuated depending on the circumstances at home and the economic climate in the receiving societies. In the 1870s, during the economic depression in the United States and a time of relative prosperity in Ireland, overseas emigration rates decreased quite significantly.[74] Between 1850 and the outbreak of the First World War in 1914, roughly another four million people left Ireland, an outflow that 'was enormous by international standards'.[75] The chief destination for the majority of Irish emigrants was North America, but many also travelled to Britain, Australia and New Zealand. The choice of destination depended on a number of factors including the pool of relatives already settled in a country, the perceived economic climate in the 'host country', and not least the price of fares.

Migration affected every county in nineteenth-century Ireland to some extent, but its impact was selective. In the pre-famine period, the provinces of Ulster and Leinster were heavily represented in the emigrant stream.[76] This point is clearly illustrated by employing cohort depletion techniques.[77] Fitzpatrick's estimates demonstrate that Ulster had the highest rate of cohort depletion, followed by Leinster, between 1821 and 1841. However, a marked change is evident during the famine when Connacht predominates. Over the next decade, a staggering 48 per cent of the population cohort aged between 5 and 24 years in 1841 in Connacht had 'disappeared' as a result of emigration and famine-related mortality.[78] For the post-famine period, official returns are available for the number of Irish emigrants from each county and province from 1852 onwards.[79] A note of caution should be sounded in relation to these statistics in that the official returns underestimate emigration to Britain, particularly from western Ireland.[80] Drawing again on Fitzpatrick's cohort depletion estimates, it is evident that the provinces of Connacht and Munster supplied the majority of the emigrants.[81] However, the point which should be made is that *all* counties were affected by emigration in post-famine Ireland, although some, such as Mayo, Galway and Cork, lost a greater proportion of their population in comparison with other counties.

As we have seen earlier, ascribing motives for emigration is a complex and vexed issue: different people emigrated from nineteenth-century Ireland for different reasons. The decision to migrate was often made at a particular stage in the life cycle and was influenced by a combination of factors.[82] Since we know relatively little about the circumstances dictating the decisions of individuals, explanations invariably centre on the economic and social environment in which the migrant previously lived. Prior to 1845, the regions where most emigrants originated, Leinster and Ulster, were severely affected by the decline in the rural textile industry.[83] The transformation in the rural economy which occurred with the shift from tillage to pasture

displaced many who had hitherto secured employment in agriculture.[84] Fewer opportunities for non-agricultural employment together
with the advances in the commercialisation of agriculture which led to
a surplus in the labour requirement, all added up to what was perceived to be a bleak and unpromising future in Ireland.[85] And as Fitzpatrick has noted, a poor harvest or the partial failure of the potato
crop – as occurred in 1829–30, 1832–34, 1836, 1839, 1841–42 – usually resulted in a rise in emigration.[86] For many, Ireland became a place
where the future was uncertain in comparison with the opportunities
available elsewhere, especially in North America.

The causes of Irish emigration during the famine need little elab-
oration. Obviously, the imperative for leaving Ireland was widespread
distress owing to the hunger and disease that occurred after the complete failure of the potato crop in 1846 and 1847 as a result of the blight
that affected most of the country. The patterns of Irish emigration
which had been established in the pre-famine years proved to be of
some consequence as relatives could pay fares and ensure that a family member escaped from the distress in Ireland. The assistance provided by landlords and the government was only a token effort when
compared with the large number of passages that were financed solely
by relatives.[87] However, it is clear that only those with some means
were able to escape the distress; the poorest strata of society, particularly in the west of Ireland, had little option but to stay and suffer. One
additional point should made about emigration during the famine: it
was the sense of sheer panic which was characteristic of this movement that was the most distressing development. Emigration was necessary for survival rather than a route to future success.

The demographic shock of the great Irish famine established a
trend of population decline which to some extent has lasted until the
present day. Almost uniquely, this population decline was a result of
the high rates of migration from post-famine Ireland. The inheritance
patterns which were established as a result of the famine ensured that
only one son (usually but not always the eldest) would inherit the family farm and one daughter could marry the inheritor of another farm.
Prior to the famine, holdings had been subdivided but the uneconomic nature of these units was underlined during the crisis. Henceforth, the family farm would be passed intact (impartible inheritance),
and the surplus sons (and daughters) would seek their livelihoods elsewhere.[88] However, the fundamental cause underpinning the movement out of Ireland throughout the post-famine era was the lack of

economic development, since the large-scale non-agricultural employment that existed in the United States, Britain and in other European states had no parallel in Ireland, with the exception of Belfast and its hinterland. The lure of America and of Britain ensured that the decision to emigrate became an integral part of the life cycle of young Irish people.[89] Many emigrated in search of a better standard of living which proved unattainable in post-famine Ireland. Migrants left to improve their life chances in the shape of higher wages and better employment prospects. Information and knowledge percolated back to Ireland from the United States and Britain in the form of letters and the ubiquitous presence of returned emigrants. The availability of information concerning the economic conditions in the intended destination was crucial for the prospective migrant when contemplating emigration.[90] Many other causes, such as the 'modernisation' of post-famine Ireland and the way in which emigration acted as a 'safety-valve' in a conservative, predominantly rural society, are also relevant. Miller weighs up the various arguments which, it must be said, do not lend themselves to quantification.[91] Nevertheless, it is perhaps worth pointing out that large-scale migration facilitated the maintenance of the social structure of post-famine Ireland by removing from the landscape a large number of marginalised (and disadvantaged) people. That these people came to regard themselves as 'exiles' is another matter, yet if anything they were exiled by the processes of uneven economic development, itself a product of the vagaries of nineteenth-century international capitalism.

Family emigration was characteristic of the transatlantic movement in the earlier part of the nineteenth century.[92] Roughly half of the Irish migrants arriving in Boston and New York in the pre-famine period were in family groups.[93] For example, an examination of the passenger lists for ships arriving in four American ports (New York, Boston, Philadelphia and New Orleans) in 1831 indicates that over three-fifths of Irish arrivals were travelling in family groups.[94] Family emigration was at its peak in the late 1840s which is obviously explained by the crisis conditions in Ireland at this time. The post-famine flow was, however, dominated by single persons travelling to North America and Britain and family movement decreased steadily after 1875.[95] An analysis of the bookings data for ships which left Londonderry for Philadelphia between 1847 and 1865 provides a stark illustration of this point. In 1847–49, 26 per cent of emigrants who booked passages from Londonderry were travelling as individuals and between 1858 and 1865 this figure had risen to over 52 per cent.[96]

Turning to the age profile of Irish emigrants, the majority of people who left Ireland in the post-famine period were under the age of 30 years. Females tended to migrate at a slightly younger age than males, especially in the later decades of the century.[97] A useful method of estimating the age profile of nineteenth-century Irish migration is to employ 'survivorship ratios', calculating the proportion of an age cohort at the time of one census who are still living in Ireland at the time of the next census ten years later. For instance, it can be seen that of 100 females aged 15–19 years in 1861, only 56 were still living in Ireland in 1871.[98] Of course, it should be borne in mind that no adjustment is made for mortality, which we know to be of significance during the entire period, although particularly so for the decade after 1841. Nevertheless, the general point which should be made is that for the most part Irish migrants were drawn from the younger sections of the population: the age cohort of 20–24 years supplied not less than a quarter and on occasions over two-fifths of the emigrants between 1852 and 1900. For the pre-famine period, the fragmentary evidence available indicates that over 60 per cent of those who left Ireland were under the age of 35 years.[99]

The occupational and social status of these emigrants is of particular interest to those interested in studying the patterns of migration out of Ireland. Again, the problem of inadequate data becomes an obstacle, but historians who have amalgamated a number of diverse sources have been able to sketch the main occupational characteristics of the people who left Ireland in the nineteenth century for North America and Britain. First and foremost, this was a movement of those who found themselves on the bottom rung of the ladder in occupational and social status terms. As Fitzpatrick observes, 'most emigrants, when asked to state their occupation on embarkation, claimed neither status or skills'.[100] Emigrants who were returned as skilled, professional or entrepreneurial constituted a very small percentage of the total flow between 1850 and 1900. In the pre-famine period labourers (agricultural and general labourers together with farm servants and other agricultural workers) made up the bulk of male Irish migrants arriving in North America and Britain. The emigration of farmers, which was of some significance in the pre-famine period, became less so relative to the total flow over the course of the century. A similar picture emerges for female migrants: the women who left

Ireland throughout the nineteenth century usually emanated from the ranks of the unpaid workers on the family farm, servants of various types and those for whom few opportunities for paid employment existed. Apart from the north-east, which benefited from the transference of the Industrial Revolution to Ireland, factory employment elsewhere did not cater for female labour as was the case in some parts of Ulster and throughout Britain. Post-famine Irish emigrants, as Miller notes, 'came largely from more-impoverished backgrounds, and consequently possessed fewer skills and less capital, than their pre-famine predecessors'.[101] Those counties which had the poorest land, such as Clare, Leitrim and Mayo, and were least urbanised with few outlets for employment other than agriculture, supplied the lion's share of the post-famine flow.

In the pre-famine period, male emigration to the United States exceeded female emigration: for example, data from passenger lists of ships arriving at New York in 1820–29 indicate that males constituted roughly two-thirds of flow from Ireland. This pattern changed somewhat over the next 25 years and in 1840–46, nearly half of Irish migrants to New York were female.[102] After 1851, the availability of detailed statistics facilitates a more comprehensive examination of the gender balance. What is most noteworthy is the relative parity in gender terms, which contrasted with most other European emigrant streams in the second half of the nineteenth century.[103] Females left Ireland in numbers roughly equal to those of males, although in the 1860s and 1870s males emigrated in greater numbers. By the end of the nineteenth century, females outnumbered males in the Irish emigrant stream, reflecting the demand for domestic servants in the United States at this time.[104] It can be seen, therefore, that, while males dominated the Irish emigrant flow in the pre-famine period, both during and after the famine the gender balance was roughly equal, with more females leaving Ireland by the turn of the century.

Throughout the nineteenth century, and especially in the post-famine period, seasonal migrants, principally from counties Donegal and Mayo, left Ireland to obtain work as harvesters in Britain.[105] As Ó Gráda has noted, the duration of the stay in Britain increased significantly over time and 'in the post-famine period for some the absences might last almost the whole year'.[106] The numbers of seasonal migrants decreased from the turn of the century as Figure 1.2 demonstrates. These estimates are derived from the adjusted figures of Handley, who argues that the official returns collected by the Royal

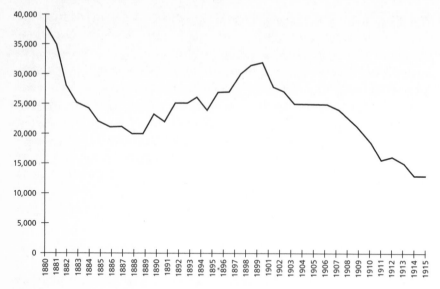

Source: J. E. Handley, *The Irish in modern Scotland*, Cork, 1947, p. 171.

Fig. 1.2 *Estimates of Irish migratory workers, 1880–1915*

Irish Constabulary considerably understate the actual number involved.[107]

   The independent Irish state did not collect statistical information regarding seasonal migration until a government-appointed committee instituted an inquiry in 1937, after ten seasonal workers were killed in a fire in a bothy at Kirkintilloch in September 1937. For the purposes of the work of the committee, the Irish Department of Agriculture prepared a statement of the numbers involved and found that approximately 9,500 persons still travelled from the province of Connacht (mostly from county Mayo) and county Donegal to Britain in 1937 for seasonal agricultural work.[108] Of this total number, it was estimated that 1,787 persons were engaged in potato picking and the remainder were employed as general agricultural workers.[109] Owing to the paucity of reliable statistical material from 1915 until 1937, and again thereafter, definitive assessments of the patterns of seasonal migration for the period under consideration are virtually impossible. O'Dowd's folklore evidence illustrates in detail the experience of Irish seasonal migrants to Scotland and England, although her analysis is focused for the most part on the nineteenth century.[110] For the mid-twentieth century, Jackson's unsubstantiated comments regarding the movement of Irish seasonal workers suggest the continuation of this pattern.[111] Seasonal migration has achieved a form of immortality since a number of works of literature describe in detail the experiences of the Irish agricultural worker in Britain.[112]

How migrants who left nineteenth- and early twentieth-century Ireland fared in their new and unfamiliar surroundings in North America, Britain, Australia, New Zealand and South Africa is another and much more complicated story.[113] The number of published accounts of the Irish in Britain, the United States and Canada is a testament to the interest in the history of the Irish diaspora. Numerous studies have updated Jackson's classic book *The Irish in Britain* and much scholarly endeavour has been devoted to investigating the patterns of settlement in Britain, hostility towards Irish migrants, communal violence and the level of social mobility.[114] In the United States, a plethora of regional studies have examined the position of Irish migrants, their political sensibilities and the patterns of employment and settlement.[115] For Canada, Akenson, Elliott, Smyth and Houston among many others have documented in detail the experiences, political affiliations and regional distribution of Irish migrants.[116] It would be well-nigh impossible to summarise this vast and ever-increasing corpus of research and accounts firmly grounded in primary source materials can be found elsewhere. Nevertheless, it is worth underlining the point that migration by its very nature involves two societies, although our concern for the most part in this study will be with the sending society.

IV

Migration from independent Ireland was therefore not a new development, rather the perpetuation of a long-established pattern of movement to other countries. Transatlantic migration, which dominated most European flows in the second half of the nineteenth century, became less significant in the years following the outbreak of the First World War in 1914 and Irish migration patterns mirrored this general development. As we shall see, certain features of the Irish migrant flow remained remarkably consistent over time, such as the age profile, the relative parity in terms of gender and the geographical origins of migrants. By 1921 migration was an established stage in the life cycle of young Irish people and this remained the case for the following 50 years.

NOTES

1 For a comprehensive survey, see Robin Cohen, ed., *The Cambridge survey of world migration*, Cambridge, 1995; see also Jan Lucassen and Leo Lucassen, eds, *Migration, migration history, history: old paradigms and new perspectives*, Berne, 1997.

2 Douglas S. Massey, Joaquín Arango, Graeme Hugo, Ali Kouaouci, Adela Pellegrino and J. Edward Taylor, 'Theories of international migration: a review and appraisal', *Population and Development Review*, Vol. 19, 1993, pp. 431–32.

3 E. G. Ravenstein, 'The laws of migration', *JRSS*, Vol. 48, 1885, pp. 167–227, and 'The laws of migration', *JRSS*, Vol. 52, 1889, pp. 214–301.

4 A. R. Zolberg, 'The next waves: migration theory for a changing world', *IMR*, Vol. 23, 1989, p. 403.

5 J. A. Jackson, *Migration*, London, 1986, p. 13.

6 Dudley Baines, *Migration in a mature economy: emigration and internal migration in England and Wales, 1861–1900*, Cambridge, 1986.

7 E. S. Lee, 'A theory of migration', *Demography*, Vol. 3, 1966, pp. 47–57.

8 Dudley Baines, 'European emigration, 1815–1930: looking at the emigration decision again', *Econ. Hist. Rev.*, 2nd ser., Vol. 47, 1994, p. 528.

9 T. J. Hatton and J. G. Williamson, 'International migration, 1850–1939: an economic survey', in *Migration and the international labour market, 1850–1939*, ed. Timothy J. Hatton and Jeffrey G. Williamson, London, 1994, p. 9.

10 T. J. Hatton and J. G. Williamson, 'Latecomers to mass migration: the Latin experience', in *Migration and the international labour market*, ed. Hatton and Williamson, pp. 62–63.

11 J. D. Gould, 'European intercontinental emigration: the role of "diffusion" and "feedback" ', *J. Eur. Econ. Hist.*, Vol. 9, 1980, p. 302.

12 Riccardo Faini and Alessandra Venturini, 'Italian emigration in the prewar period', in *Migration and the international labour market*, ed. Hatton and Williamson, p. 73.

13 Charlotte Erickson, *Invisible immigrants*, London, 1972; W. I. Thomas and Florian Znaniecki, *The Polish peasant in Europe and America*, 2 vols, New York, 1958, 1st edn, Chicago, 1920. For a useful discussion of the use of emigrants' letters, see David A. Gerber, 'The immigrant letter between positivism and populism', *Journal of American Ethnic History*, Vol. 16, 1997, pp. 3–34.

14 Dudley Baines, *Emigration from Europe, 1815–1930*, London, 1991, p. 15.

15 Arnold Schrier, *Ireland and the American emigration, 1850–1900*, Minneapolis, 1958, ch. 2.

16 David Fitzpatrick, *Oceans of consolation: personal accounts of Irish migration to Australia*, Cork, 1995; see also Patrick O'Farrell, *Letters from Irish Australia, 1825–1929*,

Sydney, 1984.

17 For a survey of European return migration in the nineteenth and early twentieth century, see J. D. Gould, 'European intercontinental emigration. The road home: return migration from the USA', *J. Eur. Econ. Hist.*, Vol. 9, 1980, pp. 41–111.

18 Baines, *Emigration from Europe*, p. 39.

19 Mark Wyman, *Round-trip to America: the immigrants return to Europe, 1880–1930*, Ithaca, 1993.

20 David Fitzpatrick, *Irish emigration, 1801–1921*, Dublin, 1984, p. 7.

21 Kerby A. Miller, *Emigrants and exiles: Ireland and the Irish exodus to North America*, New York, 1985, p. 426; Marjolein 't Hart, ' "Heading for Paddy's green shamrock shore"; the returned emigrants in nineteenth-century Ireland', *Ir. Econ. & Soc. Hist.*, Vol. 10, 1983, pp. 96–97 [thesis abstract]; see also Marjolein 't Hart, 'Irish return migration in the nineteenth century', *Tijdschrift voor Economische en Sociale Geografie*, Vol. 76, 1985, pp. 223–31.

22 't Hart, ' "Heading for Paddy's green shamrock shore" ', p. 96.

23 Donal Garvey, 'The history of migration flows in the Republic of Ireland', *Population Trends*, No. 39, 1985, p. 25.

24 Donall Mac Amhlaigh, *An Irish navvy: the diary of an exile*, trans. from the Irish by Valentin Iremonger, London, 1964, pp. 109–10, 175–82; John O'Donoghue, *In a strange land*, London, 1958, p. 146, 181–82.

25 TCD, MS 8306, rural surveys: S.8, Waterford, Dungarvan, New Ross, Carrick-on-Suir, Enniscorthy, Carlow and Bagenalstown, n.d [Oct. 1948], p. 2.

26 Oded Stark, *The migration of labour*, Oxford, 1991, p. 26.

27 Massey et al., 'Theories of international migration', p. 436.

28 Ibid., p. 439.

29 Stark, *The migration of labour*, p. 24.

30 Clifford Jansen, 'Some sociological aspects of migration', in *Migration*, ed. J. A. Jackson, Cambridge, 1969, p. 60.

31 Zolberg, 'Migration theory for a changing world', pp. 403–04.

32 Jackson, *Migration*, pp. 38–39.

33 Franklin D. Scott, 'The study of the effects of emigration', *Scan. Econ. Hist. Rev.*, Vol. 3, 1960, p. 167.

34 The most eloquent exposition of this view is that of Alexis Fitzgerald in his reservation to the report of the Commission on Emigration and other Population Problems, 1948–54 (Commission on Emigration, *Reports*, p. 222); see also Raymond Crotty, *Irish agricultural production: its volume and structure*, Cork, 1966, p. 157.

35 J. S. MacDonald, 'Agricultural organisation, migration and labour militancy in rural Italy, 1902–13', *Econ. Hist. Rev.*, 2nd ser., Vol. 16, 1963, pp. 61–75.

36 Mirjana Morokvašic, 'Introduction: migration in Europe', *Current Sociology*, Vol. 32, 1984, pp. 18–19.

37 Jackson, *Migration*, p. 52.

38 Stephen Castles and M. J. Miller, *The age of migration: international population movements in the modern world*, 1st edn, London, 1993, p. 196.

39 A useful overview is provided by John Rex, *Race and ethnicity*, Milton Keynes, 1986 and John Rex and David Mason, eds, *Theories of race and ethnic relations*, Cambridge, 1986. Specific studies sponsored by the Institute of Race Relations include E. J. B. Rose and Nicholas Deakin with others, *Colour and citzenship: a report* *on British race relations*, London, 1969; John Rex and Robert Moore, *Race, community, and conflict: a study of Sparkbrook*, London, 1967; Sheila Patterson, *Immigrants and race relations in Britain, 1960–67*, London, 1969: A. H. Richmond, *Migration and race relations in an English city: a study of Bristol*, London, 1973.

40 Zolberg, 'Migration theory for a changing world', p. 405.

41 Robert A. Divine, *American immigration policy, 1924–52*, New Haven, 1957, pp. 1–51.

42 Jackson, *Migration*, p. 64.

43 Colin Holmes, *John Bull's island: immigration and British society, 1871–1971*, Basingstoke, 1988, pp. 113–14.

44 Zig Layton-Henry, *The politics of immigration: 'race' and 'race' relations in post-war Britain*, Oxford, 1992, p. 7.

45 Jackson, *Migration*, p. 69.

46 Holmes, *John Bull's island*, p. 309.

47 For a fuller discussion of migration policy in Europe, see Sarah Collinson, *Europe and international migration*, London, 1993, pp. 46–63; Anthony Fielding, 'Migrants, institutions and politics: the evolution of European migration policies', in *Mass migration in Europe: the legacy and the future*, ed. Russell King, London, 1993, pp. 40–62. More detailed comparative studies can be found in Tomas Hammar, ed., *European immigration policy: a comparative study*, Cambridge, 1985.

48 Castles and Miller, *The age of migration*, pp. 85–96; Zolberg, 'Migration theory for a changing world', p. 405.

49 Proinnsias Breathnach and J. A. Jackson, 'Ireland, emigration and the new international division of labour', in *Contemporary Irish migration*, ed. Russell King, Dublin, 1991, GSI special publications No. 6, p. 1.

50 For an overview, see Ankie M. M. Hoogvelt, 'Theories of imperialism, dependency and underdevelopment', in *The developing world*, ed. Anna Farmar, Dublin, 1988. This reading is taken from Hoogvelt's book, *The third world in global development*, London, 1982.

51 Jackson, *Migration*, p. 22.

52 Elizabeth Petras, 'The global labour market in the modern world economy', in *Global trends in migration: theory and research on international population movements*, ed. Mary M. Kritz, Charles B. Keely and Silvano M. Tomasi, New York, 1981, p. 56.

53 Douglas S. Massey, Joaquín Arango, Graeme Hugo, Ali Kouaouci, Adela Pellegrino and J. Edward Taylor, 'An evaluation of international migration theory: the North American case', *Population and Development Review*, Vol. 20, 1994, p. 728.

54 Monica Boyd, 'Family and personal networks in international migration: recent developments and new agendas', *IMR*, Vol. 23, 1989, p. 641.

55 A. O. Hirschman, *Exit, voice and loyalty: responses to decline in firms, organizations and states*, Cambridge, Mass., 1970; Stein Rokkan, 'Dimensions of state formation and nation-building: a possible paradigm for research on variations within Europe', in *The formation of national states in western Europe*, ed. Charles Tilly, Princeton, 1975, pp. 526–600.

56 Brian Barry, 'Review article: "Exit, voice and loyalty" ', *British Journal of Political Science*, Vol. 4, 1974, p. 82.

57 Ibid.

58 S. E. Finer, 'State-building, state boundaries and border control', *Social*

Science Information, Vol. 13, 1974, p. 80.

59 A. O. Hirshman, 'Exit, voice and the state', in *Essays in trespassing: economics to politics and beyond*, Cambridge, 1981, p. 246.

60 Ibid., p. 259.

61 Stein Kuhnle, 'Emigration, democratisation and the rise of the European welfare states', in *Mobilisation, center-periphery structures and nation-building*, ed. Per Torsvik, Bergen, 1981, pp. 512–13.

62 Massey et al., 'Theories of international migration', p. 432.

63 Miller, *Emigrants and exiles*.

64 Baines, *Migration in a mature economy*, p. 9.

65 Baines, *Emigration from Europe*, table 3, p. 10.

66 Ibid., p. 7.

67 Robert James Scally, *The end of hidden Ireland: rebellion, famine and emigration*; Miller, *Emigrants and exiles*; D. H. Akenson, *The Irish diaspora: a primer*, Belfast, 1993, New York, 1995.

68 Fitzpatrick, *Irish emigration*, p. 1.

69 L. M. Cullen, 'The Irish diaspora of the seventeenth and eighteenth centuries', in *Europeans on the move: studies on European migration, 1500–1800*, ed. Nicholas Canny, Oxford, 1994, pp. 113–49.

70 David Fitzpatrick,'Emigration, 1801–70', in *A new history of Ireland, V: Ireland under the union, pt. I (1801–70)*, ed. W. E. Vaughan, Oxford, 1989, p. 565.

71 Commission on Emigration, *Reports*, p. 314.

72 Miller, *Emigrants and exiles*, p. 199.

73 Fitzpatrick, *Irish emigration*, p. 3.

74 Fitzpatrick, 'Emigration, 1871–1921', in *A new history of Ireland, VI: Ireland under the union, pt. II (1871–1921)*, ed. W. E. Vaughan, Oxford, 1996, p. 606.

75 Cormac Ó Gráda, *Ireland: a new economic history, 1780–1939*, Oxford, 1994, p. 224.

76 S. H. Cousens, 'The regional variation in emigration from Ireland between 1821 and 1841', *Trans. Inst. Brit. Geog.*, Vol. 37, 1965, p. 29.

77 Cohort depletion is a technique used by scholars to estimate rates of emigration by calculating the percentage of the population cohort most likely to emigrate, 5–24 years, who have 'disappeared' when the census is recorded ten years later (20 years in the case of 1821–41). For a brief explanation, see Fitzpatrick, *Irish emigration*, p. 43.

78 Fitzpatrick, 'Emigration, 1801–70', table 1, p. 608.

79 W. E. Vaughan and A. J. Fitzpatrick, eds, *Irish historical statistics: population, 1821–1971*, Dublin, 1978, pp. 269–353. No data are available prior to May 1851.

80 Cormac Ó Gráda, 'A note on nineteenth-century Irish emigration statistics', *Population Studies*, Vol. 29, 1975, pp. 143–49; Cormac Ó Gráda, 'Some aspects of nineteenth-century Irish emigration', in *Comparative aspects of Scottish and Irish economic history*, ed. L. M. Cullen and T. C. Smout, Edinburgh, 1977, pp. 65–73.

81 Fitzpatrick, *Irish emigration*, pp. 11–12.

82 See Timothy W. Guinnane, *The vanishing Irish: households, migration and the rural economy in Ireland, 1850–1914*, Princeton, 1997, pp. 181–92.

83 Liam Kennedy and L. A. Clarkson, 'Birth, death and exile: Irish population history, 1700–1921', in *An historical geography of Ireland*, ed. B. J. Graham and L. J.

Proudfoot, London, 1993, p. 173.

84 W. J. Smyth, 'Irish emigration, 1700–1920', in *European expansion and migration*, ed. P. C. Emmer and Magnus Mörner, Oxford, 1992, pp. 55–56.

85 Kennedy and Clarkson, 'Birth, death and exile', p. 194.

86 Fitzpatrick, *Irish emigration*, p. 27.

87 Ibid., pp. 18–21

88 Ibid., p. 30.

89 See Schrier, *Ireland and the American emigration*, pp. 18–42, for a revealing account of the 'lure of America'.

90 J. H. Johnson, 'The context of migration: the example of Ireland in the nineteenth century', *Trans. Inst. Brit. Geog.*, 2nd ser., Vol. 15, 1990, pp. 269–71.

91 Miller, *Emigrants and exiles*, pp. 335–426.

92 Baines, *Emigration from Europe*, p. 43.

93 Fitzpatrick, *Irish emigration*, p. 7.

94 Charlotte Erickson, 'Emigration from the British Isles to the USA in 1831', *Population Studies*, Vol. 35, 1981, p. 184.

95 Fitzpatrick,'Emigration, 1871–1921', p. 613.

96 Deirdre Mageean, 'Ulster emigration to Philadelphia, 1847–65: a preliminary analysis using passenger lists', in *Migration across time and distance: population mobility in historical context*, ed. I. A. Glazier and Luigi De Rosa, New York, 1986, p. 283.

97 Guinnane, *The vanishing Irish*, p. 182.

98 Commission on Emigration, *Reports*, table 92, p. 123.

99 Cormac Ó Gráda, 'Across the briny ocean: some thoughts on Irish emigration to America, 1800–1850', in *Ireland and Scotland, 1600–1850: parallels and contrasts in economic and social development*, ed. T. M. Devine and David Dickson, Edinburgh, 1983, table 1, p. 123.

100 Fitzpatrick, 'Irish emigration, 1801–70', p. 575.

101 Miller, *Emigrants and exiles*, p. 351.

102 Ó Gráda, 'Across the briny ocean', table 6a, p. 126.

103 Kennedy and Clarkson, 'Birth, death and exile', p. 176.

104 Fitzpatrick, 'Emigration, 1871–1921', p. 613.

105 An extensive literature of varying quality exists relating to nineteenth-century Irish seasonal migration: E. J. T. Collins, 'Migrant labour in British agriculture in the nineteenth century', *Econ. Hist. Rev.*, 2nd ser., Vol. 29, 1976, pp. 38–59; J. E. Handley, *The Irish in modern Scotland*, Cork, 1947, pp. 164–90; J. H. Johnson, 'Harvest migration from nineteenth century Ireland', *Trans. Inst. Brit. Geog.*, Vol. 41, 1967, pp. 97–112; B. M. Kerr, 'Irish seasonal migration to Great Britain, 1800–1838', *IHS*, Vol. 3, 1943, pp. 365–80; Gerard Moran, ' "A passage to Britain": seasonal migration and social change in the west of Ireland', *Saothar*, Vol. 13, 1988, pp. 22–31; Cormac Ó Gráda, 'Seasonal migration and post-famine adjustment in the west of Ireland', *Studia Hibernica*, Vol. 13, 1973, pp. 48–76, and 'Demographic adjustment and seasonal migration in nineteenth century Ireland', in *Ireland and France*, ed. L. M. Cullen and François Furet, Paris, 1981, pp. 181–93. Special mention should be made here of Anne O'Dowd's exhaustive if badly-organised study based for the most part on folklore evidence, *Spalpeens and tattie hokers: history and folklore of the Irish migratory agricultural worker in Ireland and Britain*, Dublin, 1991.

106 Ó Gráda, *Ireland: a new economic history*, p. 50.

107 Handley, *The Irish in modern Scotland*, pp. 169–71. Ó Gráda concludes that these adjustments provide a 'more accurate picture' (Ó Gráda, 'Seasonal migration and post-famine adjustment', p. 56).

108 *Report of interdepartmental committee on seasonal migration to Great Britain, 1937–38*, Dublin, 1938, P. 3403, p. 13.

109 Ibid., p. 14

110 O'Dowd, *Spalpeens and tattie hokers*, pp. 163–202.

111 J. A. Jackson, *The Irish in Britain*, London, 1963, p. 77.

112 For examples of this genre, see Patrick Gallagher, *Paddy the Cope: my story*, London, 1939; Michael MacGowan, *The hard road to Klondike*, trans. from the Irish by Valentin Iremonger, London, 1962; Patrick MacGill, *Children of the dead end*, London, 1914, and *The rat pit*, London, 1914; Eoin O'Donnell, *The story of Hughie Johnny*, Dublin, 1941.

113 For Australia and New Zealand, see Akenson, *The Irish diaspora*, pp. 59–122; Fitzpatrick, *Oceans of consolation*; Patrick O'Farrell, *The Irish in Australia*, Sydney, 1987: and O'Farrell, 'The Irish in Australia and New Zealand, 1791–1870', in *A new history of Ireland, V: Ireland under the union, pt. I (1801–70)*, ed. Vaughan, pp. 661–81; O'Farrell, 'The Irish in Australia and New Zealand, 1871–1990', in *A new history of Ireland, VI: Ireland under the union, pt. II (1871–1921)*, ed. Vaughan, pp. 703–24. On South Africa, see Akenson, *The Irish diaspora*, pp. 123–39.

114 Useful summaries of the current state of knowledge can be found in Donald M. MacRaild, *Irish migrants in modern Britain, 1750–1922*, Basingstoke, 1999 and Brenda Collins, 'The Irish in Britain, 1780–1921', in *An historical geography of Ireland*, ed. B. J. Graham and L. J. Proudfoot, London, 1993, pp. 366–98.

115 The best available accounts include Akenson, *The Irish diaspora*, pp. 217–69; David Noel Doyle, 'The Irish in North America, 1776–1845', in *A new history of Ireland, V: Ireland under the union, pt. I (1801–70)*, ed. Vaughan, pp. 682–725, 'The remaking of Irish America, 1845–80', in *A new history of Ireland, VI: Ireland under the union, pt. II (1871–1921)*, ed. Vaughan, pp. 725–63; C. J. Houston and W. J. Smyth, 'The Irish diaspora: emigration to the New World, 1720–1920', in *An historical geography of Ireland*, ed. Graham and Proudfoot, pp. 352–62.

116 D. H. Akenson, *The Irish in Ontario: a study in rural history*, Kingston and Montreal, 1984; Bruce S. Elliott, *Irish migrants in the Canadas: a new approach*, Belfast, 1988; C. J. Houston and W. J. Smyth, *Irish emigration and Canadian settlement: patterns, links and letters*, Toronto, 1990.

2

The interwar years, 1921–1939

The interwar years were marked by a fundamental change in the nature of international migration. The rate of overseas emigration from Europe to the Americas declined sharply throughout the 1920s, after an initial postwar boom.[1] Restrictions on both emigration and immigration were introduced by a number of states, most notably in the form of the imposition of national quotas on immigrants by the United States in 1921 and 1924, which favoured migrants from north-western Europe.[2] In Hungary, the Soviet Union and Germany the freedom to emigrate was restricted in the 1920s.[3] In Italy, notwithstanding a policy to promote emigration in the early 1920s, in 1927 the fascist regime under Mussolini adopted measures which aimed to restrict movement out of the country on the basis that emigration 'represented the loss of Italy's greatest resource'.[4] But the decline in overseas emigration was also influenced by wider developments in the international economy from the late 1920s onwards as most of the major economies were in the midst of deep recession. Opportunities for migrants to obtain employment in prospective receiving societies were few, especially with the steep rise in the level of unemployment in the United States and elsewhere. This combination of factors explains the decline in overseas emigration from Europe in the interwar period. Indeed the remainder of the twentieth century would be an 'age of migration', although transatlantic migration never regained its pre-eminence.[5] Henceforth, European migration from the 1930s onwards was in essence composed of flows across relatively short distances.

State policy in determining the level of migration was closely related to a concern about the level of population which was evident in many European countries in the interwar years. Population increase was associated with economic growth. Specific policies formulated in order to increase the level of population were adopted in France and Sweden, and more famously, in Nazi Germany and fascist Italy.[6] State intervention in order to encourage pronatalism formed a central element of population policy in France, Belgium and elsewhere. In Nazi Germany pronatalist polices were combined with eugenics with disastrous consequences.[7] The interwar years were, therefore, a period when population growth, emigration and immigration came under close official scrutiny throughout Europe. Legislative measures, official and unofficial policies and, in some cases, close state regulation formed the central elements of population policies. From December 1921 onwards with the establishment of the Irish Free State, such matters became the preserve of an independent Irish state.[8] The new government faced many difficulties, not least an internal military challenge to the legitimacy of the state, and other problems such as achieving financial stability and formulating a viable political *modus operandi* within the British Commonwealth. Questions of population increase and the level of emigration paled into insignificance when compared with the more immediate and pressing problem of establishing the authority of the new state.

I

During the period from 1911 to 1926 the total population of the Irish Free State declined by 5 per cent, whereas over the following decade (1926–36) a negligible decrease was recorded.[9] The continuing decline in population since 1851 was exacerbated between 1911 and 1926 by a number of exceptional factors, which were outlined in the detailed commentary accompanying the 1926 census.[10] Firstly, the number of soldiers from the south of Ireland who were killed in the First World War was recorded by the Registrar General as 27,405, although this figure does not include officers. Fitzpatrick estimates that by early 1916 'some 3,700 officers had obtained direct commissions in the army and navy'.[11] In addition, no information is available about the number of Irish-born persons who enlisted in the British army during the war and thereafter remained in other dominion countries. Lastly, the withdrawal of the crown officials, the British army and their dependants in 1922 accounts for the departure of somewhere in the region of 34,000 persons.[12] Finally, the disbandment of the Royal Irish Constabulary (RIC) in 1922 resulted in a significant number of policemen and

their dependants leaving the Irish Free State, some for only a temporary period, others for good.[13] In 1911 the RIC numbered over eight
thousand officers and although Kennedy has estimated that up to 80
per cent of the number enumerated in 1911 had left the Irish Free
State by 1926, this figure seems excessively high.[14] Unpublished
research, based on the claims for compensation made to the British
government by former members of the RIC and other crown officials,
reveals that while a substantial proportion of former officers did leave
permanently and joined police forces in Palestine, Northern Ireland
and England, others eventually returned after the end of the civil war
in 1923 when political stability was restored.[15] By the end of 1923,
1,436 former RIC officers had received assistance to migrate to
Canada, Australia and the United States.[16] In the face of such an array
of imponderables and, of course, the 15-year gap in census enumerations, definitive assessments of the explanations for population
decline in the first intercensal period (1911–26) are well-nigh impossible. For the later period (1926–36), as shall be demonstrated later,
the relative stability in the size of the total population may be
explained by the sharp decline in the numbers leaving for the United
States and return migration to the Irish Free State in the early 1930s
as a consequence of the Great Depression.

Comparisons of population change at county level are also of interest (see appendix 1). The pattern between 1911 and 1936 is one of
greater decline in the counties along the western seaboard, such as
Mayo, Kerry, Leitrim and Donegal, areas with traditionally high
migration rates since the mid-nineteenth century. In addition, the
noticeable decrease in the population in counties Cavan and Roscommon is also a continuation of a post-famine demographic trend. The
unusually high figure for the decline in county Kildare in the earlier
period can be explained by the withdrawal of the British army from
the Curragh army camp and the garrison towns of Kildare and Newbridge in 1922. The data for religious denominations in county Kildare indicate that the number of persons classified as adhering to
'other religions', i.e. non-Catholic, decreased from 11,943 in 1911 to
3,627 in 1926.[17] No doubt internal migration partly accounts for the
decline of population in certain counties. One possible method of estimating the level of migration within the boundaries of the state is
through analysis of the data on the county of birth available in the censuses (see appendix 2).[18] The picture obtained tends to be a rather sta-
tic one, until the 1971 census when each person's usual residence one

year previously was ascertained for the first time. This information should be treated with due caution as no indication of the length of residence is available and no account is taken of the absolute numbers involved in each county. Obviously, a certain amount of internal migration did occur. For instance, in 1926, 16 per cent of the residents of county Laois were born elsewhere in the country and 23 per cent of those born in Laois lived in other counties in the Irish Free State. Higher rates of internal migration are evident for the eastern counties as Dublin and its hinterland acted as a magnet for internal migrants. An analysis of the detailed information for 1926 and 1936 points to the fact that most of the migrants settled not far away from where they were born, and whilst internal migration was of some consequence, it tended to occur between contiguous counties, with the distance of movement usually being relatively short.[19] What is noteworthy is the absence of the large-scale rural–urban migration that was a central feature of European population patterns in the nineteenth and twentieth centuries. Guinnane's observations in relation to the low level of internal migration in the post-famine period until 1914 would apply equally to the interwar years.

> The Irish did not move within Ireland because, East Ulster excepted, no place in Ireland experienced the rapid industrial and commercial development and growth of labour demand that drew people to the north of England, to the Ruhr Valley, and to the other great centres of urban growth. But the lack of urbanisation does not mean that the Irish as a people did not become urban. Most Irish emigrants (at least in the post-famine period) ended up as city dwellers in Britain or overseas.[20]

II

Official Irish emigration statistics are not available since no frontier controls existed between the Irish Free State and Britain until the outbreak of the Second World War in September 1939. The glaring deficiencies in the available statistics regarding emigration were first noted by the Committee on Economic Statistics in 1925.[21] However, little was done to improve the quality of data, perhaps in a conscious effort to ensure that the reliability of such information, which was potentially damaging to any government, was always open to question. Several methods of estimating migration rates have been employed by statisticians and demographers in order to obtain a reasonably accurate gauge of population movement from the Irish Free State.[22] The first method provides reliable information on net migration in intercensal periods (difference between outflows and inflows) using cross-sectional data from the censuses of population in conjunction with statistics on births and deaths drawn from the reports of the Registrar-General (see Table 2.1).

Table 2.1 Average annual net Irish migration, 1901–36

	Males	Females	Persons	Number of females per 1,000 males
1901–11	–11,764	–14,390	–26,154	1,223
1911–26	–13,934	–13,068	–27,002	938
1926–36	–7,255	–9,420	–16,675	1,298

Source: Commission on Emigration, *Reports*, table 86, p. 115.

The major difficulty with this method of estimating migration rates is that the census is usually taken every ten years, and therefore no light is shed on migration on a year-to-year basis. The other difficulty relates to the lack of availability of data on gross emigration and immigration flows separately, although immigration into the Irish Free State is known to be of little consequence, apart, that is, from the return flow in the early 1930s when migrants returned home from the United States and Britain as a direct result of the impact of the Great Depression (1929–31) on employment opportunities.

For the earlier period these estimates conceal important annual differences between 1901 and 1921. These can be better explored by analysing the information available on gross migration flows. These data were collated by the Registrar-General, and later examined in detail by Ó Gráda. True enough they understate migration to Britain, as was underlined by the Commission on Emigration and Other Population Problems in 1955, but nevertheless they still remain a useful guide to annual differences (see appendix 3).[23] A number of interesting points emerge relating to pre-independence patterns of migration, such as the sharp decrease in emigration to the United States with the outbreak of the First World War in 1914, and the slowdown in migration in 1917 and 1918, stemming from a fear of sea travel owing to enemy actions in the Atlantic after the entry of the United States on the side of Britain and the allies. As Fitzpatrick observes, movement across the Irish Sea during the war was not enumerated and this remains to some extent a matter for speculation. He also points to the fact that the war 'prompted considerable short-term migration to British munitions factories, in addition to the special emigration resulting from military recruitment, overseas service, and often death or postwar settlement abroad'.[24] The increase in 1920 is related to the demand for labour which occurred as a result of the short-lived post-war economic boom in Britain and the United States.

From 1926 onwards, one other form of information relating to gross migration flows is available in the calculation of the net balance of passenger movement (the difference between the total inward and outward flows) by sea (and later air). This measure is, as Garvey has quite rightly noted, a fairly crude indication of net migration and even small measurement errors in the gross flows can result in very significant errors in the passenger balance.[25] The other complication with this method of estimating annual emigration rates was the existence of the open border with Northern Ireland and the considerable volume of cross-border traffic on foot and in passenger vehicles.[26] Notwithstanding these difficulties, a series of annual migration estimates has been calculated for the period from 1926 to 1976 using an amalgam of sources including annual population estimates and information on births and mortality. The data for the period between 1926 and 1940 are presented in Figure 2.1; however, these estimates should be treated with caution as they are 'of a residual nature, being a by-product of the methods used in compiling the annual series of population estimates'.[27] In addition, as the author pointed out, the available evidence suggests that there was considerable under-registration of births before 1942, when the introduction of rationing and the subsequent introduction of children's allowances in 1944 'provided a strong encouragement for complete registration'.[28] Therefore the absolute numbers involved should not be taken as accurate, although the annual estimates do give an indication of the trends.

Several patterns should be highlighted on the basis of these estimates, the first being the effect of the Great Depression on Irish migration rates when a net inflow occurred during 1931–32. The level of migration gradually increased throughout the following years until 1936, when migration regained pre-depression levels. The other obvious point to note is the sharp decrease in 1939, with the outbreak of

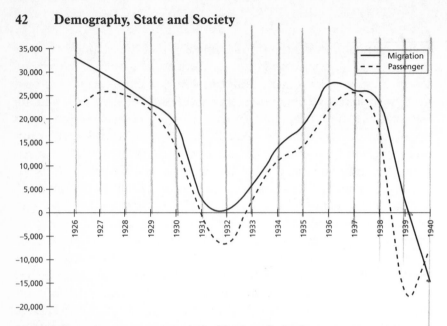

Note: Net passenger movement excludes Northern Ireland.
Source: After J. G. Hughes, *Estimates of annual net migration and their relationship with series on annual net passenger movement: Ireland 1926–1976*, Dublin, 1977, ESRI memorandum no. 122, pp. 8, 21.

Fig. 2.1 *Estimates of net Irish migration and net passenger movement 1926–40*

the Second World War. One final observation may be made with regard to the period between 1922 to 1925 which remains a lacuna in the state of knowledge. It can be presumed that the high levels of the mid–1920s did not develop spontaneously in 1926 and that they were in fact the continuation or acceleration of the pattern established in the preceding five or so years. In addition, several political factors accelerated the level of migration at this time, including those already discussed such as the disbandment of the RIC, the withdrawal of crown officials and the British army, but also the emigration to the United States of individuals from the ranks of the defeated Irregulars from 1924 onwards, after the end of the Civil War in May 1923.[29]

The principal destinations for these migrants remained the traditional receiving areas for Irish persons: the United States, Britain and to a lesser extent, Australia, Canada and New Zealand. Since our remit here is Irish migration to Britain, this aspect will be examined in more detail below. First, however, a brief overview of patterns of migration to places other than Britain will be outlined. The numbers leaving for 'overseas' destinations from 1924 until 1939 are presented in appendix 4. The classification of an 'overseas' migrant was a person travelling out of Europe and not within the Mediterranean Sea. These data were extracted from passenger manifests and British Board of Trade returns and are generally presumed to be a fairly reliable indicator of the patterns of migration to countries other than Britain and within Europe. It is well known that Irish migration to other European countries was of little consequence at this time. Of particular interest are the patterns of Irish emigration to the United States, the main destination for most migrants in the 1920s. The sharp increase in the years 1925 and 1926 – when over 30,000 persons left the Irish Free State annually – may be attributed to the changing nature of the immigration policy adopted by the authorities in the United States in this period. In 1921 an act introduced for the first time the concept of numerical limitation to restrict the number of immigrants coming from Europe after the end of the First World War. This act, which 'marked the beginning of a permanent policy of immigration restriction', was passed in the context of economic depression, increasing American nationalism and related fears about the level of immigration.[30] A quota of 77,342 persons was set for Britain and Ireland. This legislation was superseded in 1924 by an act which granted the Irish Free State a quota of 28,567 and stipulated that immigration must 'take place uniformly over the whole year and not more than 10 per cent of the annual quota would be admitted in any one month'.[31] It seems that migration to the United States accelerated in response to this legislation, perhaps in the fear of a wholesale embargo on the entry of immigrants. In 1929 the Irish quota was reduced to 17,853 persons and from 1930 onwards all prospective immigrants were required to demonstrate that they had adequate capital or a guarantor resident in the United States to ensure that they did not become a public charge.[32] It is debatable whether these restrictions or the fallout from the Wall Street Crash of 1929 and subsequent economic depression dissuaded Irish persons from wishing to travel to the United States, although the economic situation in the United States would appear to be the overriding factor which accounts for the significant decrease in migration. Gemery has underlined the fact that in the early 1930s, it was the effect of the depression on the American labour market in the form of contracting opportunities for employment rather than immigrant quotas *per se* which explains the dramatic decline in migration from Europe to the United States in the 1930s.[33] In a discussion of European emigration, Baines concludes that 'in the early 1930s, there was a drastic fall in income in all the receiving countries. Emigration would have fallen even if there had been no restriction'.[34] This analysis would also hold true for the Irish situation.

In tandem with the changes in the economy of the United States, it may also be argued that it was not so much the actual imposition of restrictions on immigration which was of consequence, but more significantly the perception that it was more difficult to enter the United States. Undoubtedly many Irish families would have access to, at the very least, one family member or friend who could act as guarantor, given the scale of nineteenth- and early twentieth-century Irish migration to the United States. However, the point which should be noted is that migrants already in the United States would not encourage relatives or friends to travel since few employment opportunities were available. In fact, as was observed earlier, there is a return flow to the Irish Free State in the early 1930s since obviously some migrants preferred to endure their spell of unemployment and poverty in the austere climate of rural Ireland rather than large American cities. There is also little doubt that the flow of information between the sending and destination societies was a key factor in determining whether the United States was a viable option for prospective migrants and this would very effectively discourage travel to the United States. What is quite telling is that the quotas for Irish citizens were never filled throughout the interwar years.[35] In short, the United States became a much less attractive option for Irish migrants in the interwar years.

Britain, on the other hand, from the mid–1930s onwards seemed to offer opportunites which the United States did not. As was noted earlier, reliable statistical measures of the level of Irish migration to Britain are not available. However, one useful compensatory method is to compare the average annual rate of migration for the intercensal period 1926–36, with the number of 'overseas' migrants and thereby arrive at a residual figure for migration elsewhere, mainly to Britain. The statisticians working on the Commission on Emigration adopted such a practice and the results are presented in Table 2.2. Whilst the changing pattern is readily apparent, it is difficult to say with any certainty in what years precisely Irish migration to Britain developed on a large scale.

Table 2.2 Net Irish migration by destination and sex, 1926–36

	Male	Female	Persons
Overseas	–42,789	–48,397	–91,186
Elsewhere (Britain, etc.)	–29,774	–45,791	–75,565
Total	–72,563	–94,188	–166,751

Source: Commission on Emigration, *Reports*, table 87, p. 116.

Walshaw constructed a series of estimates of migration from the Irish Free State to Britain using data on passenger movements in the period from 1924 until 1937, and the results are presented in Table 2.3. Between 1924 and 1930, Irish migration to Britain averaged about 9,700 persons per annum, but considerable variations are also evident. From 1934 onwards, with the beginnings of the economic recovery in Britain, Irish migration increased and in 1936 over 30,000 Irish people travelled to Britain. Since the information on 'overseas' emigration suggests that no appreciable increase occurred, it can be safely assumed that from the mid–1930s onwards Britain emerged as the principal destination for Irish migrants.

Table 2.3 Estimates of Irish migration to Britain, 1924–37

Year	Total	Year	Total
1924	18,000	1931	9,800
1925	8,800	1932	13,200
1926	11,400	1933	11,300
1927	7,500	1934	16,400
1928	5,500	1935	22,100
1929	7,900	1936	32,300
1930	8,600	1937	28,300

Source: R. S. Walshaw, *Migration to and from the British Isles*, London, 1941, table 13, p. 72.

The mid–1930s can therefore be pinpointed fairly precisely as the genesis of the 'second-wave' of large-scale Irish migration to Britain. This is not to imply that throughout the 1920s no migrant opted to improve their life chances by settling in Britain since clearly many did. For instance, in 1927 over a quarter of Irish migrants travelled to Britain.[36] However, it is the sheer scale of the movement to Britain that makes the interwar years a benchmark in the history of Irish migration. The key question is: why Britain? Firstly, it was a less traumatic move than the journey to the United States, Canada and Australia. Return movement was relatively straightforward and involved only a short passage across the Irish Sea. This was particularly relevant in the precarious climate of the international economy in the 1930s. Secondly, it was cheap and less capital was needed in order to travel to Britain. So in this uncertain environment, the risks involved in the move to Britain were considerably less than those in the North American or Australian options. If, for whatever reason, a migrant failed to secure employment, he or she could return home without suffering a great financial loss. The decision to travel to the United States was an acknowledgement that life for the foreseeable future at least would be spent abroad, since return migration, although not unknown, was an altogether more difficult process from the United States.[37] The finality associated with transatlantic migration – both in popular perception and in the minds of migrants – compared less favourably with the ease of movement across the Irish Sea. This also reflects an implicit change in the nature of Irish migration. Migration to the United States, Canada or Australia was rarely a short-term expedient, with the exceptions of times of crisis such as the Great Irish Famine. On the other hand, Britain offered the opportunity to earn income with a view to eventually returning home after a couple of years, particularly if suitable opportunities arose in the Irish Free State. The 'myth of return' which was such a central element of the deliberations of migrants might actually be realised from Britain. In some senses, migrants could 'keep a foot' in both countries because of the availability of cheap transport and the regular flow of information.

But this change in the nature of Irish migration could not have occurred without a demand for unskilled labour in the British economy. This is not the place for a detailed assessment of the performance of the British economy in the 1930s and the associated effects on the labour market, although a few observations may be made. First of all, recovery from depression occurred in the early 1930s, although the explanations for this have been the subject of some debate among British economic historians.[38] Secondly, in terms of the labour market, high rates of unemployment were concentrated in particular regions which were the centres of the 'heavy' industries such as shipbuilding, textiles, coal mining, and iron and steel manufacturing in Scotland, Tyneside and Lancashire.[39] Lastly, unemployment was at a much lower level in the Midlands and south-east England where the light manufacturing industries were located.[40] How do these changes relate to an analysis of Irish migration? In short, in the absence of a demand for unskilled Irish labour it is difficult to imagine the development of the large-scale flow of Irish migrants in the 1930s. Without employment – and with few additional resources – life in Britain would be little different from staying home in Ireland, with the obvious exception of the mechanisms of family support available at home. Related to the availability of employment, a continuous flow of Irish migrants who subsequently became a charge on the public purse as a result of unemployment would have resulted in restrictions being placed on the entry of Irish citizens to Britain. This option was, as we shall see later, one that was considered by the British authorities on a number of occasions in the interwar period.

Certain characteristics of the migrant profile may be highlighted on the basis of the evidence presented thus far. One of the pivotal issues is that of gender. In the period 1911–26, it appears that a relative degree of parity in terms of gender existed, but as the report accompanying the 1926 census explained, 'were it not for the abnormal migration in the last period [the First World War and the withdrawal of British personnel in 1921–22], it is probable that there would have been a very considerable excess of females amongst the migrants' (see Table 2.4).[41] Kennedy has constructed some rough estimates of the trend in female migration by attempting to discount the numbers involved in this 'special' emigration from the equation; he arrives at the estimate of 'normal emigration by sex, of about eight males for every ten females'.[42] Whilst his estimates of female migration under 'normal' conditions must be treated with a fair degree of

Table 2.4 Average annual rate of net Irish migration per 1,000 of the average population, 1901–36

	Male	Females	Both sexes
1901–11	–7.4	–9.1	–8.2
1911–26	–9.0	–8.7	–8.8
1926–36	–4.8	–6.5	–5.6

Source: Commission on Emigration, *Reports*, table 86, p. 115.

scepticism, it seems plausible to argue (in the counterfactual sense) that in the absence of war in Europe and the onset of independence in Ireland, the rate of female migration would have been higher than that of their male counterparts. On the basis of this assumption the excess of females over males between 1926 and 1936 may be seen as the continuation of a trend of higher female migration rather than a new development.

Another important variable is the age structure of migrants. Historically, as we have seen, migrants from Ireland have been predominantly from the younger sections of society, mostly unmarried persons. Information is available on the age distribution for 'overseas' emigration from the Irish Free State until 1939 because the age was recorded in passenger returns (see Table 2.5). Similar data for migration to Britain are not extant. One possible method of estimating the age structure is to employ 'survivorship ratios' for each age cohort, although this would include 'overseas' migrants. The Commission on Emigration applied such a procedure and the results are presented in Table 2.6a. Further data relating to mortality have been calculated and it is therefore possible to arrive at migration estimates for the age cohorts that are generally regarded as being most prone to migration (see Table 2.6b). Thus, of every 100 males aged between 15 and 19 years in 1926, 78 still lived in the Irish Free State in 1936; somewhere in the region of 4.2 died in the period and the remaining 17.8 per 100 left the country, that is, of course, assuming negligible immigration. The truism that migration affects the younger sections of the population is borne out by the data as the highest rates of migration are noted for the 15–24 age group for both sexes. The gender distribution is roughly the same, although the trend in the older female age groups is worthy of note when contrasted with the male cohorts. A similar procedure would not prove practicable for the earlier period (1911–26), owing to the effects of the First World War on male mortality rates and the withdrawal of crown officials on migration trends.

Table 2.5 Irish overseas emigration: age distribution, 1924–39 (%)

	Under 15	15–19	20–24	25–29	30 years and over
Males	9	17	35	20	19
Females	16	28	27	13	16

Source: Commission on Emigration, *Reports*, p. 122 n.1.

Table 2.6a. Survivorship ratios per 100, 1926 and 1936

Period	Males (Age at the beginning of period)					Females (Age at the beginning of period)				
	10–14	15–19	20–24	25–29	30–34	10–14	15–19	20–24	25–29	30–34
1911–26[a]	69	59	62	73	78	73	61	69	70	77
1926–36	89	78	76	91	91	83	74	77	88	87

Notes: [a] Fifteen-year period.
Source: Commission on Emigration, *Reports*, table 92, p. 123.

Table 2.6b. Cohort depletion per 100, 1926–36

	Males (Age at the beginning of period)					Females (Age at the beginning of period)				
	10–14	15–19	20–24	25–29	30–34	10–14	15–19	20–24	25–29	30–34
Decrease due to deaths (approx.)[a]	3.8	4.2	4.8	5.7	7.3	4.2	5.0	5.4	6.0	7.1
Decrease due to migration	7.2	17.8	19.2	3.3	1.7	12.8	21.0	17.6	6.0	5.9

Note: [a] These estimates for mortality are for 1935–37, based on the Census of Population (cited in Commission on Emigration, *Reports*, table 22, p. 310).
Source: Commission on Emigration, *Reports*, table 92, p. 123.

The occupations of these migrants prior to leaving the Irish Free State are difficult to ascertain as no direct information of this nature was collected for persons travelling to Britain. Whilst clearly some skilled persons did migrate, especially to Australia and Canada in the later nineteenth century, the overall impression is that of a movement of unskilled labour.[43] In the interwar years, it seems likely that the majority of migrants were drawn from the ranks of farm labourers, domestic servants, the unemployed and those who defy classification in occupational terms. An inspection by the Commission on Emigration of the data available for occupations prior to migration underlines the predominance of unskilled labour among both sexes in the migration stream to 'overseas' destinations.[44] This information is not readily available to facilitate an assessment of the occupational groupings in the case of migration to Britain, yet the point still remains that migrants, on the whole, came from unskilled and agricultural sectors of the economy. Evidence to support this general contention is provided by Breen who, in his detailed study of a rural community in county Kerry, underlines the relationship between the decline in migration in the late 1920s and 1930s and the greater availability of farm servants for hire.[45]

Similarly, the regional origins of the migrants to Britain are not readily discernible as no such information was gathered by the Irish authorities. Nevertheless, for the later intercensal period (1926–36), it is possible to calculate the rate of net migration for a particular county which includes all movement, including transatlantic and internal migration. The counties that had the highest rates of average annual net migration per 1,000 of the population were (in descending order) Kerry, Mayo, Leitrim, Roscommon, Donegal, Cavan and Clare, areas traditionally associated with migration since the second half of the nineteenth century (see appendix 5). A revealing method which sheds light on some of the factors operating in these areas is the comparison of a number of measures of population density and land-holding for each county with the migration rates. As the Commission on Emigration remarked in 1955, there is a clear relationship between counties with densely populated poor land, relatively little urbanisation and high migration rates, mainly located along the western seaboard and in the north-west: 'most of the counties which have had high rates of emigration have some or all of the following characteristics – heavy density of population, low valuation of agricultural land per head, high percentage of population living in rural areas and high percentage of land in small holdings'.[46] This pattern in terms of the regional incidence of migration was not a new one; nevertheless its continuance over time should be highlighted

Therefore, the migrant who travelled to Britain in the interwar years was typically young, unskilled and from a rural agricultural background and just as likely to be female as male. There was, of course, a skilled element in the migrant flow, although the higher rates of remuneration available for some skilled occupations in urban centres in the Irish Free State, together with restrictive British trade union regulations in relation to membership, provided little incentive to migrate.[47]

III

In general terms, Irish migration since the nineteenth century may be explained by the absence of sustained economic development, with the obvious exception of north-east Ulster, together with a demand for unskilled labour in Britain and the United States. Studies of the reasons underlying large-scale Irish migration invariably focus on the relationship between poverty and emigration. There is little doubt that endemic poverty existed in the interwar years, although assessing the extent and level of poverty is problematical to say the least, since this issue has not attracted the attention of historians and social scientists, apart from one longitudinal study of poverty in inner-city Dublin which examines the early 1920s.[48] One frequently employed method of assessing the standard of living is to examine wage levels (and later, social security levels), although clearly many persons were not in receipt of any wage, such as those who were 'relatives assisting'. Ó Gráda points to the low levels of pay for farm labourers in the 1930s and the fact that the average half-yearly wage of £16 had very limited purchasing power.[49] For the 1930s, detailed data on a county and provincial basis are available for the weekly wage rates of agricultural labourers; however, for our purposes the aggregate data for the Irish Free State are of most interest. In 1935 over three-quarters of agricultural labourers not living in, earned less than 25s. for a week's work of somewhere in the region of 55 to 60 hours.[50] The effects of the Great Depression are evident in the decline in the numbers in receipt of an average weekly wage of greater than 25s. and less than 30s. (from 30 per cent in 1931 to 17 per cent in 1937), without a significant compensating increase in the higher wage levels of over 30s.[51] As agricultural prices dropped, farmers were unable – or unwilling – to pay agricultural workers a decent wage. Of course, agricultural work, by its very nature, is seasonal and temporary, and many labourers had to rely on government assistance from 1933 in times of underemployment. The government could, by order, restrict assistance to those labourers with dependants, and farmers and relatives assisting with a farm of under £4 valuation. Such an order was in place in each of the years from 1935 to 1947 for the period between July and October.[52] In short, agricultural workers experienced a significant decline in wage levels and in their standard of living in the early to mid–1930s, especially in terms of an assessment involving the cost of living index.[53] The introduction of the Agricultural Wages Act, 1936, instituted the regulation of the position of wages for agricultural workers by establishing the Agricultural Wages Board, which fixed a minimum level of remuneration. In August 1937, the first order of the board fixed wages at a minimum of 24s. per six-day week of 55 working hours for males of 21 years of age and upwards not living on the farm.[54] Various lower rates were fixed for younger age groups.

The actual day-to-day livelihood of farm labourers at this time is a matter of speculation since no study comparable in range and scope to the pioneering work of Evans and Howkins in Britain (based for the most part on oral history) is available in the Irish context.[55] Nevertheless, when contrasted with the wages of other unskilled workers, the monies received by farm labourers seem relatively meagre. For example, a bricklayer in Dublin, where the wages were considerably higher than elsewhere (including London), earned 81s. per week in 1931, whereas an agricultural labourer in county Westmeath received roughly 22s.[56] Such a disparity between skilled workers and unskilled workers was not unusual by European standards, but in the Irish Free State male urban unskilled workers earned appreciably more than their rural counterparts. Of course, the higher paid work was difficult to obtain, especially in the provincial towns: Daly's examination of the Dublin working class underlines this point for the earlier period between 1870 and 1911.[57] However, the general picture of the worsening situation for agricultural workers *vis-à-vis* manufacturing or industrial workers in the mid–1930s is captured in a comparison of the changes in the wage rates across a number of fields of employment.[58] The problem was compounded since manufacturing or industrial employment was extremely limited, particularly in the western and north-western counties, notwithstanding the intensive efforts on the part of the new Fianna Fáil government after 1932 to increase the level of non-agricultural employment by means of a protectionist economic policy.[59] Labourers were, for the most part, employed on the larger farms engaged in cattle production in areas such as Kildare, Meath and Dublin, and mixed farming areas with considerable tillage such as north Tipperary and Wexford.[60] Other areas which had considerable numbers of paid farm workers, amounting to one-third of the total agricultural labour force, included counties Wicklow, Cork (mainly east Cork), Kilkenny, Carlow, Waterford and Limerick.[61] These areas were engaged in dairying and mixed farming, with the proportion engaged in tillage increasing over the period under consideration due to state encouragement after 1932.[62] There is little doubt that for farm labourers the interwar period was a time of acute hardship.

Despite the fact that large numbers of 'relatives assisting' figure prominently in the agricultural labour force, this elusive grouping still remains relatively neglected in the few historical studies of Irish rural society completed in the twentieth century. Clearly, many of those migrants recorded in the 'overseas' emigration returns in the generic categories of 'labourers' or 'domestic servants' came from the ranks of the relatives assisting. Relatives assisting generally worked on smaller subsistence farms, particularly along the western seaboard, areas which experienced high migration rates.[63] These holdings 'were only big enough for a family's support but not large enough to employ labour'.[64] The description of these farms in county Clare by Conrad Arensberg, a Harvard anthropologist writing in the 1930s, merits quotation:

> On the small farm, the owner relies upon the united efforts of his family. The countryman's subsistence farming is a family economy in which all members of the family take part – sons, daughters and other relatives . . . Eight out of ten people working in agriculture in Ireland work not for wages and salaries but by virtue of their family relationship.[65]

As Hannan has pointed out, 'wage labour was significant only in the larger commercialised farming regions of Leinster and east Munster'.[66] A fuller consideration of the status and position of the 'relatives assisting' category does not fall within the parameters of the present study, although some brief comments may be appropriate since many migrants came from this sector of the labour force. Firstly, the standard of living for sons and daughters working for their parents or other relatives during the interwar period is a matter of conjecture. Arensberg observed in his study of Clare during the early 1930s that a son would have little if any control of the farm income, and he recounted a revealing description of the son's limited economic status: 'If a son in Luogh and other Clare communities wants a half-crown to go to a hurley match, he must get it from his father.'[67] The sons and daughters of these farmers worked for few economic rewards, apart, of course, from that of bed and full board. The second issue relates to the imbroglio of inheritance and marriage patterns as they affected the assisting relatives in rural Ireland in the nineteenth and twentieth centuries, these being important determinants of migration patterns. It must be said that these subjects in general have spawned a large literature and attracted the attention of a number of scholars working in cognate disciplines, although much of the evidence relates to the early twentieth century rather than the interwar period. One of the central issues concerns the existence of the stem-family system. In theory, this was the practice 'of allowing only one child in each generation to inherit the family holding, marry, and produce the next generation'.[68] The application of this model to rural Ireland was first illustrated in the seminal work of Arensberg and Kimball which was based on ethnographic fieldwork in county Clare during the 1930s.[69] The pithy description contained in an earlier work by Arensberg illustrates the important features of this system: 'Usually, only the heir and one daughter are married and dowered, the one with the farm, the other with the fortune. All the rest, in the words of the Luogh residents must travel.'[70]

Other practices associated with this system include the 'match' of the son who would inherit the farm and a similar arrangement if possible for as 'many daughters as could be provided with dowries and husbands'.[71] The other key features include the 'dispersal' of the remaining children following the marriage of the male heir, either within Ireland or more probably abroad.[72] The timing of the marriage and resultant succession could be postponed indefinitely, owing to an unwillingness of the patriarch to cede ultimate authority until his death. In other cases, marriage and subsequent succession did not take place until such time as a suitable arrangement for the maintenance of the parents was arrived at.[73] These practices led in part to the postponed marriages that were such a curious and distinctive feature of Irish society until the late 1950s.[74]

The central issue of interest to this study is the relationship between household structure, inheritance practices and migration patterns. For Arensberg and Kimball, dispersal of the members of the family following the marriage of the heir formed a crucial part of the rural Irish household system.[75] Some siblings could be accommodated locally by means of a dowry or obtaining a job in, for instance, local government, but for many the only option available was that they 'must travel'.[76] Judging from their comments as recounted by Arensberg and Kimball, such migrants seemed to accept their fate in an acquiescent manner. The structural functionalist outlook of these anthropologists, it may be argued, ensured a degree of bias towards the portrayal of a social system characterised by harmonious social relations, stability and co-operation.[77] Dispersal was viewed as the logical outcome of the household system.

Viewed in the light of this family structure, the decline of population becomes interpretable not as a flight from intolerable conditions, though economic distress had a powerful effect, not as a political gesture, though political disturbance took its toll, but rather as a movement arising from the effect of all these causes upon a family system whose very nature predisposed it to disperse population and which could, therefore, accommodate itself to that dispersal when it occurred.[78]

Kennedy discusses migration within the context of postponed marriage and permanent celibacy. In Kennedy's view, the relationship between availability of land, inheritance and migration is cut and dried:

The resurgence of this type of inheritance system (one heir per holding) did not cause the permanent celibacy of the assisting relatives or the emigration of those who were unwilling to remain single; it was merely the way in which the rural Irish attempted to achieve the new minimum standard of living given the scarcity of land.[79]

It must be said that changes over time and space enter only weakly into Kennedy's schema and, as such, the analysis is vague. Nevertheless, he does underline one crucial factor in determining migration decisions, that being the expectation of the achievement of a 'minimum' standard of living in Ireland or more probably elsewhere. Furthermore, he argues that migration provided an alternative to remaining single for males, since a prospective partner would not accept the standard of living that such a small farm would provide.[80] Again little in the way of supporting evidence is deployed to substantiate and illustrate these observations, apart from a number of literary sources and a rudimentary presentation of census data. Ó Gráda examines the complexities of the relationship between emigration, inheritance and fertility in post-famine Ireland.[81] For him, 'emigration allowed the luxuries of both impartible inheritance and large families'.[82] Therefore, migration ensured the working of the social system whereby on small to medium-size farms, one son could be provided for, but the rest 'must travel'; this relationship is summed up neatly in the aphorism, 'one for the farm, and the rest for the road'.[83] In addition, high levels of marital fertility could exist, since the 'surplus' children would inevitably migrate, and through remittances provide for the younger children and eventual maintenance of the parents. An equally interesting point worth noting is that the issue of who actually inherited the holding is not as clear cut as it may once have seemed. Whereas primogeniture was regarded by scholars as the principal form of transfer in Ireland until relatively recently, the evidence for the early twentieth century suggests that other sons, rather than the oldest one, frequently inherited the farm.[84]

Drawing on an examination of manuscript census records, the most recent assessment of these issues undertaken by Guinnane demonstrates that the Irish household in the early twentieth century did not conform conveniently either to the stem-family or nuclear-family model.[85] More importantly for our purposes, he points to the fact that inheriting the family farm or migration may be viewed not necessarily as a process whereby some children were disadvantaged in order to ensure that the family holding remained intact for one son or daughter.

> By giving one son a solid farm and the others a chance at a good life elsewhere, parents were able to provide for both themselves and their children. Doubtless sometimes this system involved bitter disappointment for the son or daughter not favoured to remain in Ireland, and considerable anguish for the son who would rather leave but was expected to stay. But it is more accurate to view this situation as changes in the way families divided their properties than to cling to the notion that parents disinherited all but one or two of their children.[86]

There is much value in this suggestion that inheritance of a farm holding and migration represented two quite different outcomes for young people. With the demand for labour in other countries, well-developed migrant networks and the possibility of a far better life abroad, the fact that a child did not inherit may well have presented them with a much brighter future abroad than if they stayed.

The available evidence suggests that inheritance patterns, the limited opportunities for social mobility in this rigid social structure and the widespread prevalence of poverty among the poorer sections of the agricultural community, combined with perceptions of a better life elsewhere, are among the numerous factors which ensured that migration provided the only avenue to improve the life chances of young people in interwar Ireland. The main occupational grouping that constituted the majority of migrants evident in the available data – unpaid and paid farm labourers and domestic servants – would have been particularly susceptible to these pressures owing to their precarious position in the economic hierarchy. The interwar years in the Irish Free State were difficult times (as was the case elsewhere in Europe and the United States), especially for those with small holdings or no land at all, and therefore it is not particularly surprising that when the effects of the depression began to lessen in intensity in Britain during the mid–1930s, many decided to migrate.

IV

Emigration since the nineteenth century had been regarded as a 'problem', a movement of people which could be stemmed with the achievement of self-government for Ireland. Successive Irish nationalist political leaders, such as Daniel O'Connell in the 1830s and Charles Stewart Parnell in the 1890s, argued that the solution to the migration of large numbers of Irish persons was the end of British rule in Ireland and the encouragement of indigenous industry.[87] Of course, these facile 'solutions' made for excellent political propaganda, although a detailed policy for economic development as such was rarely enunciated.[88] This study is not strictly speaking concerned with an examination of the place of emigration in Irish nationalist political rhetoric throughout the nineteenth and early twentieth centuries, although in general terms, it may be observed that migration was explained by British misrule combined with the connivance of the landlord élite in Ireland.[89] Emigration was also seen as a tool in the British inventory of tactics designed to defeat Irish separatists during the Anglo-Irish war of 1919–21. The stimulation of emigration was regarded by the self-instituted Dáil Éireann as an avenue whereby the British administration attempted to remove young men from Ireland, and by implication, from involvement in the nationalist organisations. According to a 'manifesto' on emigration issued in August 1920, persons who left the country were to be regarded as 'deserters'.[90] This attempt to regulate migration was not a success, notwithstanding the introduction of a 'permit' system by Dáil Éireann in July 1920.[91] During these optimistic days, the achievement of independence would ensure 'that no Irishman would ever leave his native land in order to live under decent conditions'.[92] This sanguine belief that self-government would lead to an ending of emigration was, of course, not a new element of Irish nationalist ideology. In a memorable comment, Patrick Pearse suggested in 1913 that 'a free Ireland would not, and could not, have hunger in her fertile vales and squalor in her cities. Ireland has resources to feed five times her population: a free Ireland would make those resources available.'[93] In December 1921 the Anglo-Irish treaty provided for the establishment one year later of the Irish Free State. Contrary to earlier Irish nationalist rhetoric which suggested that in a 'free Ireland' emigration would soon dissipate owing to the concrete benefits of self-government, nothing could have been further from reality. The newly established Irish state did not have a policy as such on migration to other countries. Other problems were perceived to be more important throughout the 1920s. Equally revealing is the fact that no government file relating to emigration is extant for the period from 1921 to 1939, although it must be said that it is quite likely that Cumann na nGaedheal ministers did not leave any potentially embarrassing documentation for their political opponents to peruse when Fianna Fáil entered office in March 1932.[94]

Emigration in isolation rarely entered the realm of public discourse in the interwar period, but was frequently discussed in relation to the economic policies adopted by the Cumann na nGaedheal (1922–32) and Fianna Fáil administrations (from 1932 onwards). The basic tenet of the economic programme of the Cumann na nGaedheal government was 'an outward-looking commercial policy based on pursuing Ireland's comparative advantage in pastoral agriculture'.[95] The export of goods to Britain at competitive prices was the key policy element of the economic strategy adopted by this administration.[96] To quote one sympathetic admirer of Patrick Hogan, the Irish Free State minister for agriculture, 'Hogan started from the assumption that agriculture was and would remain by far the most important industry in the Free State, and that the touchstone by which every economic measure must be judged was its effect on the prosperity of farmers'.[97] By implication, therefore, the stimulation of industry or the creation of employment in the industrial sector remained a secondary objective for the Cumann na nGaedheal administration. The development of indigenous industrial concerns would involve, in the infant stages at least, some degree of protectionism. However, the Cumann na nGaedheal government was loath to introduce a general tariff on imports, since this would increase the cost of living, especially for the agricultural sector.[98] Tariff protection was granted to individual producers and each case was assessed on its merits, but in general the policy was based on the principles of free trade.[99] Towards the end of the 1920s with the onset of depression, the policy towards protection changed somewhat, and a number of authors have suggested that had Cumann na nGaedheal remained in power 'it would have undoubtedly become even more protectionist'.[100] Nevertheless, the two key elements of Cumann na nGaedheal policy throughout the 1920s – promotion of pastoral agricultural exports and limited protection of Irish industries – were, for some contemporary commentators, directly related to the continuance of emigration from Ireland. Hogan was constantly berated in *The Leader* for his perceived failure to promote an increase in the amount of land under tillage, which it was argued, would increase employment and consequently reduce migration.[101] The agricultural policy of the 'Minister for Grass', as *The Leader* acerbically labelled Hogan, was singled out for ridicule as his programme had resulted in 'continued emigration'.[102] This publication was in no doubt as to where the blame lay regarding continued migration:

> Unemployment and unnatural emigration still are rampant as if we were not free. And now that we are free we cannot blame England. Mr Hogan, our minister of lands and agriculture, if the British were in occupation would be the most abused man in Ireland. *The Leader* would not be the only paper to call him the minister for grass; he would be held responsible for emigration.[103]

The Leader, which discussed this issue at some length throughout the late 1920s, can be viewed as a fairly idiosyncratic organ of public opinion, not least for the vituperation which flowed from its columns. The fact that the main opposition party, Fianna Fáil, adopted a fairly similar line regarding the symbiotic relationship between the economic policy of Cumann na nGaedheal and migration is of far greater consequence. An election flyer published in 1927 by Fianna Fáil argued that 'from 1922 until 1926 their [Cumann na nGaedheal] policy forced an emigration which was unsurpassed since the decade after the famine'.[104] Leaving aside the cavalier approach to statistics evident in this election literature, Fianna Fáil clearly realised that figures for migration, some of fairly dubious veracity, were a useful basis for criticism with which to attack the record of the government.[105] During the 1927 election campaign, de Valera suggested that 'unemployment and emigration, if allowed to continue, will so cripple this nation that there can be little hope for it, in the immediate future at any rate'.[106] In the following year, de Valera made a comment along similar lines to that of Pearse in 1913 when he stated, 'we believe that there can be maintained on the soil of this country, in comfort, and with a proper policy, a population two or three times the size of the present population'.[107] In de Valera's view, 'everybody realises that what is happening at the present time is that the producing part of the our population is being driven out by emigration'.[108] In an unpublished memorandum on the 'industrial and economic state of the country' written in 1929, Seán Lemass, perhaps one of the more economically sophisticated thinkers in the Irish political élite at this time, provides a revealing insight into the background to the policies adopted by his party when it assumed power in 1932. According to Lemass, questions of national well-being were directly related to the issues of migration and employment.

> We are not prepared to watch calmly the depopulation and impoverishment of our country. We desire political and economic freedom so that we can take action to protect our vital national interests . . . The economic policy which in operation has produced this exodus from the country stands self-condemned. It is indeed amazing that any voices should be raised in defence of the system which in 15 years drove out of the country half a million people, a number almost equal to the entire population of the province of Connacht. Unless that drain on the country's vitality is arrested the days of the Irish nation are numbered.[109]

The attitude of the Cumann na nGaedheal administration to continued migration in the 1920s appears indifferent. Emigration is not mentioned at all in a number of party pamphlets produced for the 1927 and 1932 elections.[110] Clearly, the acknowledgment of the 'problem' of migration was not perceived as a practical vote-winner, yet outlining policies which might 'stem the flow', as it were, was a ploy used fairly effectively by the Fianna Fáil party to increase its support. It is quite revealing that Gallagher found a direct relationship between support for Fianna Fáil and high emigration rates in the period from 1927 to 1938.[111] It was the small farming communities in the west and north-west of Ireland which were particularly affected by emigration and Fianna Fáil was therefore merely reflecting the immediate concerns of its supporters or potential voters. Similarly, in the period prior to the foundation of Fianna Fáil in 1926, support for Sinn Féin in the 1923 general election tended to be strong in regions with high rates of migration, especially the west of Ireland.[112]

When the president of the Executive Council, W. T. Cosgrave, addressed the issue of emigration during a speech in September 1928 to the Cork Industrial Development Association, a protectionist lobby, his comments appeared quite bizarre.[113] The annual report for 1928 of the Cork IDA had stated that the 'annual economic loss to the state caused by the emigration of 30,000 of its best nationals is equivalent to a direct annual capital loss of 15 million pounds sterling'.[114] Cosgrave's response to this statement merits quotation as it provides a unique insight into his views with regard to emigration.

> The association suggests that the annual economic loss to the state caused by the emigration of 30,000 citizens is equivalent to a direct annual capital loss of £15,000,000. The average assessment would appear to me to be small at £500. Suitably equipped for the battle of life with a determination to succeed, it

might be reasonably assessed at double that sum. Over a lengthy period the number of emigrants have [sic] run into millions and on the basis adopted by your association the loss in cash value exceeds £1,000,000,000. It is at least an indication of the resources of the country that it would have afforded such a drain on manpower and the equivalent of the cash value you have assessed. This is however one of the problems which is helped least by its harrowing reiteration.[115]

Whether this statement can be assessed as displaying a pragmatic approach to migration and an acceptance of the inevitability of population movement, or as sheer indifference, is open to debate. For *The Leader*, Cosgrave's statement indicated that the Cumann na nGaedheal administration 'appeared to look upon emigration . . . as a matter of course'.[116] In a vigorous defence by Cosgrave of the economic policy of his administration in 1930, emigration is not mentioned, nor indeed are any long-term policies which aimed at increasing rural and urban employment.[117] But, as de Valera pointed out, Cosgrave's assessment appeared unduly optimistic: 'Why is it our people are leaving this country if everything is so fine as the president stated?'[118]

Fianna Fáil came to power in March 1932 on a populist economic programme of self-sufficiency and protectionism and, as Neary and Ó Gráda have noted, the policies pursued were 'influenced by immediate economic pressures and by the party's ideological commitments'.[119] Therefore, the effects of the worsening depression together with the economic programme which had been outlined in opposition mediated the decisions taken during the first few years of the Fianna Fáil administration. In short, the central strands of Fianna Fáil economic policy were threefold: the encouragement of tillage, protectionist tariffs and the development of economic 'self-sufficiency'.[120] A co-ordinated policy to develop native industry and increase employment in rural and urban areas would counter the related problems of unemployment and emigration. The employment gains from the policy of protection followed by the Fianna Fáil administration have been the subject of debate amongst Irish economic historians. Johnson has argued that 'it is undeniable that employment increased in the protected trades and certainly more people were employed in factory-based industries'.[121] The overall increase of 51,000 persons in industrial or manufacturing employment in the intercensal period from 1926 to 1936 which is indicated by the Census of Production is, however, 'open to doubt'.[122] Daly has questioned some of the assumptions underlying this analysis and argued that in the period 1932–36 industrial employment increased by somewhere in the region of 35,000–40,000 persons.[123] As Ó Gráda concludes, after reviewing the various strands of the debate, 'whatever the change over the 1926–36 decade as a whole, the contrast between the pre- and post-1932 period remains'.[124] The link between unemployment and migration was a direct one, according to the conventional logic of the time. For example, in 1932 Seán Lemass, the new minister for industry and commerce, acknowledged that the increase in unemployment had resulted from the substantial decrease in migration.[125] However, as was noted above in this chapter, the level of migration actually increased throughout the 1930s which in itself indicates that migration rates were to some degree influenced by exogenous events, particularly the perceived employment opportunities in Britain in the wake of the Great Depression. If we apply de Valera's litmus test of the economic state of a country – albeit uttered from the relative comfort of the opposition benches – that is, 'Is it not a definite test of prosperity whether our people can be retained in the country or not?', successive administrations under his stewardship would seem to have failed miserably.[126] This failure was not lost on members of the opposition who asked parliamentary questions on a regular basis, seeking to ascertain the numbers of migrants and to highlight the consequent embarrassment of the government.[127] When de Valera was asked in 1937 whether he would participate in the imperial conferences relating to British empire migration, he outlined the government's policy on emigration:

> The aim of the Irish government is not to provide facilities for the emigration of our people to the states of the British Commonwealth or elsewhere. Its aim is to concentrate on utilising the resources of this country and so improving the conditions of life here that our people will not have to emigrate, but will be able to find a livelihood in our country.[128]

This statement reflects an integral aspect of the ideology of nationalist Ireland, that is, migration was a problem which could be 'solved' by creating sufficient employment opportunities. In fact, the level of migration throughout the 1930s suggests that such an assumption was at best naïve and perhaps disingenuous. In 1930 de Valera indicated to a French journalist that the elimination of emigration was central to economic recovery in the Irish Free State.[129] In 1933 in the course of a post-election speech given in London to Irish migrants, de Valera again pointed to the primacy of this issue: 'We shall not rest until we have lifted the doom of exile which so long has lain upon hundreds of thousands of Irishmen in every generation.'[130]

Certain elements of the ideology that was articulated by the Fianna Fáil party – and de Valera in particular – are quite revealing on the prevailing views in relation to living standards in interwar Ireland. An appeal to traditional norms which sat rather uneasily with a commitment to industrialisation and modernisation was a central element of the ideology of this political party.[131] In a famous and oft-quoted St Patrick's Day speech in March 1943, de Valera 'evoked an ideal Irish society' in which 'people were satisfied with frugal comfort'.[132] But other statements by de Valera in the 1930s point to the romantic notions of a peasant society untouched by modernity which characterised much of his thinking in relation to Irish rural society.[133] There is an interesting parallel here with Salazar's Portugal, although this is not to imply that de Valera was a fascist dictator. According to Brettell, Salazar promoted a 'pastoral ideology' in which 'backwardness' was a virtue, which 'was designed to suppress any feelings of class antagonism'.[134] Salazar's 'pastoral ideology' did not differ greatly from de Valera's 'ideal' Ireland: 'This ideology was based on a romanticised vision of the rural way of life, medieval simplicity, freedom of Catholic belief and the love of the land which characterises the instinct of property peculiar to peasant culture.'[135]

The idealised view of Irish rural society which de Valera frequently articulated on a number of occasions was greatly at odds with the grinding poverty that labourers and small farmers endured on a daily basis. In these circumstances, migration was a means whereby young people could improve their standard of living, albeit at the expense of the leaving behind the 'simple' life of rural Ireland. Sometime later, in August 1951, de Valera displayed a remarkable lack of understanding when he stated that most migrants could find work at home 'and in conditions infinitely better from the point of view of health and morals'.[136]

Irish state policy, insofar as a distinct policy in relation to migration to Britain was formulated in the interwar years, centred on the creation of sufficient employment in order to remove the necessity for people to leave the country. The Cumann na nGeadheal administration paid little attention to the movement of population out of the newly established state because it was faced with more pressing problems, such as establishing the legitimacy of the state in 1922–23, Anglo-Irish diplomatic relations and the economic difficulties of the

1920s. Although the Fianna Fáil party frequently paid lip-service to the cessation of migration both while in opposition and on assuming power, there are few discernible differences in terms of policy. The Irish state did not attempt to control or regulate migration, but merely benefited from the steady demand for labour in Britain which reduced the level of unemployment in the Irish Free State. However in the mid–1930s the Irish state was forced to enunciate a policy on the position of Irish migrants in Britain, as a result of a number of unrelated developments and in particular by representations from Roman Catholic clergy in both countries.

The death in a fire in a bothy at Kirkintilloch in Scotland of ten young migratory labourers from Achill Island in county Mayo in September 1937 was given extensive press coverage.[137] This event mirrored a similar tragedy in November 1935 when 19 migratory labourers were drowned on a boat journey from Burtonport to Arranmore in the final stage of the return journey home from Scotland.[138] Seasonal migration, as we noted in the previous chapter, was a long-standing tradition of the movement of workers from parts of western Ireland, particularly counties Donegal and Mayo. The deaths in Kirkintilloch provoked discussion on the livelihood of seasonal migrants, and brought to light a number of revealing accounts on the plight of these workers.[139] The response of the Irish government was predictable to say the least. An interdepartmental committee on seasonal migration composed of civil servants was appointed in September 1937. This committee was charged with the task of making recommendations to improve the manner in which seasonal labour was recruited, the conditions of employment and the economic conditions in the congested areas.[140] The *Irish Times* noted that a committee with such limited scope was of 'little practical value', and that what was required was a public commission to investigate 'the living conditions which drive some thousands of citizens annually from the west to seek unworthy and humiliating employment across the channel'.[141] In addition, as the secretary of the Joint Committee of Women's Societies and Social Workers pointed out, despite the fact that migratory workers were both male and female, the committee did not include any female member.[142] The report of the interdepartmental committee was published in 1938 and dealt in detail with administrative matters relating to poorer parts of western Ireland, such as the extension of bog reclamation schemes and greater efforts at land redistribution.[143] However, the report did not include any significant recommendations regarding the flow of migratory workers to Scotland, the committee concluding that such measures would not be appropriate. The government later accepted most of the administrative recommendations, but little in the way of a programme to ensure better living conditions for seasonal workers was included.[144]

With the threat of an impending European conflict, the position of Irish citizens in Britain in the event of war became an issue for Irish civil servants and politicians.[145] The discussion centred on the possibility of Irish migrants being conscripted to serve in the British forces. William Norton, the leader of the Labour Party, requested information on this matter from the government in October and November 1938. De Valera informed Norton that Irish citizens temporarily resident in Britain would not be liable for military service.[146] The situation was more complicated for Irish citizens who were 'permanently or ordinarily' resident in Britain owing to the Irish Nationality and Citizenship Act, 1935. Under Irish law, persons who became Irish citizens under the 1922 Constitution, or the 1935 Act, were Irish nationals, and therefore not British subjects.[147] The British position was that Irish citizens were also British subjects, regardless of the legislation passed by the Dáil in 1935.[148] When the British National Service Acts were passed in June 1939, men living in Britain for longer than two years were treated as 'permanent' residents and consequently liable for conscription. However, Irish citizens who could prove that their residence in Britain was of a 'temporary' nature were specifically excluded from military service.[149] In practice, throughout the course of the war, Irish migrants who came to Britain were regarded as 'temporary' and therefore not subject to conscription.[150] The situation as regards Irish citizens who lived in Britain prior to the outbreak of the war is not as straightforward. Strictly speaking such persons would have been liable for military service after two years of residence, but the British authorities allowed 'a large number' of Irish citizens to return in 1939.[151] Presumably then, persons who were resident in Britain for longer than two years prior to the outbreak of the war and who did not return were willing to take their chances as regards conscription. However, any Irish citizen living in Britain who was called up for service could return home, and somewhat later, in 1941, an assurance was given by the British authorities that this would remain the case.[152]

Throughout the post-famine period the Irish Roman Catholic church adopted a rather ambivalent stance in relation to migration.

Most clerics realised the inevitability of population movement from Ireland, notwithstanding the fact that in principle emigration was perceived to be harmful to the Irish 'nation'.[153] From the mid–1930s onwards, with the increase in the level of Irish migration to Britain, individual clerical figures set about highlighting the perceived problems associated with this flow, in particular the difficulties faced by Irish migrants in Britain. The recurrent theme of many of the public statements was that young Irish women were especially vulnerable to the moral 'dangers' of living in 'godless' Britain. For example, the archbishop of Tuam, Dr Thomas Gilmartin, who was particularly vocal about female migration, addressed this issue in a number of statements. In 1934 Gilmartin warned young Irish women and their parents against answering advertisements for work in Britain and placed the blame for female migration firmly on the employment agencies recruiting women for positions as domestic servants: 'A number of these advertising agencies are traps, in order that Irish girls may be enticed into houses of ill-fame, and very often terrible tragedies follow.'[154] He suggested that girls should seek the advice of their parish priest before answering such advertisements.[155] In his Lenten pastoral of 1937, Gilmartin returned to the issue of the moral welfare of Irish female migrants, when he again advised prospective female emigrants to consult local clergy or Catholic agencies before responding to an advertisement for employment in Britain: women who did not follow this procedure were 'foolish girls [who] run terrible risks to soul and body'.[156] Public interest in the 'plight' of Irish female migrants in Britain is indicated by a number of newspaper articles and a pamphlet by the redoubtable Gertrude Gaffney of the *Irish Independent*, published in 1937.[157] This pamphlet describes at length the experiences of some Irish women in London, and apart from some dubious advice regarding the need to 'avoid foreign Jews', Gaffney outlines a number of the pitfalls facing young Irish women in Britain for the first time.[158] Since her writings on this matter were based on research in London and Dublin, her 'exposés' must have proved an awkward embarrassment for the Irish government.

This interest in the level of female migration to Britain, particularly for domestic service, was not confined to individual prelates or journalists since some prominent members of the hierarchy of the Roman Catholic church in England also displayed anxiety about Irish female migrants in London. In 1937 Cardinal Arthur Hinsley, the archbishop of Westminister, outlined a scheme to J. W. Dulanty, the

Irish High Commissioner in London, whereby employment agencies in London would issue prospective emigrants and their employers with leaflets, offering guidance on life in Britain in order to ensure that female migrants 'do not fall into moral danger'.[159] However, Hinsley stressed the point that 'a very large proportion of Irish girls' encountered few problems in Britain and continued to practise their religion.[160] The Irish government's response was to secure the general co-operation of Irish newspapers, although it is not clear from the available documentation whether the Irish employment agencies agreed to distribute the flyers.[161] De Valera's attitude towards increased female migration to Britain in the late 1930s, and the inherent moral dangers, was outlined in a letter to Dr Michael McGrath, bishop of Menevia, who wrote to the taoiseach in 1937 to express his concerns about the 'larger stream than usual of Irish girls' coming to Britain.[162] In de Valera's view, action on the part of the Irish state would not be possible and he added that he had arrived at the conclusion that 'this is essentially a matter in which only the close co-operation of the clergy here and in Great Britain can be effective'.[163] The comments of Joseph Walshe, the secretary of the Department of External Affairs, are revealing on the subject of the respective responsibilities of church and state:

> I have come to the conclusion that it is time for us to put the responsibility for this matter where it really belongs, namely, on the shoulders of the clergy . . . The church in this country and in England has an organisation incomparably better than any that could be set up by the state. A direction from the bishops would be enough to produce a special committee in every parish in the country within a week, but, so long as the bishops keep their heads in the sand and continue to believe that the problem does not really exist, there is no hope.[164]

The crux of the matter was where the ultimate responsibility lay for the welfare of young Irish female migrants in Britain. Walshe's comments suggest that, so far as the Irish state was concerned, the 'moral' problems posed by the migration of thousands of young women fell within the remit of the pastoral work of the Irish and British Catholic clergy and that consequently such matters were not the responsibility of the Irish state.

Sometime later, in May 1939, as if to emphasise the obligations of the Irish state, Hinsley forwarded a detailed report on welfare work by Catholic organisations with Irish female migrants living in the archdiocese of Westminster to de Valera. Hinsley again noted that the vast majority of Irish migrants were 'credits to their country and to their religion', but that the migration of young persons from a rural area to a large city presented 'grave social problems'.[165] In addition, he pointed to the number of pregnant young Irish women who came to Britain, and those who became pregnant 'in a short space of time after arriving in this country'.[166] However, Hinsley was not solely communicating his worries to de Valera about the position of Irish migrants as he requested that the Irish government should appoint a social worker to the office of the Irish High Commissioner and pay a weekly maintenance grant for each Irish girl in 'an English mother and baby home', run by a Catholic organisation.[167] According to Walshe, de Valera believed that the Irish Catholic clergy were particularly lethargic when it came to the welfare of Irish migrants in comparison with their British counterparts: Walshe remarked optimistically that with action by the Irish clergy 'the problem [of the moral "dangers" associated with female migration] would very soon disappear'.[168] For de Valera, the best possible procedure was to secure the co-operation of parish priests in the Irish Free State, presumably through the medium of fire and brimstone sermons about the evils of migration to Britain. Meanwhile, the Irish Catholic hierarchy had passed a resolution at their meeting in June 1939 calling on the Irish government to establish an emigration bureau in Dublin, to appoint a welfare officer in London and to regulate the activities of employment agencies in order to ensure that 'emigrants will obtain suitable employers and equitable conditions of employment' in Britain.[169] The documentation that refers to the response of the Irish government is not available, but a number of observations may be made.[170] Firstly, the Irish state was loath to provide financial assistance as was suggested by Hinsley and the Irish bishops, as such a decision could make continuing and indeterminate demands on the Irish exchequer.[171] Secondly, and more significantly, the principal importance of the representations made by both British and Irish Catholic bishops is the response that they evoked from the Irish state. Both civil servants and politicians alike believed that the problems which Irish migrants encountered in Britain were the preserve of their spiritual leaders, not the Irish state. In any event, the outbreak of war in 1939 and the introduction of travel restrictions ensured that the Irish authorities could regulate the flow and therefore these problems seemed less urgent. The broader significance of the representations made by Catholic clergy in the Irish Free State and Britain is that the Irish state was forced to formulate a policy on the welfare of Irish citizens in Britain. In short, the

Irish state abrogated all responsibility for the problems that Irish citizens faced and relied on the voluntary efforts of Catholic clerics. The issue of where ultimate responsibility lay for Irish migrants in Britain is an overarching theme of this study and we shall return to this issue on a number of occasions at a later stage.

V

> I call upon the government of this country to take the necessary steps to protect a grievously-wounded minority, and to defend the Protestants of west Cork from a repetition of these atrocities, and to save the Protestants there and in other parts of the South from threatened violence and expulsion from their homes. (J. A. F. Gregg, Church of Ireland archbishop of Dublin, April 1922)[172]

> Minority fears were sufficiently aroused for J. A. F. Gregg, the archbishop of Dublin, to lead a deputation [in May 1922] from the General Synod to the provisional government, enquiring 'if they were to be permitted to live in Ireland or if it was desired that they should leave the country'.[173]

The relationship between migration and religious denomination is a subject that has received relatively little scholarly attention for the period after 1921. The fate of the Protestant minority in independent Ireland has been the subject of much heated debate; accusations of the unfair treatment of minority religious groupings, leading to migration, and, on the other hand, devout protestations of religious pluralism have entered academic and popular discourse.[174] The situation is further complicated as the position and status of Protestants in interwar Ireland were on occasions compared by contemporaries with those of Roman Catholics in Northern Ireland.[175] Valuable light has been shed on this subject by Kennedy in his illuminating account of the experiences of southern Irish Protestants as reported in newspapers in Northern Ireland during the interwar period. He details the effects of the sectarian campaign embarked upon by the Irregulars in 1922–23 in reinforcing the unionist mind-set regarding the precarious position of the Protestant minority in the newly established Irish state.[176] For example, the incidents in west Cork, mentioned in the above quotation from Archbishop Gregg, were the most apparent indication of the sectarian face of extreme Irish republicanism. In one well-known massacre, ten members of the local Protestant community were murdered in April 1922, apparently in response to the killing of an IRA member who was breaking into a house.[177] According to the

Northern Whig, a Belfast newspaper with a unionist orientation, a 'mass exodus' of male Protestants occurred from west Cork after these murders, the females being left to mind the property.[178] The reliability of such assertions is impossible to verify, since for many the exodus may have been a temporary expedient, and these people may have returned when stability was restored.[179] None the less, the general point still remains that violence directed against members of the Protestant community during the 'revolutionary' period (1919–23) accelerated the trend of migration of Irish Protestants to Britain and further afield. Many other well-documented incidents of this nature occurred during the Anglo-Irish war (1919–21) and the civil war (1922–3).[180] The notorious burning of the houses of members of the landlord class, for the most part (though not exclusively) members of the Church of Ireland, is also another factor worthy of consideration.[181] It has been estimated that, in the period between 1919 and 1923, nearly 300 houses of the landlord class were destroyed.[182] But it was not only landlords who suffered at the hands of the republican extremists. For instance, in June 1922 the businesses owned by Protestants in Mullingar, county Westmeath, were attacked, and a substantial number of Protestants in the county were given 'notice to quit'; the *Church of Ireland Gazette* concluded that, 'we have little doubt that many of them have left nothing to chance'.[183] Reports of similar threats in counties Mayo and Laois reached the provisional government in 1922; what action, if any, was taken by the government is not documented.[184] In one order, issued by the local IRA commander in April 1922 to Major Browne, a Protestant landowner in Castlebar, county Mayo, the recipient was advised that he and his family were to be 'deported', and that the IRA would 'secure possession' of his property.[185] Ostensibly, his 'deportation' was justified by reference to the treatment of Roman Catholics in Northern Ireland at this time.[186] However, the manner in which Browne could directly influence his northern 'co-religionists' was not spelt out. In Ballina, also in county Mayo, local Catholic citizens petitioned Arthur Griffith, president of the provisional government, in May 1922, to 'take immediate steps to prevent the threatened expulsion of the prominent Protestant merchants and businessmen of Ballina' who were served with orders to leave the country in 48 hours.[187]

The question of the relationship between sectarian violence (and threats of violence) and patterns of migration is a sensitive subject which is often neglected in standard accounts of Irish history. In

Table 2.7 **Percentage change in population of each religious denomination in the Irish Free State, 1901–36**

Period	1901–11[a]	1911–26	1926–36
Total	−2.5	−5.3	−0.1
Roman Catholics	−2.3	−2.2	+0.8
Total other religions	−4.8	−32.5	−11.9
Anglicans	−5.6	−34.2	−11.7
Presbyterians	−2.6	−28.7	−13.5
Methodists	−8.0	−35.1	−9.5
Jews	+26.6	−3.1	+1.7
Baptists	−0.1	−54.8	−0.3
Others	+2.2	−12.7	−19.1

Note: [a]Data for the 26-county area which later constituted the Irish Free State.
Source: Census of population, 1936, III, pt. I: religions, table 1b, p. 3.

addressing this issue, it is useful to chart the decline in numerical terms of the Protestant community in the Irish Free State during the period under review. A similar range of problems emerge when analysing demographic change by religious denomination for the intercensal period from 1911 until 1926 as were encountered in the earlier section on migration patterns. The long interval between these two censuses makes it impossible to identify the precise timing of the changes over this period. With this caveat in mind, it can be seen from the 1926 enumeration that a significant decline of 32.5 per cent in the numbers of non-Catholics was recorded (see Table 2.7). Substantial decreases are evident in the cases of Methodists, Presbyterians, Baptists and Anglicans (not all members of the Church of Ireland, as one recent examination seems to assume).[188] It should be noted that the absolute numbers involved for some denominations such as the Baptists were quite small: in 1911 the census recorded 1,588 Baptists and this figure had decreased to 717 by 1926.[189] One obvious explanation for the decline in the Protestant population is the ending of the union with Britain in 1921, the uncertainty surrounding the establishment of the Irish Free State and the consequent withdrawal of the British army and other public servants, many of whom were Protestants.

It was estimated that about one quarter of the decrease or 40,000

Table 2.8 Estimate of migration from minority religious communities, 1911–26

Total decrease in population of minority religions		106,456
Numbers of members of British forces recorded as minority religions in 1911 census	21,422	
Adjustment for dependents[a]	7,926	−29,348
Estimates of mortality for the First World War, 1914–18[b]		−5,000
Natural increase 1911–26[c]		−10,000
Total estimated net migratory outflow		62,108

Notes: [a]Taking 37 dependants for every 100 British personnel (this was the known proportion for British soldiers in Dublin city).
[b]This estimate is taken from Sexton and O'Leary.
[c]On the basis of the calculations of Sexton and O'Leary.
Sources: Census of population, 1926, X: general report, p. 11, pp. 46–47; Sexton and O'Leary, 'Factors affecting population decline', pp. 301, 332 n. 22, n. 23.

persons 'can be attributed to the withdrawal of the British army and the disbandment of the police forces and the emigration of their dependants'.[190] It is possible to piece together the fragmentary evidence in order to posit some suggestions regarding patterns of migration from the minority religious communities (see Table 2.8). The tentative nature of these calculations need not be emphasised as many of these figures are, in essence, merely rough calculations with scope for a considerable degree of error either way. For instance, data on age structure of the population by religious denomination are non-existent until 1926, and Sexton and O'Leary's estimate of natural increase for minority communities for the 15-year period (which appears quite high) is based on information for the later intercensal decades of 1926–36 and 1936–46.[191] Yet despite the impossibility of calculating the *exact* numbers involved, it is clear that the migration of persons from the minority religious communities was, without doubt, substantial. At the very least over 60,000 Protestants who were not directly connected with the British administration left southern Ireland between 1911 and 1926. The numerous imponderables, such as mortality among minority religions during the First World War, the number of dependants of British personnel, and the lack of registration data of births and deaths categorised by religion prior to 1926, complicate any attempt to arrive at a more reliable estimate of migration differentiated by religious denomination.

The decline in the Protestant population between 1911 and 1926 was greater in urban areas.[192] To some degree, this can be explained by the withdrawal of personnel associated with the British administration. The population decrease on a regional basis between 1911 and 1926 is illustrated in appendix 6. The dramatic decreases for counties such as Kildare and Westmeath can be accounted for by reference to the withdrawal of British forces in 1921. Not only were members of the British forces likely to have been Protestant; also, as Bowen has remarked, the 'minority's involvement in the armed forces was particularly high'.[193] The fact that 12 of the 26 counties of the Irish Free State experienced a decrease of over 40 per cent is indicative of the scale of the decline in the Protestant population. Perhaps of most interest are the rates of decline in border counties such as Cavan, Monaghan and Donegal, where a substantial Protestant population existed prior to independence, which in contrast to other areas, particularly in Munster, appear slightly lower. For example, the decline in Clare (where admittedly the absolute number involved was quite low) may be explained by the migration of Protestant landlords and associated staff: one contemporary assessment in the 1930s found that since 1919, 70 from a total of 80 Protestant landed families had left county Clare.[194] The high figure for Cork in the earlier period reflects not only the withdrawal of British forces, but also the effects of the sectarian campaign waged in west Cork in particular during the Anglo-Irish war and the later turbulence associated with the civil war. However, establishing a direct causal link between sectarian intimidation or harassment and migration is problematic. Clearly, threats of intimidation or 'revolutionary' rhetoric did not necessarily lead to the mass exodus of Protestants. Moreover, the dearth of reliable sources, such as autobiographies or oral testimony which might provide insights into the motives for migration by members of the Protestant community to elsewhere in the British Isles or further afield, militates against any definitive conclusions being reached in this regard. None the less, what evidence there is suggests that a range of factors explain the decline in the Protestant community from 1911 to 1926, including the end of the union in 1921, the resultant political instability, and finally, the intimidation of *some* Protestants.

During the intercensal period 1926–36, the decline in the numbers of Protestants continued throughout the Irish Free State, with an overall decrease of over 16 per cent in the provinces of Munster and Connacht, and a decline in the three counties of Ulster that was not far behind at 15.5 per cent (see appendix 6, which gives an estimate of population decline through migration for each county). According to estimates by Sexton and O'Leary, roughly 18,700 persons of 'other denominations' left the Irish Free State during this intercensal decade. This corresponded to an average annual net migration rate of –9 per 1,000 of the average population; the rate for Catholics was considerably lower at –5.4 per 1,000.[195]

The question must be posed: why were Protestants migrating from Ireland in such numbers over the period under consideration? Furthermore, it must be asked whether these trends constitute simply a continuation of a long-term pattern – the 'long retreat' as Kennedy and Miller label the decline of Protestantism in Longford – or rather whether they are related to a more proximate cause, the ending of the union with Britain in 1921.[196] A number of scholarly interpretations have been advanced, which have centred around two broad explanations: firstly, the effects of Irish nationalism in all of its various guises including sectarian intimidation and harassment and secondly, wider economic and social considerations such as the decline of the landlord class. Obviously there is a certain degree of overlap between these factors, but for clarity of analysis, this artificial division will be employed.

Irish nationalism in the nineteenth and early twentieth century was characterised by a sectarian hue in a similar manner to Ulster unionism. The partition of Ireland under the Government of Ireland Act, 1920, had catered for Ulster unionism, yet in the eyes of some unionists in southern Ireland this was the 'great betrayal' since they were left to fend for themselves in a potentially hostile environment.[197] Establishing a firm link between the nationalist ethos of the Irish Free State and the perceptions of members of the Protestant community as to their medium- to long-term prospects within this environment is, by its very nature, a difficult task. The values of the nationalist élite which dominated the political scene were, in essence, Catholic and Gaelic, and thus, as Fanning has noted, 'a certain triumphalism became a hallmark of the Irish Free State'.[198] The exclusivity of these values is exemplified in a number of well-known incidences. In the realm of government, the social policy of the Cumann na nGaedheal administration (1922–32) was based largely on Roman Catholic social thought, for example, restrictive censorship was introduced on both publications and films.[199] In popular terms, the celebrations in Dublin in 1929 of the centenary of the achievement of Catholic emancipation reflected this triumphalism.[200] The Eucharistic Congress of 1932 held in Dublin, 'the greatest international celebration of Catholicism in the history of independent Ireland', was also perhaps the most obvious indication of the 'faith and fatherland' ethos which permeated the discourse regarding the exalted position of Catholicism in the Irish Free State.[201] One incident that has attracted the attention of historians on the grounds of its sectarian undertones is the infamous Dunbar-Harrison case, in which in 1930 the Mayo Library Committee refused to ratify the appointment of a librarian who had been chosen for the post by the Local Appointments Commission, a body instituted in 1926 to ensure selection on merit, a new concept for appointments in local government in Ireland.[202] Letitia Dunbar-Harrison was a Protestant who had been educated at Trinity College, Dublin, then regarded by many nationalists as the last bastion of the Protestant ascendancy.[203] The library committee, composed for the most part of prominent local Catholics, including a bishop, 'refused to endorse the nomination, ostensibly on the grounds that Miss Dunbar-Harrison's knowledge of Irish was inadequate'.[204] However, the sectarian considerations underlying the decision soon became overtly manifest as the debate intensified and the question that arose was 'could a Protestant be trusted to hand out books to Catholics?'.[205] After much rancour, including the dissolution of Mayo County Council in 1931, Dunbar-Harrison was eventually appointed and the Cumann na nGaedheal administration stood firm, in public at least, in the face of a good deal of opposition from some prominent Catholic clerics and members of the Fianna Fáil party, including de Valera.[206] Nevertheless, a boycott of the library service in Mayo ensued and Dunbar-Harrison was eventually transferred to a post in Dublin in January 1932, although it seems that an agreement for this transfer had been negotiated behind the scenes in April 1931 between the president of the Executive Council, W. T. Cosgrave, and the Roman Catholic archbishop of Tuam, Dr Thomas Gilmartin.[207] Whilst most accounts treat this case as a illuminating incident in changing church–state relations, viz. the government facing up to the opposition of the local clerics, some authors have also reflected on the impact of the sectarian sentiments which surfaced in the public debate: according to J. H. Whyte, 'the importance of the Mayo library case ... lies not in what was done but in what was said'.[208] Whyte's observation is verified by the reaction of the *Church of Ireland Gazette*, which stated that, from the Protestant perspective, it 'must inevitably increase the apprehensions which are felt by many as to the treatment which Protestants are likely to receive, if certain elements in the Free State get their way'.[209]

The Dunbar-Harrison case was exceptional in terms of the coverage it received in the public sphere. However, in the area of education, the policies pursued by the Cumann na nGaedheal administration were to prove particularly irksome for Irish Protestants during this period. It should be noted that education in the Irish Free State, as in Northern Ireland, was organised on the basis of segregation by religious denomination. In essence, the programme of 'constructive "Gaelicisation" ', applied to the educational system, was a fundamental tenet of the educational policy of the Irish Free State.[210] The first issue centred on the content of many of the school textbooks which 'were open to grave objections' in that they contained elements of Roman Catholic doctrine.[211] This matter was partially resolved in 1927 when an edition of the *Saorstát* reader which was acceptable to the Church of Ireland Board of Education was published.[212] Especially difficult in the Irish context was the teaching of history, since the new curriculum was concerned for the most part with Ireland, and aimed at ensuring 'that Irish boys and girls be brought up seeing themselves as part of a unique nation, separate from Britain, and possessed of its own distinctive cultural inheritance'.[213] As Bowen has argued, the curriculum 'brought out the dormant Irish context of their [Protestant children's] history, and it belittled their British allegiance by neglect and by the presentation of Britain's oppressive role in Ireland'.[214] Ultimately, the issue of the content of history textbooks for Protestant schools was not fully resolved to the satisfaction of the Church of Ireland educational authorities until the 1960s, when a suitable textbook on Irish history for secondary classes was eventually published.[215]

Whereas the teaching of history aroused some controversy within Protestant circles, the policy of compulsory Irish in schools, introduced by the government for primary schools in 1922 and as a compulsory subject for the Intermediate and Leaving Certificate examinations in secondary schools in 1928 and 1934 respectively, proved an insuperable problem for Irish Protestants (and some Catholics).[216] According to Bowen, 'no other government policy provoked such widespread and sustained criticism from Protestants'.[217] The problem was further compounded by the fact that a proficiency in the Irish language was required from 1925 for appointment to the civil service, the defence forces, the police force and the law courts.[218] Quite apart from the question of logistics, as Protestant teachers capable of teaching Irish were at first difficult to recruit, many Irish Protestants believed that time devoted to Irish in the classroom could be devoted to other more practical subjects.[219] The principal of the Church of Ireland teacher training college, Canon H. Kingsmill Moore, articulated in 1930 the basis upon which the Protestant community's objections to the policy introduced in the 1920s were founded. 'The compulsory Irish policy of the ministers caused trouble and anxiety. In no sense was the Church of Ireland opposed to Irish; but we feared an impossible standard, and possible danger to our faith from the teaching of the textbooks.'[220] An underlying factor, not mentioned by Moore, in the opposition to the compulsory Irish policy was that 'to most Protestants, the whole Gaelic tradition was not only alien but primitive and inferior to their own British heritage, and they deeply resented being forced to study what they contemptuously regarded as "back country gab" '.[221] It should be said that Bowen offers little in the way of supporting evidence for this general observation, although few Protestants in the Irish Free State would dare to denounce openly the Irish language for fear of being labelled as 'anti-national', especially by 'Irish-Ireland' publications such as *The Leader*, edited by the redoubtable polemicist, D. P. Moran.[222] Even the most cursory survey of the voice of educated Irish Protestant opinion for this period, the *Church of Ireland Gazette*, indicates that this issue was at the forefront of public discourse amongst Protestants.[223] When the proposal to make Irish compulsory in all schools that relied on official grants was being considered in 1924, the *Gazette* enunciated a number of objections which merit lengthy quotation:

> Despite the explanation of this and that apologist, the Free State government proposes to make the teaching of the Irish language compulsory in all the schools which depend in any way on official grants. In other words, the Irish language will be forced down the throats of thousands of Protestant – and we believe also of Roman Catholic – children merely to pander to the fanaticism of a few enthusiasts for the Gaelic state. We have no objection to the Irish language … It is not a question of culture, but of politics.[224]

The objections of members of the Protestant community to the policy of cultural 'Gaelicisation' through the education system fell on deaf ears. For President Cosgrave the 'success' of the compulsory Irish policy was regarded as 'perhaps the most striking reform' of the Cumann na nGaedheal administration.[225] When the Fianna Fáil government assumed power in 1932, it pursued the policy with even greater vigour.[226] Nevertheless, it should be noted that the issue was to all intents and purposes not sectarian as such, but rather aimed at the nebulous objective of the removal of all vestiges of British influence. However, this was viewed by Protestants as sectarian since Britishness was an integral feature of the Irish Protestant identity in the interwar period. At first sight, the issues of the teaching of history and the Irish language may seem to be of tangential interest to a study concerned for the most part with demographic changes of the minority religious community. But the 'Gaelicisation' policy was to result in some Protestant parents opting to educate their children in Britain or Northern Ireland. According to the author of an account of St Columba's, a prestigious Protestant boarding school outside Dublin, the policy of compulsory Irish contributed at least in part to a decline in numbers.[227]

In employment terms, some Protestants viewed the policy of compulsory Irish for civil service positions as 'disguised discrimination', and White suggests that the Irish language requirement contributed to 'the continuing emigration of young Protestants in search of jobs'.[228] The impressionistic nature of this comment need not be emphasised, yet some evidence to support this view is provided by the census data. Applying cohort depletion techniques to the age groups 10–14 years and 15–24 years for Protestants in the period from 1926 to 1936 yields some significant results. It can be seen that younger female Protestants were emigrating at a greater rate than their male counterparts (see Table 2.9). For the older age cohort, 15–24 years, male migration rates exceeded those for females. It should be pointed out that these figures are merely estimates since mortality rates differentiated by religion are not available, and in addition, persons changing religious denomination would further complicate the picture.[229] Such transfers were, however, rare in this period.[230] On the basis of these data the trend of migration of young adults is clearly discernible in this period, especially in comparison with the levels for the older age groups.[231] The rate for the older age groups of 'other denominations', mostly Protestant, contrasts starkly with that of Catholics which indicates that family movement also formed a significant element of the migrant stream (see Table 2.10).[232] The broad thrust of R. E. Kennedy's analysis of the census data supports this contention regarding the migration of Protestant family groups in the period 1926–36, although it may be pointed out that he makes no adjustment whatsoever for mortality.[233]

Contemporary organs of Protestant opinion such as the *Irish Times* and the *Church of Ireland Gazette* were acutely conscious of the decline

Table 2.9 Irish Protestants: cohort depletion, 1926–36[a]

	Males	Females	Total
10–14 years in 1926	8,952	8,275	17,227
20–24 in 1936	7,745	6,614	14,359
Survivorship ratio per 100	86.5	79.9	83.4
Average annual mortality ratio per 1,000[b]	–3.8	–4.2	–4.0
Average annual migration rate per 1,000	–9.7	–15.9	–12.6
15–24 years in 1926	16,775	16,470	33,245
25–34 in 1936	13,553	13,572	27,125
Survivorship ratio per 100	80.1	82.4	81.6
Average annual mortality ratio per 1,000[b]	–4.8	–5.4	–5.1
Average annual migration rate per 1,000	–15.1	–12.2	–13.3

Notes: [a] 'Protestants' includes Anglicans, Methodists, Presbyterians and Baptists.
[b] Calculated from the life tables in Commission on Emigration, *Reports*, table 22, p. 310.
Sources: Census of population, 1926, III, pt. I: religions, table 13a, p. 99; *Census of population, 1936, III, pt. I: religions*, table 13a, p. 103.

Table 2.10 Average annual rates of net Irish migration per 1,000 of the average population by age group and religion, 1926–36

Age in 1926	Roman Catholic	Other denominations
0–4	+2.3	–1.8
5–14	–6.9	–10.5
15–24	–19.4	–16.7
25–34	–4.6	–7.5
35–44	–1.5	–5.0
45–54	–1.8	–4.9

Note: 'Other denominations' includes those enumerated as having 'no religion' or refusing to provide any information as regards religious denomination.
Source: After Sexton and O'Leary, 'Factors affecting population decline', table a.6, p. 324.

in numbers. According to the *Gazette*, the decline in the earlier period 1911–26 was due not only to factors mentioned above, such as the removal of British personnel in 1921, but also to the 'forced exodus of large numbers during the time of the "troubles" '.[234] However, the comments of the *Gazette* on the migrant stream since 1922–23 are particularly revealing:

perhaps the most serious factor of all is the sheer economic pressure which forces so large a proportion of our young people to seek careers abroad, if they have any desire to better themselves. Emigration by families there has been to some extent, but more evil is emigration of the young as individuals . . . It is plain that we, like other Protestant bodies, have a wholly disproportionate number of old people compared with young, in comparison with Roman Catholics. Our people marry later, have fewer children, and a dreadfully large proportion of the young men and women seek careers abroad . . .[235]

For the *Irish Times*, the results of the 1926 census were not so much an issue deserving consideration by the Protestant community in isolation. The decline affected the Irish Free State as a whole, since Protestants played a very significant role in the commercial and cultural activities of the country. In short, 'the continuation of the drain of the minority would be exceedingly serious for the Free State'.[236] According to *The Leader*, however, the high representation of Protestants in the various professions and the landowning sector was in fact related to the effects of penal legislation of the eighteenth century and the contemporary influence of freemasonry![237] The continued decline recorded in the 1936 census reignited interest in this issue. The *Gazette* reflected on the inevitability of migration from Ireland, not only for Protestants, but for the population as a whole.[238] In comparison with the coverage afforded to the results of the 1926 census, the *Gazette* in 1939 was rather muted in its observations regarding the continuing decline. The somewhat depressed coverage in the *Irish Times* was later republished by the Ulster Unionist Council as an indication of the fate of southern Protestants in the Irish Free State and by implication the fate of *all* Protestants in a united Ireland.[239]

Another important aspect of this assessment of the population decline of the Protestant community in this period centres on the economic and social withdrawal of Protestants from Ireland or the 'long retreat', to use Kennedy and Miller's phrase. To view the decline in the Protestant population within a short- to medium-term analysis, focusing on the years from 1911 to 1926, is to create a distorting framework in the sense that these trends may have been evident well before 1911. A number of long-range and regionally orientated assessments which straddle the history of Ireland under the union and independent Ireland highlight the necessity of such a perspective. Kennedy and Miller observe that the key period in which the decline in numbers in county Longford occurred was between the Great Irish Famine (1845–50) and the First World War.[240] The reasons for this decline posited by the authors are socio-economic and political reasons which are 'best understood as mutually reinforcing'.[241] The Protestant community in county Longford, members of which were predominantly of a higher socio-economic status than their Catholic counterparts, was subject to a range of political, economic and social forces, not least the fact that many were aware of 'wider opportunities, as well as developed migrant pathways, [which] facilitated recourse to emigration'.[242] Evidence to support this contention is to be found in the work of Glenfield on the Protestant population in south-east Leinster during the nineteenth and twentieth centuries.[243] Glenfield argues that the trend of Protestant migration had been established well before the political developments of the first two decades of the twentieth century. In fact, in Glenfield's view the second half of the nineteenth century is the crucial time period for the demographic changes. In a similar manner to Kennedy and Miller, Glenfield links the decline in numbers to 'a retreat in their economic, social and political influence'.[244] Maguire's research on the Protestant working class in Dublin between 1870 and 1926 offers a useful corrective to the common perception that every member of the Protestant community was a landowner or a member of the professions.[245] He argues that the marriage patterns of working-class Protestants in this period were related to the 'decline' of working-class Protestants in Dublin. The propensity to marry British soldiers resulted in members of the Protestant working class moving from Dublin to other parts of the British Isles when the soldiers' tour of duty came to an end.[246] The children of mixed marriages between Protestants and Roman Catholics were usually raised as Catholics. Even before the *Ne Temere* decree of 1907, nearly 80 per cent of the offspring of such unions were brought up as Catholics, according to the census returns of 1901.[247] Maguire's sample indicates that in the intercensal period 1901–11, mixed marriages constituted roughly 15 per cent of marriages by Protestant males.[248] It seems likely that mixed marriages declined in the later period (1911–26), due not least to the fact that religious differences became much more contentious: however, this deduction remains speculative until this important aspect of the decline of religious minorities is investigated fully. Some impressionistic evidence exists which suggests that this issue was the subject of discourse in Church of Ireland intellectual circles throughout the 1920s and 1930s, although the disparity between perception and reality can, of course, be substantial.[249] The other explanation that Maguire offers for the decline of the skilled Protestant working class is the effect of the First World War on Dublin's industry, when 'the city was deindustrialised by war-time controls'.[250] The practicalities of how this deindustrialisation affected the decline of the Protestant working class are not spelt out in detail, although presumably Maguire is referring to the migration of skilled workers.

On the basis of these three detailed case-studies, examining the aspects of the demographic experience of the Protestant population in different circumstances, it seems reasonable to conclude that the decline in numbers was a process initiated before the advent of Irish independence in 1921–22. The need for more local case-studies in order to establish conclusively the reasons for the long-term decline of Irish Protestants is obvious. The question of whether and how the establishment of Irish independence accelerated this process is clearly worthy of reflection and opinions vary on this issue. R. E. Kennedy argues that the 'emigration of native-born Irish Protestants ... was a voluntary movement and was not caused by any governmental policies directed against them as a religious group' and 'because the Irish government was careful to protect the rights of the Protestant minority, it seems reasonable to conclude that the Protestants left voluntarily'.[251] While, in religious terms, the Protestant minority suffered from few *overt* discriminatory policies at the hands of central government, some fragmentary evidence exists to indicate that in the realm of local government the case may not have been so cut and dried: the Dunbar-Harrison case in 1930 is the most obvious example. The Irish Free State prided itself on its exemplary record in the treatment of religious minorities, even though the policy of introducing compulsory Irish was clearly offensive to Irish Protestants. The protestations of religious liberty had more to do with the aspiration for a united Ireland, and the consequent need to reassure Protestants in Northern Ireland of equal treatment in a prospective 32-county Ireland.[252] In reality, however, as D. H. Akenson has cogently argued, 'the Protestants were tolerated and well treated as a religious minority but were penalised and ill-treated as a cultural minority'.[253] The compulsory Irish policy was the most obvious indication that, in cultural and ethnic terms, Irish Protestants were clearly disadvantaged by the policies pursed by successive Irish governments in the educational sphere. The *Church of Ireland Gazette* summed up in a pithy manner the effect of this policy which 'undoubtedly hurt our sensibilities and injured our national pride'.[254] Thus, while Kennedy is, strictly speaking, accurate in arguing that 'Protestants left voluntarily', it seems that he has seriously underestimated the role of cultural factors, such as the triumphant Catholicism and the compulsory Irish policy, in creating an environment that a significant number of Irish Protestants were unable to stomach. Perhaps the final action to highlight the exclusivity of the Gaelic Catholic nationalist ethos was the Irish constitution of 1937 which recognised the Protestant churches, but acknowledged the 'special position' of the Roman Catholic church.[255] In essence, the constitution merely enshrined in law what had been obvious to most observers since the foundation of the Irish state in 1922: 'Irishness' was equated with Gaelic and Catholic values and there was no scope for the British, Protestant identity which was a fundamental characteristic of the Protestant minority, most of whom were born before the advent of Irish independence. Archbishop Gregg, the Church of Ireland primate of all-Ireland, in his address to the General Synod in 1939 provides a sense of the apprehension with regard to the decline evident from the 1936 census results:

> Widespread attention has been drawn to the statistics of the last census held in Eire as they concern the respective religious denominations. These statistics, as they bear upon the position and prospects of our church, demand serious and anxious consideration . . . But when men speak of the 'suicide' of our community, I would reply: 'the wholesale adoption of the culture of the majority, with the consequent loss of our distinctive identity as a community that would be our "suicide" '. There is too much at stake – much more than mere numbers – for us to consent to imperil out identity.

> It is not necessary to be Gaelic in order to be Irish. On the other hand, the Gaelicisation which is recommended to us, added to other factors or our environment, would involve our absorption, the incorporation of the minority into the majority, with the inevitable loss of the religion we prize (which is an integral part of our identity).[256]

This issue of the relationship between migration and religious denomination will be returned to at a later stage to examine whether Irish Protestants migrated at a higher rate than Catholics during the postwar period.

VI

Immigration into Britain, particularly from the 'New Commonwealth', became a major political issue in the 1950s and 1960s, but in the interwar period, especially at times of acute economic depression, the question of Irish migrants was also a matter of discussion and debate. For the post–1921 period the reaction to the continuous flow of Irish migrants to Britain is relatively uncharted territory. Glynn's account of British policy with regard to Irish migration is useful; however, he did not consult the full range of records available, including valuable material in the files of the Home Office.[257] It should perhaps be noted here that citizens of the Irish Free State (Éire from 1937) had unrestricted entry to Britain up to June 1940 when restrictions on travel were introduced by both the British and the Irish governments. In addition, Irish citizens enjoyed the same voting and residence rights as British citizens under the Anglo-Irish treaty of 1921. In the 1920s, Irish migration to Britain was substantial, with approximately 10,000 persons annually travelling across the Irish Sea (see Table 2.3). Even though the total number of Irish-born in Britain declined during the period prior to 1921, it can be seen that the Irish-born population in England and Wales increased significantly in the following decade. However, in Scotland a noticeable decrease is evident, clearly reflecting the impact of the depression on Scottish 'heavy' industries in the interwar period (see Table 2.11). On a regional basis, cities such as Liverpool, Manchester and Glasgow contained a substantial Irish-born population, a reflection of the earlier trends of settlement from the second half of the nineteenth century. According to Walter, the 1931 census marks a turning point in that, between this census and the 1951 census, the South-East, West Midlands and to a lesser extent, the East Midlands become the main centres of Irish settlement.[258] These areas exhibited a significant increase in the settlement of Irish-born, 'largely at the expense of Scotland and the North West'.[259] These settlement patterns are also related to the demand for labour in particular areas of Britain.

Table 2.11 Irish-born population in Britain, 1911–31

Period	England and Wales		Scotland	
	Number	% of total population	Number	% of total population
1911	375,325	1.0	174,715	3.7
1921	364,747	0.9	159,020	3.3
1931	381,081	1.4	124,296	2.6

Source: J. A. Jackson, *The Irish in Britain*, London, 1963, p. 11.

The issue of Irish migration first arose in the 1920s and was discussed within the confines of the upper echelons of British governmental circles. At first, concerns were raised in Scotland regarding the extent and level of Irish migration. From 1922 onwards, intermittent protests regarding the Catholic Irish presence in Scotland emanated from the General Assembly of the Church of Scotland.[260] One report which outlined the results of an investigation of Irish immigration conducted by a committee of the General Assembly was published under the alarmist title of *The menace of the Irish race to our Scottish nationality*.[261] Bruce urges caution in viewing the receipt of this report as indicating that 'even a majority of members' of the General Assembly agreed with these sentiments; in his view, support for these views was localised and representative only of a small group of ministers.[262] Brown, on the other hand, points to the broad level of support within the General Assembly for measures to restrict Irish migration to Scotland.[263] Scottish fears regarding Irish migration must be viewed within the context of economic depression, anti-Catholic Irish prejudice, a growth in Scottish nationalism and the fact that the 'emigration of the young and vigorous of the nation naturally alarmed those who had the prosperity of Scotland at heart'.[264] The murky underworld of sectarianism in Scotland is not the subject of this study, although its ramifications on government policy have a direct bearing on the analysis here.[265] Populist works appeared in the late 1920s warning of the 'dangers' of Irish migration and several newspaper articles dealt with this issue.[266] The response of the Conservative government (1924–29) was to set up an interdepartmental conference to examine the issue. This conference was held during July 1927, and received submissions from a number of interested government departments. In the view of the Scottish Board of Health, it seemed logical to restrict Irish migration, as likewise 'foreign' immigration, 'for the purpose of relieving a congested labour market'.[267] But as an official from the Dominions Office (which had had sole responsibility for Irish affairs since 1925) pointed out, 'persons described as of "Irish Free State" nationality were British subjects by birth in one of His Majesty's dominions and as such could neither be excluded nor deported from this country'.[268] An integral aspect of the Anglo-Irish treaty of 1921 was that the Irish Free State was constituted as a dominion of the British Commonwealth, and therefore it would be most inappropriate for entry to the 'mother country' to be restricted.

The issue re-emerged on the agenda when a Scottish church

deputation travelled to London in July 1928 to meet the home secretary, Sir William Joynson-Hicks, to request 'that immigration be controlled so that Scotland should not be turned into a dumping ground
for masses of undesirable Irishmen'.[269] The deputation stated that they
did not object to Irish persons coming to Scotland, but 'they did object
to their coming in such quantities that they could not be assimilated'.[270] In short, they requested that the government restrict entry
into Scotland, a point which was much publicised in the press.[271] The
upshot of this meeting was a number of investigations by the various
arms of government into Irish migration throughout Britain. One
quite astonishing report on Irish migrants in Britain was prepared by
the aliens' branch of the Home Office, which was based on interviews
with police chief constables in areas that had traditionally received
large numbers of Irish migrants, namely Lancashire and the west of
Scotland. This report provides a revealing insight into some official
perceptions of Irish migrants in Britain.

> Every chief constable interviewed repeated the same assertion, that, except in
> rare cases, the Irish labourer never rises in the social or industrial scale and
> remains content to be a hewer of wood and drawer of water, in fact almost a
> class of helots living in an alien land . . . The general feeling expressed to me
> was that the newly arrived Irishman is a decent, law-abiding, hardworking fel-
> low; but that after a few years he degenerates, depresses the whole standard of
> living and quite frequently falls into criminal habits, in fact I got the impres-
> sion that the elimination of the Irish from Scotland would reduce the crime
> statistics by 75–80 per cent.[272]

The unscientific nature of this analysis need not be emphasised, and
the procedure which would have been adopted to 'eliminate' the Irish
population in Scotland is not elucidated. A further interdepartmental
conference was held in July 1928 under the chairmanship of Sir John
Anderson of the Home Office to consider the perceived influx of Irish
labour into Britain.[273] Anderson's solution, as outlined at this conference, was to introduce a work permit system which would limit the
length of employment of any person not ordinarily resident in
Britain.[274] In addition, when a permit was granted, a particular occupation and employer would be specified and no permit would be
issued if suitable workers were available locally.[275] Anderson also recommended that no warning should be given in order to reduce the
possibility of an influx of Irish migrants in the period prior to the
permits being introduced, and curiously, the representatives from the
various departments advised that the restriction would also apply to

workers from Northern Ireland.[276] The conference also suggested that, if the government of Northern Ireland did not seem willing to co-operate, 'use might be made of the fact that a substantial contribution is at present made from the exchequer to the government of Northern Ireland in aid of the cost of unemployment benefit'.[277] The political ramifications of this proposal were potentially explosive as the application of such a restriction to Northern Ireland citizens would seem to contravene the status of the province as an integral part of the United Kingdom under the Government of Ireland Act, 1920.

When the matter reached cabinet level during August 1928, an addendum was attached which indicated that the government of the Irish Free State had been asked to agree to a reciprocal arrangement for the removal of persons who became a charge on the poor rate in Britain and vice versa.[278] It is not surprising that no reply had been received from the Irish government as the prospect of hundreds of poverty-stricken migrants returning to the Irish Free State was understandably, not one that, the Cumann na nGaedheal administration wished to contemplate. The decision of the cabinet on this matter was to secure further information on the extent of Irish migration and to request that pressure should be applied to the Irish government on the question of the repatriation of Irish migrants who became a charge on the poor law.[279] The constitutionally delicate question of the application of any restriction to Northern Irish citizens was not raised. Records of specified labour exchanges in Lanarkshire and Glasgow were monitored for the period from October 1928 until December 1928 to gauge the level of Irish migration, and the results indicated that there was 'no evidence of any considerable immigration from Ireland to Scotland'.[280] When the matter was discussed again at cabinet in 1929, Joynson-Hicks advised his colleagues that his inquiries both independently and through various departments 'suggest that the mischief of which the representatives of the Scottish churches who came to see me in last July complained has already been done'.[281] He concluded at this time that Irish migration to Scotland was of little consequence: 'the immigration of natives of the Irish Free State to Scotland is not now such as to effect materially the position created by the presence in Scotland of large body of persons of Irish extraction'.[282] Therefore, there would be no need to implement the suggestions regarding the work permit system advanced by Anderson's interdepartmental conference in 1928, and the secretary of state for Scotland, Sir John Gilmour, concurred with this view.[283] The controversy which

had arisen in Scotland, largely propelled by alarmist statements emanating from the Scottish churches, had to some degree run its course
since, after exhaustive inquiries by government departments, it was
found that Irish immigration was of relatively little consequence. It
should be borne in mind that contemporary commentators in Scotland (and civil servants in London) frequently confused Irish-*born*
persons with second- and third-generation Irish.[284] In fact, as we have
noted, by the mid–1920s Irish migration to Scotland had substantially
decreased.[285] Whereas, the higher fertility levels of Catholics may have
resulted in a proportional increase in the total share of the population,
most contemporary commentators attributed the rise in the Catholic
population during the 1920s to Irish migration.[286] Of course, this
merely underlines the point that perception is often more powerful
than reality when issues of migration are discussed. In governmental
terms, it can be seen that the Conservative government (1924–29) was
reluctant to restrict the entry of Irish citizens for two reasons. Firstly,
the status of the Irish Free State as a dominion ensured that Irish persons were British subjects and therefore to restrict entry would be 'a
complete reversal of immemorial policy for the government to take
power to keep out or send out any British subject from this country'.[287]
Secondly, inquiries initiated by the various arms of government did
not support the contention made by the Scottish churches that there
was a dramatic increase in Irish immigration at this time.

Nevertheless, the issue of Irish migration remained a matter of
concern for both the Labour (1929–31) and National (1931–35,
1935–37) governments. When the Committee on Empire Migration, a
sub-committee of the Economic Advisory Council (a body of outside
economic experts, including Keynes, instituted by Ramsay MacDonald in 1930), considered the effects of immigration *vis-à-vis* the policy
of empire settlement, the question of Irish migration to Britain was
again examined.[288] A. M. Carr-Saunders, the distinguished demogra-
pher, prepared a memorandum in October 1930 for the Committee on
Empire Migration (of which he was a member) which argued that the
restrictions imposed by the United States in 1929 resulted in an
increase in Irish migration to Britain.[289] Carr-Saunders also commented on the anomalous position regarding the deportation of Irish
citizens who became a charge on the poor rate. In addition, he argued
that the migrant flow from Northern Ireland had decreased substantially due to the worsening economic conditions in Britain, but the
depression 'had no such effect upon the southern Irish'.[290] In response

to a request from the committee for the views of the Home Office, yet another detailed memorandum was prepared in January 1931, this time for the Labour government to consider. The Home Office reaffirmed its earlier position and stated that 'it is . . . the Irish population already established that presents the main problem, and the comparatively small migration does not appear to warrant any departure from the traditional policy of allowing the free admission into this country of all British subjects of whatever origin'.[291] In the meantime, the Scottish secretary, William Adamson, had during May 1930 received yet another deputation from the Scottish churches, who informed him that 'the position is now becoming so acute that fresh efforts should be made to stem the flow of undesirable immigrants into Scotland'.[292] The usual round of reports was requested from the interested parties in an effort to obtain an accurate assessment of the level of Irish migration into Scotland. The conclusions advanced were similar to those arrived at in 1929, that is to say, it was extremely difficult to establish that the number of Irish immigrants was increasing; in fact, the general opinion was that it had decreased.[293]

When the draft report of the Committee on Empire Migration was prepared in July 1931, it included a substantial section on the impact of Irish migration. Apart from highlighting the need for more comprehensive statistics (a common complaint), the members of the committee suggested that Irish migration to Britain 'materially reduces the benefits' of the Empire Settlement Act of 1922.[294] Whilst acknowledging the inherent problems involved in legislative action to restrict Irish citizens coming to Britain, the members of the committee concluded that the question merited 'serious consideration' by the British government.[295] When the Home Office was asked to respond to a request from the committee earlier in 1931 for its views on Irish migration to England and Wales, the memorandum prepared reiterated the position that the level of movement from the Irish Free State did not require a change in policy.[296] On the question of the deportation of Irish persons who became a public charge, the home secretary advised the committee that he was not satisfied that the problem warranted legislation, and the new departure involved in such a policy 'could only be justified by the clearest necessity'.[297] When MacDonald read the report in 1931, before it was presented to parliament, he instituted inquiries with the Dominions Office, the Home Office and Scottish Office, obviously because of a certain degree of frustration with the anomalous position regarding Irish immigration during a period of depression in Britain. The Dominions Office viewed the question as 'one of labour supply, not of migration', but assured the prime minister that the dominions secretary, J. H. Thomas, would press the Irish government on the issue of repatriation of Irish citizens in receipt of relief.[298] The home secretary, J. R. Clynes, reiterated the position of his department that the 'problem' did not demand legislation and commented on the inherent difficulties of the enforcement of any prospective controls.[299] The Scottish Office concurred with the views of the other departments that Irish migration to Britain had decreased substantially, and suggested that a decision should be made when the 1931 census returns became available.[300] On the thorny question of the repatriation of Irish migrants who became a charge on the poor rate, the Scottish Office urged that a reciprocal arrangement should be instituted. However, this was not confined to Irish migrants alone, and support was provided by the Scottish Office for the Committee on Empire Migration's recommendation that the issue of repatriation of immigrants who become a public charge be discussed at the next meeting of the Imperial Conference.[301] After considering the various positions, MacDonald instructed his private secretary to make further inquiries, as 'we should refuse to be a dumping ground of Dominion refuse'.[302] To be fair to MacDonald, he was not referring solely to Irish migrants, but he seems to have been particularly incensed by the curious position of Irish citizens who became a charge on the poor rate. One ministerial colleague, Sir Archibald Sinclair, the secretary of state for Scotland, later alluded to his 'special interest' in the question of Irish immigration.[303] Within the wider context of MacDonald's determined (if unsuccessful) efforts to find a path through the painful economic mire of the early 1930s, it is perhaps understandable that he should be annoyed by the small number of Irish migrants who became a charge on the British poor relief system. However, the available statistics and observations of the officials from various departments did not support the contention that there was an increase in Irish migration to Britain, in fact quite the reverse. Yet MacDonald realised that the repatriation issue did seem to place the 'mother country' in an inequitable position.

When the Irish government did eventually reply in January 1932 to an official request for the introduction of a reciprocal scheme for the deportation of persons who became a charge on the poor rates, Patrick McGilligan, the minister for external affairs, stated that they would be prepared to consider individual cases, but a scheme 'would give rise to unnecessary expenditure and hardship and incessant irritation'.[304] The irritation foreseen by McGilligan if such a scheme was introduced was nothing compared with that of MacDonald sometime later on reading the reply; for MacDonald the issue was 'becoming a perfect scandal, and even if the Irish gov[ernmen]t showed a greater spirit of unity than it does, the question ought not to be allowed to arise'.[305] Of course, the sands had shifted somewhat with the general election in the Irish Free State of February 1932, when Fianna Fáil gained power on a programme of dismantling elements of the Anglo-Irish treaty of 1921, particularly the removal of the oath of allegiance to the king taken by Irish members of parliament.[306] Henceforth, Irish migration became one of a number of issues that was of far greater political significance in the tangled relationship between the Irish Free State, under de Valera's premiership, and Britain.

When the Fianna Fáil administration set about removing the oath of allegiance in 1932, the restriction of Irish migration to Britain was seriously considered by British ministers as one of a number of tactics designed to dissuade de Valera and his colleagues from this course of action. In May 1932, in response to the deteriorating political climate surrounding the removal of the oath, the Home Office considered the feasibility of a scheme to restrict the entry of Irish citizens by the imposition of a system of permits for employment for those 'not ordinarily resident' in Britain. The scheme was based on the recommendations of the interdepartmental conference held in 1928 under Sir John Anderson's chairmanship discussed above. The officials at the Home Office commented on the possibility of 'widespread evasion', but since the proposals aimed 'to bring home to the Free State government and the people of the Free State the disadvantages which might result from a severance of their relations with the British Commonwealth', even 'a partial success ... would be sufficient to achieve this result'.[307] When the cabinet's Irish Situation Committee (ISC) considered possible courses of action during April 1932 in response to the introduction of a bill in the Dáil which would remove the oath, a restriction on Irish migration was one of a number of options discussed, together with special duties on Irish imports.[308] No decision was taken on the matter, but the ISC again examined the possible restriction of the entry of Irish migrants sometime later in June 1932. The Ministry of Labour argued that such a restriction would lead to some 'temporary dislocation' for firms employing Irish labour; however, the substitution of British labour would pose no great difficulty.[309] This move would help alleviate some unemployment and provide 'a small but, in present circumstances, desirable relief to the employment situation'.[310] The Irish government was alive to the possibility of such action and was thinking along similar lines in preparing a memorandum during March 1932, in the early stages of the dispute, which examined the position of Irish nationals in Britain in the event of Irish-born residents being declared 'aliens' in the legal sense. According to the unnamed official who drafted the memorandum, the category of Irish citizens who could clearly be subject to deportation would be those migrants who became a public charge, a group for which no information was readily available.[311] The deportation issue was still fresh in the minds of the Irish officials, since the British representations on this matter had occurred only two months earlier, albeit when the Cumann na nGaedheal administration was in power. In the event, neither the Irish-born in Britain nor Irish migrants travelling across the Irish Sea in search of employment were subject to any restrictions, as the British retaliation eventually took the form of special duties on Irish imports. It is worth noting that when the report of the Committee on Empire Migration, which in draft form had initiated the unease in the minds of MacDonald and other ministers, was published in May 1932, the substantial section on Irish immigration was omitted and only one brief benign reference to the possibility of Irish migration reducing the effects of empire migration on unemployment levels remained.[312] Clearly, the turbulence in Anglo-Irish relations at this time ensured that a report which considered the exclusion of Irish citizens from Britain, and by implication cast doubt on the Irish Free State's status as a full dominion of the Commonwealth, would have been valuable propaganda for de Valera in his attempts to sever the constitutional link with the United Kingdom.

Throughout the 1930s, Irish migration to Britain was of intermittent interest to policy makers in Britain. In January 1934, the home secretary, Sir John Gilmour, placed before the cabinet a detailed memorandum on the subject. This document outlined the size of the Irish-born population in Britain based on the results of the 1931 census, but as was noted by the author, it was impossible to distinguish between pre- and post–1922 migrants, as information about the length of residence was not available.[313] Other questions under consideration included the numbers in receipt of unemployment benefit and public assistance, although reliable data on how many Irish migrants were receiving such payments were difficult to procure.[314] The issue of the repatriation of Irish citizens who became chargeable to the poor rate was again highlighted, although in the face of the continued negative response to the suggestions of a reciprocal arrangement with the Irish authorities, it seems little could be done.[315] The chief significance of this memorandum is that it provides evidence that concern still existed in government circles regarding the level of Irish migration to Britain in the mid–1930s, and the possibility that this issue could enter the gamut of measures to be deployed in the continuing trade dispute.[316]

The final occasion when concern was vented about the issue of Irish migration occurred in 1937. The focus of attention, in both the public and the official sphere, was Liverpool, an established centre of Irish settlement. Concerns regarding Irish migration were voiced in Liverpool on numerous occasions throughout the 1930s, which it must be said merely represented the continuation of a trend evident since the mid-nineteenth century.[317] In 1931, one candidate in the general election, H. D. Longbottom, representing 'Protestant Democracy', recommended that all Irish persons should be required to be resident for at least five years.[318] However, such sentiments were not confined solely to the greasy pole of local politics, as an apparent proponent of eugenics, G. R. Gair, argued in the *Liverpool Review* that the Irish in Merseyside were to be 'found in the lower stratum of our society', and that Irish migrants in general were prone to criminality and lunacy and therefore ought to be excluded.[319] There was some degree of truth in Gair's first assertion as a comprehensive social survey of Liverpool conducted in the early 1930s found that nearly two-thirds of Irish male migrants were in the unskilled worker category.[320] The authors of the survey commented that 'the Irish immigrant (from both rural and urban areas) seems to be of a very different calibre from the majority of immigrants on Merseyside'.[321] Concern had been expressed in Liverpool as early as 1931 about the repatriation of destitute Irish migrants. Dr Albert David, the Anglican bishop of Liverpool, had requested that the Home Office provide him with information on this matter in July 1931.[322] It was David who again raised the issue in the public sphere in an interview in April 1937 published in a Church of England weekly, *The Guardian*. According to the report of this interview, David claimed that 'Liverpool will be dominated by Roman Catholics'.[323]

Meanwhile, behind closed doors at Whitehall, the Dominions Office had requested that the Ministry of Labour provide information

on the numbers of Irish workers coming to Britain, and the possibility of these workers becoming a public charge.[324] The secretary of state
for the dominions, Malcolm MacDonald, had responded to a number
of parliamentary questions on this subject in early 1937.[325] MacDonald
was considering a complete re-examination of the unrestricted entry
of Irish migrants, if it could be demonstrated that citizens of the Irish
Free State were 'a serious burden on public funds'.[326] The response
from the Ministry of Labour was predictable in that information of
the nature required by the Dominions Office was not readily available,
but the departments with an interest in the issue agreed that an interdepartmental conference would be the most appropriate forum in
which to investigate the matter.[327] The conference, which was held in
April 1937 (although supplementary information was collected for the
report which was finalised in August 1937), concluded on the basis of
passenger movement data that 'there is clear evidence of an increasing
emigration from the Irish Free State into Great Britain but that the
immigrants are being absorbed into employment and are not tending
to increase disproportionately the unemployment figures'.[328] This conclusion is in accordance with the data on cross-channel passenger
movement discussed earlier in this chapter, which indicate a gradual
rise in the number travelling to Britain from 1934 onwards. Clearly
the majority of these migrants were obtaining employment in Britain,
due in part to the easing of the economic depression during the
mid–1930s. The conference obtained information on public assistance
from 'confidential inquiries' in London, Liverpool and Glasgow,
which indicated 'no marked increase in the number of persons of Irish
Free State origin applying for relief'.[329] The main conclusions of the
report were outlined to the House of Commons by Malcolm MacDonald in December 1937, but the document was never published in full,
possibly, as Glynn has argued, owing to the lack of detailed information to support the general conclusions.[330]

The final incident that aroused interest in Irish migrants in
Britain was the bombing campaign embarked upon in the country by
the IRA in January 1939, which involved over 200 explosions and cul-
minated in the notorious Coventry explosion when five people were
killed and 70 others were injured on 25 August 1939.[331] In response to
the terrorist threat, the British government introduced the Prevention
of Violence Act in July 1939 which bound Irish citizens to register
with the police.[332] Most of the IRA members involved, including the
writer Brendan Behan, travelled from Ireland to complete the

campaign and there is no evidence that the Irish migrant population were involved in these atrocities.[333] However, the bombing campaign did cast a veil of suspicion over the Irish in Britain, especially as we shall see, during the Second World War, when security issues became of paramount importance.[334]

Given that significant numbers of Protestants left the Irish Free State in the interwar years, it is somewhat surprising that this grouping disappeared with little trace in Britain. It would not be expected that Irish Protestants would attract the same level of attention from the British state, since few would be in receipt of poor relief, an overarching issue in relation to Irish migrants. The explanation for this 'disappearance' centres around two factors. In the first instance, members of the Protestant landowning élite who left the Irish Free State would have assimilated with relative ease into the ranks of the British ascendancy class as a result of similarities in terms of educational background, social mores and interests. Secondly, for the majority of those Protestants who left who were not landowners, the socio-economic profile of the Irish Protestant community would suggest that most were equipped with skills and expertise which enabled them to find a niche within the ranks of the British middle classes.[335] As such this analysis remains speculative, but in the absence of a detailed investigation of the experience of Irish Protestants in interwar Britain, this issue remains a lacuna in the current state of knowledge.

It may be concluded on the evidence presented thus far that anxiety existed on occasions in British official circles regarding Irish immigration throughout the interwar period. The interest in the matter was intermittent and on occasions clearly related to public opinion, as illustrated by the Scottish church protests in the late 1920s. However, a further concern for politicians and civil servants alike was the possibility that the unrestricted entry of Irish citizens was increasing the level of unemployment in the areas where Irish persons traditionally settled. Numerous investigations failed to establish such a link, notwithstanding the sectarian bluster of local figures as in the case of Liverpool in 1937. What is also worthy of note is that many of the protests and representations about Irish migration emanated from the traditional areas of sectarian conflict, Liverpool and Glasgow. The extent to which these statements must be viewed within a local rather than national context is equally worthy of reflection. In general, the various government departments displayed a pragmatic approach to Irish migration and based their recommendations on the available data. For the Conservative, Labour and National governments, the issue of Irish migrants was of some interest, especially in the 1930s, yet their actions were circumscribed by the fact that as a dominion of the Commonwealth any legislative action to restrict the entry of Irish citizens would be seen to contravene policy of long standing. None the less, exceptional steps were taken when national security was at stake, as evidenced by the reaction to the bombing campaign undertaken by the IRA in 1939, and more starkly, by the introduction of travel restrictions when war broke out in September 1939.

VII

Britain became the chief destination for Irish migrants from the mid–1930s onwards, and the United States, previously the choice of the majority of migrants prior to the Great Depression, declined in significance as a 'receiving society'. The explanations underlying this movement of population from the Irish Free State are numerous, but clearly for many migrants the decision to leave was based on the perception that better economic opportunities could be had elsewhere. The rate of migration for Irish Protestants in the interwar period is somewhat higher than for their Catholic counterparts, and this can be attributed to a range of factors including the long-term decline of the Protestant community, apprehension about sectarian violence during the Anglo-Irish war (1919–21) and the civil war (1922–23), and the cultural ethos of the Irish Free State, particularly in the sphere of education. However, there is no evidence of a mass exodus of Irish Protestants as a result of sectarian intimidation or religious discrimination on the part of the Irish state.

A central tenet of Irish nationalist rhetoric was that migration from Ireland was the result of British rule; however, the Irish nationalist leaders who governed the country until the outbreak of the Second World War found that such an explanation was fallacious. Not surprisingly political independence in 1921–22 did not result in the cessation of migration. The Cumann na nGaedheal government did not seem unduly troubled by the migration of Irish citizens, although the numbers leaving during the 1920s were quite low. Successive Fianna Fáil governments placed an emphasis on ensuring that migration would be reduced, in their rhetoric at least; in practice this was easier said than done. In Britain, anxiety about the level of Irish migration was evident in official circles in the late 1920s and 1930s. After numerous inquiries, the British government decided not to take action to restrict Irish migration and by the late 1930s controversy regarding Irish migrants in Britain had dissipated. With the outbreak of war in September 1939, the position of Irish migrants again came under official scrutiny.

NOTES

1 Dudley Baines, *Emigration from Europe, 1815–1930*, London, 1991, p. 71.

2 Robert A. Divine, *American immigration policy, 1924–1952*, New Haven, 1957, pp. 1–51.

3 Baines, *Emigration from Europe*, p. 72.

4 Carl Ipsen, *Dictating demography: the problem of population in Fascist Italy*, Cambridge, 1996, p. 51.

5 Stephen Castles and Mark J. Miller, *The age of migration: international population movements in the modern world*, 1st edn, London, 1993.

6 See D. V. Glass, *Population policies and movements in Europe*, Oxford, 1940, chs 4–7; Ipsen, *Dictating demography*, chs 2–4; Maria Sophia Quine, *Population politics in twentieth-century Europe: fascist dictatorships and liberal democracies*, London, 1996. A valuable review of the current literature can be found in Carl Ipsen, 'Population policy in the age of fascism: observations on recent literature', *Population and Development Review*, Vol. 24, 1998, pp. 579–92.

7 See Quine, *Population politics in twentieth-century Europe*, pp. 89–128.

8 Strictly speaking a provisional government was in place until the establishment of the Executive Council of the Irish Free State in December 1922.

9 *Census of population, 1936, I: population, area and valuation of each district electoral division . . .*, Dublin, 1938, P. 2913, table 4, p. 7.

10 *Census of population, 1926, X: general report*, Dublin, 1934, P. 1242, pp. 11–12. A census was not taken in 1921 as the unofficial Dáil Éireann 'passed a decree prohibiting the census' thereby ensuring the probability of wholesale non-co-operation (Arthur Mitchell, *Revolutionary government in Ireland: Dáil Éireann, 1919–22*, Dublin, 1995, p. 241).

11 David Fitzpatrick, 'The logic of collective sacrifice: Ireland and the British Army, 1914–1918', *Hist. J.*, Vol. 38, 1995, p. 1017. For estimates of Irish mortality during the war, see J. M. Winter, 'Some aspects of demographic consequences of the First World War in Britain', *Population Studies*, Vol. 30, 1976, pp. 539–52; see also David Fitzpatrick, 'Militarism in Ireland, 1900–1922', in *A military history of Ireland*, ed. Thomas Bartlett and Keith Jeffery, Cambridge, 1996, p. 388.

12 *Census of population, 1926, X: general report*, p. 11.

13 Ibid., p. 12.

14 R. E. Kennedy, *The Irish: emigration, marriage and fertility*, Berkeley, 1973, p. 80.

15 Dr Niamh Brennan, who has conducted research on approximately 4,000 documentated claims from crown public servants, informs me that many of the RIC officers who fled to Britain during the civil war (1922–23) returned to the Irish Free State eventually (personal communication to the author, 16 May 1995). For officers who went to parts of the empire, see J. D. Brewer, *The Royal Irish Constabulary: an oral history*, Belfast, 1990, p. 12; Kent Federowich, 'The problems of disbandment: the Royal Irish Constabulary and imperial migration, 1919–29', *IHS*, Vol. 30, 1996–97, p. 105. For the issue of compensation, see Niamh Brennan, 'A political minefield: southern Loyalists, the Irish Grants Committee and the British government, 1922–31', *IHS*, Vol. 30, 1996–97, pp. 406–19.

16 David Fitzpatrick, *Politics and Irish life, 1913–1921: provincial experience of war and revolution*, Dublin, 1977, p. 39.

17 *Census of population, 1926, III: pt. I, religions*, Dublin, 1929, table 9, p. 13.

18 For more sophisticated methods of estimating internal migration, see Dudley E. Baines, 'The use of published census data in migration studies', in *Nineteenth-century society: essays in the use of quantitative methods for the study of social data*, ed. E. A. Wrigley, Cambridge, 1972, pp. 311–35.

19 *Census of population, 1936, IX: general report*, Dublin, 1942, P. 5620, p. 43. There is, of course, the possibility that some of the people recorded as 'internal migrants' were simply relatives or friends visiting across county boundaries on the census night.

20 Timothy W. Guinnane, *The vanishing Irish: households, migration, and the rural economy in Ireland, 1850–1914*, Princeton, 1997, p. 124.

21 *Report of the Committee on Economic Statistics*, Dublin, 1925, p. 6.

22 This section relies heavily on Commission on Emigration, *Reports*, pp. 115–22, 'Statistics of emigration and passenger movement', *Irish Trade Journal and Statistical Bulletin*, n.v. (June 1951), pp. 76–84, and NAI, DT S11582 D, Department of the Taoiseach, memorandum for the government: methods of compilation of emigration statistics, 5 May 1953. These difficulties are experienced by migration specialists in other countries. For a useful assessment of some of the inherent problems with cross-sectional migration statistics, see Dennis P. Hogan and David I. Kertzer, 'Longitudinal approaches to migration in social history', *Historical Methods*, Vol. 18, 1985, pp. 20–30.

23 Commission on Emigration, *Reports*, p. 119; Cormac Ó Gráda, 'A note on nineteenth-century Irish emigration statistics', *Population Studies*, Vol. 29 (1975), pp. 148–49.

24 David Fitzpatrick, 'Emigration, 1871–1921', in *A new history of Ireland, VI: Ireland under the union, pt. II (1871–1921)*, ed. W. E. Vaughan, Oxford, 1996, p. 631.

25 Donal Garvey, 'The history of migration flows in the Republic of Ireland', *Population Trends*, No. 39, 1985, p. 26.

26 'Statistics on emigration and passenger movement', p. 82.

27 NESC, *The economic and social implications of emigration*, Dublin, 1991, Pl. 7840, p. 55.

28 J. G. Hughes, *Estimates of annual net migration and their relationship with series on annual net passenger movement: Ireland 1926–1976*, Dublin, 1977, ESRI memorandum no. 122, p. 13; for a full discussion of the birth under-registration, see John Coward, 'Birth under-registration in the Republic of Ireland during the twentieth

century', *Economic and Social Review*, Vol. 14, 1982, pp. 1–27.

29 Erhard Rumpf and A. C. Hepburn, *Nationalism and socialism in twentieth-century Ireland*, Liverpool, 1977, pp. 87–88.

30 Divine, *American immigration policy*, pp. 9, 5–10.

31 Commission on Emigration, *Reports*, app. v: summary of immigration policy of the United States of America, p. 266.

32 Ibid.

33 Henry A. Gemery, 'Immigrants and emigrants: international migration and the US labour market in the Great Depression', in *Migration and the international labour market*, ed. Timothy J. Hatton and Jeffrey G. Williamson, London, 1994, p. 195.

34 Baines, *Emigration from Europe*, p. 72.

35 Commission on Emigration, *Reports*, p. 266.

36 R. S. Walshaw, *Migration to and from the British Isles: problems and policies*, London, 1941, p. 72.

37 For an assessment of the comparatively low level of return migration of post-famine Irish migrants from the United States, see Mark Wyman, *Round-trip to America: the immigrants return to Europe, 1880–1930*, Ithaca, 1993, pp. 10–11.

38 Derek H. Aldcroft, *The British economy: I, the years of turmoil, 1920-1951*, Hassocks, 1986, pp. 55–59; B. W. E. Alford, *Depression and recovery? British economic growth, 1918–1939*, London, 1972, pp. 80–82; Sean Glynn and Alan Booth, *Modern Britain: an economic and social history*, London, 1996, pp. 135–41.

39 Glynn and Booth, *Modern Britain*, pp. 90–91.

40 Ibid.

41 *Census of population of Ireland, 1926, X: general report*, p. 19.

42 Kennedy, *The Irish*, p. 80.

43 David Fitzpatrick, *Irish emigration, 1801–1921*, Dublin, 1984, p. 13; T. J. Hatton and J. G. Williamson, 'After the famine: emigration from Ireland, 1850–1913', *J. Econ. Hist.*, Vol. 53, 1993, pp. 588–89.

44 Commission on Emigration, *Reports*, p. 127.

45 Richard Breen, 'Farm servanthood in Ireland, 1900–40', *Econ. Hist. Rev.*, 2nd ser., Vol. 36, 1983, p. 99.

46 Commission on Emigration, *Reports*, p. 131.

47 See Kevin O'Rourke, 'Did labour flow uphill? International migration and wage rates in twentieth century Ireland', in *Labour market evolution: the economic history of market integration, wage flexibility and the employment relation*, ed. George Grantham and Mary MacKinnon, London, 1994, pp. 139–60.

48 Jacinta Prunty, *Dublin slums, 1800–1925: a study in urban geography*, Dublin, 1997.

49 Cormác Ó Gráda, *Ireland: a new economic history, 1780–1939*, Oxford, 1994, p. 435.

50 For detailed data, see Department of Industry and Commerce, *Some statistics of wages and hours of work in 1937, with comparative figures for certain previous years* Dublin, 1938, P. 2904, p. 43.

51 Ibid.

52 Dan Bradley, *Farm labourers: Irish struggle, 1900–1976*, Belfast, 1988, p. 18. For the unemployment assistance scheme and its coverage, see *First report of the Department of Social Welfare, 1947–9*, Dublin, 1950, P. 9807, pp. 16–21; details of the various orders can be found in this report, table 4, pp. 175–9.

53 Ó Gráda, *Ireland: a new economic history*, table 17.4, p. 435.

54 Department of Industry and Commerce, *Some statistics of wages and hours of work in 1937*, pp. 8–9.

55 See, for example, George Ewart Evans, *Ask the fellows who cut the hay*, 2nd edn, London, 1965; Alun Howkins, *Poor labouring men: rural radicalism in Norfolk, 1872–1923*, London, 1985.

56 Department of Industry and Commerce, *Some statistics of wages and hours of work in 1937*, table 1, p. 13; table 8, p. 40.

57 Mary E. Daly, 'The social structure of the Dublin working class, 1871–1911', *I.H.S.*, Vol. 23, 1982, p. 133.

58 See Department of Industry and Commerce, *Some statistics of wages and hours of work in 1937*, pp. 9, 40.

59 See pp. 61–62.

60 Bradley, *Farm labourers*, p. 11; T. W. Freeman, *Ireland: its physical, historical, social and economic geography*, London, 1950, fig. 37, p. 196; fig. 38, p. 199.

61 Bradley, *Farm labourers*, p. 11.

62 D. A. Gillmor, 'The political factor in agricultural history: trends in Irish agriculture, 1922–85', *Agric. Hist. Rev.*, Vol. 37, 1989, p. 169.

63 Freeman, *Ireland: its physical, historical, social and economic geography*, fig. 37, p. 196.

64 Damian Hannan, 'Peasant models and the understanding of social and cultural change in rural Ireland', in *Ireland: land, politics and people* ed. P. J. Drudy, Irish studies 2, Cambridge, 1982, p. 144.

65 C. M. Arensberg, *The Irish countryman*, New York, 1937, pp. 53–54.

66 D. F. Hannan, *Displacement and development: class, kinship and social change in Irish rural communities*, ESRI paper no. 96, Dublin, 1979, p. 36.

67 Arensberg, *The Irish countryman*, p. 66.

68 Kennedy, *The Irish*, p. 151.

69 C. M. Arensberg and S. T. Kimball, *Family and community in Ireland*, 1st edn, Cambridge, Mass., 1940; 2nd edn, 1968. All subsequent references are to the second edition.

70 Arensberg, *The Irish countryman*, p. 82.

71 Peter Gibbon and Chris Curtin, 'The stem family in Ireland', *Comp. Stud. Soc. & Hist.*, Vol. 20, 1978, p. 432.

72 Arensberg and Kimball, *Family and community*, pp. 140–52.

73 Gibbon and Curtin, 'The stem family in Ireland', p. 433.

74 For a useful discussion, see Kennedy, *The Irish*, pp. 139–72.

75 Arensberg and Kimball, *Family and community*, pp. 140–52.

76 Ibid., p. 143.

77 For a penetrating critique, see Peter Gibbon, 'Arensberg and Kimball revisited', *Economy and Society*, Vol. 2, 1973, pp. 492–96.

78 Arensberg and Kimball, *Family and community*, p. 150.

79 Kennedy, *The Irish*, p. 154.

80 Ibid., pp. 162–63.

81 Cormac Ó Gráda, *Ireland before and after the famine: explorations in economic history, 1800–1925*, 2nd edn, Manchester, 1993, pp. 180–212; see also his earlier paper,

'Primogeniture and ultimogeniture in rural Ireland', *Journal of Interdisciplinary History*, Vol. 10, 1980, pp. 491–97.

82 Ó Gráda, *Ireland before and after the famine*, p. 197.

83 Quoted in Liam Kennedy, 'Farm succession in modern Ireland: elements of a theory of inheritance', *Econ. Hist. Rev.*, 2nd ser., Vol. 44, 1991, p. 481.

84 Ó Gráda, *Ireland before and after the famine*, pp. 189–92; Kennedy, 'Farm succession in modern Ireland', pp. 483–90; Guinnane, *The vanishing Irish*, pp. 151–54.

85 Guinnane, *The vanishing Irish*, p. 146.

86 Ibid., p. 164.

87 K. A. Miller, *Emigrants and exiles: Ireland and the Irish exodus to North America*, New York, 1985, p. 244; Liam Kennedy, 'The economic thought of the nation's lost leader: Charles Stewart Parnell', in *Parnell in perspective*, ed. D. G. Boyce and Alan O'Day, London, 1991, p. 184.

88 Brian Girvin, *Between two worlds: politics and economy in independent Ireland*, Dublin, 1989, p. 11; perhaps the most detailed attempt to outline an economic programme was Arthur Griffith, 'The Sinn Féin policy', appendix to *The resurrection of Hungary*, Dublin, 1918, pp. 139–67.

89 This theme is explored in Kerby Miller's *magnum opus, Emigrants and exiles.* For the 'official' reaction see G. R. C. Keep, 'Official opinion on Irish emigration in the later nineteenth century', *Irish Ecclesiastical Record*, Vol. 81, 1954, pp. 412–21, and 'Some Irish opinion on population and emigration', *Irish Ecclesiastical Record*, Vol. 84, 1955, pp. 377–86. For the views of economists and other thinkers, see R. D. C. Black, *Economic thought and the Irish question, 1817–70*, Cambridge, 1960, pp. 203–38.

90 NLI, MS 8415, Manifesto from the Department of Defence of Dáil Éireann, 5 June 1920; Mitchell, *Revolutionary government in Ireland*, p. 240

91 Fitzpatrick, 'Emigration, 1871–1921', p. 633.

92 NLI, MS 8415, Manifesto from the Department of Defence of Dáil Éireann, 5 June 1920.

93 Ruth Dudley Edwards, *Patrick Pearse: the triumph of failure*, paperback edn, Dublin, 1990, p. 183.

94 The fact that the most revealing papers on this period were subsequently deposited in the Archives Department of University College, Dublin, seems to reinforce this point. In fact, government documentation in general for the earlier period is scanty, which may well be explained by the destruction of a considerable mass of documents during the Second World War.

95 Ó Gráda, *Ireland: a new economic history*, p. 385.

96 K. A. Kennedy, Thomas Giblin and Deirdre McHugh, *The economic development of Ireland in the twentieth century*, London, 1988, p. 35.

97 George O'Brien, 'Patrick Hogan: Minister for Agriculture, 1922–1932', *Studies*, Vol. 25, 1936, p. 355.

98 David Johnson, *The interwar economy in Ireland*, Dublin, 1985, pp. 22–23. For further details see Mary E. Daly, *Industrial development and Irish national identity, 1922–39*, Dublin, 1992, pp. 37–57; Girvin, *Between two worlds*, pp. 47–87.

99 Kennedy et al., *Economic development*, p. 36.

100 Ó Gráda, *Ireland: a new economic history*, p. 387; see also Johnson, *Interwar economy*, p. 26.

101 On the general context of the views of *The Leader* throughout the 1920s, see

Patrick Maume, *D. P. Moran*, Dublin, 1995, pp. 43–52.

102 *The Leader*, 10 Nov. 1928, p. 342.

103 Ibid., 25 Aug. 1928, p. 77.

104 UCDA, Sean MacEntee papers, P67/346, Fianna Fáil, *Five years of policy and panic*, [Dublin], 1927.

105 Fianna Fáil, *A national policy outlined by Eamon de Valera, delivered at the inaugural meeting of Fianna Fáil at La Scala Theatre, Dublin, May 1926*, Dublin, n.d. [1927], p. 31. Fianna Fáil's election literature included such statements as 'Stop emigration – end unemployment' (Fianna Fáil election handbill, 1927) and 'You voted for ... employment ... You got ... emigration rampant' (UCDA, MacEntee papers, P67/348), Fianna Fáil, *The greatest failure in Irish history* [an attack on the economic record of the Cumann na nGaedheal administration], Dublin, n.d. [1932].

106 Maurice Moynihan, ed., *Speeches and statements by Eamon de Valera, 1917–73*, Dublin, 1980, p. 152.

107 *Dáil Éireann deb.*, XXV, 12 July 1928, col. 477.

108 Ibid., col. 475.

109 NLI, MS 18339, Frank Gallagher papers, typescript of paper or article by Lemass on industrial and economic state of the country 'some time in 1929 or 1930', p. 3, 11. John Horgan (*Sean Lemass: the enigmatic patriot*, Dublin, 1997) notes that this document was sent to Frank Gallagher on 26 July 1929.

110 William Cosgrave, *Policy of the Cumann na nGaedheal party*, Dublin, 1927; *Fighting points for the Cumann na nGaedheal speakers and workers, general election, 1932*, Dublin, 1932; Cumann na nGaedheal, *To the electorate of the Irish Free State*, Dublin, n.d. [1932].

111 Michael Gallagher, *Electoral support for Irish political parties, 1927–73*, London, 1976, p. 19; see also Richard Dunphy, *The making of Fianna Fáil power in Ireland, 1923–1948*, Oxford, 1995, pp. 94–96.

112 Peter Pyne, 'The third Sinn Féin party, 1923–26, pt. ii', *Econ. Soc. Rev.*, Vol. 1, 1969, p. 238

113 On this protectionist lobby, see Daly, *Industrial development*, p. 27.

114 NAI, DT S5729, Cork IDA, copy of twenty-fifth annual report adopted at the Annual General Meeting of the council of the association held in July 1928, p. 5.

115 NAI, DT S 5983/20, text of speech by Cosgrave to Cork IDA, 5 Sept. 1928, pp. 10–11.

116 *The Leader*, 15 Sept. 1928, p. 155.

117 *Dáil Eireann deb.*, XXVI, 19 Nov. 1930, cols 62–71.

118 Ibid., col. 73.

119 J. P. Neary and Cormac Ó Gráda, 'Protection, economic war and structural change: the 1930s in Ireland', *IHS*, Vol. 27, 1991, p. 250.

120 A considerable body of literature has attempted to gauge the success or otherwise of these policies up to the outbreak of the Second World War. On agriculture, see Gillmor, 'The political factor in agricultural history: trends in Irish agriculture, 1922–85', pp. 169–73; James Meenan, *The Irish economy since 1922*, Liverpool, 1970, pp. 95–102; Ó Gráda, *Ireland: a new economic history*, pp. 389–96. On industry, see Daly, *Industrial development and Irish national identity*, pp. 59–102; Girvin, *Between two worlds*, pp. 88–130; Johnson, *The interwar economy*, pp. 20–30; Kennedy et al., *Economic development of Ireland*, pp. 40–49; James Meenan, 'Irish industrial policy,

1921–43', *Studies*, Vol. 32, 1943, pp. 209–18; Ó Gráda, *Ireland: a new economic history*, pp. 396–403.

121 Johnson, *The interwar economy*, p. 30.

122 Ibid.

123 Mary E. Daly, 'The employment gains from industrial protection in the Irish Free State: a note', *Ir. Econ. & Soc. Hist.*, Vol. 15, 1988, p. 75. On the accuracy of the timing of these changes and the actual composition, see David Johnson's rejoinder to the above article, 'Reply', *Ir. Econ. & Soc. Hist.*, Vol. 15, 1988, pp. 76–80.

124 Ó Gráda, *Ireland: a new economic history*, p. 397.

125 *Dáil Éireann deb.*, XLI, 12 May 1932, col. 1673.

126 *Dáil Éireann deb.*, XXVI, 19 Nov. 1930, col. 73.

127 E.g. *Dáil Éireann deb.*, XLI, 21 Apr. 1932, col. 327; *Dáil Éireann deb.*, LXII, 13 Aug. 1936, cols 2726–27.

128 *Dáil Éireann deb.*, LXV, 17 Feb. 1937, col. 332.

129 M.-L. Sjoestedt, 'L'Irlande d'aujourd'hui, ii: Dublin', *Revue des Deux Mondes*, 1 July 1930, p. 187. According to one unpublished thesis, de Valera stated in 1930 in a widely publicised interview that if Fianna Fáil came to power his administration would end emigration (Nicholas R. Burnett, 'Emigration and modern Ireland', Ph.D. thesis, The John Hopkins University, 1976, p. 186). The author does not, however, provide a source, but presumably this is a reference to the same interview in *Revue des Deux Mondes*.

130 Quoted in Joseph Lee and and Gearóid Ó Tuathaigh, *The age of de Valera*, Dublin, 1982, p. 129.

131 Tom Garvin, 'The destiny of the soldiers: tradition and modernity in the politics of de Valera's Ireland', *Political Studies*, Vol. 26, 1978, p. 346.

132 Ibid.

133 Gearóid Ó Crualaoich, 'The primacy of form: a "folk ideology" in de Valera's politics', in *De Valera and his times*, ed. J. P. O'Carroll and John A. Murphy, 2nd edn, Cork, 1986, pp. 47–61.

134 Caroline Brettell, 'Emigrar para voltar: a Portuguese ideology of return migration', *Papers in Anthropology*, Vol. 20, 1979, p. 7.

135 Antonio de Figueiredo, *Portugal: fifty years of dictatorship*, London, 1975, p. 164.

136 NAI, DFA 402/222, text of speech by Eamon de Valera at Galway, 30 Aug. 1951, p. 2.

137 *Irish Independent*, 17 and 18 Sept. 1937; *Irish Press*, 17, 18 and 19 Sept. 1937; *Irish Times*, 17 Sept. 1937. Useful accounts of this tragedy can be found in Handley, *Irish in modern Scotland*, pp. 187–90; O'Dowd, *Spalpeens and tattie hokers*, pp. 196–98.

138 Michael McInerney, *Peadar O'Donnell: Irish social rebel*, Dublin, 1974, p. 47.

139 Peadar O'Donnell, *The bothy fire and all that, with a reprint of [an] article on [the] Arranmore disaster from the Irish Press*, Dublin, 1937, and 'Achill, Arranmore and Kirkintilloch', *Ireland To-day*, Vol. 2, 1937, pp. 45–50; League of Social Justice, *The Achill island tragedy*, Dublin, 1937.

140 *Report of the interdepartmental committee on seasonal migration*, Dublin, 1938, P. 3403, p. 6.

141 *Irish Times*, 24 Sept. 1937.

142 Ibid., 27 Sept. 1937.

143 *Report of the interdepartmental committee on seasonal migration*, pp. 23, 51–53.

144 For the government's acceptance of the majority of the recommendations, see Lemass's statement on the matter, *Dáil Éireann deb.*, LXXIV, 1 Mar. 1939, cols 1106–07.

145 This issue was also the subject of some newspaper coverage, see *Irish Press*, 27 and 28 Apr. 1939, 18 May 1939.

146 *Dáil Éireann deb.*, LXXIII, 26 Oct. 1938, col. 3.

147 Ibid., LXXIII, 2 Nov. 1938, col. 182.

148 Deirdre McMahon, *Republicans and imperialists: Anglo-Irish relations in the 1930s*, New Haven, 1984, p. 143.

149 *Dáil Éireann deb.*, LXXVII, 27 Sept. 1939, cols 192–93.

150 International Labour Office, 'The transfer of Irish workers to Great Britain', *International Labour Review*, Vol. 48, 1943, p. 341. This information was provided by the British Ministry of Labour and National Service.

151 *Dáil Éireann deb.*, LXXVII, 27 Sept. 1939, col. 194.

152 NAI, DT S 11582A, 'Copy of written assurances which have been received from the British authorities', with a note from J. P. Walshe (Secretary, Department of External Affairs) to Maurice Moynihan (Secretary, Department of the Taoiseach), 31 Mar. 1941.

153 Arnold Schrier, *Ireland and the American emigration, 1850–1900*, Minneapolis, 1958, p. 64; Fitzpatrick, 'Emigration, 1871–1921', pp. 629–30. See also Enda Delaney, 'The churches and Irish emigration to Britain, 1921–60', *Archivium Hibernicum*, Vol. 52, 1998, p. 98–114.

154 *Irish Catholic Directory, 1935*, 12 June 1934, p. 607.

155 Ibid.

156 *Irish Catholic Directory, 1938*, 7 Feb. 1937, p. 584, see also *Irish Times*, 10 Aug. 1936 for a similar statement by Gilmartin.

157 *Irish Times*, 13 Apr. 1937, 30 Oct. 1937; Gertrude Gaffney, *Emigration to England: what you should know about it, advice to Irish girls*, Dublin, n.d. [1937].

158 Gaffney, *Emigration to England*, p. 29.

159 NAI, DFA 402/218/1, copy of a letter from Hinsley to Dulanty, [6 Feb.]1937, p. 1.

160 Ibid.

161 NAI, DFA 402/218/1, James Hurson (Secretary, Department of Local Government and Public Health) to J. P. Walshe (Secretary of the Department of External Affairs), 8 Sept. 1937.

162 Ibid., McGrath to de Valera, 30 Oct. 1937.

163 Ibid., copy of a letter from de Valera to McGrath, 15 Nov. 1937.

164 Ibid., copy of a letter from Walshe to Hurson, 25 Oct. 1938.

165 Ibid., letter from Hinsley to de Valera, 25 May 1939, p. 2

166 Ibid., pp. 2–3. For a useful, if uneven, discussion of the provision by Catholic organisations for Irish single mothers in London, see Lara Marks, ' "The luckless waifs and strays of humanity": Irish and Jewish unwed mothers in London, 1870–1939', *Twentieth Century British History*, Vol. 3, 1992, pp. 113–37.

167 NAI, DFA 402/218/1, letter from Hinsley to de Valera, 25 May 1939, pp. 7–8.

168 Ibid., copy of a letter from Walshe to Hurson, 27 May 1939.

169 Ibid., copy of a letter from Jeremiah Kinane (bishop of Waterford and secretary to the Irish hierarchy) to Hurson, 15 Aug. 1939.

170 Although the files do exist, they could not be located for the present study and 'there is little prospect of their appearing in the near future' (private communication from Caitriona Crowe (Archivist, National Archives, Dublin) to the author, 25 Oct. 1995).

171 NAI, DFA 402/218/1, Hurson to Walshe [15 Dec. 1939].

172 Quoted in George Seaver, *John Allen Fitzgerald Gregg, archbishop*, London, 1963, p. 121.

173 Kurt Bowen, *Protestants in a Catholic state: Ireland's privileged minority*, Dublin, 1983, p. 24.

174 See, for example, *Irish Times*, 9 and 19 Apr. 1996.

175 For unionist rhetoric referring to the fate of southern Protestants, see Ulster Unionist Council, *Southern Ireland's census returns: serious decline in Protestant population*, [Belfast, 1939].

176 Dennis Kennedy, *The widening gulf: northern attitudes to the independent Irish state, 1919–1949*, Belfast, 1988.

177 See Peter Hart, *The IRA and its enemies: violence and community in Cork, 1916–23*, Oxford, 1998, pp. 273–315.

178 Kennedy, *Widening gulf*, pp. 117–18.

179 For an account of one such returnee, George Applebe Byran, after the end of the civil war in 1923, see Peter Hart, 'The Protestant experience of revolution in southern Ireland', in *Unionism in modern Ireland*, ed. Richard English and Graham Walker, Dublin, 1996, p. 94.

180 See Bowen, *Protestants in a Catholic state*, pp. 22–25; Patrick Buckland, *Irish unionism, I: the Anglo-Irish and the new Ireland, 1885–1922*, Dublin, 1972, pp. 278–81; T. A. M. Dooley, *The decline of unionist politics in Monaghan, 1911–1923*, Maynooth Historical Series no. 6, Maynooth, 1988, pp. 20–21, and 'Monaghan Protestants in a time of crisis', in *Religion, conflict and coexistence in Ireland*, ed. R. V. Comerford, Mary Cullen, J. R. Hill and Colm Lennon, Dublin, 1990, pp. 235–51; Kennedy, *Widening gulf*, pp. 114–29; W. Alison Phillips, *The revolution in Ireland, 1906–1923*, 2nd edn, London, 1926, pp. 273, 290; Jack White, *Minority report: the Protestant community in the Irish Republic*, Dublin, 1975, pp. 83–90. For details of specific incidents, see *Church of Ireland Gazette*, 26 May 1922, pp. 320–21, 16 June 1922, pp. 362–63, 23 June 1922, p. 382, 12 Jan. 1923, p. 22, 2 Feb. 1923, p. 53.

181 Buckland, *Irish unionism, I*, p. 279.

182 T. A. M. Dooley, 'The decline of the big house in Ireland, 1879–1950', *Ir. Econ. & Soc. Hist.*, Vol. 25, 1998, p. 105 [thesis abstract of unpub. PhD thesis, National University of Ireland, Maynooth, 1997].

183 *Church of Ireland Gazette*, 16 June 1922, p. 362.

184 NAI, DT S566, unsigned report of a number of incidences in county Laois in which 'the agitation has been directed against the Protestants alone' [mid–1922].

185 NAI, DT S565, copy of order sent by Thomas Hevey, commandant adjutant, no. 1 brigade, 4th western division, Oghlaigh na hÉireann, west Mayo brigade, to Major Browne, Breaffy, Castlebar, 29 Apr. 1922.

186 Ibid.

187 NAI, DT S565, unsigned petition from a number of the Catholic citizens of Ballina to Arthur Griffith [an appeal 'to prevent the threatened explusion of the prominent Protestant merchants and businessmen of Ballina'], 4 May 1922.

188 Sexton and O'Leary refer only to members of the Church of Ireland in their recent discussion, which for the earlier period is not accurate as many Anglican British soldiers and officials would have been members of the Church of England (J. J. Sexton and Richard O'Leary, 'Factors affecting population decline in minority religious communities in the Republic of Ireland', in *Building trust in Ireland: studies commissioned by the Forum for Peace and Reconciliation*, Belfast, 1996, pp. 255–332).

189 *Census of population, 1926, III: pt. I, religions*, Dublin, 1929, table 1a, p. 1.

190 Ibid., p. 46.

191 Sexton and O'Leary, 'Factors affecting population decline', p. 301.

192 For detailed data, see *Census of population, 1926, III, pt. I: religions*, table 5b, p. 6; *Census of population, 1936, III, pt. I: religions*, table 5b, p. 8.

193 Bowen, *Protestants in a Catholic state*, pp. 21–22.

194 Quoted in L. P. Curtis, 'The Anglo-Irish predicament', *Twentieth Century Studies*, Vol. 4, 1970, p. 57; on Clare, see also Fitzpatrick, *Politics and Irish life*, pp. 80–84

195 Sexton and O'Leary, 'Factors affecting population decline', table 9, p. 302.

196 Liam Kennedy and Kerby A. Miller with Mark Graham, 'The long retreat: Protestants, economy and society, 1660–1926', in *Longford: essays in county history*, ed. Raymond Gillespie and Gerard Moran, Dublin, 1991, pp. 31–61.

197 This phrase is taken from perhaps the most enlightening account of life as a Protestant in the Irish Free State, Brian Inglis's, *West Briton*, London, 1962, p. 12.

198 Ronan Fanning, *Independent Ireland*, Dublin, 1983, p. 59.

199 J. H. Whyte, *Church and state in modern Ireland, 1923–79*, 2nd edn, Dublin, 1980, pp. 34–39.

200 Fanning, *Independent Ireland*, pp. 59–60.

201 Ibid. pp. 129–30.

202 Whyte, *Church and state in modern Ireland*, p. 44.

203 On the perceptions regarding Trinity College in the Irish Free State, a much-neglected essay by F. S. L. Lyons is very informative (F. S. L. Lyons, 'The minority problem in the twenty-six counties', in *The years of the great test, 1926–39*, ed. Francis MacManus, Cork, 1967, pp. 92–103).

204 J. J. Lee, *Ireland, 1912–1985: politics and society*, Cambridge, 1989, p. 161.

205 White, *Minority report*, p. 100.

206 Whyte, *Church and state in modern Ireland*, pp. 45–46.

207 Lee, *Ireland, 1912–1985*, pp. 161–67; Whyte, *Church and state in modern Ireland*, p. 45; Gerard Moran, 'Church and state in modern Ireland: the Mayo county librarian case, 1930–32', *Cathair na Mart*, Vol. 7, 1987, pp. 92–99.

208 Whyte, *Church and state in modern Ireland*, p. 47.

209 *Church of Ireland Gazette*, 5 Dec. 1930, p. 684.

210 The quotation is taken from Margaret O'Callaghan's incisive article, 'Language, nationality and cultural identity in the Irish Free State, 1922–7: the *Irish Statesman* and the *Catholic Bulletin* reappraised', *IHS*, Vol. 24, 1984, pp. 226–45 (quotation on p. 241).

211 Séamas Ó Buachalla, *Educational policy in twentieth century Ireland*, Dublin, 1988, p. 243; for a detailed assessment, see Valerie Jones, 'The attitude of the Church of Ireland Board of Education to textbooks in national schools, 1922–1967', *Irish Edu-*

cational Studies, Vol. 11, 1992, pp. 72–81.

212 Ó Buachalla, *Educational policy in twentieth century Ireland*, p. 244.

213 E. Brian Titley, *Church, state, and the control of schooling in Ireland, 1900–1944*, Kingston and Montreal, 1983, p. 83.

214 Bowen, *Protestants in a Catholic state*, p. 159.

215 For discussion of this issue, see Bowen, *Protestants in a Catholic state*, pp. 158–60; Ó Buachalla, *Educational policy in twentieth century Ireland*, p. 244.

216 Ó Buachalla, *Educational policy in twentieth century Ireland*, p. 348.

217 Bowen, *Protestants in a Catholic state*, p. 156.

218 Fanning, *Independent Ireland*, p. 82.

219 Bowen, *Protestants in a Catholic state*, p. 157.

220 H. Kingsmill Moore, *Reminiscences and reflections*, London, 1930, p. 287. For the other objections of the Church of Ireland, see Ó Buachalla, *Educational policy in twentieth century Ireland*, pp. 244–46.

221 Bowen, *Protestants in a Catholic state*, p. 60.

222 For acerbic criticisms a long these lines, see *The Leader*, 11 Dec. 1926, pp. 443–45. For an assessment of the background to the views of this publication on compulsory Irish, see Maume, *D. P. Moran*, pp. 43–47.

223 E.g., *Church of Ireland Gazette*, 24 Feb. 1922, p. 102, 10 Mar. 1922, p. 135, 27 June 1924, p. 392, 11 Feb. 1938, p. 82

224 *Church of Ireland Gazette*, 12 Dec. 1924, p. 742.

225 William Cosgrave, *Policy of the Cumann na nGaedheal party*, Dublin, 1927, p. 11.

226 Sean Farren, *The politics of Irish education, 1920–65*, Belfast, 1995, pp. 142–52.

227 Quoted in ibid., p. 121.

228 White, *Minority report*, p. 98.

229 These estimates broadly conform with those of Bowen, *Protestants in a Catholic state*, table 5, p. 33, and Sexton and O'Leary, 'Factors affecting population decline', table a.6, p. 324. However, the former account is concerned only with members of the Church of Ireland and the latter with 'other denominations' in general, including the small Jewish community in Ireland.

230 Sexton and O'Leary, 'Factors affecting population decline', p. 300.

231 Bowen, *Protestants in a Catholic state*, p. 33.

232 Sexton and O'Leary, 'Factors affecting population decline', p. 300.

233 Kennedy, *The Irish*, p. 113, table 37, p. 114.

234 *Church of Ireland Gazette*, 1 Mar. 1929, p. 126.

235 Ibid.

236 *Irish Times*, 15 Feb. 1929.

237 *The Leader*, 23 Feb. 1929, p. 78.

238 *Church of Ireland Gazette*, 31 Mar. 1939, p. 169.

239 See Ulster Unionist Council, *Southern Ireland's census returns*.

240 Kennedy et al., 'The long retreat', p. 60.

241 Ibid.

242 Ibid.

243 Ferran Glenfield, 'The Protestant population of south-east Leinster,1834–1981', *Ir. Econ. & Soc. Hist.*, Vol. 20, 1993, pp. 82–83 [thesis abstract of unpub. MLitt. thesis, University of Dublin, 1990].

244 Ibid., p. 82.

245 Martin Magire, 'A socio-economic analysis of the Dublin Protestant working class, 1870–1926', *Ir. Econ. & Soc. Hist.*, Vol. 20, 1993, pp. 35–61, and, 'The Church of Ireland and the problem of the Protestant working-class of Dublin, 1870s–1930s', in *As by law established: the Church of Ireland since the Reformation*, ed. Alan Ford, James McGuire and Kenneth Milne, Dublin, 1995, pp. 195–203.

246 Maguire, 'A socio-economic analysis', p. 50.

247 Ibid., p. 49.

248 Ibid.

249 See the contemporary pamphlets published by APCK: Richard Babbington, *Mixed marriages*, Dublin, 1928; Dudley Fletcher, *Rome and marriage: a warning*, Dublin, 1936; T. C. Hammond, *Marriage: what shall it be?*, Dublin, 1936.

250 Maguire, 'A socio-economic analysis', p. 57, and 'The Church of Ireland and the problem of the Protestant working-class of Dublin', p. 202.

251 Kennedy, *The Irish*, pp. 129, 138.

252 For instance, de Valera's statement in 1938 that 'in a united Ireland fair play and equal justice is guaranteed to all citizens. As for freedom of conscience, the historic Irish nation has a splendid record of religious toleration' (quoted in *Irish Press*, 1 Feb. 1938).

253 D. H. Akenson, *A mirror to Kathleen's face: education in independent Ireland*, Montreal, 1975, pp. 118–19.

254 *Church of Ireland Gazette*, 12 Dec. 1924, p. 742.

255 Whyte, *Church and state in modern Ireland*, p. 54.

256 *Church of Ireland Gazette*, 12 May 1939, p. 256.

257 Sean Glynn, 'Irish immigration to Britain, 1911–1951: patterns and policy', *Ir. Econ. & Soc. Hist.*, Vol. 8, 1981, pp. 50–69.

258 Bronwen Walter, 'Time-space patterns of second-wave Irish immigration into British towns', *Trans. Inst. Brit. Geog.*, new series, Vol. 5, 1980, p. 298.

259 Ibid.

260 Tom Gallagher, *Glasgow: the uneasy peace*, Manchester, 1987, p. 136. For an extended discussion of the attitudes of the Scottish Presbyterian churches to Irish migration to Scotland, see Stewart J. Brown, ' "Outside the convenant": the Scottish Presbyterian churches and Irish immigration, 1922–1938', *Innes Review*, Vol. 42, 1991, pp. 19–45.

261 Edinburgh, 1923.

262 Steve Bruce, *No Pope of Rome: anti-Catholicism in modern Scotland*, Edinburgh, 1985, p. 46.

263 Brown, ' "Outside the covenant" ', p. 41.

264 Handley, *The Irish in modern Scotland*, p. 304; R. J. Finlay, 'Nationalism, race, religion and the Irish question in interwar Scotland', *Innes Review*, Vol. 42, 1991, pp. 46–67. On empire migration, see Stephen Constantine, *The making of British colonial development policy, 1914–1940* London, 1984 and Stephen Constantine, ed., *Emigrants and empire: British settlement in the dominions between the wars*, Manchester, 1990.

265 Good treatments of this issue include Bruce, *No Pope of Rome*; Gallagher, *Glasgow*, and 'Protestant extremism in urban Scotland, 1930–1939: its growth and contraction', *Scottish Historical Review*, Vol. 64, 1985, pp. 143–67.

266 Handley, *The Irish in Scotland*, pp. 309–15; Gallagher, *Glasgow*, pp. 167–68.

267 PRO, LAB 2/1346, Scottish Board of Health: memorandum for joint conference on Irish immigration, 24 June 1927, p. 11.

268 Ibid., minutes of interdepartmental conference held on 27 July 1927 on the subject of Irish immigration: comments of Whiskard (Dominions Office), p. 2.

269 PRO, HO 45/14634, draft note of proceedings at a deputation to the home secretary and the secretary of state for Scotland from the Church of Scotland, the United Free Church of Scotland, and the Free Church of Scotland, 19 July 1928, p. 2.

270 Ibid., p. 3.

271 *Daily Telegraph*, 20 July 1928; *Morning Post*, 20 July 1928; *The Times*, 18 and 20 July 1928.

272 PRO, HO 45/14634, report prepared by Chief Inspector, Aliens' Branch, 27 Aug. 1928, p. 3.

273 Anderson was sometime joint-undersecretary in Ireland (1920–22), formerly governor of Bengal, and later chancellor of the exchequer and home secretary.

274 PRO, CAB 24/197 (1928), Irish immigration: memorandum by the home secretary and the secretary of state for Scotland, note of interdepartmental conference on the possibility of controlling Irish immigration into Scotland and England, 31 July 1928, p. 2.

275 Ibid.

276 PRO, HO 45/14634, note of conference on the influx of Irish labour into Great Britain, held at the Home Office on 25 July 1928, p. 4.

277 Ibid.

278 PRO, CAB 24/197 (1928), Irish immigration: memorandum by the home secretary and the secretary of state for Scotland, note of interdepartmental conference ..., p. 2.

279 PRO, HO 45/14634, extract from cabinet conclusions, 1 Aug. 1928.

280 PRO, LAB 2/1346, copy of letter from J. A. Dale (Ministry of Labour) to A. S. Hinshelwood (Home Office), 7 Jan. 1929, and enclosed summary of returns.

281 PRO, CAB 24/201 (1929) Irish immigration: memorandum by home secretary, 20 Feb. 1929, p. 1.

282 Ibid.

283 Ibid., p. 6; PRO, CAB 24/201 (1929), Irish immigration: memorandum by the secretary of state for Scotland, 21 Feb. 1929.

284 Handley, *The Irish in modern Scotland*, pp. 305–06.

285 Brenda Collins, 'The origins of Irish immigration to Scotland in the nineteenth and twentieth centuries', in *Irish immigrants and Scottish society in the nineteenth and twentieth centuries*, ed. T. M. Devine, Edinburgh, 1990, p. 15; Walshaw, *Migration to and from the British Isles*, pp. 73–74.

286 It should be noted that a series of articles in the *Glasgow Herald* in March 1929 pointed to this explanation (Gallagher, *Glasgow*, p. 167; Handley, *The Irish in modern Scotland*, pp. 312–15).

287 PRO, LAB 2/1346, minutes of interdepartmental conference held on 27 July 1927 on the subject of Irish immigration: comments of Prestige (Home Office), p. 2.

288 For further information on the composition and activities of the Economic Advisory Council, see S. S. Wilson, *The cabinet office to 1945*, London, 1975, pp. 83–84, 150–52.

289 PRO, HO 45/14635, Economic Advisory Council, EAC (E.M.) 60, Committee on Empire Migration: Irish Free State emigration, note by Professor A. M. Carr-Saunders, 27 Oct. 1930, p. 2.

290 Ibid., pp. 2–3.

291 PRO, HO45/14635, memorandum by the home secretary on Irish immigration, n.d. [Jan. 1931], pp. 3–4.

292 PRO, 30/69/358, Ramsay MacDonald papers, copy of a letter from the secretary of state for Scotland (William Adamson) to the prime minister (J. R. MacDonald), 5 June 1930.

293 Ibid., migration from Ireland into Scotland: memorandum by the Ministry of Labour, 1 July 1930.

294 Ibid., Economic Advisory Council, Commitee on Empire Migration, report, 11 July 1931, p. 45.

295 Ibid.

296 PRO, HO45/14635, memorandum by the home secretary, pp. 3–4.

297 Ibid., p. 4.

298 PRO, 30/69/358, MacDonald papers, letter from E. H. Marsh (Dominions Office) to H. G. Vincent (private secretary to the prime minister), 5 Aug. 1931.

299 Ibid., Clynes to MacDonald, 13 Aug. 1931.

300 Ibid., note for prime minister by H. G. Vincent on Irish immigration, 14 Aug. 1931, p. 1.

301 Ibid., p. 2; Economic Advisory Council, Commitee on Empire Migration, report, 11 July 1931, p. 45.

302 Ibid., handwritten note by MacDonald.

303 Ibid., Sir Archibald Sinclair (secretary of state for Scotland) to MacDonald, 24 Mar. 1932.

304 Ibid., copy of a letter from Patrick McGilligan to J. H. Thomas, 21 Jan. 1932.

305 Ibid., MacDonald to Sinclair, n.d. [Mar. 1932].

306 The definitive exposition of the impact of this changeover on Anglo-Irish relations is contained in McMahon, *Republicans and imperialists*, pp. 4–28.

307 PRO, LAB HO 45/14635, Home Office memorandum on certain restrictions unpon the employment of immigrants from IFS, 10 May 1932, p. 2.

308 PRO, CAB 27/525, ISC (32) 16, possible courses of action at present stage: memorandum by the secretary of state for dominion affairs, 29 Apr. 1932, p. 5.

309 Ibid., ISC (32) 32, immigrants from the IFS: memorandum by the Ministry of Labour, 16 June 1932, p. 6

310 Ibid.

311 NAI, DFA pre–100 series, 5/9, memorandum on the position of Irish nationals in Great Britain and British nationals in the Irish Free State in the event of the removal of oath of allegiance for members of Dáil Éireann, 24 Mar. 1932, p. 1.

312 *Report, to the Economic Advisory Council, of the Committee on Empire Migration*, p. 13, 1931–32, IX, 333.

313 PRO, CAB 24/247, CP 5 (1934), p. 1.

314 Ibid., pp. 1–2.

315 Ibid., p. 3.

316 For more details about this memorandum, see Glynn, 'Irish immigration to Britain', pp. 64–65.

317 Good treatments of this issue include Frank Neal, *Sectarian violence: the Liv-*

erpool experience, 1819–1914, Manchester, 1988, and 'English–Irish conflict in the north-east of England', in *The Irish in British labour history*, ed. Patrick Buckland and John Belchem, Liverpool, 1992, pp. 59–86; P. J. Waller, *Democracy and sectarianism: a political and social history of Liverpool*, Liverpool, 1981.

318 Colin Holmes, *John Bull's island: immigration and British society, 1871–1971*, Basingstoke, 1988, p. 149; Waller, *Democracy and sectarianism*, p. 329.

319 G. R. Gair, 'The Irish immigration question: pt. 3', *Liverpool Review*, vol. 9, 3 Mar. 1934, pp. 86–88; for his other articles on this matter, see 'The Irish immigration question: pt. 1', *Liverpool Review*, vol. 9, 1 Jan. 1934, pp. 11–13 and 'The Irish immigration question: pt. 2', *Liverpool Review*, vol. 9, 2 Feb. 1934, pp. 47–49. This source was first discussed in Holmes, *John Bull's island*, p. 149.

320 David Caradog Jones, ed., *The social survey of Merseyside*, 2 vols, Liverpool, 1934, Vol. I, p. 202.

321 Ibid., p. 206.

322 PRO, HO 45/14635, David to R. R. Bannatyne, 10 July 1931; Bannatyne to David, 14 July 1931; David to Bannatyne, 15 July 1931. This issue received some coverage at the time in the national press, see *The Times*, 5 Aug. 1931.

323 PRO, LAB 8/16, *The Guardian*, n.d. [April 1937].

324 Ibid., Stephenson (Dominions Office) to secretary, Ministry of Labour, 6 Mar. 1937.

325 One memorable question tabled on 2 March 1937 by Lt.-Col. Moore asked, 'Would it not be possible to put an import duty on southern Irish human beings as is placed on southern Irish animals?' (quoted in Glynn, 'Irish immigration to Britain', p. 65).

326 PRO, LAB 8/16, Stephenson (Dominions Office) to secretary, Ministry of Labour, 6 Mar. 1937.

327 Ibid., Wolfe (Ministry of Labour) to undersecretary of state (Dominions Office), 6 Apr. 1937.

328 Ibid., migration to Great Britain from the Irish Free State: report of interdepartmental committee, August 1937, p. 3.

329 PRO, LAB 8/16, migration to Great Britain from the Irish Free State: report of interdepartmental committee, August 1937, p. 3; on the cities chosen, see ibid., Stephenson (Dominions Office) to Mongomerie (Ministry of Labour), 15 Oct. 1937.

330 *Hansard* (Commons), CCCXXIX, 3 Dec. 1937, cols 2514–17; Glynn, 'Irish immigration to Britain', p. 67.

331 Kevin O'Connor, *The Irish in Britain*, rev. edn, Dublin, 1974, p. 55; for a detailed discussion, see T. P. Coogan, *The IRA*, London, 1970, pp. 127–35.

332 O'Connor, *The Irish in Britain*, p. 52.

333 Ibid., p. 51. For Behan's subsequent and ultimately successful attempts to enter Britain, see Colin Holmes, 'The British government and Brendan Behan, 1941–54: the persistence of the Prevention of Violence Act', *Saothar*, vol. 14, 1989, pp. 125–28.

334 Ibid., p. 55.

335 On the socio-economic profile of Irish Protestants, see Kennedy, *The Irish*, pp. 131–36.

3

Enter the state, 1940–1946

Total war inevitably resulted in the displacement of population such as refugees fleeing persecution or transported foreign workers who were compelled to become involved in the war effort as was the case in Nazi Germany.[1] But the Second World War also created opportunities for migrants to take advantage of the incessant demand for labour that is fuelled by the exigencies of total war. Conscription and increased levels of wartime production ensured that female, over-age and migrant workers were required to fill the gaps in the labour force left by those who joined the armed forces. During the First World War Irish migrants travelled to Britain to work in munitions factories.[2] A similar movement of population across the Irish Sea occurred during the Second World War, although in contrast with the 1914–18 period, these workers were now the citizens of a neutral state, and this caused both the British and Irish governments a whole host of difficulties, as we will see later.

Whereas the First World War undoubtedly had a beneficial effect on Ireland's prosperity, the onset of the Second World War exposed the vulnerability of a small, heavily protected economy, reliant on imports from one of the principal combatants – Britain.[3] The wartime experience in neutral Ireland was characterised by austerity, the most obvious example being the fact that supplies of essential products were subject to rationing. In addition, the shortage of raw materials seriously affected production in agriculture and industry alike.[4] The objective of economic self- sufficiency, which had been pursued as an aspiration in the 1930s, became an enforced harsh reality as essential products proved increasingly difficult to procure during the war. As Kennedy, Giblin and McHugh have noted, 'economic survival took over from economic development as the main thrust of policy'.[5] It might be expected in theory that one measure of the grave economic

situation facing the fledgling Irish state would be the level of unemployment. However, unemployment statistics for this period are
acknowledged to be notoriously difficult to interpret, and the official
estimates for the live register suggest what at first glance appears a surprising decrease from 15 per cent to roughly 10 per cent during the
war years.[6] As we shall see, this development had much to do with the
significant increase in Irish migration to Britain together with the
expansion in the total number employed in the Irish defence forces.[7]
In monetary terms, Irish wages were frozen by an emergency powers
order from 1942 to 1946.[8] The purchasing power derived from wages
in both agriculture and industry decreased substantially as the cost of
living rose by 70 per cent.[9] The official cost of living index (July 1914
= 100) had risen from 205 in 1940 to 282 in 1943, reaching the extraordinary figure of 295 in 1944.[10] The degree of poverty and hardship in
Ireland (strictly speaking Éire from 1937 onwards) during the rather
euphemistically entitled 'emergency' is a matter for speculation,
although one unpublished attempt to ascertain the level of poverty,
employing Rowntree's classic 'human needs standard', found that 45
per cent of households in Cork city were living in poverty in 1944.[11] In
many senses, the demand for labour in Britain provided the outlet
from the grim hardship of wartime Ireland, despite the fact that Ireland was in theory a neutral state and Britain a belligerent power.

I

The population of the 26 counties that constituted Éire remained relatively stable in the decade from 1936 until 1946, a slight decrease in
the total population of 0.4 per cent being recorded in the 1946 census.[12]
On a provincial basis, Connacht suffered the most significant decline
with a decrease of 6.2 per cent in the intercensal period between 1936
and 1946, although the figure for the north-western counties was a
comparable one of just under 6 per cent (see appendix 7). The demographic changes in the population on a county level are similar to
those for the previous decade (1926–36). The population decline in
counties along the western seaboard such as Leitrim, Sligo, Mayo,
Clare and Kerry continued, but some of the highest figures are also to
be found for a number of other counties, namely Cavan and Monaghan. In the case of the most striking example, county Leitrim,
which experienced a decline of nearly 13 per cent or over 6,000 persons

in the period 1936–46, clearly migration, either internal or international, played no small part in ensuring that any of the gains which would occur through natural increase drained away. Minor increases in the total population for the majority of the counties in Leinster were recorded in 1946, with Dublin and its adjoining counties enjoying a quite substantial gain in population. In short, therefore, the decline was concentrated in the north-west and along the western seaboard which, as we noted earlier, was the continuation of a post-famine demographic trend.

Patterns of internal migration shed some light on the population redistribution evident for this period. On an initial inspection of these data, the Irish population appear to have been remarkably mobile (see appendix 8). However, the problem – as we observed in the previous chapter – with the county-level data is that they include even movement of a relatively short distance across an administrative county boundary. This distorts the overall picture since no indication of the duration of residence is provided. In addition, the levels of in-migration and out-migration for a county depended on several factors including its size, the number of urban settlements within the county boundary and the existence of any industries.[13] A further factor to be considered is that the decision to move from one county to another, particularly a contiguous one, would not have presented much difficulty for many people at this time. Without doubt, a degree of consciousness existed in regard to county origins when it came to sport, particularly Gaelic football and hurling, but in other less visceral circumstances a decision to cross a county boundary for the purposes of employment or marriage would not have troubled most internal migrants.

The other feature that is evident from the data is the growth of Dublin city and county and its surrounding areas. Dublin's population had increased by 49,000 persons between 1936 and 1946.[14] The question of whether this increase merely reflects a growing trend towards the urbanisation of the Irish population or, on the other hand, a pattern peculiar to Dublin, merits some reflection. By 1946, nearly 40 per cent of the Irish population lived in an urban area (see Table 3.1), a slight increase on the figure of 37 per cent in 1936. In contrast with the striking enlargement in the size of the population of Dublin during the previous decade (1926–36), the following intercensal period witnessed a slower rate of growth. A crucial point which should be underlined is that, whilst the population of Dublin grew steadily,

Table 3.1 Population of towns as a percentage of the total Irish population, 1936–46

Year	Éire	Leinster	Munster	Connacht	Ulster
1936	37.1	57.5	33.2	11.8	8.2
1946	39.3	59.0	34.5	13.0	9.5

Source: Censuses of population of Ireland 1946 and 1951: general report, table 4, p. 24.

the rate for other towns was relatively modest, except in the case of those with an average population of between 500 and 1,000 persons.[15] The comments of the Commission on Emigration in 1955, when discussing the growth of Dublin, equally apply to this earlier period: 'a weakness does exist, but is due not to the absolute size of Dublin, which is not abnormal for a capital city of a country such as Ireland, but to its relative size, that is, its size compared with the remaining town population of the country'.[16] In essence, the growth in the total urban population is primarily an indication of the enlargement of the population of Dublin, rather than an increase in the size of towns throughout rural Ireland.

In terms of religious denomination, the number of Roman Catholics rose by 0.4 per cent between 1936 and 1946.[17] For other religious denominations, however, a decrease of 13 per cent spread fairly evenly across the main Protestant denominations was recorded in this decade.[18] The proportion of Catholics in the Irish population, therefore, rose gradually to 94 per cent in 1946 compared with 93 per cent in 1936 and 92 per cent in 1926.[19] The decrease in the number of Protestants was general throughout the country, although of somewhat less significance in the province of Leinster.[20] The effect of migration on the age distribution of Catholics and other religious denominations (mostly Protestant) is illustrated in Table 3.2. Net migration for the 'other religious denominations' category was significantly higher by age and gender. On the basis of these calculations, somewhere in the region of 25 to 30 per cent of male non-Catholics aged between 10 and 24 years in 1936 had left the country by 1946. The rate for females was lower but still above their Catholic counterparts. As was noted by the statisticians working on an analysis of the 1946 census results, the demographic features exhibited by the Protestant community, viz. a low marriage rate, a low fertility rate, a high migration rate and significantly higher rates of mortality owing to the large proportion of elderly people, explain the decline in population which was evident in this decade, but this was a continuing trend, as was demonstrated in the previous chapter.

Table 3.2 Persons in 1946 per 1,000 of those who were 10 years younger in 1936, by religious denomination

Religious denomination	Males				Females			
	Age in 1936				Age in 1936			
	10–14	15–19	20–24	25–34	10–14	15–19	20–24	25–34
Catholics	827	760	776	880	818	802	844	914
Other religious denominations	723	654	699	832	735	747	809	881
Total population	821	754	771	877	814	799	842	912
Decrease in 10 years due to mortality (approx.)	26	37	40	47	28	38	43	48
Net emigration per 1,000 persons								
Catholics	147	203	184	73	154	160	113	38
Other religious denominations	251	309	261	121	237	215	148	71

Source: After *Censuses of population of Ireland 1946 and 1951: general report*, table 155, p. 169.

II

The involvement of the state in the regulation of migration between Ireland and the United Kingdom is the most significant development of the wartime period. State regulation and control of migration inevitably resulted in the generation of a voluminous corpus of documentation on both sides of the Irish Sea. Much of the British documentation was consulted by A. V. Judges in the course of the preparation of his extremely valuable account of Irish labour in Britain between 1939 and 1945, a document that was utilised for the work on the official histories of the Second World War.[21] Judges was, an economic historian based at the London School of Economics in the 1930s, who subsequently became professor of the history of education at King's College, London, in 1949.[22] During the war he was attached to the Ministry of Labour and National Service, and he remained there after the war to work on a part-time basis. Judges's account was never published, ostensibly because the information suggested that the Irish government facilitated the migration of Irish citizens to Britain. One British civil servant who was closely involved in the recruitment of Irish workers advised that it was 'dangerous in the extreme'.[23] The edited version was marked 'for consumption in the United Kingdom only', and since 1949 it has languished in the records of the Ministry of Labour. The fact that Judges had unlimited access to the records of the Ministry of Labour makes his history of Irish migrants who travelled to Britain during the war a key source for this period. The present study draws on Judges's account supplemented with other official documents available from British government departments. The Irish documentation, on the other hand, is of a different nature both in its diversity and scope. For the first time the Irish state became closely involved in the regulation of migration and this generated a mass of documentation of varying quality and interest. A further boon is that detailed statistical records were kept by both governments, thereby facilitating a fuller analysis of certain characteristics of the migrant flow.

Prior to the outbreak of war in September 1939, as was demonstrated in the previous chapter there was no restriction on the free movement of labour from Ireland to Britain. With the onset of war, the British authorities moved quickly to ensure that all persons travelling to Britain had a valid identity card. In response to this requirement, identity cards were issued by the Irish Department of External Affairs and all Irish citizens wishing to travel to Britain applied at the local station of the Garda Síochana.[24] However, the identity card requirement should not be regarded as a restriction as such, but merely a sensible security precaution on the part of the British authorities. In addition, as was stated in the previous chapter, because of the IRA bombing campaign in 1939 Irish citizens were required to register with the local police station in Britain. After the fall of France in June 1940, and the consequent impending threat of the invasion of Britain, the severe measures that were already in place under the defence regulations drafted in September 1939 were implemented whereby travel across the Irish Sea was strictly curtailed, including travel from Northern Ireland.[25] Permission to enter the country was only given for 'business of national importance', and those who returned to Ireland were not permitted to re-enter Britain.[26] The reasons for this restriction were obvious: the movement of persons between Ireland and Britain resulted in a security risk since information could be carried, either intentionally or unintentionally, and it was also feared that some Irish persons in Britain might prove receptive to a German invasion – a type of fifth column.[27] A permit office was set up in Dublin by the British government in June 1940 to consider applications for visas to travel to Britain.[28] From June 1940 until the spring of 1941, the only significant degree of movement which occurred under official auspices was that of seasonal agricultural workers who were allowed to enter Britain on a six-month visa for the 1940 harvest.[29] These seasonal migrants were required to stay working in agriculture in order to reduce the possibility of exposure to industrial sites of military importance.[30] The Irish government had issued a statement in April 1940 assuring seasonal migrants that they would not be liable for conscription in Britain after a large number of enquiries were received by the Department of External Affairs.[31]

Throughout late 1940 and early 1941 a considerable amount of unofficial co-operation occurred between the British Ministry of Labour and National Service and the Irish Department of Industry and Commerce, whereby particulars relating to unemployed persons wishing to travel to Britain for work were forwarded from Dublin to London, although the numbers involved were not great.[32] However, that situation changed when in late February 1941 applications to be considered for employment in Britain began to flood into the Dublin Employment Exchange. In the space of only two weeks 1,500 people applied as information regarding employment opportunities in Britain became widely available.[33] Even though the officials explained to the applicants that they had no information on employment vacancies in Britain, all requested to have their applications for work in Britain recorded. The employment exchange refused to consider any further cases after two weeks. Officials feared that this development would spread throughout the country and result in thousands of requests for employment in Britain.[34] Clearly, the situation would by necessity involve a decision by the Irish government on the principle of facilitating the migration of Irish workers to Britain. A crucial determinant in such a decision was the alleviation of Irish unemployment that was assumed would be the result of allowing those without work to travel to Britain. A further factor was that large groups of disgruntled unemployed workers who wished to go to Britain could pose a significant threat to the social order, if they were prevented from doing so. On the British side, a recognition existed that the pool of unemployed labour in Ireland would prove a useful additional source of labour for the demand created by the war. The severity of the British labour situation was illustrated by the emergency powers act which was introduced in May 1940 whereby workers could be directed to place ' "themselves, their services and their property" at the disposal of the government'.[35] Therefore the dilemma for the Irish government was to weigh up the obvious advantage of allowing unemployed workers to travel to Britain against the possibility of a labour shortage in Ireland at some future date and the concomitant danger of being seen to aid a belligerent power, notwithstanding the policy of neutrality adopted in September 1939. Furthermore, the public criticism which could result from a policy of facilitating emigration to Britain was also a source of worry for the Irish government. Another difficulty emerged after the spring of 1941, with the acceleration in unregulated recruiting of Irish workers by individual 'agents' for large British firms involved in wartime production, such as ICI and Ford.[36]

These matters came to a head in the summer of 1941 when the Irish and British governments arrived at a *modus operandi*. In the first instance, the Irish government sought an assurance from the British authorities that migrants would not be subject to conscription and would be entitled to receive compensation for war injuries. These assurances were received by June 1941 after a good deal of diplomatic wrangling.[37] Secondly, and not surprisingly, the Irish authorities discussed a number of mechanisms which would enable the state to control the type of workers who were migrating, particularly rural workers who would be required at home to participate in harvesting and turf-cutting work.[38] In the event, strict restrictions of this nature were not imposed from the outset and the only stipulation was that 'a travel permit is not to be refused to any person unless it is clear that there is employment available for him [*sic*] in Éire in producing food or fuel'.[39] Of course, establishing whether employment was available or not would always prove a difficult task for officials.

In July 1941 representatives of the British Ministry of Labour and National Service and the Irish Department of Industry and Commerce met in Dublin to consider the details of an agreement which would be acceptable to both sides. The framework developed at this conference provided the basic mechanism by which Irish citizens travelled to

Britain for employment throughout the war. The central figure in the machinery that was instituted in August 1941 was the British liaison officer for labour who co-ordinated all recruitment in Ireland for employment in Britain.[40] The duties of this official included supervising recruitment 'agents' for large British firms; advising all prospective applicants for employment in Britain to enrol with the local employment exchanges; assessing and allocating applications from employers in Britain for Irish labour; and ensuring all applicants were interviewed by representatives of the liaison officer.[41] The Irish state was able to retain control by ensuring that only people who were without work (and for whom no employment was apparently available) received permits.[42] Since the enrolments for employment in Britain were processed through the local employment exchanges, in theory a system of monitoring ensured that these stipulations were adhered to, and detailed statistical information on the migrant flow was collected to assess the possibility of a future labour shortage. A number of modifications were introduced to the scheme, such as a requirement from October 1941 that persons applying for a travel permit be over 22 years of age.[43] In the same month, the role of recruitment agents for British employers was curtailed because their overt activities had caused some public outcry in the national press.[44] Henceforth direct recruitment by British firms was prohibited[45] and the censor was instructed to ensure that no advertisements which offered employment outside the country appeared in the national press.[46] The role of the agents was limited to interviewing prospective applicants, rather than the controversial one of actively encouraging Irish citizens to travel to Britain.

A significant modification was introduced in May 1942 when workers who resided outside incorporated towns and who had any experience of agricultural or turf-cutting work were to be refused permits to travel to Britain.[47] In practice, most workers from rural Ireland would have at least some experience of agricultural work. Prior to this decision, some debate had occurred within the upper echelons of the Irish civil service with regard to the wisdom of such a decision. When a similar suggestion to limit the migration to Britain of rural residents was first mooted by the Department of Industry and Commerce in September 1941, the reaction of the bastion of economic orthodoxy – the Irish Department of Finance – is revealing in that it sheds light on the divergent priorities of the various arms of the state in relation to Irish migration to Britain. A detailed memorandum was prepared by finance officials, most probably by the redoubtable secretary of the

department, J. J. McElligott.[48] According to this document, 'in regard
to emigration to Britain from rural areas, the minister for finance
[Seán T. O'Kelly] is definitely of the opinion that it is preferable that
rural residents should be employed in Britain, rather than remain
unemployed at home'. Apart from a paternalistic desire to ensure that
workers in rural areas retained their motivation to work, other factors
were also cited:

> From both moral and economic points it is preferable that workers should be
> allowed to obtain employment outside the country than that they should be
> compelled through circumstances outside their control to remain in idleness
> at home.
>   Involuntary idleness tends to sap the ability to work and the courage of
> workers and the minister feels that it is better that they should be employed at
> good wages in Great Britain than that they should remain without work at
> home, dependant [sic] for existence on unemployment assistance or other
> forms of public assistance. Moreover, the worker employed at good wages in
> Great Britain is in a position to send substantial contributions to his depen-
> dants at home, and thereby break for them the monotony of continuous
> poverty.[49]

Needless to say other concerns apart from moral or economic principles entered the discussion, as the Department for Industry and
Commerce had proposed that unemployment assistance be paid all
year round for persons living in rural areas, and a weekly retainer be
paid to unemployed workers who were prepared to volunteer for food
and turf production in any part of the country.[50] This would place a
further strain on the exchequer which was already finding it difficult
to meet the costs of existing services, let alone the additional burden
of £330,000 per annum that it was estimated these proposals would
involve.[51] The first part of this proposal was not implemented by the
government in October 1941, but when the similar suggestion to
refuse travel permits to men who had experience in agricultural or turf
work was put before the cabinet in May 1942, opposition to the
Department of Finance position arose from an unexpected quarter, the
Department of External Affairs. A lengthy and detailed memorandum
on the subject was drafted by F. H. Boland, then assistant secretary of
the department, and subsequently a well-respected international
diplomat. This frank and thoughtful exposition of the issues surrounding the migration of Irish workers deserves some analysis as it
underlines a number of the fundamental concerns of the Irish body
politic. In Boland's view, the British authorities, in response to a pro-

hibition on the migration to Britain of workers from rural areas (the main source of Irish labour), might restrict the supply of raw materials to industries in Ireland, which would therefore increase unemployment in the urban areas and in turn lead to an increase in emigration.[52] Boland was emphasising the reliance of Irish industry on British goodwill and the informal *quid pro quo* as regards the availability of Irish migrants. He acknowledged that it was only speculation that these matters would be linked, but the campaign of 'economic pressure' adopted by the British from January 1941 onwards served to exemplify Ireland's vulnerability in terms of the procurement of essential supplies.[53]

With a frankness not generally acknowledged to be the preserve of civil servants, Boland mused further on the position of the Department of Finance on the migration of Irish workers to Britain. He was not completely convinced by McElligott's arguments regarding the benefits of the continuance of Irish migration to Britain:

> In a recent conversation, Mr McElligott mentioned to me some of the arguments which are, no doubt, being urged very strongly in favour of allowing the traffic to continue. He claims that it provides a safety-valve against revolution, that the resulting inflow of ready money – he put it as high as £100,000 or £150,000 a week – did a great deal to relieve distress and maintain economic activity, and that it would be contrary to sound social ethics and inequitable to prevent the poor man from marketing his most valuable asset – that is to say his labour – in his best market. No doubt, a further argument, which Mr McElligott was not so indelicate to mention, is the saving on unemployment assistance which results to the exchequer![54]

The similarities in the arguments for the continuance of labour migration to Britain advanced by McElligott to Boland and those outlined in the earlier Department of Finance memorandum provide further evidence that the views are those of McElligott rather than Seán T. O'Kelly, the minister for finance. In the event, Boland was sceptical about the value of these propositions since they seemed to him to lack foresight:

> To my mind, all these arguments are open to the criticism that they are largely theoretical and do not take sufficient account of practical realities, such as the danger of social revolution and extreme distress which is likely to result if we are entirely thrown back on our own resources and find ourselves short of adequate manpower.
>
> There is just one final point. Whatever the danger of social revolution in this country may be, it is certain to be in its maximum during the last year of the war and during the next year or two after it. Now, if there is one thing more cer-

tain than another, it is that immediately the 'cease fire' order is given, the whole aim and purpose of the British authorities will be to rush all these workers back to this country as quickly as they can . . . Therefore, no problem that we are likely to have to face during the war is likely to be so serious as the problem we will have when up to as many as 100,000 or more unemployed men (who will, no doubt, have imbibed a good deal of 'leftism' in Britain) are dumped back here within the course of a few weeks after the conclusion of the war, to have piled on top of them, in the course of a short time afterwards all the Irish citizens demobilised from the British armed forces.[55]

Boland was not merely outlining the potential hazards ahead, but rather suggesting that some arrangement should be negotiated with the British authorities whereby Irish migrants would be returned on a gradual basis.[56] No such formal agreement was arrived at with the British Ministry of Labour and National Service, although the Department of Industry and Commerce received an assurance in November 1942 that the British authorities would be willing to discuss the matter 'when the time comes'.[57] For Boland, an injudicious approach to the control of migration to Britain could result in either a labour shortage during the war or the large-scale return migration of Irish citizens after the war ended.

It can be seen that within the Irish political and administrative élite, a degree of unease existed in some quarters about the migration of Irish workers to Britain in 1941 and 1942. Yet there was a realisation that it would be extremely difficult to prohibit migration to Britain whilst unemployment continued and no obvious labour shortage was evident. The Irish minister for industry and commerce, Seán Lemass, was reported as saying in October 1941 that the government shared the dislike of the manner in which workers were leaving the country, but since the Irish state could not provide full employment, they were very reluctant to prohibit migration to Britain.[58] However, when a labour shortage did pose a threat, the government acted, as in May 1942, to prevent those who had experience in agricultural or turf work from leaving. It is curious that civil servants frequently referred to migration as an outlet for the reduction of potential social unrest, or in other words, the large-scale movement of Irish citizens to Britain was a 'safety-valve' against revolution. Although clearly this was a useful point to make during governmental deliberations about the introduction of restrictions on migration, the extent to which this alleged potential for revolution existed in reality was conjectural. Nevertheless, it illustrates the element of double-thinking in the Irish official mind. On the one hand, large-scale migration to Britain was undesirable since it was damaging to national morale. Yet, on the other hand, this movement of unemployed and underemployed people – in theory at least – reduced the possibility of social unrest. As Boland noted, the return of these migrants when the war ended was ostensibly to be welcomed, but the prospect of thousands of Irish migrants returning from Britain and adding to the level of unemployment was difficult to contemplate. Therefore, even though on a general level the Irish state encouraged return migration, it suited civil servants and politicians that these migrants remained in Britain.

Despite the fact that direct recruitment by 'agents' or employers' representatives for British firms had been prohibited in October 1941, the Irish government moved in December 1942 to proscribe any advertisements offering employment in Britain which appeared in the national newspapers. Earlier efforts in October 1941 to restrict newspaper advertisements had effectively been circumvented by employers not stating that the location of the employment was in fact in Britain. These advertisements created the impression of 'almost unlimited opportunities for employment at high wages' in Britain and Northern Ireland and, it was argued, generated dissatisfaction amongst Irish workers at home since higher wages in Britain were more attractive.[59] The government by virtue of the emergency powers legislation, required all advertisements for employment for more than two workers to specify the location of the employment within the Irish state, thereby enforcing strictly the ban on recruitment by British firms.[60] This was a clear cut case of ensuring that fields that were not so far away did not appear 'greener'!

In March 1944 the British authorities imposed a ban on travel from the country owing to the security precautions in preparation for the D-Day invasion.[61] Hitherto, Irish workers in Britain had been entitled to one visit home every six months, subject to the various travel restrictions and the agreement of their employer in Britain.[62] The Irish response was to stop facilitating any further involvement in recruitment at employment exchanges. Lemass announced in the Dáil in April 1944 that 'it has been decided to suspend, for the time being, the facilities previously available to workers who desired to register for employment outside the country'.[63] In fact, as Judges noted, recruitment at employment exchanges for civilian work in Britain had ceased from mid-March, although workers who had received official authorisation continued to travel in March and April.[64] Whereas the decision by the British authorities provided the immediate impetus to implement the embargo on recruitment, the concerns which were aired with regard to the possibility of a labour shortage at an earlier juncture re-emerged in the first half of 1944. A decision had been taken earlier, in December 1943, to prohibit the issuing of travel permits to males living in counties Mayo and Galway who, in the two years before their application was made, had experience in agriculture or turf production work.[65] However, the officials monitoring the migration controls became increasingly uneasy about the volume of persons leaving the country. An estimate of the total number who obtained travel permits for employment outside the state in the period from September 1939 to March 1944 indicated that 188,254 people had applied for and were issued with the appropriate documentation; of course, not all these people actually left the country.[66] This was a vast number from a relatively small economically active population of approximately 1.3 million people in 1936. According to the Department of Industry and Commerce the moment had come to safeguard the Irish national interest:

> There is no means of measuring precisely the reserve of effective labour available for the production of food and fuel and other essential services, but having regard to the extent of emigration during the past 4½ years, there appears to be a danger that the supply of labour may become seriously depleted if emigration is allowed to continue at the present rate. This would constitute a national danger if, owing to the cessation of imports, it became necessary to produce within the country the food and fuel needed to meet the requirements of the people.[67]

It should be remembered that by 1944 shortages had become acute in Ireland. One obvious manifestation of the dearth of supplies was the suspension of the Dublin tram service in the summer of that year as a result of fuel shortages.[68] Lemass was sounding a portentous note, and recommended that four measures should be taken: firstly, an embargo should be placed on the emigration of men from rural areas and towns with a population of 5,000 persons or fewer; secondly, a complete ban ought to be enforced on the emigration of persons aged 22 years or less (subject to exemption in special cases, e.g. trainees and 'professionals'); thirdly, a ministerial power should be instituted, either for a temporary or permanent period, to restrict, migration by all persons over 22 years of age not living in the specially designated areas where restrictions were already in place; and lastly, the ban in place on the migration of workers with agricultural or turf work experience should continue.[69] This last ban would in theory have affected virtually all male rural dwellers. The government accepted Lemass's recommendations which granted him widespread powers in controlling migration to Britain, with the added proviso that his department should endeavour to negotiate an agreement with the British authorities for the return of Irish workers after the end of the war.[70]

As was the case in 1942, these recommendations were the subject of some implicit criticism by the Department of External Affairs. In a lengthy and involved memorandum on the issues surrounding the migration of Irish workers to Britain, a number of revealing comments were made. The unrealistic nature of the regulation regarding the restriction on travel permits for men from towns with a population of 5,000 or fewer was underlined, unless applications for permits were subjected to vigorous checks to ensure that the place of residence given was in fact the correct one.[71] Otherwise, the new regulations would be rendered ineffective as 'full advantage will be taken of the loopholes to evade the restriction'.[72] According to this document, the earlier regulations imposed by the Irish government in 1942 and 1943 were not effective as the number of male migrants from rural areas actually increased.[73] A further, and equally interesting, reflection is that the police officers at the point of application may have been dealing with people who displayed an uncanny knowledge of the myriad regulations and rules imposed by both states, an aspect noted wryly by British officials.[74] This observation also serves as a salutary reminder that, even though a range of restrictions were in place, some may not have been strictly observed by the numerous officials who processed the applications for travel permits. It is not unrealistic to suggest that public servants did not wish to prevent an unemployed person seeking a livelihood in Britain rather than surviving on the meagre level of unemployment assistance in Ireland.

The embargo on recruitment in Ireland existed from March until June 1944 and the ban on travel from British ports was lifted gradually from July of the same year.[75] Thereafter the revised Irish regulations discussed above came into force, albeit somewhat late in the day. During the intervening period of the embargo, the British Ministry of Labour had implemented a reform of the recruitment system for Irish labour whereby all prospective applicants would be centralised in the hands of the liaison officer in Dublin from September 1944 onwards.[76] The procedure by which individual representatives of British firms or government departments such as the Ministry of Supply recruited

Irish workers specific to their own needs was dispensed with, and complete control and discretion was given to the officials of the British Ministry of Labour in Dublin.[77] These changes were indicative of the altered demand for Irish migrant labour within the British wartime economy by the closing years of the war as construction workers became increasingly important and the requirements of the industries manufacturing military supplies tapered off. A further modification was introduced by the Irish government during the closing months of the war in April 1945 which prohibited the granting of travel permits to persons under 19 years of age rather than the age limit of 22 years previously in force.[78]

This corpus of somewhat intricate regulations comprised the gamut of measures adopted by both the Irish and British states during the period of the war. In theory, the various schemes for recruitment of Irish workers appeared workable. However, in reality frequent delays occurred in the issuing of travel permits and employment visas. Inevitably, the British authorities attributed these delays to staffing deficiencies within the Irish departments concerned with these matters and vice versa.[79] It was estimated in early 1942 that the delay in the processing of material could be up to two months.[80] But what the British officials seem to have missed is the implication that for the Irish state to devote significant resources to facilitating the migration of its citizens would have been anathema. In many Irish minds it was bad enough that workers were leaving the country in large numbers, let alone the possibility of apportioning extra clerical staff to ensure that delays were minimised during the 'emergency'.

In many respects this scheme closely resembled the bilateral labour agreements which were negotiated between western European and southern European countries in the 1950s and 1960s.[81] The sending state retained ultimate control on both the numbers leaving and the types of workers who were allowed to travel. The receiving country could recruit migrants in a selective manner to help meet the demand in specific areas of the labour force. From the point of view of the Irish state, this was a convenient means by which the level of unemployment was reduced, which in turn ensured that fewer financial resources were required for unemployment benefit or assistance. For the British authorities, these schemes provided a useful pool of additional labour and, apart from inherent security considerations, there appeared to be few other obvious disadvantages. The British state retained the right to send all the migrants who travelled to

Britain during the war back to Ireland since they were 'conditionally landed', not unlike 'guestworkers' in postwar Europe, notwithstanding attempts by Irish officials to negotiate a staggered return at the end of hostilities. To some extent, both states had much to gain from this informal labour agreement.

III

The control and regulation of migration by both states involved the collection of a range of statistics on both sides of the Irish Sea. These data facilitate a unique analysis of certain features of the Irish migrant flow. First, let us turn to the total number of workers who migrated from Ireland to Britain between 1940 and 1946. The Irish authorities collected information on the number of new travel permits issued to persons travelling from Ireland for this period (see Table 3.3). A note of caution should be sounded because this information does not record how many people actually travelled or the fact that the same person could receive more than one travel document.[82] A senior British official involved in the recruitment of Irish workers during the war was later to state that there was a substantial difference in numerical terms between those who received permits and those who actually travelled.[83] In addition, a considerable amount of movement occurred to and from Ireland during the later years of the war and the immediate postwar period, which these statistics do not take into account.[84]

For the purposes of comparison, the data collected by the British Ministry of Labour and National Service are presented here also (see Table 3.3). No statistical data exist on the British side for 1940 and these figures only refer to group labour recruitment schemes. It can be readily noted that a considerable disparity exists between the two sets of estimates, which is not fully explained by the deficiencies in the Irish data mentioned above or indeed by labour migration to Northern Ireland. According to Blake, 'some thousands of Éire citizens came into Northern Ireland', although he does not cite any source to substantiate this statement.[85] In order to ensure that Irish citizens did not present a security problem and, perhaps more importantly, that suitable employment would be available for Northern Irish workers at the end of the war, a residence permit requirement was introduced by the Stormont administration in 1942.[86] In the years for which detailed statistics are available, from 1943 to 1946, only 1,680 persons applied

Table 3.3 Numbers going to employment in Britain, 1940–46

Year	Number of new Irish travel permit cards issued[a]			British Ministry of Labour group recruitment schemes		
	Male	Female	Total	Male	Female	Total
1940	17,080	8,884	25,964	–	–	–
1941	31,860	3,272	35,132	4,688[b]	–	4,688
1942	37,263	14,448	51,711	27,792	3,867	31,659
1943	29,321	19,003	48,324	29,551	7,653	37,204
1944	7,723	5,890	13,613	11,330	2,670	14,000
1945	13,185	10,609	23,794	11,736	1,434	13,170
1946	10,547	18,956	29,503	18,510	12,883	31,393
Total	146,979	81,062	228,041	103,607	28,507	132,114

Notes:[a]Includes permits received by those travelling to Northern Ireland.
[b]September to December only.
Sources: Commission on Emigration, *Reports*, table 96, p. 128; A. V. Judges, 'Irish labour in Great Britain', table 4, p. 78; Ministry of Labour and National Service, *Report for the years, 1939–1946*, p. 55, 1947, XII, 459; PRO, LAB 8/1487, recruitment of group labour in Eire: number of persons who travelled in 1946.

for permits to travel to Northern Ireland.[87] Another factor that goes some way in explaining the disparity between the two sets of estimates is that Irish recruits for the British forces would for the most part have passed through Belfast. Irish military intelligence estimated, on the basis of the interception of mail destined for the combined recruiting centre in Belfast, that in June 1944 at least 200 recruits per week were joining the British forces; by April 1945 the estimated number of recruits had dropped to approximately 30 per week.[88] A somewhat surprising statistic was the number of deserters from the Irish army, the majority of whom joined the British forces. The Irish Department of Defence reported that the total number of deserters by the end of the war in Europe reached almost 5,000 men.[89] In August 1940 the total strength of the Irish army was somewhere in the region of 42,000 men.[90] In any case, it was suspected by the Irish authorities that any volunteers for the British forces who made their way to the border with Northern Ireland did not require a permit to enter the territory.[91] Another more plausible explanation for the difference between the statistics produced by both governments relates to the varying estimates of the numbers of females migrating to employment in Britain. As can be seen from Table 3.3, the British and Irish figures diverge considerably for female migrants for the period between 1941 and 1945. After considering the various possibilities for these differences, Judges concluded that 'quite a lot of these [women] must have gone into private domestic service or institutional domestic service', and thereby bypassed the British group labour recruitment schemes.[92] Notwithstanding the quite significant differences in the estimates of the total number of those who migrated to Britain for employment during the war, it can be stated with a degree of certainty that over 100,000 people left Ireland for civilian employment in Britain and as many as 150,000 migrants may well have travelled.

The timing of this vast movement of population is also worthy of examination. As Figure 3.1 reveals the demand for Irish labour peaked in 1942–43.[93] From March 1942 onwards Irish workers were being recruited at a rate of 1,000 persons per month solely for the munitions industries.[94] The cumulative effect of the recruitment of Irish migrants is underlined in Table 3.4 which presents data on the number of conditionally landed Irish workers who were registered with the British police. Irish workers were 'conditionally landed' as they were

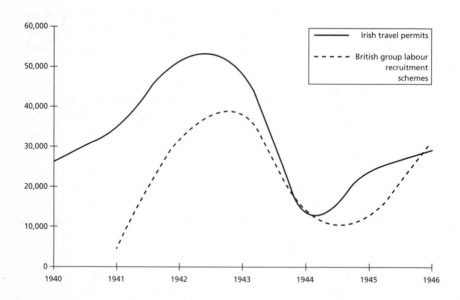

Sources: as Table 3.3.

Fig. 3.1 *Irish labour recruitment, 1940–46 (p.a.)*

Table 3.4 Conditionally landed Irish workers registered with the police as living in Britain, 1942–45 (000)

Date	Agricultural	Non-agricultural	Total
September 1942	7.3	47.8	55.2
September 1943	11.6	74.9	86.6
July 1944	11.4	87.7	99.1
September 1945	15.5	90.4	105.9

Source: Judges, 'Irish labour in Great Britain', table 2, p. 75.

required to work in the employment specified on their permit, and also to register with the police.[95] The scale of migration to Britain in 1942–43 is evidenced by the sharp increase in Irish workers, amounting to some 30,000 people over a 12-month period. By July 1944 nearly 100,000 Irish people were working in Britain and in September 1945, after the war had ended, this figure had exceeded 105,000.

Detailed information relating to certain characteristics of the profile of the migrant flow is available from 1943 onwards. The geographical origins of those who received travel permits during the war are presented in appendix 9. In rank order, county Mayo had the highest rate of males in receipt of travel permits per annum, followed by Dublin city and county, Donegal, Louth, Wicklow and Waterford. For females, the counties with the highest rates of issue of travel documents per annum were Mayo, Kerry, Sligo and Leitrim. All of these counties were located along the western seaboard where paid employment opportunities for females were few. These data are not, however, estimates of migration since applicants may never have travelled and no account is taken of return migration. The surprisingly high rate for Dublin can be explained by the intensive recruitment which occurred in this county in 1941 and 1942 as agents for British employers were most active in the capital at this time.[96] In addition, prospective migrants may have stayed with relatives in Dublin when applying for the permit and hence used temporary Dublin addresses. Of course, the fact that restrictions were imposed at various stages throughout the war on turf-cutting and agricultural areas and those living outside towns helps explain the comparatively high rates for males in eastern counties such as Louth and Wicklow. In the case of females, the situation is less influenced by external factors and areas that were traditionally associated with female migration such as Sligo and Leitrim feature prominently.

The age distribution of persons who received Irish travel permits indicates that this was primarily a movement of young persons. Over three-fifths of males who received travel permits in these years were under 30 years of age and representation of the older age cohort of 35 years and over declined during the course of the war (see Table 3.5). The age distribution of females who were in receipt of travel permits is even more skewed towards young people with 82 per cent of the successful applicants being under 30 years of age, and nearly 66 per cent between 16 and 24 years. Despite the decision by the Irish government in October 1941 to prohibit the migration of persons under 22 years of age (and then to lower this age regulation to 19 years of age in 1945), a significant proportion of those who received travel permits were below this age. R. E. Kennedy underestimates the degree to which females under 22 years of age could travel to Britain and seems to imply that these regulations were strictly enforced, which on the basis of the available statistics does not appear to have been the case.[97] These regulations included a clause which allowed exceptions in 'cases of very special hardship', and this obviously opened the door for a degree of flexibility on the part of the issuing officials. Judges remarked that 'as regards volunteers under 22 they [the regulations] proved in practice very elastic, nor were the Éire authorities generally disposed to make difficulties by refusing travel permits to persons for whom jobs *might* be available at home' (emphasis as in original).[98]

In terms of gender, a far greater number of males migrated to work in Britain during the war, but in the immediate postwar year of 1946, female migration exceeded the rate of male migration and this may be explained by the lifting of regulations on the migration of females in July 1946 (see Table 3.3).[99] The numbers of females applying for permits increased over time and by 1946 substantially more females than males made applications. In a similar manner to males, the majority of female migrants came from rural areas. For the period 1943–46 nearly two-thirds of females in receipt of travel permits came from rural districts, reflecting the distribution of the total population between rural and urban areas.[100] Towards the end of the period under consideration, the extent of female migration to Britain attracted some interest among policy makers in Ireland. In June 1944 a detailed memorandum which dealt with aspects of Irish female migration to Britain was prepared by the Department of External Affairs. The unnamed official

Table 3.5 Percentage age distribution of persons in receipt of Irish travel permits, 1943–46

	Males					Females				
	16–19	20–24	25–29	30–34	35 years and over	16–19	20–24	25–29	30–34	35 years and over
1943	6.9	26.4	20.9	14.5	31.3	20.3	39.3	18.5	9.1	12.8
1944	12.3	28.8	18.1	13.1	27.7	22.2	38.8	18.1	8.9	12.0
1945	12.8	33.8	17.9	12.5	23.0	29.2	40.7	14.7	6.9	8.5
1946	10.7	34.9	22.3	13.5	18.6	31.7	41.5	13.9	6.1	6.8
1943–46	**10.7**	**31.0**	**19.8**	**13.4**	**25.1**	**25.9**	**40.0**	**16.3**	**7.8**	**10.0**

Source: Commission on Emigration, *Reports*, table 97, p. 129.

who drafted this document was not convinced that the regulations with regard to the issuing of permits to females were being adhered to, because evidence existed that employment was available in Ireland for domestic servants and nurses.[101] According to this official, there was an upward trend in wages in these jobs owing to the scarcity of available labour and competition with the higher wages available in Britain.[102] A specific local case was cited in the memorandum: one colleague in the Department of External Affairs advertised for a domestic servant three times and did not receive a single reply![103] But other, more profound, issues were also at stake.

> Another point to be borne in mind is the deep public uneasiness at the number of young girls in the late teens and early twenties who are being allowed to leave the country. It is certainly disturbing to find that in spite of the government's decision against allowing out young people under 22, no less than 7,002, or 36 per cent, of the 19,003 women who went to work in Britain last year [1943] were under that age. This is a good example of an exception becoming, in time, wider than the rule. In the case of women, the rate of emigration is actually heavier under the age of 22 than over it. From every point of view, the consequences are bad. We have had cases of Irish girls being sent back to this country by the British police on the ground that they were too young and immature to be away from home! The taking of employment in Britain by young girls of 18 and 19 may be justifiable on other grounds, but it is certainly not good for the girls themselves and, in many cases, it is very humiliating for the country.[104]

These observations bring to mind the objections to female migration to Britain which were articulated in the 1930s. However, a more pragmatic approach was adopted in this instance by the members of the Irish Roman Catholic hierarchy, particularly Dr John Charles McQuaid, archbishop of Dublin. The Catholic Social Welfare Bureau was established by McQuaid in June 1942 to care for the spiritual and moral welfare of emigrants, 'principally women and girls'.[105] The purpose of this bureau, directed by the Legion of Mary, a Catholic lay organisation noted for its zeal, was to arrange introductions to the local clergy for emigrants in Britain, to aid in the continuance of religious practise, and finally, to provide assistance in terms of welfare.[106] It appears that McQuaid was applying pressure on ministers behind the scenes to ensure that the spiritual welfare of Irish migrants was catered for. In 1942 in talks with the minister for justice, Gerard Boland, he requested that the passport office provide the Catholic Social Welfare Bureau with lists of names, destinations and prospective places of employment of people who received travel permits.[107]

Obviously the provision of such confidential information was not the function of a government department, although the request does shed some interesting light on the consensual nature of church–state relations in Ireland at this time. McQuaid displayed a genuine concern for the plight of Irish migrants and, as we shall see in the following chapters, in the mid-1950s he was at the forefront of a scheme for Irish priests to look after the pastoral interests of migrants in Britain. Condemnation rather than action was the response of some clergy. The redoubtable bishop of Galway, Dr Michael Browne, for example, suggested that there was a 'tendency for even girls to emigrate, deceived by "fairy tales about wages and conditions abroad" '.[108]

Browne's statement is illustrative of the view which failed to recognise that those females who opted to travel to Britain were the most economically disadvantaged in Ireland. An analysis of the skills composition of the migrant flow illustrates this point clearly (see Table 3.6). Women who recorded their last occupation as domestic service constituted a very substantial proportion of the migrant flow between 1940 and 1946. Domestic service may not have been literally interpreted by the applicants and would include those involved in cleaning and catering work in institutions such as hospitals. In some cases it may have indicated weak aspirations rather than previous work experience. Other occupations such as nursing also provided a significant section of the total number of female migrants. Nursing proved to be a source of employment for many young Irish women, largely explained by reference to the shortage of trainee nurses in Britain from the late 1930s onwards.[109] The sharp increase in the 'other' category, mainly factory work, is also worthy of note for the years 1941–44. Therefore those who had least to lose and much to gain in economic

Table 3.6 Females in receipt of Irish travel permits and identity cards by last occupation, 1940–46 (%)

	1940	1941	1942	1943	1944	1945	1946
Domestic service	59.5	41.0	41.8	48.0	46.9	44.5	62.9
Nursing	18.4	24.0	15.5	15.0	19.1	33.2	20.3
Agriculture	5.5	5.4	4.5	2.2	5.2	4.4	1.7
Clerical	3.9	5.5	3.2	1.9	1.8	1.9	1.3
Other (factory work, etc.)	12.7	24.1	35.0	32.9	27.0	16.0	13.8

Source: Calculated from Commission on Emigration, Reports, table 31, p. 322.

terms sought perceived better opportunities by travelling to Britain. When Louie Bennett of the Irish Women Workers' Union, a distinguished campaigner for women's rights, was asked before the Commission on Youth Unemployment in May 1944 whether many domestic servants were out of work, she replied: 'not at the moment because a great many have gone to England where conditions are very much better. In fact, there is a great scarcity of domestic workers at the present time.'[110] In general terms, the predominance of unskilled female labour was the overriding characteristic of the wartime migrant flow.

What employment did these women become involved in on arrival in Britain? Clearly, the demand created by wartime requirements dictated the placement of Irish workers within the British economy. Detailed data are not available for every year with regard to female migrants, but statistics from the group labour schemes collected by the British Ministry of Labour and National Service for the period from 1942 until 1946 afford some insight into the nature of the employment of Irish women workers in Britain. In the years for which statistics are extant, the vast majority of women recruited under the British group schemes (95 per cent) were allocated to the Ministry of Supply, mostly for the munitions industries, as a result of a campaign initiated in 1942.[111] By 1945 this figure had dropped to 65 per cent.[112] One official in the Ministry of Supply noted in 1943 that some 2,500 women had been recruited for work in the munitions factories when 'supplies from other sources were not forthcoming'.[113] As was noted above, certain categories of employment such as nursing and domestic service did not fall within the remit of the Ministry of Labour schemes, but according to the official historian of British wartime labour policy, 'for [Irish] women there were plenty of openings in domestic and hospital service'.[114] Domestic service in Britain during the interwar period had become an increasingly unpopular occupation and since more – and better paid – opportunities existed for female employment in factories, and the war accentuated these demands, the shortage became more acute in a time of total war.[115]

Similarly, the male migrant flow was dominated by unskilled labour, encompassed in the generic official term of 'unskilled workers' (see Table 3.7). There is a strong likelihood that this category also includes agricultural workers who, in order to circumvent the restrictions on the migration of agricultural workers, were recorded as 'unskilled workers'. This category constituted over half of the

Table 3.7 Males in receipt of Irish travel permits and identity cards by last occupation, 1940–46 (%)

	1940	1941	1942	1943	1944	1945	1946
Unskilled workers[a]	34.5	66.0	64.0	62.4	56.2	47.4	54.7
Agriculture	31.7	5.6	12.8	12.2	17.6	23.9	22.3
Industry	20.5	18.5	12.9	13.5	7.9	12.9	10.4
Other skilled workers and clerks	13.4	9.9	10.3	11.9	18.3	15.8	12.6

Note: [a]Builders' labourers are included in the industry group.
Source: Calculated from Commission on Emigration, *Reports*, table 31, p. 322.

applications for travel permits and, when it is taken together with agricultural workers, the predominant characteristic which emerges is the movement of a large number of unskilled males, destined for the British wartime industries. Irish males were for the most part required for heavy work where the demand was greatest.[116] Civil engineering and building accounted for the lion's share of males recruited in the early years of the war: it was estimated that up to the autumn of 1941, 80 per cent of men travelling to Britain from Ireland were to be employed by building contractors.[117]

Labour for agriculture proved at first more difficult to secure owing to the unattractive nature of the work – land drainage – and the wages paid were above the British minimum rate in order to attract Irish workers.[118] By 1943 the demands of wartime industrial production, both in the munitions and iron and steel industries, ensured that many workers were recruited for essential supply contracts.[119] In one area of the wartime economy, shipbuilding, security considerations dictated that only a small number of Irish workers were employed. The Admiralty was a late entrant to the recruitment of Irish labour, in 1942, and in total only 2,000 men were involved in shipbuilding work.[120] Security considerations prevented the employment of Irish workers on the south coast of England, and employers in the North-East 'refused to have Irish workers at any price', presumably in part due to security considerations, and therefore only firms on the Clyde used Irish labour.[121] In the latter part of the war, the range of industries in which Irish male migrants were involved diversified as military supply industries became less important and demand for workers in the munitions industries diminished. Transport, food production and the building industries were of increasing importance throughout 1944 and 1945.[122]

It would be incorrect to deduce that the migrant flow was wholly unskilled, as a small but steady trickle of skilled workers travelled to Britain. Information on this movement of skilled workers is scarce and much of it is impressionistic in nature. The figures for 'industry' and 'other skilled workers and clerks' do not make a distinction between unskilled and skilled workers, but regardless of the obvious degree of variation inherent in these statistics, it is clear that some workers with marketable skills did travel to Britain (see Table 3.7). As O'Rourke has demonstrated, however, wage levels in a number of skilled trades were actually higher in Dublin than in Britain, and consequently migration made little economic sense for individuals with these skills.[123] In any case, difficulties with the transfer arrangements between trade unions with membership in both Britain and Ireland hindered the placement of skilled workers.[124] A further barrier existed in that the uniformity agreement in the building trades guaranteed workers the same wages as were paid in their localities. In theory, skilled building workers from Dublin would be entitled to a higher wage in Britain than the indigenous workers, which would obviously result in a great deal of resentment on the part of British people working on the same site.[125]

Notwithstanding the skill element within the migrant flow, it can be seen that Irish labour filled a void in the British wartime economy by acting as a reservoir of unskilled male and female labour. In general terms, the types of work engaged in by these Irish migrants were the occupations that had been traditionally those of Irish workers: for males heavy labouring work, and for females domestic service. The unrelenting demand for labour during the Second World War also opened up to migrants a range of other occupations which hitherto had little or no significant Irish presence, such as transport, factory work and other areas of industry. Jackson points to the fact that the 1951 census reveals that Irish migrants were represented across a range of occupations:

> Before the war the new arrival was almost bound to go into 'the building', general labouring or domestic service. Industrial occupations, transport, catering and the like were now open to the Irish worker. The war served the purpose of opening the way for far greater occupational choice and mobility for the Irish immigrant [sic] to Britain and paved the way for direct Irish infiltration into almost every branch of industry in the period since the end of the war.[126]

These changes in the occupations that Irish migrants entered were not brought about solely by British government policy, but also as the result of the general scarcity of civilian labour. It would be naive to argue that this development was universally welcomed by either British employers or workers. Holmes has unearthed some valuable evidence in the files of the British Ministry of Information which suggests that some of the attitudes expressed were far from harmonious. The usual complaints of drunken and disorderly behaviour – which were an immutable feature of views with regard to Irish migrants in Britain – were also voiced during the Second World War. It was claimed in 1942 that Irish workers were 'the terror of law-abiding citizens in the Leicestershire area'.[127] More significantly a report on the reactions to Irish workers completed in 1944 noted that they were the objects of distrust and hostility, and that many of these attitudes were fuelled by Ireland's neutrality, but also, and more interestingly, by the fact that Irish migrants were reaping the benefit of good wages when British men were compelled to serve in the armed forces.[128] Women workers in the factories were also the subject of some resentment. Summerfield has noted that 'prejudice against Irish women was ... strong' on the part of some employers who preferred not to recruit Irish women or did so reluctantly.[129] Fragmentary evidence from a survey undertaken by the social research organisation Mass Observation indicates that a degree of hostility existed between Irish women workers and their colleagues in Birmingham in 1942, due in part to the fact that it was perceived that the Irish did not mix.[130] The problem of interpreting isolated outward manifestations of prejudice or hostility as indicative of a widespread attitude is obvious. Such sentiments must also be placed within the wider context of British society during the Second World War since undoubtedly meeting the demand for labour was the overriding concern, particularly for government officials. It is also worth noting that the few incidents of overt prejudice which have been unearthed by historians mostly emanate from the Midlands, an area which until the war was not a region of significant Irish settlement.

IV

It was a great adventure for me. I'd never been anywhere. I'd never been on a train – only once in my life before that, I went to Galway and that was the only

time I'd ever been on a train – so I'd never been to Dublin even. I thought it
was marvellous. I often think now that I was stupid, and I shouldn't have come
... but, anyway, I did come, and you know, I did like it, I enjoyed it.

(Julia Griffin, an Irish emigrant who travelled to Britain in November 1943:
punctuation as in original)[131]

There were thousands of people coming here at that time to work. I got in the
long queue and got my visa stamped and boarded the boat to Holyhead. I was
going to work at Closey mental hospital near Reading. They were very short
staffed and they were delighted to see me. I was given a blue serge uniform, a
belt and a bunch of keys. It was rather like a policeman's uniform with a peaked
cap.

(Brian Watters who travelled to Britain in June 1941)[132]

The sense of excitement, mingled with apprehension, felt by Irish
migrants who travelled to Britain during the Second World War is
well captured by these two personal accounts of leaving Ireland and
the subsequent arrival in Britain. For most migrants, the first experience of Britain was the port of Holyhead through which the majority
of the migrant flow passed.[133] Then the long train journey to the
intended destination, followed shortly thereafter by starting work in a
factory, hospital, construction site, or private home in the case of
domestic servants. Most of these migrants were young and not by any
stretch of the imagination worldly-wise since for many it was the first
experience of life outside their local communities in Ireland. In recent
years a number of valuable collections of life-histories employing oral
history have been published, thereby facilitating an insight into
aspects of the Irish migrant experience.[134] Without doubt, evidence
derived from oral testimony has, in a similar manner to any form of
historical source, its inherent problems. The techniques of oral history have been effectively exploited by those concerned with the experience of ethnic minorities in Britain and elsewhere.[135] Unpublished
documentation concerning welfare issues is also available, which facilitates an assessment of welfare measures instituted by the British
authorities. British officials went to considerable lengths to ensure the
alleviation of many of the hardships faced by Irish migrants travelling
and working in Britain. Naturally, some of these initiatives were more
successful than others.

The first of many obstacles faced by most Irish migrants travelling
to Britain was the reception arrangements in Holyhead, including the
checking of the appropriate documentation by British officials and
subsequent allocation to the intended destination. As Judges noted,

the administrative formalities could take hours, despite the fact that a reception officer drawn from the ranks of the Ministry of Labour and National Service was appointed in March 1942 to oversee the arrangements in an effort to ensure speedy processing of the arrivals.[136] In the same year a temporary welfare officer was seconded, 'to whom the authorities ... entrusted the full time task of looking after the spiritual, moral and general well-being of the transferred Irish workers'.[137] After a visit to Dublin in June 1942, this official recounted to his superiors that Archbishop McQuaid had expressed his 'keen appreciation and gratitude' for his appointment.[138] However, according to one migrant, British officialdom as first encountered in Holyhead appeared to have an unsympathetic attitude towards Irish migrants:

> When we arrived at Holyhead, I heard a rather harsh English voice saying, 'Irish passports this way. If your passport has a harp on it, you're Irish.' Young as I was, I realised that this was a put down.
> (Christina Pamment who travelled in 1946)[139]

The next hurdle was ensuring the efficient transportation of Irish migrants by train to their place of employment. Welfare officers were posted at the train station in Crewe to help guide the Irish workers to their ultimate destination.[140] Inevitably delays and mix-ups occurred, as with any movement of population, and errors were made by both British officials and the Irish migrants.[141] To compound the difficulties even further, those involved in the organisation of the reception arrangements for the workers throughout Britain were frequently given incorrect information regarding the number, destination and itinerary of the migrants.[142] One migrant from Wicklow, who was located in Scotland and whose letter was intercepted by the British postal censor, wrote home in March 1942 to tell his mother of the ordeal in graphic terms:

> We had a terrible time coming here, we did not land till 11 p.m. at night and no one to meet us it was spilling rain nowhere to go it was terrible cold if I would have got back I would have run ... I never gave in till I got off the boat we were from 11 till 2.30 standing in the road in the cold and rain and no one to tell us or take us anywhere ... [grammar and punctuation as in original][143]

No doubt a certain element of exaggeration coloured this person's description as he had just arrived in Britain and may well have been homesick. The British authorities were sensitive to any form of criticism on this score, as it was realised that such tales of woe, if they became common currency, would adversely affect the numbers volunteering in Ireland for employment in Britain.

The provision of accommodation for Irish wartime migrants was a complicated issue and caused British officials numerous problems. British workers who transferred from one region to another for essential war work were usually billeted in private homes close to their employment, but finding appropriate accommodation frequently proved troublesome.[144] One regional officer of the Ministry of Labour and National Service spelt out the special difficulties involved in the housing of Irish migrants in August 1941:

> There is no doubt that, if southern Irishmen are to be imported in large numbers, it will be necessary for many of them to be housed in hostels. Whether or not they are justified in doing so, the majority of householders in England are strongly unwilling to have Irishmen in their houses as lodgers and it may be difficult to persuade local authorities to compel their citizens to accept Irishmen, even of the better type. In some parts of the country also, the religious question will arise and it is presumed that the majority of these men will be Roman Catholics.[145]

In particular the situation was extremely acute in towns and villages which were not accustomed to the 'ways of life of industrial workers' from elsewhere within Britain, let alone Irish workers who were frequently stereotyped as having a propensity towards drunkenness and violence, and in some extreme cases were associated with disease.[146] An official involved in the allocation of Irish migrants summed up the situation in a pithy manner: 'only a small proportion of the Irish were verminous, dirty, drunken and diseased, but their number was sufficient to terrify the ordinary housewife'.[147] Even in large cities such as Birmingham and Coventry the housing of Irish migrants presented an intractable problem and in the spring of 1942, special hostels were established to provide for those employed in drop-forging factories.[148] The British authorities found that the most efficient manner in which to accommodate Irish workers was to allocate large groups to industrial employers who were in a position to cater for them in hostels, rather than to employ a policy of dispersal.[149] Construction and agricultural workers were also generally accommodated within hostels, in close proximity to their employment and separate from the home population.[150]

On the question of disease, in 1943 as a result of unease on the part of the British authorities a scheme for the delousing of Irish migrants at Holyhead or Liverpool was proposed in order to eliminate the possibility of louse infestation.[151] An outbreak of typhus in western Ireland during 1943 raised the possibility of transmission of this disease by body louse into Britain.[152] When the Irish authorities were given the option of delousing the migrants before they left Ireland or leaving the job to the British, they reluctantly decided on the former course of action, perhaps owing to the resonances associated with these dehumanising procedures and emigration during the Great Irish Famine of 1845–50.[153] The Irish government instituted a health embarkation scheme under which each migrant was examined and certified before travelling to Britain. From 1943 until 1947 approximately 55,000 people were processed by the health embarkation centres in Dublin.[154] James Deeny, who was chief medical adviser to the Department of Local Government and Public Health, recounts that it was 'a fairly hush-hush affair and people did not talk much about it lest national feelings should be hurt'.[155] In an effort to secure extra funding from the Irish Department of Finance for public health measures to help combat infectious diseases, a group of senior civil servants including J. J. McElligott, secretary of the Department of Finance, and Deeny visited the depots to inspect the working of the scheme. Deeny's revealing description of what they found offers some indication of the humiliating nature of this procedure.

> We went first to the Globe Hotel in Talbot Street [Dublin] where there was quite a crowd of people milling around trying to make their way into the hotel. We pushed our way and saw that in various rooms doctors in white coats were examining the people for lice. This was the health embarkation scheme in action. From the Globe Hotel we went to Iveagh Baths. There I saw something I will not forget. The baths had been emptied. On a floor of a pool were large sherry half-casks. Men with rubber aprons and wellington boots were hosing people down and bathing them with disinfectant in the casks. All around were naked men, seemingly in hundreds. The place was full of steam and the smell of disinfectants.
>
> Now naked men *en masse* are not a pretty sight and the atmosphere of shame, fear and outrage was easy to feel . . . J. D. [McCormack, senior medical official in the Department of Local Government and Public Health] prided himself on the thoroughness of the operation and took MacElligott [*sic*] along to the place where a fellow with an electric iron was killing the lice in cap-bands and braces since steam disinfection, which the clothes were receiving, would perish leather and rubber. MacElligott [*sic*], a man with proper sensibilities, promptly came over faint and had to be taken outside and revived in the fresh air. Then we adjoined [*sic*] to the Dolphin for a good dinner.[156]

Deeny's graphic portrait of the treatment meted out to those found to be carrying infectious diseases illustrates the sheer humiliation these people had to endure. The visit also served another purpose. When Deeny and James Hurson, the secretary of the Department of Local Government and Public Health, attended a meeting the following morning to discuss the provision of money for a bill designed to increase levels of public health, they 'did not need to do any arguing or pleading since MacElligott [sic] did it for us against his own people', and the previous position of the Department of Finance on the matter was reversed.[157] The British liaison officer was later to heap praise on the effectiveness of the procedures instituted by the Irish authorities; he claimed they were 100 per cent efficient, and, given the seeming thoroughness of the procedure, albeit with little respect for human dignity, this is not altogether surprising.[158]

When Irish migrants reached Britain and commenced work in their new employments, it appears for the most part that the majority settled down to the humdrum existence of life in wartime Britain. Homesickness, the familiar sentiment experienced by many migrants, was for one woman, Julia Griffin, particularly exacerbated during certain times of the year, such as St Patrick's day: 'I can remember crying often, being homesick, especially when St Patrick's day came, that was heartbreaking ...'[159] For Noreen Hill from Cork, who made the journey to Britain in 1945, the first three months were a time of longing for her family back at home.[160] Irish women (and men) who came over to Britain to train as nurses entered an atmosphere characterised by discipline and authority, yet the institutional ethos provided a sense of security for young migrants.[161] Many aspects of the Irish experience of life in wartime Britain are difficult to recover owing to the paucity of sources, particularly those focused at local level. Hickey's study of the long-established Irish community in Cardiff found that the Second World War 'contributed a great deal to the ending of the period of isolation',[162] although it may be noted that migrants who came during the war specifically were not the concern of the author. Those migrants who have come forward with their recollections seem on the whole to be positive about their experiences in Britain at this time; for example, Margaret Quirke who travelled to work in the munitions industries recalled that they 'were treated well in the factories'.[163] Holmes rightly argues that attitudes towards the Irish migrants during the war and the resultant ramifications in terms of treatment are complex, and an optimistic picture of relative assimilation and, on the other hand, isolation within the host community are the vastly divergent poles of the range of reactions experienced by those people who travelled to

Britain.[164] On the basis of the oral testimony that is available, however, it appears that for the most part Irish migrants were not subject to any overt hostility. Incorporation into the mainstream of British society was a wholly different matter, and such a process would not occur within such a short time period, if ever. In any event, many of the migrants viewed their stay in Britain as a short-term expedient, thereby obviating the need to develop lasting bonds with the host country.

This brings us lastly to the question of the changes in the geographical patterns of Irish settlement in Britain brought about as a result of the various schemes of recruitment during the war. As was noted in the previous chapter, prior to the mid-1930s Irish migrants predominantly settled in the areas which had traditionally been large centres of Irish population: lowland Scotland, Lancashire and London. However, since Irish migrants were directed by government departments to those locations such as construction sites and factories where the workers were most needed, the patterns of Irish settlement in Britain during the war were significantly different from previous periods. The majority of those migrants who were recruited for agricultural work went to Scotland.[165] In the early years of the war the largest share of Irish labour in regional terms was taken by the Midlands civil defence region (see appendix 10). The airfield construction programme resulted in considerable numbers of Irish workers being located in the North Midlands and Eastern regions in 1942 and 1943. Whereas at the outset of the war, the proportion of new Irish migrants residing in the London and South Eastern regions was of little consequence, by September 1945 because of the V-bomb repair programme and the development of munitions factories in this region, the majority of Irish people registered with the police were located there.[166] Therefore, it can be seen that the policy adopted by the British government in directing Irish labour to specific locations ensured that substantial communities developed in areas such as the Midlands. For example, in Coventry the Irish-born as a percentage of the total population had risen from 1.2 per cent in 1931 to 3.9 per cent in 1951.[167] The patterns of settlement during the war established migrant pathways which were to prove significant determinants in the distribution of the Irish migrants in Britain throughout the 1950s and 1960s. However, as before, the South-East, mainly London, was also the focus of Irish settlement.[168]

V

In July 1946 the Irish government decided to discontinue the controls on the emigration of female workers that had been put in place during the war.[169] This decision was the result of the lifting of regulations on the entry of female workers by the British government which would 'render obsolete the existing machinery for the control of emigration'.[170] When the Irish government first learnt of the British plans for the removal of controls in May 1946, an official stated that the Irish government 'would prefer the present arrangement to go without alteration', since it provided 'a complete check upon the emigration of Éire citizens which satisfied both political and economic considerations'.[171] In effect, the visa hitherto required by females for employment in Britain would no longer be issued and they could enter Britain without hindrance. However, females wishing to travel to Britain still required a travel permit issued by the Department of External Affairs which allowed for some element of regulation, but it would prove impossible to ensure that those travelling to Britain to visit friends and relatives would not take up employment there, and the controls were discontinued.[172] Therefore from July 1946 females could leave Ireland for Britain without having firstly to prove that suitable employment was not available at home.[173] In any case, prior to this time, as noted already, these restrictions were fairly liberally interpreted by the police officers who issued the permits. Males, on the other hand, were still subject to the range of restrictions put in place by the Irish state with regard to length of unemployment and geographical origin.[174] The Irish regulations on male migration to Britain were eventually abolished in 1952. Gradually it became clear that the Irish government was no longer able to ensure effective control of migration to Britain. An essential component of the machinery instituted during the war was the corresponding regulations put in place by the British authorities which were soon to be regarded as obsolete. The demand for labour in Britain ensured that Irish migrant workers were able to take advantage of the numerous opportunities created by the programme of postwar reconstruction.

This demand also prevented the mass return of displaced workers which Irish officials had feared during the early years of the war. When this question was considered in 1943 by the prominent Irish economist, James Meenan, he concluded that there would be plenty of opportunities available in postwar Britain for certain types of occupations such as construction workers. He also pointed to the fact that people who had been required to do factory work during the war, such as those over the working age and married women, would withdraw from this sphere leaving gaps which could be filled by Irish migrants.[175] Meenan's prescient analysis proved accurate and the mass return of some 100,000 or more migrants never occurred. In a counterfactual sense this was most fortunate for the Irish state, since providing employment or even unemployment assistance would have placed a strain on the already limited exchequer resources and might even fundamentally have altered the character of postwar Irish economic and social policy. There was also the possible threat to social order posed by hundreds of thousands of disgruntled returned migrants seeking to maintain the standard of living which they had enjoyed in Britain during the war. Had the British government decided to revoke all visas and in short send all Irish workers home, particularly post-haste over a short time period, the effects would have been incalculable and would perhaps have altered the course of Irish history in the immediate postwar period. Fortunately, from the point of view of Irish politicians and civil servants, this never came to pass.

This is an apposite point at which to consider the Irish contribution to the British war effort and the concomitant ramifications for the policy of neutrality pursued with some vigour by the Irish government throughout the Second World War. Undoubtedly the pool of available Irish labour contributed significantly to the achievement of production levels in factories, the building of aerodromes throughout Britain and many other activities. Despite the fact that the official report of the British Ministry of Labour and National Service for the war years devotes some attention to the Irish contribution to the overall war effort, relatively little attention has been paid to this not insubstantial movement of population across the Irish Sea.[176] British official histories which deal with the mobilisation of civilian workers examine the recruitment of Irish migrant workers more thoroughly, albeit at an administrative level, but the best account is to be found in Holmes's monograph on immigration and British society.[177] The explanations for this seeming reluctance to acknowledge the Irish contribution are twofold. In the first instance, the Irish government was loath to admit that thousands of workers had to travel to Britain to earn a living and this apparent shortcoming was not one for inclusion in the pantheon of Irish national achievements, unlike neutrality which was, as Salmon has cogently argued, the stuff of future myths and something which was portrayed as 'a specifically Irish success, the crowning glory of independence, and the confirmation of distinctiveness from Britain'.[178] Secondly, reaction in Ireland to the migration to Britain of large numbers of Irish citizens was muted by the strict censorship of newspapers and other printed avenues for public discussion. The controller of censorship, T. J. Coyne, stated in July 1941 that images of 'thousands of starving Irish workers flocking across to the bombed areas of England or to join the British forces, or maybe to throw themselves into the sea, have simply got to be stopped if public morale is not to be hopelessly compromised'.[179] It is therefore not surprising that Irish migration to Britain during the war received little coverage in the press, if the principal official involved in censorship believed this issue would lower morale amongst the populace at large. A recent study demonstrates how seriously these officials viewed their duties in ensuring that such censorship was rigorously enforced.[180]

On the other side of the Irish Sea, a desire not to offend Irish sensibilities with regard to the cherished myth of neutrality helps explain the reticence in relation to the Irish contribution to the British war effort. When Judges's account of Irish labour in Britain was completed in 1948, he encountered resistance from certain quarters to the suggestion that the Irish authorities co-operated with the British government. The Commonwealth Relations Office (formerly Dominions Office) was 'most anxious that nothing should get into print under official auspices which suggests that the Éire government helped forward plans for emigration of Irish nationals, or were really co-operative at all'.[181] Judges thought it 'wrong to play down the importance of Irish labour', but acknowledged that references to the Irish government would have to be vetted by diplomats.[182] Another official referred to the fact that the word 'recruitment' in Judges's narrative 'could have been interpreted by our enemies as a breach of Éire's neutrality'.[183] This discussion was a hypothetical one in that Judges's account was never published and therefore such considerations did not arise. Yet the point still remains that the Irish state facilitated, but most definitely did not encourage, migration to Britain, although the diplomatic climate in the postwar period did not allow for the airing of such unpalatable facts, especially in Ireland during the late 1940s when the numbers leaving the Irish Republic were steadily rising.

To what extent can the Irish government's provision of facilities for those wishing to migrate to Britain be viewed as a breach of Ireland's neutrality? This is a vexed issue, but a number of points can be

made. On the level of Irish participation in the actual war, it is difficult to agree with Salmon's suggestion that 'with regard to attitudes to
neutrality, it must be remembered that thousands of Irishmen voted
with their feet by going to Britain'.[184] If he is referring to enlistment in
the British forces there may be some element of truth in this comment. Estimates of the total number who followed this course of action
vary considerably. Jeffery, drawing on official figures produced by the
Dominions Office in 1946 in response to a question in the House of
Lords, estimates the total figure as being 43,000 people.[185] At the other
end of the scale, a former senior British army officer, General Sir
Hubert Gough, in a letter to *The Times* in April 1946, stated that
165,000 southern Irish people served in the British forces.[186] According to confidential Irish government sources, this estimate was based
on information derived from the next-of-kin records held by the War
Office and therefore may be taken as a useful top-of-the-range figure.[187]
Of course, the fact that servicemen gave the address of the next-of-kin
as being in Ireland does not necessarily demonstrate that they left Ireland to join the British forces during the war as the Irish-born population in Britain prior to 1939 may well have supplied a substantial
proportion of these recruits. R. M. Smyllie, the editor of the *Irish
Times*, stated in 1946 that 'it is fairly safe to say that between 150,000
and 180,000 young Irishmen served under the British flag, and it must
not be forgotten that every one of them was a volunteer'.[188] Fisk pours
scorn on the higher estimates and underlines the political significance
of such claims in the immediate postwar period, viz. attempts to
demonstrate the limited contribution of Northern Ireland in terms of
volunteers in the armed forces as compared with the number of
recruits from the south.[189] He opts for the lower figure of 42,000 Irishmen who served in the British armed forces, but readily admits that
the methods of estimation are not an exact science.[190] However, it is
clearly inappropriate to view those who travelled for civilian work as
consciously expressing any judgement on the policy of neutrality. In
short, these migrants left in order to earn a livelihood which was not
available in Ireland; perceived better opportunities in Britain, unemployment in Ireland and the general economic malaise are more plausible explanations of the migrants' decision to travel to Britain rather
than a high-minded rejection of de Valera's policy of neutrality. Since
the Irish government did not encourage enlistment in the British
forces, and of course, a state cannot be equated with its citizens as
Salmon acknowledges, the charge of '*de facto* partiality' seems at best

ill-founded.[191] The question of legislation to prohibit enlistment in
foreign armies can also be dismissed as both unrealistic and failing to
take due account of the circumstances of the time. The relatively high
level of desertion from the Irish army, which was itself an act subject
to legal punishment, illustrates the unrealistic nature of a prohibition
of enlistment in foreign forces.

There is more value in Salmon's other suggestion, that the indirect
involvement of the Irish state in the provision of migration facilities
'cannot be ignored'.[192] Smyllie, an independent-minded commentator,
outlined in 1946 the most cogent exposition of Ireland's rather peculiar
brand of neutrality in the sense that material assistance was given,
albeit discreetly, to the allies. As Smyllie noted, the Irish state refrained
from encouraging migration to Britain, 'but it did nothing to stop it'.[193]
Some restrictions were put in place, although, as has been demonstrated, these had more to do with the requirements of the Irish economy than anything else. Possible explanations as to why the Irish state
did not prevent the migration of its citizens would include the idea that
such a prohibition was contrary to natural justice, that it would be difficult to enforce with the land border adjoining Northern Ireland and,
the argument most frequently put forward by the Department of
Finance, that it was the prerogative of the individual to decide how best
they could 'sell' their labour. On a more basic level, it is also worth noting that the political will to prohibit emigration simply may not have
been in evidence, especially as conditions worsened in Ireland. Lastly,
one of the reasons posited by Smyllie for the lack of action is without
doubt a major factor in any evaluation of Irish policy: the migration to
Britain of over 100,000 Irish people reduced the level of unemployment.[194] It also provided a means for the alleviation of potential social
unrest since, as was noted above, the age profile of the migrant flow was
heavily skewed towards the young in their mid-twenties and early thirties, a grouping which, if prevented from 'selling their labour', might
have challenged the maintenance of law and order during a time of
shortages, rationing and general austerity. Salmon's general assessment
of the Irish policy of neutrality as a misnomer, and better encapsulated
in the term 'non-belligerency', would seem to apply with a fair degree
of accuracy with regard to migration.[195] Of course, Ireland was not the
only non-belligerent state to provide aid to either the allies or the Axis
powers, although it could not be reasonably argued that had the Irish
state prevented migrants from travelling to Britain this would have
seriously affected British wartime production levels.[196]

VI

The outbreak of the Second World War compelled both states to formulate concrete policies on migration from Ireland to Britain. The overriding feature of the policies adopted, to some extent on a piecemeal basis, was control of the migrant flow. The Irish government was prepared to facilitate but not actively encourage migrants who wished to travel to Britain. The British policy in relation to labour recruitment from Ireland was determined by both security considerations and the need to obtain labour for essential industries. Unlike in the postwar period, the migration of Irish citizens to Britain during the war attracted little attention in the political sphere and the subject of migration rarely entered Irish political discourse.[197] The involvement of the state in the regulation of migration receded in the immediate postwar period. When all of the British restrictions were lifted in 1947, Irish migrants could travel to Britain with little or no hindrance, providing that they were eligible to receive an Irish travel permit in the case of males. The medium-term effect of the large-scale movement during the war was to complete the process of the spatial shift in Irish settlement from Scotland and Lancashire to the Midlands, an area which became a region of substantial Irish-born population in the 1950s, as shall be demonstrated in the following chapters. The South-East, or more accurately London, still retained its traditional importance as a centre of Irish settlement. In the long-term, the patterns of Irish migration to Britain during the war mark a turning point in that migrant pathways and networks were established which were to prove of vital importance for the postwar period when the 'second-wave' of Irish migration to Britain reached its zenith.

NOTES

1 Alan S. Milward, *War, economy and society, 1939–45*, London, 1977, pp. 212–15; Stephen Castles and Mark J. Miller, *The age of migration: international population movements in the modern world*, 1st edn, London, 1993, p. 70.

2 David Fitzpatrick, 'Emigration, 1871–1921', in *A new history of Ireland, VI: Ireland under the union, pt. II (1871–1921)*, W. E. Vaughan, Oxford, 1996, p. 630.

3 On the effects of the First World War on the Irish economy, see David Johnson, *The interwar economy in Ireland*, Dublin, 1985, p. 3.

4 James Meenan, 'The Irish economy during the war', in *Ireland in the war years and after, 1939–51*, ed. Kevin B. Nowlan and T. Desmond Williams, Dublin, 1969, pp. 36–37.

5 K. A. Kennedy, Thomas Giblin and Deirdre McHugh, *The economic development of Ireland in the twentieth century*, London, 1988, p. 50.

6 J. J. Lee, *Ireland, 1912–1985: politics and society*, Cambridge, 1989, p. 226.

7 By March 1941 the Irish defence forces numbered some 41,463 people (Denis Parsons, 'Mobilisation and expansion, 1939–40', *Irish Sword*, Vol. 19, 1993–94, p. 18 [special issue on *'The Emergency', 1939–45*]).

8 James Meenan, *The Irish economy since 1922*, Liverpool, 1970, p. 66. In 1947 a new index was introduced; there was a great deal of public criticism of the cost of living index in the late 1940s and early 1950s. For a trenchant defence penned by the state's chief statistician, see R. C. Geary, *The official cost of living index number and its critics*, Cork, 1951.

9 Liam Kennedy, *The modern industrialisation of Ireland, 1940–1988*, Dublin, 1989, p. 6.

10 Meenan, *The Irish economy since 1922*, p. 66.

11 Liam Ryan, 'Urban poverty', in *One million poor?*, ed. Stanislaus Kennedy, Dublin, 1981, p. 35. The study was carried out under the supervision of Dr Alfred O'Rahilly, president of University College, Cork, and John Busteed, professor of economics at the same institution. A final report was never published.

12 *Censuses of population of Ireland 1946 and 1951: general report*, Dublin, 1958, Pr. 4511, table 3, p. 18.

13 Ibid., p. 174.

14 Commission on Emigration, *Reports*, p. 13.

15 Ibid., table 4, p. 284.

16 Ibid., p. 15.

17 *Census of population of Ireland, 1946, III: pt. I, religions*, Dublin, 1952, Pr. 158, table 1b, p. 1.

18 Ibid.

19 *Censuses of population of Ireland 1946 and 1951: general report*, p. 163.

20 Ibid., table 3b, p. 4.

21 PRO, LAB 8/1528, A. V. Judges, 'Irish labour in Great Britain, 1939–45', (hereafter cited as Judges, 'Irish labour in Great Britain').

22 'Judges, Arthur Valentine', *Who was who, 1971–1980*, London, 1989, p. 424.

23 PRO, LAB 8/1528, H. Toms (United Kingdom Liaison Officer) to E. A. Mossman, 17 Sept. 1948.

24 This information is derived from Commission on Emigration, *Reports*, app. vi: note on travel permits, identity cards and passports, p. 267.

25 Judges, 'Irish labour in Great Britain', p. 3; J. W. Blake, *Northern Ireland in the Second World War*, Belfast, 1956, pp. 84, 171–74.

26 H. M. D. Parker, *Manpower: a study of wartime policy and administration*, London, 1957, p. 335.

27 Judges, 'Irish labour in Great Britain', p. 3.

28 Ibid.

29 Ibid., pp. 5–6.

30 'The transfer of Irish workers to Great Britain', *International Labour Review*,

Vol. 48, 1943, p. 338; Judges, 'Irish labour in Great Britain', pp. 5–6.

31 NAI, DFA 220/530, copy of press statement on the position of seasonal agricultural workers, 1 Apr. 1940.

32 Ibid., memorandum on employment of Irish workers in Great Britain prepared by the Department of Industry and Commerce, 13 Mar. 1941, p. 2. For confirmation on the British side of this informal arrangement, see Judges, 'Irish labour in Great Britain', p. 7.

33 NAI, DT S 11582 A, memorandum on employment of Irish workers in Great Britain prepared by the Department of Industry and Commerce, 13 Mar. 1941, p. 3.

34 Ibid.

35 Margaret Gowing, 'The organisation of manpower in Britain during the Second World War', *Journal of Contemporary History*, Vol 7, 1972, p. 151.

36 P[hylis]. Inman, *Labour in the munitions industries*, London, 1957, p. 168.

37 NAI, DT S 11582 A, Department of Industry and Commerce: recruitment of citizens of Éire for employment in Great Britain, 23 June 1941, pp. 1–3.

38 Ibid., pp. 4–6.

39 NAI, DT S 11582, memorandum for the government: employment of Irish workers in Great Britain, 18 Aug. 1941, p. 1.

40 The British liaison officer for labour throughout the war was H. Toms, an official of the Ministry of Labour and National Service.

41 For a detailed exposition of the wartime machinery, see Commission on Emigration, *Reports*, app. vii, pp. 268–70.

42 Ibid., p. 268.

43 NAI, DT S 11582 A, extract from cabinet minutes, GC2/300, 2 Oct. 1941.

44 See, for example, the statement by Dr Michael Browne, the Roman Catholic bishop of Galway: 'The country has been invaded by agents of foreign firms who are trying to get strong young Irishmen to leave the country for work abroad ... I am surprised that these people are allowed to operate so freely, for they are a danger to their victims and to the nation.' (*The Standard*, 22 Aug. 1941).

45 Judges, 'Irish labour in Great Britain', p. 16.

46 Donal Ó Drisceoil, *Censorship in Ireland, 1939–1945: neutrality, politics and society*, Cork, 1996, p. 112.

47 NAI, DT S 11582 A, extract from cabinet minutes, GC2/352, 19 May 1942. It should be noted that this prohibition did not apply to the Congested Districts.

48 For a considered assessment of McElligott's role, see Ronan Fanning, *The Irish Department of Finance, 1922–58*, Dublin, 1978, pp. 490–92; see also Lee, *Ireland, 1912–1985*, pp. 279–88.

49 NAI, DT S 11582 A, memorandum for the government: observations of the minister of finance on the memorandum submitted to the government by the minister for industry and commerce on the subject of the employment of Irish workers in Britain, 19 Oct. 1941, p. 2.

50 Unemployment assistance was limited at certain times between March and October for rural workers.

51 NAI, DT S 11582 A, memorandum for the government: observations of the minister of finance . . . 19 Oct. 1941, p. 5.

52 NAI, DT S 11582 A, memorandum by F. H. Boland on a proposal from the Department of Industry of Commerce for the restriction on the emigration of persons from rural districts with experience of agricultural or turf work, 14 May 1942. This document was passed by J. P. Walshe, the secretary of the department, to de Valera, the taoiseach and minister for external affairs.

53 For more details, see J. T. Carroll, *Ireland in the war years*, Newtown Abbot, 1975, pp. 78–94; Trevor C. Salmon, *Unneutral Ireland: an ambivalent and unique security policy*, Oxford, 1989, pp. 147–51.

54 NAI, DT S 11582 A, memorandum by F. H. Boland on a proposal from the Department of Industry and Commerce ... 14 May 1942, p. 3.

55 Ibid., p. 5.

56 Ibid.

57 NAI, DT S 11582 A, memorandum for the government from the minister for industry and commerce on permits to reside in Northern Ireland, 12 Nov. 1942, p. 1.

58 Judges, 'Irish labour in Great Britain', p. 16.

59 NAI, DT S 11582 A, memorandum for the government: restrictions on advertisements for Irish workers from the minister for industry and commerce, 25 Nov. 1942.

60 Ibid., extract from cabinet minutes, G2/404, 1 Dec. 1942; *Emergency Powers (no. 241) Order, 1942*, P. 5775; for further information on the use of emergency powers legislation in relation to the national press during the Second World War, see Ó Drisceoil, *Censorship in Ireland*, pp. 95–158.

61 Judges, 'Irish labour in Great Britain', p. 66.

62 'The transfer of Irish workers to Great Britain', p. 341.

63 *Dáil Éireann deb.*, XCIII, 18 Apr. 1944, cols 855–56.

64 Judges, 'Irish labour in Great Britain', p. 66.

65 NAI, DT S 11582 A, extract from cabinet minutes, GC3/32, 21 Dec. 1943.

66 NAI, DT S 11582 B, Department of Industry and Commerce, memorandum for the government: employment in Great Britain and Northern Ireland, 28 Apr. 1944, p. 4.

67 Ibid., p. 5.

68 Meenan, 'The Irish economy during the war', p. 36.

69 NAI, DT S 11582 B, Department of Industry and Commerce, memorandum for the government: employment in Great Britain and Northern Ireland, 28 Apr. 1944, p. 6.

70 NAI, DT S 11582 B, extract from cabinet minutes, GC4/1, 15 June 1944.

71 NAI, DT S 11582 B, Department of External Affairs, memorandum on new proposals regarding restrictions on travel permit issues to workers, n.d. [9 May 1944], p. 1. The document can be dated from the covering letter from J. P. Walshe (secretary, Department of External Affairs] to K. O'Connell (Department of the Taoiseach).

72 Ibid.

73 Ibid., p. 2.

74 Judges, 'Irish labour in Great Britain', p. 15.

75 Ibid., p. 68.

76 Parker, *Manpower, p. 341.*

77 Ibid.

78 NAI, DT S 11582 B, extract from cabinet minutes, GC4/93, 17 Apr. 1945.

79 Judges, 'Irish labour in Great Britain', p. 20.

80 Ibid.

81 John Salt, 'International labour supply: the geographical pattern of demand', in *Migration in postwar Europe: geographical essays*, ed. John Salt and Hugh Clout, Oxford, 1976, p. 64.

82 Commission on Emigration, *Reports*, p. 128.

83 Judges, 'Irish labour in Great Britain', p. 70 n. 1.

84 Commission on Emigration, *Reports*, p. 128.

85 Blake, *Northern Ireland in the Second World War*, p. 177.

86 Ibid.

87 Commission on Emigration, *Reports*, table 36, p. 321.

88 NAI, DFA, Secretary's files, P. 81, G2/X/0123, extent of recruitment from 26 counties for British forces, Apr. 1945.

89 NAI, DFA, Secretary's files, P. 81, Department of Defence, memorandum for the government: deserters from the defence forces, 20 June 1945, p. 1.

90 Robert Fisk, *In time of war: Ireland, Ulster and the price of neutrality, 1939–1945* paperback edn, London, 1985, p. 159.

91 NAI, DFA, Secretary's files, P. 81, memorandum prepared on the number of Irishmen who served in the war, Dec. 1946, p. 1.

92 Judges, 'Irish labour in Great Britain', p. 79.

93 Gowing, 'Organisation of manpower during the Second World War', p. 155.

94 Parker, *Manpower*, p. 339.

95 Judges, 'Irish labour in Great Britain', p. 14.

96 Ibid., p. 81.

97 R. E. Kennedy, Jr., *The Irish: emigration, marriage and fertility*, Berkeley, 1973, pp. 72–73.

98 Judges, 'Irish labour in Great Britain', p. 17.

99 NAI, DT S 11582 B, extract from cabinet minutes, GC4/176, 28 June 1946.

100 Calculated from the Commission on Emigration, *Reports*, table 30, p. 321. The figure for males is 61 per cent.

101 NAI, DT S 11582 B, Department of External Affairs, memorandum on new proposals regarding restrictions on travel permit issues to workers, n.d. [9 May 1944], p. 4.

102 Ibid., pp. 4–5.

103 Ibid., p. 7.

104 Ibid.

105 *Irish Catholic Directory, 1943*, 17 June 1942, p. 629.

106 Ibid., p. 630.

107 NAI, DT S 11582 A, letter from Gerard Boland to de Valera, 14 July 1942.

108 *Irish Catholic Directory, 1944*, 4 Oct. 1943, p. 700.

109 For further information, see *Report of the working party on the recruitment and training of nurses*, 1947 [Non. Parl.]; Brian Abel-Smith, *A history of the nursing profession*, London, 1960, pp. 161–90.

110 NAI, ICTU records, 1163/6122, Commission on Youth Unemployment: minutes of evidence taken before the commission on 29 Mar. 1944.

111 PRO, AVIA 22/1184, D. P. T. Jay (Ministry of Supply) to A. Patterson (Ministry of Labour and National Service), 24 Dec. 1941; statistic calculated from Judges, 'Irish labour in Great Britain', app. 1, p. 82; see also ibid., p. 31, on the role played by unskilled female labour in the Royal Ordnance factories.

112 Judges, 'Irish labour in Great Britain', app. 1., p. 85.

113 PRO, AVIA 22/1184, A. D. Murray to Secker, 15 Apr. 1943.

114 Parker, *Manpower*, p. 335.

115 Ministry of Labour and National Service, *Report on postwar organisation of private domestic employment*, 1944–45, Cmd. 6650, V, 1, pp. 6–7; see also Pamela Horn, *The rise and fall of the Victorian domestic servant*, Dublin, 1972, pp. 166–83.

116 Parker, *Manpower*, p. 334.

117 Judges, 'Irish labour in Great Britain', p. 22 n. 1.

118 Ibid., p. 21.

119 Inman, *Labour in the munitions industries*, p. 174.

120 Ibid., p. 139.

121 Ibid.

122 Judges, 'Irish labour in Great Britain', pp. 72–73.

123 Kevin O'Rourke, 'Did labour flow uphill? International migration and wage rates in twentieth century Ireland', in *Labour market evolution: the economic history of market integration, wage flexibility and the employment relation*, ed. George Grantham and Mary MacKinnon, London, 1994, p. 143.

124 Judges, 'Irish labour in Great Britain', p. 26.

125 Ibid.

126 J. A. Jackson, *The Irish in Britain*, London, 1963, p. 104.

127 Quoted in Colin Holmes, *John Bull's island: immigration and British society, 1871–1971*, Basingstoke, 1988, p. 198.

128 Ibid.

129 Penny Summerfield, *Women workers in the Second World War: production and patriarchy in conflict*, London, 1984, p. 59.

130 Kenneth Lunn, ' "Good for a few hundred at least": Irish labour recruitment into Britain during the Second World War', in *The Irish in British labour history*, ed. Patrick Buckland and John Belchem, Liverpool, 1992, p. 107.

131 Pam Schweitzer, ed., '*Across the Irish sea*', 2nd edn, London, 1991, p. 81.

132 Ibid., p. 169.

133 Judges, 'Irish labour in Great Britain', p. 39.

134 Mary Lennon, Marie McAdam and Joanne O'Brien, *Across the water: Irish women's lives in Britain*, London, 1988; Schweitzer, ed., '*Across the Irish sea*'; Anne Lynch, ed., *The Irish in exile: stories of emigration*, London [1988].

135 For a useful review of the issues surrounding oral history, see Paul Thompson, *The voice of the past*, 2nd edn, Oxford, 1988, pp. 100–49. On oral history and the experience of ethnic minorities, see Alistair Thomson, 'Moving stories: oral history and migration studies', *Oral History*, Vol. 27, 1999, pp. 24–37; Rina Benmayor and Andor Skotnes, eds., *International yearbook of oral history and life stories, iii: migration and identity*, Oxford, 1995.

136 Judges, 'Irish labour in Great Britain', p. 39

137 Ibid., p. 47.

138 PRO, LAB 26/9, report on visit to Ireland from 8–19 June 1942 by an unnamed official [Tom Leyland, welfare officer for Irish workers], [June] 1942, p. 2.

139 Schweitzer, ed., '*Across the Irish sea*', p. 149.

140 Judges, 'Irish labour in Great Britain', p. 41.

141 Ibid., p. 40.

142 See the voluminous correspondence in PRO, LAB 26/9, arrangements for the reception and accommodation of workers travelling in this country from Éire, 1941–44.

143 PRO, LAB 26/9, interception of mail from 'Dan', Stranraer, Scotland to M. Quinn, Kilcool, Co. Wicklow, 10 Mar. 1942. It should be noted that the permanent British reception officer was appointed in the same month.

144 Inman, *Labour in the munitions industries*, p. 160.

145 PRO, LAB 26/9, B. W. Vincent (Manchester) to headquarters, 29 Aug. 1941.

146 Judges, 'Irish labour in Great Britain', p. 42. On the stereotypical views associated with Irish workers, see Lunn, ' "Good for a few hundred at least" ', pp. 109–10.

147 B. W. Vincent (Ministry of Labour regional officer for north-west England) quoted in Judges, 'Irish labour in Great Britain', p. 43.

148 Inman, *Labour in the munitions industries*, p. 160.

149 Parker, *Manpower*, p. 338.

150 Judges, 'Irish labour in Great Britain', p. 42.

151 Ibid., p. 43.

152 Ibid., p. 44.

153 Ruth Barrington, *Health, medicine and politics in Ireland, 1900–1970*, Dublin, 1987, p. 139.

154 Ibid.

155 James Deeny, *To cure and to care: memoirs of a chief medical officer*, Dublin, 1989, p. 77.

156 Ibid., p. 78.

157 Ibid.

158 H. Toms (British liaison officer) quoted in Judges, 'Irish labour in Great Britain', p. 44.

159 Schweitzer, ed., *'Across the Irish sea'*, p. 82.

160 Lennon, McAdam and O'Brien, *Across the water*, p. 95.

161 See the comments of Nancy Lyons who left Kerry in February 1943 in Lennon, McAdam and O'Brien, *Across the water*, p. 172; in addition the recollections of Brian Watters are valuable on his experience as a psychiatric nurse (Schweitzer, ed., *'Across the Irish sea'*, pp. 169–70).

162 John Hickey, *Urban Catholics: urban Catholicism in England and Wales from 1829 to the present day*, London, 1967, p. 124.

163 Anne O'Grady, *Irish migration to London in the 1940s and 1950s*, London, 1988, p. 11.

164 Holmes, *John Bull's island*, p. 199.

165 Judges, 'Irish labour in Great Britain', p. 76.

166 Ibid.

167 Russell King, Ian Shuttleworth and Alan Strachan, 'The Irish in Coventry: the social geography of a relict community', *Ir. Geog.*, Vol. 20, 1989, table 2, p. 68.

168 On this point, see Bronwen Walter, 'Time-space patterns of second-wave Irish immigration into British towns', *Trans. Brit. Inst. Geog.*, new series, Vol. 5, 1980, p. 301. This aspect is examined exhaustively in her unpublished thesis, 'The geography of Irish migration to Britain since 1939 with special reference to Luton and Bolton', unpub. DPhil. thesis, University of Oxford, 1979, ch. 2.

169 NAI, DT S 11582 B, extract from cabinet minutes, GC4/176, 28 June 1946.

170 NAI, Department of Industry and Commerce, emigration to employment: summary of attached memorandum for the government, 21 June 1946. These measures were closely related to the decision of the British government, under pressure from industry, to abolish controls on the location of labour within the economy.

171 PRO, LAB 8/1480, notes on meeting held at the Department of Industry and Commerce (Dublin), 14 May 1946.

172 Commission on Emigration, *Reports*, app. vii: control on emigration to employment in Great Britain, p. 268; NAI, DT S 11582 B, Department of External Affairs, memorandum on emigration control, 22 July 1947, p. 1.

173 NAI, DT S 11582 B, Department of External Affairs, memorandum on emigration control, 22 July 1947, p. 1.

174 Ibid, p. 2.

175 James Meenan, 'Irish industry and postwar problems', *Studies*, Vol. 32, 1943, pp. 362–63.

176 Ministry of Labour and National Service, *Report for the years, 1939–1946*, pp. 55–56, 1947, Cmd. 7225, XII, 439; see, for example, the very brief discussion in Dermot Keogh, *Twentieth-century Ireland: nation and state*, Dublin, 1994, pp. 122–23.

177 Inman, *Labour in the munitions industries*, pp. 167–75; Parker, *Manpower*, pp. 334–41; Holmes, *John Bull's island*, pp. 164–65, 194–99.

178 Salmon, *Unneutral Ireland*, p. 153.

179 Quoted Ó Drisceoil, *Censorship in Ireland*, p. 257.

180 Ibid., p. 285.

181 PRO, LAB 8/1528, A. V. Judges to E. A. Mossman, 1 Oct. 1948.

182 Ibid.

183 Ibid., H. Toms, notes on A. V. Judges, 'Irish labour in Great Britain, 1939–1945', 16 Dec. 1948.

184 Salmon, *Unneutral Ireland*, p. 142.

185 Keith Jeffery, 'The British army and Ireland since 1922', in *A military history of Ireland*, ed. Thomas Bartlett and Keith Jeffery, Cambridge, 1996, p. 438.

186 *The Times*, 3 April 1946; Gough, born in county Waterford, was involved in the Curragh mutiny of 1914; however, he is most remembered for his recall to Britain in March 1918 following the disorganised retreat of the British Fifth Army then under his command in the face of German advances (see 'Gough, Sir Hubert de la Poer', in *Dictionary of National Biography, 1961–70*, Oxford, 1981, pp. 446–48.

187 NAI, DFA Secretary's files, P. 81, memorandum prepared on the number of Irishmen who served in the war, Dec. 1946.

188 R. M. Smyllie, 'Unneutral neutral Eire', *Foreign Affairs*, Vol. 24, 1946, p. 320.

189 Fisk, *In time of war*, pp. 522–24.

190 Ibid., p. 524.

191 Salmon, *Unneutral Ireland*, p. 129.

192 Ibid., p. 130.

193 Smyllie, 'Unneutral neutral Eire', p. 321.

194 Ibid.

195 On the question of 'non-belligerency', see Salmon, *Unneutral Ireland*, pp. 120–54.

196 See, for example, A. S. Milward, 'Could Sweden have stopped the Second World War?', *Scandinavian Economic History Review*, Vol. 16, 1967, pp. 127–38.

197 Enda Delaney, 'State, politics and demography: the case of Irish emigration, 1921–71', *Irish Political Studies*, Vol. 13, 1998, p. 35.

4

Postwar exodus, 1947–1957

Christina Pamment (b. 1929) from Croom, county Limerick, left Ireland in 1946 just after her seventeenth birthday. She travelled to near Egham in Surrey where she started work as a domestic in a local hospital after replying to a newspaper advertisement. On turning eighteen years of age, she was accepted for nurse training at a hospital in Shooter's Hill, south-east London. A short time later, she met another Irish migrant who was employed as a labourer and they became engaged to be married. In 1948 she broke off this engagement to marry a much older English widower. Notwithstanding considerable opposition from her family, she married this man in October of the same year. She settled down to life in Britain and had two children. After more than forty years in Britain, when interviewed in 1989, Christina still hoped to return to her native Limerick. It is unclear if she ever realised this aspiration.[1]

The story of Christina Pamment contains many elements of the principal themes of this chapter. All too often migration is viewed solely as a movement of population which is subject to rigorous quantitative analysis. But the process of migration involves real people with real stories. A sense of displacement, a desire to return home and the sometimes painful adaptation to the norms of the new society feature prominently in the oral testimony of all migrants.[2] Christina was one of the thousands of young people who left Ireland during the immediate postwar period. Notwithstanding her tender years, she travelled to Britain on her own and arrived in London at Euston Station, where she encountered 'all these people speaking in what sounded to me like a foreign language'.[3] On arrival she observed the widespread devastation from wartime bombing and wondered 'where was the wonderful London of the picture palace?'.[4] Many of her compatriots would be involved in the postwar programme of reconstruction which created a seemingly insatiable demand for Irish labour. As was the case with many other Irish female migrants, she trained as a nurse in Britain, which provided an avenue for social mobility as her family in Limerick lived in a small cottage with only one acre of land. In Britain she became aware of the advantages of living in a consumer society as she purchased new clothes with her hard-earned wages, something which was a completely new experience for her. On a return trip home she believed that she had 'travelled the world' since she was living in England. She felt 'great, coming home full of style'.[5] In many ways, the holiday back at home underlined the stark differences between life in rural Ireland and everyday existence in postwar industrial Britain.

Why did Christina, like thousands of other young Irish people, leave home and migrate to Britain in the immediate postwar period? To a large degree the answer is to be found in the lack of sustained economic development in postwar Ireland. The stagnation which affected the Irish economy is, in part, reflected in the results of the censuses of 1951 and 1956. In the first intercensal period (1946–51), the total population of the Irish Republic increased by 0.2 per cent, the first gain recorded in census enumerations since 1841.[6] However, the following five years from 1951 until 1956 witnessed a decrease of 2 per cent and the total population in 1956 of 2.9 million people was the lowest figure recorded since reliable enumeration began in 1841.[7] Population decline was concentrated in the west and north-west of Ireland. Dublin and the contiguous counties such as Meath and Louth experienced gains in population, albeit a very slight one for the later period (appendix 11). The counties which fared the worst were Leitrim, Roscommon, Cavan, Donegal, Monaghan, Clare and Sligo, all of which, as was demonstrated in previous chapters, experienced significant population decline over a long period of time. In essence, therefore, the picture was a familiar one, but the scale of decline was on an altogether different plane.

I

The acceleration in migration from Ireland during the period under consideration is clearly evident from an inspection of the varying types of data available. Firstly, the evidence derived from the published censuses is examined before turning to more detailed, if less reliable, information on travel identity cards collected by the Irish government until 1951. The data on the average annual net migration for 1946–51 demonstrate that nearly 25,000 people left the Irish Republic each year compared with 18,711 per annum over the whole preceding decade (see Table 4.1a).[8] The increase is perhaps more sharply illustrated by the average annual rate of net migration per 1,000 of the average population which rose to –8.2 persons as compared with –6.3 persons in the previous ten years (see Table 4.1b). A further noteworthy trend is the number of females who migrated annually, which nearly doubled in the years 1946–51. In fact, the overall increase in net migration is accounted for by the volume of female migration. Undoubtedly, the immediate postwar period witnessed a new development in terms of the sheer scale of Irish migration, since the departure of at least 120,000 emigrants virtually negated the higher rate of natural increase.[9] The rise in the rate of natural increase was accompanied by a higher migration rate, thereby ensuring that the size of the total population remained relatively stable.[10]

For the following five years (1951–56) the census data indicate that the total net migration reached nearly 200,000 persons (see Table 4.1a). The average annual net migration of –39,353 people was the highest figure recorded since 1900.[11] The average annual rate of net migration per 1,000 persons was –13.4 (see Table 4.1b). The only comparable

Table 4.1a Average annual net Irish migration, 1936–56

Period	Males	Females	Total	Number of females per 1,000 males
1936–46	–11,258	–7,454	–18,712	662
1946–51	–10,309	–14,075	–24,384	1,365
1951–56	–21,657	–17,696	–39,353	817

Table 4.1b Average annual rate of net Irish migration per 1,000 of the average population, 1936–56

Period	Males	Females	Total
1936–46	–7.5	–5.1	–6.3
1946–51	–6.9	–9.7	–8.3
1951–56	–14.6	–12.2	–13.4

Sources: Commission on Emigration, *Reports*, table 86, p. 115; *Census of population of Ireland, 1956, I: population, area and valuation of each district electoral division and of each larger unit of area*, Dublin, 1957, Pr. 3983, table x, p. xxi.

figure since 1871 was recorded during the intercensal period of 1881–91 when the average annual rate of migration per 1,000 was –16.3 persons.[12] The number of males exceeded females, thus reversing the trend which characterised the previous five years. An indication of the gross migration flows between 1947 and 1951 is afforded by an analysis of the number of travel identity cards issued.[13] It can be seen that nearly 135,000 persons applied for travel permit cards in this five-year period (see Table 4.2). The rather large figures for 1947 and 1948 are explained by an administrative change which was introduced whereby travel permit cards were made obsolete from January 1948 and those wishing to leave the Irish Republic using a previously issued document were required to obtain a new travel identity card.[14] Therefore, statistics on the number of travel identity cards issued are not as useful for monitoring migration from Ireland in the immediate post-war period as they were for the war years.

Table 4.2 Number of new Irish travel identity cards issued, 1947–51

Year	Number issued
1947	31,328
1948	40,075
1949	25,491
1950	17,356
1951	20,246
Total	134,496

Source: Commission on Emigration, Reports, table 96, p. 128.

As state regulation of migration between the two countries receded from July 1946 onwards, the resultant data become less reliable. In any event, movement between the Irish Republic and Britain was not solely one-way traffic as wartime migrants returned in the mid- to late 1940s and were, in turn, replaced by the next wave of the migrant flow. Statistics of health insurance transfers from Ireland to Britain and vice versa for the period until 1951 reinforce the observation that 'the outgoing traveller was not, in any sense, a permanent emigrant and frequently came and went like a seasonal migrant'.[15] An analysis of the information derived from the sample passenger card inquiry for 1950 also underlines the importance of return movement in this year, although the numbers involved are very much a matter for speculation owing to the small size of the sample.[16] It is difficult to capture with any degree of certainty the level of movement back and forth across the Irish Sea. Nevertheless, the available evidence suggests that the finality associated with transatlantic migration was not a feature of the postwar flow to Britain. A migrant might work for a few months in Britain, return home for a short spell and then travel back to Britain. The nature of this movement between the two countries is not readily quantifiable, although there is little doubt that the relatively straight-forward journey to Britain facilitated considerable two-way traffic across the Irish Sea.

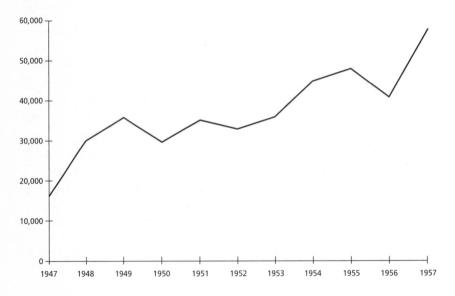

Source: J. G. Hughes, *Estimates of annual net migration and their relationship: with series on annual net passenger movement: Ireland 1926–76,* Dublin, 1977, ESRI memo-randum no. 122, p. 8.

Fig. 4.1 *Estimates of net Irish migration, 1947–57 (p.a.)*

Hughes's estimates of annual net migration, which were evaluated at some length in Chapter 2, are also worthy of mention here. It will be remembered that these estimates are not an accurate indication in absolute terms of the numbers involved, but rather, as Hughes noted, 'they give a reliable picture of the trend in Irish migration behaviour'.[17] After an initial decrease in net migration in 1946 – explained by return migration after the end of the war – the trend in Irish net migration was upward until 1950 (see Figure 4.1). Notwithstanding the brief hiatus in 1950, throughout the following years net migration accelerated at an unprecedented rate and 1957 may be regarded as the nadir of movement out of the Irish Republic on the basis of Hughes's estimates: according to his calculations over 58,000 people left the country in this year.

In the war years virtually all documented migration was to Britain, for obvious reasons, but in the postwar period movement to 'overseas' destinations, that is, not within the British Isles or the rest of Europe, became increasingly significant, although the vast majority of migrants still travelled to Britain. In the period 1946–52, 16 per cent of Irish emigrants, or some 19,400 persons, migrated to 'overseas' destinations, mostly the United States.[18] To take 1948 as an example, over 70 per cent of 'overseas' migrants left Ireland for the United States, and the remainder were divided between Australia, Canada and diverse other places.[19] Nearly 3,000 Irish migrants travelled to Canada between 1945 and 1949.[20] However, it would be erroneous to imply anything other than that for the majority of Irish migrants the intended destination was not Boston, Toronto, Wellington or Sydney, but rather London, Coventry or Birmingham. It is, none the less, worth reiterating that not all Irish migrants travelled to Britain in the immediate postwar period and a small but significant degree of movement occurred to places outside the British Isles.

A fairly similar trend in the age profile of migrants emerges as has already been identified in previous chapters. The information available on the age of prospective migrants from the data relating to travel identity cards until 1951 demonstrates the youthful composition of the flow (see Table 4.3). Ó Gráda and Walsh's cohort depletion estimates illustrate starkly that the vast majority of Irish emigrants were young (see Table 4.4). The age cohort that was most prone to migration was individuals aged 20–24 years at the end of the intercensal period, followed by those aged 25–29 years. In the case of males, over 70 per cent of applicants for travel documents between 1947 and 1951 were under the age of 30 years. In addition, the percentage of males aged 15–19 years applying for travel identity cards increased significantly in 1950–51. Perhaps of more interest is the evidence which suggests that females were migrating at a younger age than their male counterparts. Roughly 72 per cent of female applicants were under the age of 24 years, with a relatively small proportion over 30 years of age opting to leave Ireland (see Table 4.3). Explaining the younger age profile of the female migrant flow is a complex matter. The limited opportunities for females to obtain casual work is an important factor here since males could secure temporary labouring with a local authority or agricultural work, thereby postponing the eventual decision to migrate. Of equal significance is the nature of the demand for female labour in Britain. Nurse training in particular was one of the principal sources of employment for Irish migrant women in Britain and this is usually embarked on in the late teens.

Lastly, we shall briefly examine the geographical origins of the migrants. The average annual rate of net migration per 1,000 of the population for each province and county for the decade 1946–56 is presented in appendix 12. These data demonstrate that migration affected every county in the Irish Republic with the exception of Dublin in the first intercensal period, rather than being a purely regional phenomenon. The counties that experienced the highest average annual rates of net migration per 1,000 in the period 1946–51 were (in descending order) Leitrim, Kerry, Longford, Clare, Roscommon, Cavan, Galway and Mayo: all counties that have figured prominently in our previous discussions of regional migration rates. County Leitrim also had the honour (a dubious one) of having the highest rate of migration in the previous decade. However, in the following five years (1951–56), the rate for almost every county rose appreciably, with the exception of some midland counties such as Kilkenny, Meath and Offaly. For example, the rate for Kildare, a prosperous midlands county, rose from −8.8 per 1,000 in 1946–51 to −15.5 per 1,000 of the average population in the following five years. The counties with the highest rate per 1,000 were (in descending order) Leitrim, Donegal, Monaghan, Mayo, Wicklow, Cavan, Sligo, Longford, Roscommon and Clare. The rate for Leitrim recorded in the 1956 census of −23.1 persons per 1,000 was an all-time high. The majority of these counties are in the west, north-west midlands and north of the country, with the obvious exception of Wicklow located on the eastern seaboard. Of particular interest is the relationship between the net migration rates for each county between 1946 and 1956. It emerges that the rates of county migration in the two time periods (1946–51 and 1951–56) were positively associated, pointing to continuity in migration patterns over time.[21]

Table 4.3 Percentage age distribution of persons in receipt of Irish travel identity cards, 1947–51

	Males					Females				
	16–19	20–24	25–29	30–34	35 years and over	16–19	20–24	25–29	30–34	35 years and over
1947	12.1	35.3	22.4	12.9	17.3	33.3	38.2	15.0	6.2	7.3
1948	12.7	35.6	21.6	12.5	17.6	30.1	35.5	15.6	7.8	11.0
1949	16.8	40.0	19.0	8.8	15.4	36.0	36.9	12.5	5.1	9.5
1950	20.0	39.0	18.1	8.0	14.9	40.6	33.6	12.0	4.5	9.3
1951	20.1	35.5	14.1	8.2	22.1	41.8	33.1	11.2	5.5	8.4
1947–51	16.3	37.1	19.0	10.1	17.5	36.4	35.5	13.3	5.8	9.1

Source: Commission on Emigration, *Reports*, table 97, p. 129.

Table 4.4 Net Irish external migration by age group (gain or loss of population over intercensal period as a percentage of initial cohort), 1946–56

Period	\multicolumn{8}{c}{Age at end of intercensal period}
	0–14	15–19	20–24	25–29	30–34	35–39	40–64	65+
1946–51	–0.5	–7.5	–18.8	–13.1	–6.7	–0.3	–1.5	+3.1
1951–56	–2.6	–10.7	–25.3	–15.4	–10.8	–3.9	–3.4	+2.0

Source: After Cormac Ó Grada and Brendan Walsh, 'The economic effects of emigration: Ireland', in *Emigration and its effects on the sending country*, ed. Beth J. Asch, Santa Monica, 1994, table 4.3, p. 99.

A further noteworthy contrast between the two periods relates to Dublin city and county. Between 1946 and 1951, Dublin was the only county of net in-migration, and without doubt a proportion of those recorded as having 'emigrated' from a county ended up in Dublin. A total net inflow of about 18,000 people was recorded for Dublin during these years.[22] A significant trend is evident for the later period (1951–56) in that the average annual rate of net migration per 1,000 for Dublin may not appear unduly high (–9.7), but in terms of volume, net emigration from this county constituted over one-sixth of movement from the Irish state during these five years.[23] Dublin, which had hitherto gained in population terms at the previous censuses – excepting that is the decade 1936–46 – had become a county of net migration. This also explains the not insubstantial increase in the rate of net migration for the complete province of Leinster. Taking the broader view, from 1926 until the early 1970s regional migration rates 'remained stable over long periods of time'.[24]

II

All researchers of Irish demographic history are much indebted to the authors of the *Reports* of the Commission on Emigration and Other Population Problems for the extremely valuable compendium of statistical material which forms the core of this publication.[25] For the present purposes, our principal concern is with the detailed findings that resulted from inquiries made at the instigation of this body. Sadly the official papers and minutes of the meetings of the commission are not extant. However, the documents relating to the work of the commission were fortuitously deposited by the family of one commissioner, Arnold Marsh, in the library of Trinity College, Dublin. This unpublished documentation is a particularly valuable source for the study of postwar Irish migration to Britain and it contains much information that is unique and original, which to date has not been exploited by scholars.[26]

In late 1948 and early 1949, the commissioners conducted personal surveys throughout the country in order to investigate the factors affecting migration at a local level. In addition, over 200 males who applied for work in Britain were interviewed at employment exchanges and the results were incorporated into the surveys.[27] The British Ministry of Labour continued to recruit Irish males for work under its group schemes until 1954, but after 31 December 1947, there were no restrictions imposed on the employment that migrants could take up in Britain.[28] Therefore, both males and females who received Irish travel permits could migrate to Britain without official assistance from the Ministry of Labour. The advantage of taking up a place on the British scheme was that a post could be secured before leaving Ireland and the fare was paid. A fraction of these surveys were actually dated, but it can be stated with a fair degree of certainty that they were conducted in late 1948 and early 1949 on the basis of the few reports which include some reference to the date of completion. Inevitably, the quality of the information varies considerably and the observations are coloured by the commissioners' attitudes and prejudices. Ideally, it would be more revealing to have a systematic survey of each county, with a focus on both rural and urban areas. Nevertheless, for the purposes of this study, these at times rather impressionistic reports furnish new evidence of the selective impact of migration throughout Ireland firmly grounded in local case-studies.

The topography of the impact of Irish migration to Britain is illustrated in the surveys completed for various parts of the country. For instance, in Kilkenny it was found that migration to Britain had relatively little impact and that males only left Ireland when no work was available locally or if the wage levels for agricultural labourers in Britain were reported to have been 'much higher than at home'.[29] However, the crucial determinant of the minimal amount of male migration from rural areas was the fact that work was available all year around as local farmers were engaged in mixed farming and dairying.[30] Female migration from Kilkenny and the surrounding area was of some significance, especially for employment as a domestic servant in Britain.[31] The situation in Kilkenny contrasted sharply with that observed in counties Mayo and Sligo as recorded by J. P. Beddy, a distinguished public servant and chairman of the commission. As Beddy noted, this region with its backdrop of poor land and overcrowded holdings, which as we have seen in appendix 12 had higher than average rates of net migration had little to offer by way of industrial employment, apart from a scattering of factories.[32] One interesting observation related to the parish of Lahardane in east Mayo. To all intents and purposes the parish appeared prosperous to the outside observer, yet on closer inspection, when Beddy spoke with the Roman Catholic curate, he discovered that this appearance of relative luxury concealed the salient fact that the wealth of the inhabitants was based on emigrants' remittances, particularly from relatives in the United States.[33] Farms in the locality were often too small to support the sons and daughters and given that no other forms of employment were available, a long-standing tradition of migration to the United States and Britain had been established. The curate noted that migration to Britain from his parish had 'increased greatly' in recent times.[34] It should be borne in mind throughout this discussion that the comments of informants were influenced by the context in which they were proffered. When a commissioner interviewed local luminaries, invariably they tended to exaggerate the 'problem' of emigration. According to Beddy's informants, it was not unusual for sons and daughters living abroad not to return home to take over the farm on the death or old age of their parents. Some sons who did inherit renounced their inheritance claim when marriage opportunities appeared scarce in the locality, as prospective partners were 'unwilling to share in the hard work of farming when they can emigrate to where they consider there is easier work, better conditions, more money and improved prospects for marriage'.[35] Beddy concluded solemnly that in this region there 'seems to be no ambition other than to emigrate'.[36]

A similar picture emerges in county Leitrim, another area which as already noted had a high rate of out-migration over a long period of time. Notwithstanding the fact that the Arigna coal-mines provided well-paid and reasonably secure employment for some 600 people, there was no other industry in the vicinity of Carrick-on-Shannon. The employment exchange manager frankly remarked that there were 'practically no openings in industry for females and very few for males'.[37] Moreover, the tradition of migration was particularly strong in the area, and family and kin networks with people already living in Britain were a significant factor in sustaining the migrant flow.[38] In addition, migrants home on holidays naturally reported favourably on the conditions in Britain.[39] In a similar manner to the survey of county Mayo, it was noted by the vocational education committee in Leitrim in evidence given before the commission that the small size and uneconomic nature of farms in the county led to young people refusing to take on the family holding, which was regarded as a most deleterious development.[40] In post-famine Ireland the inheritance of the family farm by a son was a rite of passage, and the spurning of this 'honour' was viewed with some alarm by contemporary observers.

The importance of seasonal migration to the local economy was demonstrated in the survey of two towns in county Donegal, Killybegs and Dungloe. Male migratory workers left Killybegs in September for sugar-beet work in Britain until February when they returned to tend their holdings.[41] The size of these holdings was on average ten acres with about three acres of arable land. Although these workers stated that they would have preferred to be employed in the local fishing industry, it was difficult to secure a position on a trawler.[42] Females migrating from Killybegs tended to take up permanent work such as nursing, presumably nurse training in the first instance.[43] The manager of the employment exchange in Letterkenny observed that there was considerable female migration to domestic service and nursing in Britain.[44] In Dungloe, it was noted that the majority of those travelling to Britain were migratory workers going to Scotland: 'Scotland was always regarded as Dungloe's America.'[45] It was estimated that equal proportions of males and females were migrating for this seasonal work. Limited employment was available for females involved in home crafts and a co-operative employed over a hundred people. But as Geary observed, 'migratory movement is born in the people', and remittances sent back by the migratory workers ensured that this pattern was maintained.[46]

Moving down the west coast to county Galway, the principal reasons for leaving this county offered by prospective migrants to Britain who were interviewed at employment exchanges in Tuam and Galway city were economic in nature. In Tuam, the majority of prospective male migrants cited the lack of steady paid work as the fundamental determinant in the decision to travel to Britain. Some of the men stated that plenty of work was available on the small family holding but completely without payment, hence the decision to carve out a decent livelihood in Britain.[47] When asked if they would stay at home if they had full-time employment at lower wages than in Britain, all respondents replied in the affirmative, although we should be a little suspicious about the sincerity of these responses.[48] Four female intending migrants interviewed in Galway city stated that they were 'fed up in Ireland' owing to the lack of status associated with domestic workers and the harsh conditions of work including the long hours.[49] According to the member of the commission who conducted the survey, 'the groups from which [female] emigrants are mostly drawn are domestics, under-paid shop assistants in small shops, and unemployed and casual workers'.[50] In Loughrea, east Galway, all of the people interviewed stated that 'there was no industry in the town and so no chance of constant employment'.[51] Therefore, it can be seen that those who stood to gain most in economic terms left Ireland, whereas people employed in well-paid steady industrial jobs had little incentive to leave. The crux of the matter was that such industrial employment was extremely limited and geographically biased towards the cities and the larger towns. Perceptions of what constituted an acceptable standard of living were gradually changing, but such comparisons of working and living conditions were not solely based upon observations of conditions in Ireland. Migrants at home on holidays, newspaper reports, letters from relatives and returned emigrants all ensured that conditions in Ireland were compared unfavourably with those in Britain. Undoubtedly the regular contact with migrants living in Britain ensured that the norms of industrial Britain in terms of wages and working conditions were transposed into rural Ireland. As Hannan has argued, 'the widespread existence of British points of reference for judging the adequacy of conditions at home is probably one of the most influential local consequences of our recent emigration history'.[52] In short, the sporadic spells of underemployment and unemployment added up in many minds to a bleak future in Ireland which contrasted starkly with the well-paid and steady employment opportunities available in Britain.

The report from Clare is less informative than other surveys in that it comprises a plethora of suggestions regarding the causes and possible remedies for Irish migration with little or no supporting analysis. The manager of an employment exchange in Ennis underlined the importance of permanent work, whereas a local doctor suggested that agricultural methods should be improved.[53] Of course, the implicit explanation for migration from Clare was similar to that for other counties which had poor land: few opportunities existed for non-agricultural employment. Fortunately the reports for counties Cork and Kerry are much more informative. Both counties are regarded as having been particularly affected by migration since the initial demographic shock of the famine in the 1840s. By the late 1940s the situation had changed little. In the period 1946–51, Cork and Kerry figured prominently in the six counties that accounted for over 55 per cent of the volume of net migration; Cork was top of the list and Kerry was in third place.[54] Interviews with managers at employment exchanges throughout Cork county pointed to the lack of industrial development which accounted for the large number of people migrating to Britain. A further revealing observation was that prospective migrants had 'lost confidence in this country to provide them with a permanent job'.[55] But, as the manager of the exchange in Midleton in east Cork noted, the seasonal nature of the industries that were in existence, such as the local distillery, ensured that when workers were laid off in the summer, the option of migration became particularly important.[56] The fact that the town was classified as a rural area and hence no unemployment assistance was available in the summer months without doubt accelerated the movement of people to Britain. In Cork city, males applying for work in Britain struck the commissioners as a transitory grouping 'clearly of the "migratory" type, going to England for a period to earn some money, coming home to spend it and using the British scheme to get their fares paid for to England again'.[57]

Reports from employment exchanges in Kerry adopted a similar despondent tone. For the manager of the exchange in Cahirciveen in west Kerry, the only course of action available to any person who desired permanent employment was to migrate.[58] In addition, the attractions of city life in Britain were an inducement to leave Ireland, as were the regular wages and steady employment opportunities.[59] In Tralee it was males from rural areas rather than from the town who sought better prospects abroad, but as the manager remarked, the older men would not leave even if two weeks work per month was available.[60] In some inland counties, an analogous situation was evident. The chairman of Tipperary South Riding County Council, Daniel Kennedy, stated in evidence given before the commission that 'it is so very difficult to find employment in county districts that emigration is the only alternative'.[61]

One consistent feature emerges from an analysis of the surveys of those areas most affected by migration: the lack of steady employment in a locality was a key determinant in the decision to migrate. But employment in itself was not the remedy since temporary employment was available at certain times during the year in most rural areas, be it working for the local authority on roads or assisting local farmers. In its final report the commission stressed the type of employment that was required: 'Employment all year round, and as far as possible on a quasi-permanent or permanent basis, is the only type of employment which gives a feeling of economic security and enables a person to be content and plan for the future.'[62]

Surveys conducted in a number of towns in the midlands where various types of industrial employment were available endorse this analysis. For instance in Newbridge, county Kildare, a cutlery factory, a rope factory, civilian employment at a military camp and public service jobs all ensured that the manager of the employment exchange could state with a degree of confidence that 'any young man earnestly seeking employment can obtain it'.[63] Apparently, females in the town preferred factory employment to the arduous work of domestic service and these industrial jobs could be had in this prosperous town.[64] Similarly in Edenderry, county Westmeath, the footwear and furniture factories in the town were going at 'full blast' and few people had left the region for Britain.[65] It was reported to the commission that another town in the midlands, Athlone, was 'well industrialised' and experienced little by way of unemployment or emigration.[66]

Notwithstanding the perceived economic causes of migration, a range of other factors was observed by the commissioners as they reported from throughout the country. Better prospects for marriage were cited in a number of surveys: for example, in Sligo, the economic situation of males in the area 'prevented them from marrying and in some areas prospective partners were difficult to find'.[67] In Tuam, in east Galway, male migrants stated that their economic conditions prevented them from marrying.[68] The commission devoted a complete chapter of its report to a discussion of Irish marriage patterns and associated issues, and the analysis of the relationship between a low rate of marriage and migration is worthy of quotation:

> Unmarried people, having fewer ties or responsibilities than married people, can more easily leave their surroundings, and they respond more readily to the attractions (including the more favourable marriage prospects) of other countries, or if they live in rural areas, the more favourable marriage prospects of towns.[69]

However, the dearth of non-agricultural employment compounded these difficulties:

> In rural areas, and especially in the congested areas in the west, girls find few opportunities for remunerative employment. The men have little prospect of employment either, but in each farming family, responsibility for his parents prevents one son at least from emigrating, even though he may consider the holding insufficient to support a home. In such a setting girls are attracted towards emigration. They may not realise that the poor marriage prospects enter deeply into their decision to emigrate, but it is the opinion of the commission that until men can find employment which can support homes, even those girls who could find employment locally will continue to emigrate. On the other hand, both men and women even from an early age often have the intention to emigrate, and this militates against early marriage.[70]

It was concluded by the commission that there was a symbiotic relationship between migration and marriage patterns. People did not want to marry because of their economic circumstances, and the fact that migration was an intrinsic aspect of the life cycle of young people contributed to a low rate of marriage.[71] There was also a well-known pattern of permanent celibacy, especially among males, which was a curious characteristic of Irish demographic patterns.[72] In Longford, the survey reported that 'in a number of houses in the surrounding rural areas there are no women' and males (generally brothers) lived alone.[73]

Social factors were also underlined by the commissioners. A frequent observation was that the drab and austere nature of rural life in Ireland provided little enticement to young people to remain at home. One respondent recounted in some detail her social life in London, including dances at Catholic clubs two nights a week, and summed up her reasons for staying in Britain as being the fact that she had 'a better life in Croydon than Sligo'.[74] Written and oral evidence to the commission from community development bodies and other interested individuals emphasised the importance of enhancing the social life of rural Ireland:

> We were impressed by the unanimity of the views presented to us in evidence on the relative loneliness, dullness and generally unattractive nature of life in many parts of rural Ireland at present, compared with the pattern of life in urban centres and with that in easily accessible places outside the country.[75]

As is implicitly acknowledged in this statement it was the sharp contrast between life in rural Ireland and that associated with the cities of Britain that contributed to the sense of discontent with the perceived stagnant social environment. It is of some interest that it was for the most part local figures rather than the migrants themselves who tended to highlight the mundane existence of those living in rural communities. Indeed, this is a case where the perceptions of parents, clerics and teachers were imposed on the calculations of migrants. One final factor that should be mentioned can be rather colloquially labelled the 'crowd mentality', or in other words, the view that migration was a self-perpetuating phenomenon. In Clonmel it was found that 'there appeared to be a large element of following the crowd and, in the case of some of the younger men, a – perhaps justifiable – desire for wider horizons ...'.[76] In the town of New Ross in county Wexford a worrying development was noted:

> The New Ross men would not be prepared to take work in Ireland at the same wages as they hoped to get in England; all the good men in their neighbourhood, they said, had gone to England and were reported to be doing very well. They considered it a sign of inferiority to remain at home, unless they were in regular employment or had strong home ties. In other words it is 'the thing' to go to work in England.[77]

The fact that some prospective migrants would not take on employment at home at the same rate of remuneration was a reflection of the sense of malaise which pervaded many regions in Ireland at this time.

III

When the commissioners visited employment exchanges around the country in late 1948 and interviewed prospective male migrants, the resultant data were recorded in the papers circulated to members of the commission. From 1 July 1946 onwards females were not subject to any restrictions and this information relates only to male migration to Britain.[78] Male migrants were still subject to restrictions and were therefore required to present at the local employment exchange before a travel permit was granted. As we noted earlier, male migrants could obtain free travel and special grants from the British Ministry of Labour if they took up employment in essential industries and services.[79] One caveat that should be added at this juncture is that this is not in any way a scientific or representative sample, such as that designed by Hannan for use in his survey of migration intentions among Irish school leavers in the 1960s.[80] This body of data is simply the responses provided by over 300 prospective male migrants to a list of questions posed by a member of the commission when they were interviewed in late 1948.[81] There is therefore an element of self-selection in this sample since many male migrants travelled to Britain without any form of official assistance. In essence, these interviews result in the creation of individual life-histories, some inevitably defying classification. These data do, however, shed light on matters such as the age and marital status of prospective migrants. The age distribution of the sample is outlined in Table 4.5. One half of all the prospective migrants interviewed were under the age of 25 years, thereby reinforcing the earlier observations regarding the youthful composition of the migrant stream. Perhaps of equal interest were the numbers of those aged 35 years and over applying for work in Britain at employment exchanges throughout Ireland: 4 per cent of the total sample were over 50 years of age, with two applicants being over 60 years of age. In terms of conjugal status, the majority of males interviewed were single, but roughly a quarter were married (see Table 4.6).

Table 4.5 Age distribution of Commission on Emigration sample of prospective male migrants, 1948–49 (%)

Age group	%
16–19	10.9
20–24	38.9
25–29	19.8
30–34	7.6
35+	22.8

n = 303
Source: TCD MS 8306, rural surveys.

The other types of data collected by the commissioners are fragmentary and vary widely in terms of comprehensiveness and quality. They are useful, however, for identifying a number of patterns. Firstly, a significant proportion of the sample had family members and friends already living in Britain. It is difficult to ascertain whether each individual was actually asked if they had relatives in Britain, although on the basis of the available data this would seem to have been the case. Detailed information is extant for 208 individuals, and of those roughly a third, or 72 people, reported that they had one or more

Table 4.6 Conjugal status: Commission on Emigration sample, 1948–49

Conjugal status	Number
Single	178
Married	65
Widowed	3
Separated[a]	1

n = 247

Note: [a] Divorce was prohibited by a constitutional ban in the Irish Republic until 1995.
Source: TCD MS 8306, rural surveys

relatives from their immediate family living in Britain.[82] Many others stated that they had other relatives and friends from the locality in Britain. For one prospective 29-year-old migrant from Tullow, county Carlow, all nine of his siblings were working in Britain.[83] This factor should not be underestimated: relatives and friends in Britain provided sound and much sought after advice regarding employment opportunities and wages and, in addition, crucial exhortations to come to a place where things were better, in theory at least. Numerous studies have found that family and kin networks facilitate migration as they act as 'conduits of information and social and financial assistance'.[84] The location of relatives in Britain also determined the initial destination of migrants since accommodation could be provided in the first instance. The second pattern revealed by the data is that many of those who were migrating had had various types of temporary work, for example, labouring jobs with the local authority on the roads or agricultural employment and either had been laid off or were dissatisfied with the uncertain nature of the work. For example, a 26-year-old man from county Clare lived with his parents on a small-holding of nine acres and worked as a labourer as well. Two of his four sisters were in Britain and sent home remittances on a weekly basis, and he was migrating because of the lack of constant employment.[85] Another example was a man aged 19 years from Ballina in county Mayo, who had been working casually with the county council but who was leaving as he sought a 'steady job abroad'.[86] Roughly a quarter of the sample had worked in Britain on a previous occasion or had served in the British forces during the Second World War.[87] Therefore the migrant pathways that had been established during the war and the immediate postwar period proved of importance for those who returned home and subsequently experienced difficulty securing employment.

Networks, prior experience of working in Britain and a lack of steady employment were therefore significant factors in determining who migrated to Britain and who did not. Without doubt, underemployment or casual employment would not be unusual in an agriculturally based economy, although it is evident that this form of precarious livelihood was becoming increasingly unacceptable, especially since relatives and friends could obtain secure and reasonably well-paid employment in Britain. The eagerness to leave is illustrated by the fact that the majority of the positions on offer under the British recruitment scheme were in the coal-mines or heavy foundry work at Ford's in Dagenham, near London. The British coal industry experienced considerable difficulty in meeting the demand for labour in the late 1940s. In 1947 and 1948, roughly 20,000 men left the coal industry annually on the completion of their national service obligations and Irish migrants, together with European Volunteer Workers and other 'displaced persons', were recruited for this unattractive employment.[88]

Data on the last occupation of the prospective migrants are available and these confirm our earlier observations with regard to the unskilled nature of the male migrant flow. For some cases, the occupation can only be ascertained by inference, but for the majority this information is readily available. The findings that emerge from an analysis of this sample are particularly revealing with respect to the categories most heavily represented (see Table 4.7). The effects of the demobilisation of the Irish army in the immediate postwar period can be noted in the small yet significant proportion of the sample whose last employment was as a member of the defence forces. Skilled workers constituted a minor element of the migrant flow, which is a continuation of previous trends. In any case, skilled workers could secure work in Britain without having to rely on the official recruitment schemes. The bulk of the prospective migrants to Britain were non-agricultural unskilled workers: this broad category includes those involved in transport, such as lorry drivers, shopworkers and builders' labourers, but the grouping which is most heavily represented is that without any specified occupation. These men were employed on an intermittent basis on road maintenance and repair work for the local authority or were involved in turf-cutting and other types of casual labouring. Lacking training or education, such unskilled workers

Table 4.7 Male occupational profile (last occupation): Commission on Emigration sample, 1948–49 (%)

Occupation	%
Farmers	1.4
Farm workers	13.0
Relatives assisting	6.7
Skilled workers	3.3
Non-agricultural unskilled workers	66.9
Ex-Irish army	3.8
Not available	4.9

n = 209
Source: TCD MS 8306, rural surveys.

were unable to find steady well-paid work in Ireland, but in Britain the wage levels that applied to similar types of employment were much higher. This general picture is confirmed by the aggregate data derived from the applications for travel identity cards in the period from 1947 until 1951.

The Commission on Emigration highlighted this contrast in the remuneration of these unskilled workers which was one of the principal causes of Irish migration to Britain:

> The higher levels of wages in Britain are not, of course, strictly comparable with wage levels here, because costs of living, taxation, food standards, factory amenities and social services are not the same in both countries. There is, however, no doubt that the rather wide difference between what the unskilled worker earns in this country and what he could earn in Britain has been a strong incentive to emigration. Emigration which is due to the attraction of British wage rates would be slowed down by narrowing the gap between wage levels in the two countries, but we do not believe it would be necessary for the levels of wages here to be in all cases identical with those prevailing in Britain.[89]

Nevin has noted the widening gap between industrial wage levels in Ireland and those in Britain in this period.[90] However, Irish migrants were not for the most part engaged in industry, but rather the intermittent casual work discussed above. The level of remuneration for such employment clearly does not lend itself to quantification. Impressionistic evidence does nevertheless shed some light on this point. For example, a male prospective migrant, aged 41 years, from

Killybegs in county Donegal, who worked as a cook at the rate of £4
per week, stated that he could earn up to £7 1s. per week plus overtime
in Britain.[91] A 29-year-old labourer from Tullow in county Carlow,
who could not remember when he last had a constant job and who was
surviving on casual employment yielding roughly £3 10s. per week,
was going to work in agricultural employment in Britain at a rate of
£5 10s.[92] The sharp contrast of the wages that unskilled male workers
could earn in Britain relative to those on offer in Ireland was a very
significant determinant in Irish migration in the immediate postwar
period.

The proportion of the sample with a background in agricultural
work is lower than the statistics for last occupation of the applicants
for Irish travel permits and identity cards indicate for the period from
1947 until 1951 (see Table 4.8). This may be explained by the fact that
the sample does not reflect accurately the distribution of the incidence
of migration. There is no weighting of these data to ensure that areas
with a higher rate or volume of migration are represented to a greater
degree. This point is well illustrated by the small proportion of those
applicants for work who were recorded as 'relatives assisting', that is,
unpaid workers on the family farm. The decline of the male agricultural labour force was not a new development, but in the immediate
postwar period from 1946 onwards, this decline was greatly accelerated. Between 1926 and 1946 2,235 males left agriculture per annum.
However, in the period 1946–51 the total number of males fell by
61,800 or 12,360 per annum, a fivefold increase on the decline in the
earlier period.[93] This decline was spread evenly across all sizes of
farms, unlike the decline prior to 1946 which was experienced mainly

Table 4.8 Occupational distribution (last occupation) of males in receipt of Irish
travel permits, identity cards and passports to go to employment, 1947–51 (%)

	1947	1948	1949	1950	1951	1947–51
Unskilled workers[a]	44.4	49.1	42.3	33.6	31.0	42.0
Agriculture	36.8	25.0	27.9	33.0	40.0	31.3
Industry	7.1	8.0	9.4	11.4	11.4	9.1
Other skilled workers and clerks	11.7	17.9	20.4	22.0	17.6	17.6

Note: [a]Builders' labourers are included in the industry group.
Source: Commission on Emigration, Reports, table 31, p. 322.

by farms of less than 15 acres.[94] In regional terms this development affected all provinces, although of particular significance are the higher rates of decline for paid farm labourers throughout the country (see Table 4.9). The agricultural labour force was in a spiral of decline, and it was this grouping that formed a substantial segment of the pool of migrants in the postwar period.

Table 4.9 Decline in Irish male agricultural labour force, 1946–51 (%)

	All males	Employees	Relatives assisting
Leinster	15.4	22.9	9.8
Munster	11.9	20.4	8.3
Connacht	12.2	28.1	10.1
Ulster	11.5	24.8	8.6
Irish Republic	12.7	24.1	9.2

Source: Commission on Emigration, *Reports*, p. 47.

Perhaps the most novel aspect of the sample drawn from the interviews conducted by the members of the Commission on Emigration are the 208 individual case-histories which underline the variety of factors that influenced the migration 'decision'. Understandably some of the respondents sought to justify their decision to leave Ireland, whereas others bitterly complained about the economic conditions that they were expected to endure. In an effort to give some indication of the individual circumstances, the information provided by eight respondents chosen at random from the total sample is presented in Figure 4.2. As can be seen, these individual case-histories confirm the observation that lack of constant work was a key determinant in the decision to migrate, although family circumstances and other factors such as relatives in Britain also were of some significance. A further revealing observation is the frequency of a declaration of intention to stay in Britain 'permanently'. No doubt 'permanence' as such was rare in the closely integrated Irish and British labour markets, yet an express statement of intention is revealing in itself. These people were not confident that a secure and steady job could be obtained in Ireland and therefore their short- to medium-term future lay in Britain.

A   25 years old; male; married with two children; living in Athlone town, county Westmeath; last employment casual with Electricity Supply Board at £5 per week; prior to that worked in the coal-mines in Britain but returned home owing to wife's illness; very anxious to return to Britain and remain there permanently; present family income £1 2s. of unemployment assistance.

B   18 years old; male; single; from Kilkee in county Clare; son of a tailor; eldest of seven children; two sisters working as domestic servants in Britain; does 'odd jobs'; wishes to get away to obtain constant work.

C   36 years old; male; married with one child; from rural area in county Longford; wife working in cigarette factory in Britain since July earning £3 15s. per week; he is going to tile-making plant and will earn £7 per week; stated that he had worked casually dealing in horses and cutting timber for sale; intends to stay in Britain.

D   25 years old; male; single; living in town of Boyle, county Roscommon; ex-British navy carpenter; out of navy three months and unemployed since; staying in house with uncle and his wife and four children; total money coming into the house is £3 2s. 6d.; no work in Boyle and determined not to be unemployed; going to work in coal-mines; intends to stay in Britain.

E   20 years old; male; single; from town of Bray in county Wicklow; builders' labourer who was earning £5 12s. 6d. per week; five weeks unemployed; living at home with mother and sister in three-roomed flat; one brother in RAF; rejected because he had only one eye; would take any kind of non-agricultural work in Britain; thinks there is little chance of constant work at home; while wage rate is good in building industry, work is far too casual and annual earnings therefore pretty small; 'no future in employment of that kind'.

F   20 years old; male; single; from rural area in the hinterland of Thomastown, county Kilkenny; blacksmith's assistant; lives with parents; 16 in the family home, father, mother and 14 children; unemployed two months; would like factory work in Britain but not coal mining; wishes to travel; gave the impression that he was not seriously troubled about being unemployed but would like a change of scene.

G   21 years old; male; single; from Clonmel, county Tipperary; four brothers and two sisters; one brother in Britain; was demobilised from Irish army in May 1948; would like to go to kitchen gardening near Hammersmith where he has friends; will stay here if he gets a good job; did not try elsewhere in Ireland.

H   29 years old; male; single; living in Ballina, county Mayo; ex-RAF ground staff, 1943–46; farm labourer since his return but only casual work available; going to Ford's at Dagenham for foundry work; considers that Britain offers a steady job with prospects.

Source: TCD MS 8306, rural surveys.

Fig. 4.2 *Eight migration case histories, 1948–49*

Unfortunately, the sample based on the surveys completed for the Commission on Emigration is almost exclusively concerned with male migration, although in order to obtain information on female migration, one commissioner, Stanley Lyon, the former director of statistics at the Department of Industry and Commerce, interviewed 12 returned female migrants applying again for work in Britain at an employment exchange in Dublin. As Lyon noted, 'few general and reliable conclusions can be drawn from the evidence received' owing to the limited size of the sample and the geographical concentration in Dublin city.[95] Nevertheless, the rural surveys conducted by the commissioners raise a number of important issues relating to female migration to Britain. The average annual rate of female net migration (−9.7 per 1,000) exceeded that for male migration (−6.9 per 1,000) between 1946 and 1951, as we already noted above (see Table 4.1b). In the following five years, males migrated at a slightly higher rate (−14.6 per 1,000) in comparison with females (−12.2 per 1,000). A theme evident in many of these surveys is a sense that male migration to Britain was for purely economic reasons – and by implication comprehensible – whereas female migration was for altogether different reasons, primarily sociological in nature. For example, in Galway, a commissioner noted that 'it would appear that men are not subject to the pull of a new environment to the same extent as women'.[96] This comment reflects the prejudices of the author, although a similar statement was made in a survey of a number of towns in the south-east of Ireland. According to Lyon, he was told by people he encountered on his tour that 'the lure of England, emphasised by the "grand" appearance of the returned emigrants when they came home on holidays, was a [sic] main factor [in female emigration]'.[97] This distinction between the predominantly economic causes of male migration and the broader range of factors associated with female migration was contained in the final report of the commission:

> Although female emigration, like male, is the result of a variety of causes, the purely economic cause is not always so dominant. For the female emigrant improvement in personal status is of no less importance than the higher wages and better conditions of employment abroad and some of the evidence submitted to us would suggest that the prospect of better marriage opportunities is also an influence of some significance.[98]

However, what the commissioners failed to acknowledge was that the status associated with female work in Ireland was considerably lower than was the case in Britain. Domestic servants, for instance, were viewed as an inferior form of life by both employers and the community at large. As was underlined in evidence submitted to the commission by the Irish Housewives' Association, 'the domestic worker in Great Britain gets recognition as a human being while she does not get it here'.[99] If females left Ireland because of factors other than economic concerns, this may well be an indication of the low status associated with women's work (both paid and unpaid) in Ireland rather than the standard explanation which was advanced that females were more susceptible to the 'lure' of Britain. In addition, Louie Bennett of the Irish Women Workers' Union stated in evidence before the commission that those women who were in factory employment in Ireland and subsequently migrated to Britain found the conditions there 'a thousand times better'.[100] British employers were more concerned than their Irish counterparts with ensuring that the conditions of work in terms of hours, environment and remuneration were substantially better than was the case in Ireland.

Female migration to Britain in the immediate postwar period has attracted the attention of a number of scholars. Moser argues that the changing nature of the agricultural economy in the west of Ireland resulted in political agitation in the form of agrarian organisations on the part of males, but for females, migration to Britain was the favoured option:

> Men and women on the farms acted and reacted differently. The men tried to save their socio-political interests through the formation of political pressure groups. The women, however, didn't organise themselves politically but rather tried to escape the increasingly difficult situation individually through emigration.[101]

At best this analysis is inchoate since female migration from the west of Ireland was not a novel development peculiar to the postwar period; and on a more fundamental level, *some* men may have become involved in political organisations, although many more left the country. Clearly, Moser's suggestive comments do not shed much light on the causes of female migration in the immediate postwar period. Travers attempts to construct a more rounded treatment, yet his findings still appear rather impressionistic. On the basis of an 'as yet incomplete survey of Irish female emigration', he states that 'the vast majority of respondents cite employment as a major determinant of their decision to emigrate but most also cite other factors including restlessness, dissatisfaction with their lot, poor or unattractive social conditions, marriage and the influence of an emigrant network'.[102] These factors were, without doubt, determinants in the migration decision, although Travers pays scant attention to the economic factors and discusses at some length government schemes to promote early marriage, female reaction to the Irish constitution of 1937 (with its implicit message regarding the subservience of women), and 'the unfriendly nature of Irish society and particularly the state apparatus as far as many women were concerned'.[103] Similarly, Walter's paper specifically concerned with gender and Irish migration to Britain is equally opaque on the actual causes of female migration from postwar Ireland, apart from an analysis of the 'complex interaction between patriarchy and colonialism'.[104] There is much more of practical value in Hannan's suggestion that the higher rates of female migration in the postwar period can be explained by reference to the lack of female industrial employment coupled with an increased commercialisation of agriculture.[105] Factory and clerical work which would absorb surplus female labour were extremely difficult to obtain in rural Ireland.[106] There is also some evidence to demonstrate that the creation of employment for females was regarded as being of secondary importance.[107] For instance, the Commission on Emigration concluded that it would be more 'advantageous' if industrial employment was provided for males rather than females.[108] In addition, as Daly has posited, there is also some indication of a distinct change in mentality: 'The rising emigration of young women meant that they were placing their personal interest above those of family and society: a change from a family-based system to one which gave greater weight to the woman as an individual.'[109] Nevertheless, on the other hand, it may be argued that migration was in itself placing the family's interest over the individual because, in order for uneconomic farming units to survive, the non-inheriting children, both male and female, had little option but to leave the family holding.[110] However, Daly is surely correct in pointing to the changing priorities of women in rural Ireland. The bleak future that was mapped out for many young females was rejected in favour of paid employment in Britain and a stark contrast in terms of status and remuneration.

IV

The controls on migration established during the Second World War were gradually dismantled in the years following the end of the war in

1945. From July 1946, Irish restrictions on female migration for employment in Britain were discontinued after the British authorities lifted wartime regulations on the direction of all female labour.[111] Females wishing to travel to Britain were still required to apply for an Irish travel permit but no restrictions were applied by the Irish authorities. The British restrictions on Irish male employment continued to remain in force until December 1947 and henceforth all forms of employment were open to Irish males.[112] However, as noted earlier, Irish restrictions on those males eligible to obtain a travel permit remained until April 1952.[113] In theory, those males in employment or for whom employment was available or would be available in a 'reasonable time' were to be refused travel permits.[114] Professionals were excluded from these restrictions.[115] There was, however, a loophole in that persons wishing to travel to Britain for reasons other than employment were issued with a travel identity card without an employment visa.[116] In theory, British employers were required to check that there was an employment visa on the identity card but whether this was the case in practice is a matter for conjecture.

In the late 1940s two closely related subjects, a possible wholesale ban on migration and anxiety regarding female emigration with a view to prohibition of this movement, dominated all official discussions with regard to population movement from Ireland. In August 1947, after a detailed examination of the issues, the Department of External Affairs drafted a memorandum on the subject of female migration to Britain for consideration by the government. According to this document, female migration to employment was 'extremely high', although no statistical evidence to corroborate this statement was furnished.[117] In addition, since this flow was not regulated, many women under the age of 21 years were leaving for work in domestic service owing to the better conditions of work and pay.[118] This movement of population had, according to the memorandum, consequences which could only be limited by refusing permits to applicants under a specified age such as 21 or 22 years:

> The moral and social dangers of emigration are obviously the greater the younger and more inexperienced the emigrant and the most effective method of protecting the interests of young female emigrants is the imposition of an age limit below which girls would not be allowed to emigrate. This method would have the additional advantage of going some way to protect our own population from an alarming loss of women of marriageable and child bearing age.[119]

This memorandum was postponed on numerous occasions and eventually withdrawn from the cabinet agenda; perhaps the Fianna Fáil government of the day found these issues too uncomfortable to contemplate. The Department of External Affairs again raised the issue of emigration in December 1947 with a memorandum prepared by F. H. Boland, then assistant secretary at the department, for consideration by the taoiseach and minister for external affairs, Eamon de Valera. The most radical question Boland raised was the possibility of the wholesale prohibition of emigration or restriction by means of a quota. The idea of such a ban was not a novel one, as we have seen in previous chapters, but it is of significance that Boland thought it fitting to assess the merits of such a proposal at this time. He underlined the patent difficulties of enforcing a prohibition, although the issue at stake was one of principle rather than of practicality:

> Is any government entitled – and, if so, in what circumstances – to tell a citizen that he [sic] must not leave the country but remain at home to be available if his services are needed? No doubt there are circumstances in which a government would be justified in saying that. It could do it in time of war if men were required for the national defence ... In our view, it can do it, too, in time of scarcity, to prevent people in key positions in production, by wantonly withdrawing their labour, causing widespread hardship and suffering to the community at large.[120]

Notwithstanding these special circumstances, Boland stated in unequivocal terms what ought to be the position of the Irish government:

> Any such prohibition would involve an unjustifiable and dangerous infringement of the freedom of the individual. It would mean the government substituting its own judgement for that of the individuals concerned and their parents. It would be an unwarranted invasion of human responsibility. It would lower national morale. Far from effectively countering the psychological causes of emigration, it would turn the country into a prisonhouse in the eyes of those who wanted to emigrate, making far-off hills greener than ever.[121]

Boland was surely correct in emphasising the effect such a prohibition would have on morale: to prevent the citizens of a country leaving for employment elsewhere would have been a very difficult step for any government to take.

The Roman Catholic church was to the fore in stimulating debate regarding migration to Britain and working directly with migrants during the war years. In the postwar period the church hierarchy in Ireland became increasingly involved in making representations to various governments in relation to migration to Britain. For example, at its meeting in October 1947, the bishops passed a resolution which expressed their 'alarm' at the continuing high level of female emigration, and deplored the activities of 'foreign agents' who were involved in recruitment of female labour for work in Britain.[122] De Valera requested that the issues raised by the hierarchy be investigated by the various departments concerned. His reply acknowledged that female migration was 'causing the government particular anxiety', but outlined the policy of his government on the subject of migration for employment in Britain:

> Among the principal objects of the government's policy are the development of the national resources to the maximum extent and the encouragement of increased production in agriculture and manufacturing industry. These would seem to be the most effective means available to the state for dealing with the problem of emigration.[123]

In addition, he ruled out the possibility of a prohibition on emigration as this would constitute 'the restriction of a fundamental human right which could only be justified in circumstances of great national emergency'.[124] The public statement issued by the hierarchy in October 1947 focused on the recent increase in migration and warned migrants of the dangers 'to their religious and moral well-being'.[125] When members of the hierarchy travelled to Rome in October and November 1947 for their *ad limina* visits, Pope Pius XII raised the issue of Irish emigration. Joseph Walsh, the archbishop of Tuam, stated that the pontiff was 'perturbed by the mass emigration from Ireland' and the associated dangers to the faith of emigrants.[126] Such high-profile expressions of anxiety regarding emigration must have acutely embarrassed the de Valera government.[127] However, after the election of February 1948, it was the first inter-party government (1948–51) led by John A. Costello that was faced with the seemingly insurmountable 'problem' of Irish emigration.

One of the first steps taken by the inter-party government was to establish in March 1948 the Commission on Emigration and Other Population Problems under the chairmanship of James Beddy, the distinguished public servant.[128] The genesis of the body lay in a cabinet decision that was taken on 24 February 1948 by the inter-party government, which had come to power a few weeks earlier. The cabinet resolved to establish a commission of inquiry to investigate the related problems of emigration and rural depopulation.[129] The commission was publicly announced in March 1948 by the then minister for social welfare, William Norton, the leader of the Labour party and tánaiste (deputy prime minister). It is particularly noteworthy that emigration is not specifically referred to in the terms of reference of the commission:

> To investigate the causes and consequences of the present level and trend in population; to examine, in particular, the social and economic effects of birth, death, migration and marriage rates at present and their probable course in the near future; to consider what measures, if any, should be taken in the national interest to influence the trend in population; generally, to consider the desirability of formulating a national population policy.[130]

The similarities with the terms of reference of the British Royal Commission on Population instituted in 1944 are remarkable, the remit of the latter being

> ... to examine the facts relating to the present population trends in Great Britain; to investigate the causes of these trends and to consider their probable consequences; to consider what measures, if any, should be taken in the national interest to influence the future trend of population and to make recommendations.[131]

Clearly, originality was not the forte of Irish civil servants. Nevertheless, it was evident from the title of the commission that the principal concern of this body was emigration rather than mortality, fertility or nuptiality.

The institution of the commission was generally welcomed in the press coverage, although its composition was the source of some disquiet as the membership was predominantly drawn from the ranks of the professional and academic strata of Irish life, apart that is from the notable exception of Peadar O'Donnell, the campaigner for the rights of the underprivileged and sometime republican propagandist, and Aodh de Blacam, a former Fianna Fáil party activist who resigned over the question of rural depopulation and subsequently joined Clann na Poblachta.[132] R. C. Geary, M. D. McCarthy, Stanley Lyon, James Meenan and G. A. Duncan were members with backgrounds in economics and statistical techniques. Geary and McCarthy were statisticians of international repute, Lyon was the former director of statistics at the Department of Industry and Commerce, and Meenan and Duncan were based at economics departments in University College, Dublin, and Trinity College, Dublin, respectively.[133] In some senses, the establishment of a commission – an age-old method of kicking issues to touch – deflected criticism on the increasing rates of emigration away from the inter-party government. If this were the aim underlying the institution of the commission, it was grossly misjudged as the issue was debated with increasing frequency over the following few years.

The commission considered the question of a ban on the emigration of young women under the age of 21 in November 1948 as a result of a request from the then minister for external affairs, Seán MacBride, who was the driving force behind this proposal.[134] After a lengthy discussion the commission stated that it was not prepared to recommend such a ban.[135] Divergent views emerged during the course of this discussion. Despite the fact that a letter in favour of the ban was received from the archbishop of Tuam, Joseph Walsh, two priests on the commission, Thomas Counihan and Cornelius Lucey, objected to the ban on the basis of moral law.[136] Counihan stated that he did not think the bench of bishops would uphold the archbishop's view, and Lucey, the professor of ethics at the Catholic seminary, Maynooth College, argued that the state had 'no right to check the movement of minors into moral danger', if they had their parents' permission.[137] This ran contrary to some informal advice that MacBride had received the previous September which suggested that such a proposal would, to quote him, 'secure the warm approval of the hierarchy'.[138] It may well be that MacBride obtained this advice from John Charles McQuaid, the Roman Catholic archbishop of Dublin, as they corresponded about the matter of emigration, although McQuaid was cautious in his dealings with MacBride.[139] It is noteworthy that the issue was viewed very much within the context of state control versus the rights of the individual, but perhaps the point which should be underlined is that it was a government minister from a radical socialist republican party, Clann na Poblachta, rather than a clerical figure who was actively promoting the idea of a ban on female emigration for those aged less than 21 years.[140] MacBride had stated in a letter to a member of the commission that a prohibition was 'the only satisfactory solution of the problem'.[141] In the event, the commission rejected the idea of such a ban and a number of government departments were not pleased at the prospect of enforcing this prohibition.[142] Lastly, when a query on the matter was published some months later in the scholarly theological periodical, *Irish Ecclesiastical Record*, a ban was adjudged to be morally inadmissible on the grounds that it would conflict with parental rights, and the rights of the minors themselves.[143] In its final report, the commission rejected a proposal of this nature on the grounds that it was 'drastic inference by the state with the liberty of movement of its citizens'.[144]

In December 1949 the inter-party government embarked on a novel campaign to encourage skilled Irish migrants to return from Britain to help meet the shortage of skilled labour in urgent housing and hospital building schemes. The number of skilled workers who left Ireland to work in Britain was, as noted earlier, quite small relative to the total flow, but as one newspaper observed, 'many men who were unskilled when leaving home have now qualified as skilled workers'.[145] This skilled labour was particularly required for the hospital building programme introduced by Noël Browne, the energetic minister for health, in July 1948.[146] A glossy brochure was produced outlining plans for housing and hospital building schemes and included a commentary which adopted a rather sanguine tone:

> Ireland looks to great numbers of her sons, who were obliged to emigrate for employment in other days, to return to the motherland and help in building up the national fabric ... Many emigrants have left their native land through a sense of adventure and enterprise. This was not unusual in days when Ireland was backward and unprogressive. Today, Ireland offers her sons the grand adventure of building up a state.[147]

Over 10,000 of these brochures were printed for distribution in the Irish Republic and Britain.[148] The taoiseach, John A. Costello, made a speech in early January 1950 requesting that skilled workers come home to help in the building programmes.[149] The minister with responsibility for the local authority housing schemes, M. J. Keyes, spoke on Irish radio in January 1950 in an effort to encourage carpenters, bricklayers and plasterers to come back home for work, presumably in the hope that relatives would pass on details of the appeal.[150] Within a short time, reports published in the *Daily Express* in the same month suggested that all was not well with the campaign. Only 100 men actually came back: some found accommodation impossible to obtain, others were refused union cards and made their way back to Britain and recounted details of the difficulties to their colleagues.[151] There was also some opposition from the trade unions to the possibility of large numbers of skilled workers returning home, presumably on the basis of the possible effects on wage levels.[152] Conor Cruise O'Brien, then an aspiring civil servant, warned his minister, Sean MacBride, that 'this campaign is becoming a débâcle I fear'.[153] In July 1950 the campaign was officially wound up owing to its lack of success.[154] These endeavours on the part of the inter-party government denote a significant nuance in official policy with regard to migration to Britain in the immediate postwar period. By appealing for skilled workers to come back home, the Irish government was explicitly acknowledging the fact that migration to Britain resulted in a shortage of labour (albeit skilled labour). Outwardly the Irish state encouraged return migration, but in reality it was only migrants with marketable skills who were needed. The possibility of thousands of unskilled workers returning was not something that the Irish state wished to encourage.

The actual conditions of Irish migrants in Britain were the subject of some controversy in the summer months of 1951. Maurice Foley, a full-time official of the Young Christian Workers' Association, prepared a comprehensive report in July 1951 on all aspects of the conditions of Irish workers in Birmingham. It is noteworthy that Foley was later (in March 1965) to become the junior minister in the Labour government (1964–66) in charge of the co-ordination of policy on the integration of immigrants.[155] The results were quite shocking: in one house he found 50 Irishmen living together with 15 people sleeping in one room.[156] At this time there was an acute housing shortage in Birmingham and Foley estimated that over half of the Irish-born population there lived in groups of between 15 and 20 people.[157] Many were employed in small firms and the working environment was basic at best.[158] The 'morals' of Irish migrants in Britain were also the source of particular anxiety. Unmarried mothers, married men whose wives were in Ireland and who were then living with other women, and the inevitable drunk and disorderly behaviour of Irish males were noted. Apparently, on one Monday morning, of 75 people before the courts for drink-related charges, 48 were Irish.[159] In terms of religion, Foley reported that in one hostel of 300 Irish workers only 8 per cent practised their religion regularly.[160] While the report is not in any sense of a scientific nature, there is no reason to believe that Foley was exaggerating the deplorable conditions of Irish people in Birmingham. Boland, now elevated to the position of Irish ambassador to Britain, observed that Foley's report was 'objective, trustworthy, and not exaggerated in any way'.[161] Nevertheless, reports of this nature tend to highlight what is wrong rather than what is right with a particular situation. Having learned of the details of this report, de Valera decided that he would publicise some of the accounts of conditions of accommodation of Irish workers in a speech at Galway on 29 August 1951, to which he added his own observations about the British–Irish wage differential.[162] The logic behind the decision was twofold: firstly, to warn prospective migrants of the situation in Birmingham, and secondly, to draw attention to the plight of Irish migrants in Britain in the hope that pressure would be brought to bear on the British Ministry of Labour and employers in these cities 'to realise and fulfil the responsibilities in this matter which they have hitherto so shamefully neglected'.[163] De Valera's comments about Irish migrants 'living in conditions of absolute degradation' in cities such as Birmingham, Coventry and Wolverhampton caused absolute uproar when they were widely reported in the British and Irish press at the end of August 1951.[164] His references to the wage differential between Ireland and Britain are of particular interest:

> The saddest part of all this is that work is available at home, and in conditions infinitely better from the point of view of health and morals. In many occupations, the rates of wages are higher at home than they are in Britain. It is true that, in some cases, an Irish worker's total earnings in Britain are high, but this is often due to the fact that the conditions in which he finds himself obliged to live are so unattractive that he prefers unduly long hours of overtime to a leisure which he cannot enjoy. There is no doubt that many of those who emigrate could find employment at home at as good, or better, wages – and with living conditions far better – than they find in Britain.[165]

De Valera was being disingenuous on the matter of the wage differential. Whilst wage levels for skilled and semi-skilled workers in a number of industries were higher in Ireland than in Britain, these jobs were simply not available, especially in the areas with high rates of net migration, and hence the decision to leave.[166] To imply otherwise was being economical with the truth to say the least.

The British response to these allegations was to investigate the charges made by de Valera which were conveyed to the Commonwealth Relations Office in more temperate language by an Irish diplomat in London. But as one British embassy official in Dublin noted, the Irish state was placed in a dilemma regarding the migration of thousands of its citizens to Britain: 'It was once admitted unofficially in private conversation by a senior civil servant here that if this country could not export at least 30,000 labourers to the United Kingdom each year an impossible unemployment situation would result in the Republic.'[167] Nevertheless, such an admission did not make for a practical course of action in political terms.

> It is however the case that it would be political suicide here for any government to give open encouragement to emigration and for that reason Harris-Green

[British Liaison Officer for Labour in Dublin] has always – in our view quite rightly – taken the line that if we wish to continue to receive emigrant labour from this country we must not ask the Irish Republican [sic] authorities to give their open approval to recruitment. This is a typical Irish arrangement.[168]

A detailed report was prepared by the Ministry of Labour which outlined the provisions in place for the inspection of accommodation offered to workers from Ireland, as was the case with other persons recruited under the official schemes.[169] In addition, there was already a widespread welfare organisation under the auspices of the British Ministry of Labour in Birmingham and other industrial centres.[170] It was difficult to refute de Valera's specific allegations as no details were provided. However, as a British official in Dublin reported, it had come to light that Foley's original investigation was conducted 12 months previously and was not 'necessarily still valid'.[171] The ensuing debate in the Irish newspapers underlined an important point: the situation for many in Ireland was no better than was the case in Birmingham, and if de Valera wished to prevent migration to Britain, he should in the first instance try to improve the conditions at home.[172] What is perhaps most ironic is that the United Kingdom liaison officer for labour in Dublin, Harris-Green, reported that 'there was an immediate and marked increase in the number of personal and written applications for employment in Great Britain following Mr de Valera's speech'.[173] A British official in the Commonwealth Relations Office observed ruefully that de Valera had his own motives in drawing public attention to the unenviable position of Irish migrants in Birmingham:

we know that Mr de Valera's objective in this matter is political. As a nationalist and a Roman Catholic churchman [sic] he is not so much anxious to improve the material or moral welfare of emigrant Irish workers as to stop them from leaving the Republic. This is brought out by his conduct in the publishing of his complaints in the Irish Republican [sic] press simultaneously with the making of diplomatic representations. The reasons are that the habit of Irish workers leaving for work in Great Britain offends national pride by casting a no doubt merited slur on the conditions and prospects provided for them in Southern Ireland, and that the Roman Catholic church, to whose views any Irish Republican [sic] government is very deferential, regards contact with the relative sophistication of Birmingham as corrupting the emigrant worker.[174]

In many ways, this unnamed official was correct. De Valera was not so much interested, in public at least, with the living conditions in Britain as in the broader objective of discouraging migration to

Britain. The fact that he discussed the disparity in British and Irish wages in the original speech reinforces this point. Associated with the political ramifications of continued migration to Britain were the concerns of the Roman Catholic church which, as we shall see, became increasingly significant in the mid-1950s.

The British were prepared to let the matter drop and in the absence of any further representations on the issue no further comment on the conditions of Irish workers in Britain is evident. In May 1952, de Valera requested that Boland ascertain what the current position was with regard to Irish migrants in Birmingham.[175] Boland's response was that the conditions had improved somewhat but were still unsatisfactory. However, he advised against any publicity on the matter as unemployment was rising in Britain and public comment on the matter might bring 'unfavourable reactions'.[176] Boland visited Birmingham on 27 January 1953 and reported that the situation had changed appreciably in that unemployment was high, owing to the lack of export orders, and his contacts indicated that many Irish migrants had gone elsewhere in Britain; consequently the accommodation problem had eased.[177] The change in the conditions over such a short time period would seem to add some weight to the British criticisms regarding the gap between the time when Foley completed the research for his report and the report's eventual submission to the Irish government.

Further controversy was to arise on the question of migration to Britain, but in this instance it was the scale of the numbers leaving the country that was the matter of debate. From 1951 onwards no annual statistics of emigration were published as the Central Statistics Office considered that the standard methods of compiling such statistics (net passenger balance, passenger card inquiry and travel documents) could not be relied upon 'to give dependable figures'.[178] During parliamentary debates a number of members of the opposition, particularly Seán MacBride, the former minister, had suggested that the statistics were not published owing to the possibility of embarrassing the government.[179] The context for these accusations was one of rising unemployment and by implication higher levels of migration to Britain. In January 1953 the number on the live register was 87,000 people, the highest figure since January 1943.[180] De Valera instituted an inquiry in February 1953 whereby the Central Statistics Office was required to investigate 'the method by which emigration statistics should be compiled in future'.[181] The Central Statistics Office prepared a detailed and involved memorandum and outlined the difficulties involved in the collection of annual emigration statistics (gross or net). In short, frontier controls would have to be instituted, an expensive and unrealistic option.[182] It was suggested that the most reliable method of estimating net migration was the use of census returns in conjunction with the statistics on births and deaths. The memorandum concluded that 'the Central Statistics Office is strongly of the opinion that no attempt should be made to compile annual statistics of gross and net emigration'.[183] A caveat added at the end of the document is of particular interest:

> Under existing conditions net emigration is far more important than gross emigration which, in view of the great mobility of labour between Ireland and Britain, is a highly misleading statistic. On this point it may be well to emphasise the great qualitative change in the character of emigration in its being directed in recent years towards Britain, instead of overseas as formerly. Emigrants to Britain maintain their ties with the homeland by frequent visits, and movement between jobs in the two countries reaches such dimensions that, to a large extent, the movement can scarcely be regarded as 'emigration' in the traditional meaning of the term.[184]

R. C. Geary, the director of the Central Statistics Office, was emphasising the point that many migrants left only for a short period and that, in many ways, the British and Irish labour markets were closely integrated, at least in the minds of many of those who left Ireland.

By the time the reports of the Commission on Emigration and Other Population Problems were eventually presented in April 1954, some six years after this body was established, a second inter-party government (1954–57) was in power.[185] The delay had much to do with the fact that a special census was instituted in 1951 at the request of the commission in order to ensure that the members had the most up-to-date statistical material. After the reports were made available in stencilled form in July 1954 (one majority report and two minority reports), they received extensive newspaper coverage: for example, the *Irish Independent* devoted 17 consecutive articles to the findings of the commission.[186] Similarly, periodicals such as *The Leader* examined the contents of the reports in some detail.[187] In the realm of government, it was decided at a cabinet meeting in August 1954 that each department should prepare a memorandum on the findings as they related to that department's activities.[188] It would be well-nigh impossible to summarise the findings contained in these valuable reports, but in so far as they directly relate to Irish migration to Britain, a number of points should be made.[189] For the most part, we shall be concerned with the majority report and its numerous notes, addenda and reservations, rather than the two minority reports by Cornelius Lucey and James Meenan, both of value, if a little idiosyncratic in approach. Whilst the majority report acknowledged that the fundamental cause of migration was economic in nature, other factors such as those touched upon earlier in the present chapter were also outlined: 'The other principal reason for emigration is the desire for improved material standards together with a dissatisfaction with life on the land, whether in its economic or its social aspects.'[190] Therefore a distinction was made between economic causes of migration, albeit of a relative kind, and economic expectations. The commission found that this dissatisfaction was in some senses fuelled by a knowledge of better conditions abroad gained through emigrants' letters or the pervasive influence of returned migrants with accounts of higher wages and an abundance of employment opportunities.[191] The commission rightly recognised the interaction of a range of factors which affected the decision of an individual to migrate, although the basic contention which underpins much of the analysis is that the lack of suitable employment opportunities was the principal determinant of migration. In relation to the consequences of the large-scale migration, the commission concluded that no obvious labour shortage was evident and the large number of people leaving the country had 'not prevented economic development'.[192] But this movement of population had both advantages and disadvantages for those who remained at home:

> The ready outlet of emigration has provided the remaining population with a reasonably satisfying standard of living and this has been responsible for an acquiescence in conditions of underdevelopment which are capable of considerable improvement. The absence, over the country as a whole, of severe population pressure on resources has failed to establish the need for drastic action, and has made the need for full development of our economic resources less compelling.[193]

This observation was one that was rarely mentioned in contemporary discussions of Irish migration to Britain. The movement of population out of rural Ireland ensured that any clamour for sustained policies which would spur on economic development was muted. The economic stagnation of underdeveloped areas in Ireland was perpetuated by continued migration and had these people stayed in at home, the demands for development would undoubtedly have been more vocal. The effect of high levels of emigration on national morale was also examined by the commission: 'The failure of the economy to support and retain a larger population and the fact that, at present, emigration amounts to more than one out of every three persons born, weakens national pride and confidence which of itself retards the efforts required for national progress.'[194]

Naturally, the commission could offer no miracle panacea to stem the exodus of people to Britain. As one former member of the commission, George Duncan, professor of economics at Trinity College, Dublin, remarked, the commission had shied away from outlining a 'simple, bold plan'.[195] Facile 'solutions' were shunned by the commission and its detailed findings relate to the broader economic and social environment rather than endeavouring to devise strategies aimed at discouraging emigration in particular.[196] For example, the recommendations on decentralisation of industry and of the state's administrative apparatus constituted a practical policy for the distribution of the available employment opportunities.[197] Another significant suggestion was that local authorities should try and ensure that public employment was of 'a more permanent character' in contrast with the sporadic and temporary work which had hitherto been available.[198] The commission also recognised that not all migration was a bad thing and that people leaving the country for employment elsewhere was an inevitable fact of life.[199] As regards the specific question of formulating a national population policy, the commission rejected direct intervention on the part of the state to influence population patterns, such as marriage loans or grants, on the grounds that 'the influences which determine population growth are matters which should properly depend upon personal decisions'.[200]

When each government department considered the reports of the commission, naturally the civil servants were anxious to defend previous policy positions and, of course, to protect their own fiefdoms. The Department of Agriculture boldly stated that 'the report contains nothing which is novel in its comments or recommendations on the subject of agriculture' and 'merely repeats the constant injunctions of the Department of Agriculture'.[201] The Land Commission, which had been the subject of much adverse criticism in Lucey's minority report, excoriated the Roman Catholic bishop of Cork for his sweeping statements and ill-founded analysis.[202] It is perhaps worth noting that a minority report prepared for the Commission on Banking, Currency and Credit, 1934–38, was subject to the same level of scorn from within the senior ranks of the civil service.[203] Lucey had recommended that 50,000 new holdings of 20 to 30 acres could be created by acquiring land from larger farms.[204] In the Land Commission's view, this proposal 'was so sweeping as to be entirely impolitic' and would cost somewhere in the region of £125 million.[205] However, the Department of Defence agreed with the commission's suggestions regarding the decentralisation of government departments outside Dublin from the point of view of defence:

> There is always a danger of a sudden attack without warning and in particular the threat of atomic bombing must be seriously considered. So long as Dublin continues to be the centre of administration, both governmental and commercial, and contains such a high proportion of the national population, there would be great danger from the defence point of view that the morale of the nation could be swiftly broken if this centre of administration were knocked out in the initial stages of attack.[206]

This was a valid observation but the commission had the question of rural depopulation in mind when it formulated this recommendation rather than atomic attack, which did not seem all that likely as the Irish Republic could hardly be regarded as a major player in the Cold War of the 1950s. The Department of Industry and Commerce accepted the principle of administrative decentralisation but noted that 'it is not feasible to decentralise any of the offices of the department'![207] The officials in this department then set about answering each of the commission's recommendations relating to the encouragement of industry and only one minor recommendation – the importance of manufacturing design – was endorsed.[208] The Department of Finance did not even bother to submit a memorandum for consideration.[209] The fact that government departments were still considering the reports of the Commission on Emigration and other Population Problems in July 1956, some two years after the document was first presented, is indicative of the dilatory approach to the subject.[210] An interdepartmental committee was instituted in the same month to examine further the recommendations but it appears that no subsequent action was taken.[211] No substantive recommendation contained in the majority report was ever put into practice, and the findings of the commission descended into relative obscurity, similar to the fate of the work of many other government-appointed commissions and committees.

The significance of the Commission on Emigration and Other Population Problems is twofold. Firstly, its establishment in March 1948 by the first inter-party government was an explicit acknowledgement by members of the Irish political élite that large-scale emigration was a structural feature of Irish society. Thus the commission was a landmark in the recognition on the part of the Irish body politic that emigration could not be attributed to British misrule or some ill-defined colonial legacy, but rather that people emigrated because of the economic and social circumstances in which they found themselves. Secondly, the commission represented an exhaustive (if not the most complete) examination of the economic and social structure of Irish rural society in the first half of the twentieth century. It conducted extensive surveys throughout the country in 1948 and 1949, received written evidence from a wide range of interested parties and agencies, including government departments, rural development organisations such as Muintir na Tíre, trade unions and women's organisations, and it also examined witnesses representing diverse points of view.[212] Politicians and civil servants recognised that it contained much sensible analysis relating to the broader context of Irish economic and social development, although the policy measures which the report identified as being the means to address the structural problems that rural Ireland faced were not taken up by the politicians of the day.

Whereas practical proposals which might reduce the level of Irish migration did not attract much attention from within the confines of the Irish political establishment, the Irish Roman Catholic hierarchy had taken steps in 1953 to ensure that the 'moral' and 'spiritual' welfare of Irish migrants was catered for. Perversely when this initiative to provide for migrants was first made known to the Irish government, a decision taken in December 1953 to appoint a welfare officer based at the Irish embassy in London was reversed in March 1954 on the convenient grounds that it would involve the duplication of effort.[213] Meanwhile, in June 1953 a committee of Irish bishops was established to liaise with the hierarchy of England and Wales to examine the question of whether more provision should be made for the spiritual welfare of Irish migrants in Britain.[214] In June 1954, Archbishop McQuaid appointed two social workers who were members of the Legion of Mary (a Catholic lay organisation) to investigate the position of the Irish in Britain.[215] By January 1955 the Irish hierarchy adopted McQuaid's proposals for a scheme to foster the Legion of Mary among Irish emigrants and for a co-ordinated programme of missions to be given by Irish priests in Britain.[216] This scheme was announced by Cardinal Bernard Griffin of Westminister in his pastoral letter for

Trinity Sunday, June 1955.[217] A pastoral letter was issued by the Irish hierarchy in the following month asking the faithful to pray for the success of these missions and warning intending emigrants of the possible dangers of travelling to Britain.[218] This mission work laid the foundations for the Irish emigrant chaplaincy scheme which was instituted in May 1957 and involved the placement of Irish priests in areas where large numbers of Irish workers were concentrated such as hostels, hotels and road building sites.[219] It can be seen, therefore, that after some delay, the Roman Catholic church in Ireland and Britain took concrete steps to make provision for the welfare of Irish migrants, and in some senses absolved the Irish state of responsibility in this regard; this was no doubt the source of some relief for civil servants and ministers alike.

Emigration to Britain was a live political issue in the postwar period. Travers has underlined the fact that in the campaign prior to the general election of February 1948, many speeches by opposition leaders were devoted to the subject in order to attack the record of the Fianna Fáil party.[220] According to Travers, 'in no general election before or since, even 1957, has emigration been a bigger issue'.[221] Fine Gael and Labour candidates roundly condemned the government's record on emigration in election speeches during the campaign, one Fine Gael candidate even going as far as to suggest that Fine Gael would end emigration. Clann na Poblachta, a party which did not offer an alternative vision but attacked 'the failure of Fianna Fáil to live up to the hopes vested in it', also criticised the government's record on emigration.[222] Rising emigration and the associated rural depopulation loomed large in their critique of the economic record of Fianna Fáil during the 1948 election. A Clann na Poblachta candidate declared that the Fianna Fáil slogan for young people could be 'to hell or to England', an original variant of Cromwell's famous declaration of 'to hell or to Connacht'.[223] But, as the newly installed inter-party government quickly discovered after entering office, bluster, rhetoric and promises did little to stem the haemorrhage. Of course, the inter-party government could point to the establishment of the Commission on Emigration and Other Population Problems in March 1948 as hard evidence of its commitment to 'solving' the emigration 'problem'. Throughout the period of office of the inter-party government, from February 1948 until June 1951, members of the opposition frequently inquired about the progress of the report of the commission in order to harry government ministers.[224] In April 1951, one prominent opposition member, Frank Aiken, made some political capital out of the long delay with the completion of the report: 'The coalition's alternative to doing something about emigration is to have a commission go out to inquire.'[225] But on the return to government of the Fianna Fáil party in June 1951, the tables were turned. In response to a parliamentary question in October 1951, the policy of the new government was outlined in vague if optimistic terms: 'The whole objective of the economic and social policy of the government and of the implementation of that policy through the various departments of state concerned is to create such economic and social conditions in this country as will lead to the stopping of emigration.'[226]

But clearly one of the first steps that was necessary to bring about a reduction in the levels of migration to Britain was increasing employment, especially in western Ireland. This was, however, particularly difficult in the economic climate of the late 1940s and the early 1950s. An initial postwar boom, from 1947 until 1951, was 'followed by a deflationary fiscal stance for most of the remainder of the 1950s'.[227] In 1952 a deflationery budget was introduced, subsidies on food were removed and both direct and indirect taxes were increased.[228] The fiscal policy adopted by the government had a deleterious effect on the building and construction industries as public expenditure was reduced.[229] In early 1953, as was noted above, unemployment peaked and in Dublin in particular, the slowdown in the construction industry led to the displacement of many workers. Unemployed workers took to the streets of Dublin and increasingly discussions of unemployment were coupled with discourses on the emigration 'problem'.[230] The Irish economy experienced a severe crisis in the 1950s and Kennedy observes that 'more so than the years of total war, the 1950s constituted the dark hour of nationalist Ireland'.[231]

It is within this context that the collection of essays edited by the Rev. John O'Brien and including contributions from writers such as Seán O'Faolain and Bryan MacMahon, entitled *The vanishing Irish*, was published in 1953.[232] This volume was in no way a professional study of demographic patterns, but rather a literary reflection on the perceived abnormal demographic trends. Yet it summed up a frequently articulated view that, if the Irish population continued to decline as a result of late and infrequent marriages and continued migration from Ireland, the 'Irish will virtually disappear as a nation and will be found only as an enervated remnant in a land occupied by foreigners'.[233] This improbable thesis was challenged in March 1954 by

R. C. Geary who noted in an acerbic comment that 'one would have thought that perhaps statisticians, economists or sociologists might have been found worthy of election to the august roster of contributors'.[234] One of the contributors, the Rev. Patrick Noonan, had asserted that 'the saddest feature of this tragedy [the decline in population] is the universal unconcern of the Irish themselves'.[235] As Geary caustically commented, 'if Fr Noonan had to sit for six years on a population commission he would not speak of unconcern'.[236] In reality, statistical evidence derived from the 1951 census illustrated the inaccuracy of these authors' assessment of Irish demographic trends since, as Geary pointed out, the 1951 census actually recorded a slight increase in the total population.[237] In addition, the high rate of marital fertility in the Irish Republic 'more than outweighed' the level of emigration and low marriage rate.[238] According to Geary, the statistical evidence available demonstrated that there was little chance of the Irish population vanishing: 'The Irishman [sic] domiciled in Ireland is not likely to vanish, or even to reduce his present population level in foreseeable time unless he is passed off into oblivion by the atomic bomb.'[239]

Geary was again in the fray at a symposium on the 'population problem' held in Dublin on 9 May 1954. He stated boldly that there was no 'good reason that the nation should have a guilt complex about the fact of emigration'.[240] He also illustrated the link between attitudes towards emigration and recent Irish history and in addition the ramifications for current thinking:

> Perhaps I have said enough to suggest that it is high time that the Irish people examined the validity of their traditional attitude toward emigration. This attitude is largely an inheritance from the long period of the struggle for independence. It was then an effective political argument. It had, in addition, some justification on economic and sociological grounds since emigration during the latter half of the nineteenth century was the sole cause of the continuing decline in population. In those days the view was tenable that the survival of the nation was endangered. It is quite otherwise today. It is reasonable and proper to aspire to a reduction in emigration; it is quite another matter to regard all emigration as bad.[241]

These remarks were widely reported in the national press, with some adverse reaction, the *Irish Times* referring to his views in an editorial as 'cynical comfort'.[242] Geary's discordant note in challenging the orthodoxy was in some ways reflected by the comments of John A. Costello, who had been taoiseach since June 1954. During a Dáil debate in July 1955, Costello noted that 'in recent years growing doubts have been cast on the previously held view that emigration was a bad thing in itself'.[243] It is evident that there was an increasing tendency to confront the causes of Irish migration, but also implicitly an acceptance of the inevitable reality of people leaving Ireland.

Such sentiments were, however, somewhat muted when the preliminary results of the 1956 census were published in June of the same year. As we noted at the outset of the present chapter, the 1956 census indicated a decline in the total population, explained principally by migration. Extensive newspaper coverage was devoted to the population decline and migration in particular; the *Irish Times* devoted at least three editorials to the subject in June 1956 and the other newspapers also provided extended analyses of the census findings.[244] The attitude of politicians on all sides was lambasted by the *Irish Times*:

> The remedy for this wasting disease, however, does not necessarily lie in the ejection of the present government – not, anyhow, until there is some reason to assume that Fianna Fáil will do any better. On the party's past record, there is no ground for that assumption . . . That is not to say that the inter-party government has justified itself. It is just as effective as Fianna Fáil at talking, and just as ineffective at getting things done . . . There was plenty of sense in the reports, majority and minority, of the emigration commission; but these reports might as well have been banned by the censorship board for all the respect that the government has paid them.[245]

The only way for the government to proceed, according to this leader writer, was through adoption of a national long-term policy for agriculture.[246] Indirectly responding to these criticisms, Costello read out long extracts from the reports of the Commission on Emigration in a speech in the Dáil which was essentially a defence of the economic policy of the second inter-party government (1954–57), but he noted that these reports were not a 'blueprint' nor did they offer 'any cut and dried solutions'.[247] What Costello advocated was the continuation of the policy of developing the resources of the country, creating employment opportunities and raising the average standard of living, all noble enough aspirations, although few specific details were outlined.[248]

The general election in March 1957 was dominated by the crisis which the Irish economy faced. Inevitably, the continued high rate of emigration was taken as evidence of the disastrous state of the Irish economy.[249] The return of Fianna Fáil to power marked the beginnings of economic planning in the Irish Republic, with the publication of T. K. Whitaker's *Economic Development* in 1958. The sense of despondency resulting from the upsurge in Irish migration to Britain, was one factor among many that heralded the first attempts at economic planning in Ireland. The effects of this policy, in turn, have implications for migration from Ireland in the 1960s, which shall be examined in the next chapter.

V

A common fear expressed by Irish civil servants and politicians during the war was that thousands of Irish migrants would be forced to return from Britain as soon as the hostilities ended. This was not to be the case owing to the acute labour shortage in Britain at this time. The *Economic Survey for 1947* identified this labour shortage and stressed the fact that in industries such as coal-mining the situation was particularly acute.[250] From 1945 to 1951, during the period of office of the Labour government, immigrants from the dominions, European Volunteer Workers, 'displaced' persons from continental Europe and migrants from Ireland helped meet the demand for labour.[251] The Royal Commission on Population, which reported in 1949, observed in the context of a discussion of future sources of immigrants that 'Éire is likely to be a continuing source of emigrants to Great Britain'.[252] This assessment was to prove extremely accurate. The 1951 British census recorded a total number of 537,709 persons who were born in the Irish Republic.[253] It was estimated by the Commission on Emigration that over 100,000 persons migrated from the Irish Republic to Britain between 1946 and 1951.[254] The Irish-born population in 1951 was concentrated within certain regions of Britain: Greater London, the West Midlands, Merseyside, south-east Lancashire, West Yorkshire and Tyneside accounted for more than half of the total Irish-born population.[255] The regional figures, however, conceal the fact that distinct concentrations of Irish migrants had developed in particular areas of these large urban settlements. For example in the borough of Paddington in London, 8.4 per cent of the population were Irish-born.[256] Given the small percentage relative to the total population, this does not imply that Irish ghettos as such existed, but rather that some areas of large cities contained clusters of Irish migrants.

Not surprisingly, taking account of the earlier discussion on the basis of the Irish data, the age profile of the Irish-born population in 1951 indicates that this was a grouping of young people for the most part. For females, nearly three-fifths were between the ages of 20 and 39 years, and roughly half of all Irish males were within the same age group.[257] Jackson has analysed the detailed census data for 1951 on the occupational structure of the Irish-born in Britain, although it should be said that no distinction is made between those born in the Irish Republic and migrants from Northern Ireland. In terms of male employment, the construction industry, metal manufacturing and 'general labouring' are the main categories in which Irish male migrants were represented. However, as Jackson notes, 'the broad pattern remains the same in that unskilled general labour is the typical employment for the Irishman in Britain but a far higher proportion are now found in skilled occupations, in administrative and commercial categories and in the professions than was formerly the case'.[258] For instance in England and Wales, one in ten doctors were born in Ireland.[259] The drive undertaken by the Ministry of Labour to recruit Irish women for nurse training both during and after the war is reflected in the census data: 11 per cent of Irish-born women in Britain were nurses or midwives.[260] There was an acute shortage of nurses for the National Health Service in postwar Britain: one official in the Ministry of Labour reckoned in January 1947 that somewhere in the region of 34,000 nurses were required.[261] Nevertheless, the majority of Irish women were not employed in the professions and worked in domestic service, clerical employment and manufacturing industries.[262] What is perhaps the most striking point to emerge from Jackson's detailed analysis is the sheer range of occupations in which Irish migrants were employed, although the largest share were still involved in the traditional occupations such as construction work and domestic service.

The legal status of Irish-born persons resident in Britain was a matter of some concern when the Irish taoiseach, John A. Costello, announced his intention during a press conference on 7 September 1948 in Ottawa to repeal the External Relations Act, 1936, thereby declaring Ireland a republic and breaking the link with the Commonwealth.[263] Whilst Irish political leaders made great political capital out of this move, the ramifications for Irish citizens living in Britain could have been far-reaching. If Ireland left the Commonwealth and thus became a 'foreign state', Irish migrants in Britain would have to be treated as aliens with the consequent requirement for an employment permit, registration with the police, and immigration control at points of entry.[264] An anonymous letter sent to Costello the day after he

introduced the Republic of Ireland Bill in parliament on 17 November 1948, as Fanning remarks, 'exposes the gulf separating the
world of Irish emigrants in Britain from the world of their erstwhile
political leaders':[265]

> I am an Irishman working in England. My foreman is an Englishman, my fel-
> low workers are English, I live with an English family.
>   Since your government announced its proposal to sever the last link with the
> crown and commonwealth, I have been asked questions by forementioned [sic]
> persons, viz. what are the advantages of such action by your gov[ernmen]t? All
> the disadvantages are outlined for me and a very gloomy list it is for us, report-
> ing to the Ploice [sic] station, having to return to Ireland, unemployment, a
> lower standard of living.[266]

In the event, the British government decided that it would not treat
Ireland as a foreign country or its citizens as 'foreigners', and Irish citizens retained a special non-foreign status under the Ireland Act of
1949.[267] In addition, this legislation ensured that Irish citizens, who
were no longer British subjects, were to be treated with the same rights
as those conferred on them under the British Nationality Act of 1948,
notwithstanding the fact that the Irish Republic had left the Commonwealth.[268] As a number of authors have observed, this granted
Irish citizens a unique legal status since the Irish Republic was no
longer part of the Commonwealth, yet its citizens could still enter
Britain and take up employment without restrictions and were entitled to the same welfare and voting rights as British citizens.[269]
Whether this anomaly was the result of an appreciation by the British
authorities of the sheer difficulties involved in enforcing immigration
controls of the demand for Irish labour or of a perception that white
workers were in some senses preferable to migrants from Africa, the
Indian sub-continent or the Caribbean is a matter of debate. Several
studies point to the fact that the Labour government was less than
eager to encourage workers from British colonies to come to the
'mother country' despite the fact that there was a serious shortage of
labour.[270] In private, civil servants expressed disquiet that immigration
from the 'New Commonwealth' would result in racial 'tensions', but in
public at least the Labour government was committed to an 'open
door' policy and no action to restrict entry was taken.[271]
    By the mid-1950s the level of immigration from the Common-
wealth precipitated the formulation of a policy towards immigration
and this necessarily had implications for Irish migrants. In the context of an increase in West Indian immigration to Britain from 1954

onwards the question of controls was raised both in parliament and among civil servants and ministers.[272] An interdepartmental working party, which dealt directly with the issue of Irish migration to Britain, reported to the Conservative cabinet in August 1955 on the 'problems arising from the growing influx into the United Kingdom of coloured workers from other Commonwealth countries'. It was noted that Irish immigration since the war 'had been very heavy' and estimated that in the period from July 1954 to June 1955, some 58,700 Irish people had entered the British national insurance scheme for the first time.[273] However, a telling and revealing distinction was made between Irish and black migrants:

> Many of the Irish are accustomed to living in their own country in conditions which English people would not normally tolerate and are accordingly less discriminating in their choice of accommodation here. There have been a number of complaints from local authorities that they live in condemned premises and by doing so establish a prior claim on the local authorities' resources of accommodation. When all this has been said, however, it cannot be held that the same difficulties arise in the case of the Irish as in the case of coloured people. For instance, an Irishman looking for lodgings is, generally speaking, not likely to have any more difficulty than an Englishman, whereas the coloured man is often turned away. In fact, the outstanding difference is that the Irish are not – whether they like or not – a different race from the ordinary inhabitants of Great Britain, and indeed one of the difficulties in any attempt to estimate the economic and social consequences of the influx from the Republic would be to define who is Irish.[274]

The accuracy of the statement regarding accommodation is open to question: Michael Banton, the distinguished British sociologist, noticed more 'no Irish' than 'no coloured' signs when completing fieldwork in Sparkbrook in Birmingham during July 1952, although admittedly this was prior to large-scale immigration from the Caribbean and elsewhere.[275] It is particularly noteworthy that a distinction was made between the Irish migrants and other migrant groupings in terms of 'race'. This benevolent view in relation to Irish migrants contrasted sharply with a report from the Irish ambassador, Boland, earlier in the year which had observed that, if restrictions were imposed on the immigration of British subjects, 'the regulations or restrictions would certainly be applied to Irish citizens to the same, if not a greater extent'.[276] It was also suggested by the interdepartmental committee that if legislation to control immigration were introduced, citizens from the Irish Republic should be excluded as the 'Irish not only provide much needed labour, but have always done so', and the imposition of controls would 'be tiresome' for the thousands of travellers who traversed the Irish Sea each year, let alone the problem of the staffing implications.[277] Layton-Henry is surely correct to point to the inherent implications of the working party's analysis: 'It is extraordinary that, at a time when Irish immigration was estimated to be 60,000 a year, immigration controls should have been considered in order to prevent the entry of a mere 3,000 people who, as colonial and Commonwealth citizens, were British subjects.'[278] It could also be argued that the historical and geographical relationship between the two countries established a precedent for the 'special' treatment of Irish migrants, although skin colour and the perceived lack of a distinctive ethnicity were the overriding determinants. Nevertheless, when the government outlined its position in November 1955, the prime minister, Anthony Eden, stated that no legislation to control immigration was envisaged at that particular point in time and, in fact, he noted that the largest number of immigrants were from Ireland rather than elsewhere.[279]

Inevitably, the controversy surrounding immigration from the Commonwealth did not rest there. Beyond the gaze of parliament and the public, Eden appointed a committee of ministers in November 1955 under the chairmanship of Lord Kilmuir, the lord chancellor, to consider 'what form legislation should take, if it were decided that legislation to control the entry into the United Kingdom of British subjects from overseas should be introduced'. It was also instructed to explore other allied matters such as the effectiveness of legislative action and how such legislation 'could be justified to parliament, the public and the Commonwealth countries concerned'.[280] After reviewing the various issues at some length, the majority of the committee concluded that 'control over coloured immigration will eventually be inescapable, but that balance of advantage lies against imposing it now'.[281] The Kilmuir committee recognised that if legislation were introduced, the position of Irish citizens would be anomalous but observed 'that this could be defended on the grounds of proximity and the practical problems which it generates'.[282] There was obviously some unease within the cabinet regarding the exemption of Irish citizens from possible controls, as well as the public perception of this anomaly, as the committee of ministers examined this issue in a later supplementary report. This report found that 'there are sound and convincing practical reasons for continuing to exclude citizens from the Irish Republic from immigration control, even if it is eventually decided to regulate the entry of Commonwealth citizens'.[283] These reasons included the sheer difficulties involved in the regulation of passenger traffic, the border between the Republic and Northern Ireland, and the staff needed to regulate controls, but perhaps of most importance, the 'ready flow of Irish labour ... which has long been a vital source of manpower to industries and services in Great Britain'.[284] But one other fundamental issue was at stake: 'It is also to be noted that the presence in the United Kingdom of comparatively large numbers of Irish Republican [sic] citizens does not give rise to the same kind of problems or forebodings as the presence here of similar numbers of coloured people might be thought to justify.'[285]

The unrestricted entry of Irish migrants was therefore justified on three quite distinct grounds. Firstly, it would be difficult in practice to impose a set of controls. Secondly, Irish migrant workers were a valuable source of labour, in particular for certain industries. Lastly, and perhaps most importantly, Irish migrants were white and it was perceived that the entry of Irish citizens would not result in tension on the part of the British population. Another group of members of the Conservative party – albeit a less powerful one – did not view the matter in the same light. The 'Birmingham Young Conservatives' in their report in October 1956 on 'the problem of coloured peoples in Britain' argued that controls should be applied to all immigrants seeking to enter Britain, including workers from Ireland.[286] The housing situation in Birmingham was extremely acute at this time which explains the desire to limit all forms of immigration to Britain regardless of the country of origin. An Irish embassy official who paid a visit to Birmingham in June 1956 for the purpose of assessing the position of the Irish community there observed that the lack of housing was 'chronic'.[287] Without doubt, if the pool of available housing were limited, tensions would arise when immigrants sought suitable accommodation.

What was the actual day-to-day experience of Irish migrants in Britain? In an effort to assess the economic and social conditions of Irish migrants, the Commission on Emigration undertook an investigation in late 1948. Stanley Lyon travelled to Britain and visited a number of factories, hospitals and building sites and interviewed those with special knowledge of the situation of Irish workers such as clerics and officials of the British Ministry of Labour and the Home Office.[288] What is perhaps most revealing is the fact that for the greater part the report is concerned with the views of clerics and officials rather than with those of the migrants themselves. Lyon observed that those engaged in factory work were well catered for by their employers and the working environment was 'far ahead of anything provided for factory workers in Ireland'.[289] Men who worked in construction and civil engineering were found to be earning good wages and 'the employers gave the Irish workers full credit for their hard work'.[290] When he discussed female migrants, Lyon's prejudices came to the fore: 'There is a great temptation in the path of those young girls who suddenly find themselves in England with no restrictions as regards late hours or associations. Many of the unwary got into bad company soon after the arrival and the sequel was bad.'[291] It should be said that much of this analysis relating to females was based on the accounts of clerics and nuns involved with Irish migrants. Such persons tended to highlight the problem cases rather than the majority of Irish migrants who never came to their attention. The most striking conclusion to emerge from Lyon's report is the relative prosperity of Irish migrants in November 1948 despite the fact that he had a tendency to underline the negative aspects of life in Britain. It should be noted that for many the stay in Britain was viewed as a temporary expedient: oral testimony of Irish migrants who came to London in the 1950s demonstrates that most migrants only anticipated staying in Britain for a short period.[292] Whether in fact this turned out to be the case was determined by economic conditions at home, marriage and possible future opportunities in Britain.

VI

Irish migrants proved to be a useful pool of largely unskilled labour which helped meet the shortage that Britain experienced during the immediate postwar period. Why people left Ireland has been examined at some length in this chapter on the basis of the local surveys conducted as part of the inquiries of the Commission on Emigration and other Population Problems. The principal finding which emerges from the plethora of so-called 'causes' is that the lack of steady employment was of crucial significance, both for females and males. Dissatisfaction with the economic and social conditions in Ireland is also evident, especially when compared with the higher rates of remuneration available for unskilled employment in Britain. Information about the migrant lifestyle in Britain percolated back to friends and relatives, and undoubtedly was a determinant of migration; this was particularly so in areas with high rates of out-migration. Once the decision to migrate was arrived at, the pathways established during the Second World War eased the dislocation and natural apprehension experienced by those who travelled to Britain.

The reaction to large-scale Irish migration to Britain can be assessed on a number of levels. The political reaction was predictably based along political lines, although clearly its impact was greatest in terms of public opinion. It is perhaps worth noting that all interested parties looked to the government of the day to devise a policy that would stem the flow. Therefore, the state was regarded as the focal point for all representations in relation to migration from Ireland. Whereas in the war years, large-scale Irish migration to Britain was regarded as a temporary phenomenon, in the immediate postwar period it was recognised not only that people were still leaving Ireland but that they were doing so in greater numbers. Few 'solutions' were advanced and the lukewarm response from the body politic to the detailed reports of the Commission on Emigration when they were first made available in July 1954 is indicative of the lack of any concrete programme to develop non-agricultural employment which might have absorbed some of these migrants. However, the institution of the commission by the inter-party government in March 1948 was an attempt to come to grips with the issue. It must be remembered at this point that the independent Irish state had been in existence barely 25 years. The principal contribution made by the Commission on Emigration was to investigate fully the broader economic and social factors that were determinants in the migration of persons out of Ireland. Naturally, it was beyond the remit of the commission to devise policies which in essence were concerned with the complete economic structure of the country. The inaction on the part of the state in terms of the provision of welfare facilities precipitated the institution of measures in 1955 by the Roman Catholic church, both in Ireland and Britain, which would ensure that the 'moral' and 'spiritual' needs of Irish migrants were catered for.

That the British authorities were keen to secure Irish labour is illustrated by the 'special position' afforded Irish citizens wishing to travel to Britain. Even though immigrants from the Caribbean and Africa constituted a minor element of the total flow, both the Labour government under Attlee and the two Conservative governments led by Churchill and Eden respectively seriously considered imposing

immigration controls on them, despite the fact that the greater proportion of immigrants were coming from Britain's nearest neighbour.
However, the significant difference was that the Irish were white and
this ensured that the 'open door' policy continued in force. In addition, as was frequently posited by British officials, there was a historical precedent for unrestricted entry of Irish persons to Britain. As
immigration from the Commonwealth increased in the mid- to late
1950s, so too did Irish migration to Britain.

NOTES

1 This material is taken from an interview with Christina Pamment in Pam
Schweitzer, ed., 'Across the Irish sea', 2nd edn, London, 1991, pp. 146–52.
    2 For a useful review, see Alistair Thomson, 'Moving stories: oral history and
migration studies', Oral History, vol. 27, 1999, pp. 24–37.
    3 Schweitzer, 'Across the Irish sea', p. 149.
    4 Ibid.
    5 Ibid., p. 151.
    6 Censuses of population of Ireland, 1946 and 1951: general report, Dublin, 1958, Pr.
4511, p. 16.
    7 Census of population of Ireland, 1956, I: population, area and valuation of each dis-
trict electoral division and of each larger unit of area, Dublin, 1957, Pr. 3983, table x, p. xi.
    8 The intercensal period 1946–51 was slightly less than five years and total net
emigration was 119,568 (Commission on Emigration, Reports, p. 115, table 86, note a).
    9 For further discussion of this point, see Censuses of population of Ireland, 1946
and 1951: general report, p. 38.
    10 Ibid.
    11 Census of population of Ireland, 1956, I: population, area and valuation ..., table
x, p. xxi.
    12 Commission on Emigration, Reports, table 86, p. 115.
    13 Travel identity cards were introduced as a replacement for travel permits in
June 1947 (Commission on Emigration, Reports, app. vi, p. 267).
    14 Ibid., app. vi, p. 267.
    15 Ibid., p. 128.
    16 [R. C. Geary], 'Statistics of emigration and passenger movement', Irish Trade
Journal and Statistical Bulletin, n.v., June 1951, pp. 83–84.
    17 J. G. Hughes, Estimates of annual net migration and their relationship with series
on annual net passenger movement: Ireland 1926–76, Dublin, 1977, ESRI memorandum
no. 122, p. 28.
    18 Commission on Emigration, Reports, table 27, p. 317.
    19 Ibid. Migration patterns from 1921 onwards to places other than Britain and

the United States remain largely *terra incognita*, but for Australia, see Seamus Grimes, 'Postwar Irish immigrants in Australia: the Sydney experience', in *The Irish-Australian connection*, ed. Seamus Grimes and Gearóid Ó Tuathaigh, Dublin, 1989, pp. 137–59, and his 'Postwar Irish immigration in Australia', in *Contemporary Irish migration*, ed. Russell King, GSI special publications no. 6, Dublin, 1991, pp. 42–54; A. J. Rose, 'Irish migration to Australia in the twentieth century', *Ir. Geog.*, vol. 4, 1959, pp. 79–84. For the Irish in New Zealand, see D. H. Akenson, *Half the world from home: perspectives on the Irish in New Zealand, 1860–1950*, Wellington, 1990 and for Irish in Canada, see Akenson, *The Irish diaspora: a primer*, Belfast, 1993, pp. 259–69.

  20 Julius Issac, *British postwar migration*, Cambridge, 1954, table 58, p. 117.

  21 The emigration rates for the two time periods are positively correlated (a Pearson product-moment correlation coefficient of 0.51, with 26 observations).

  22 *Censuses of population of Ireland, 1946 and 1951: general report*, p. 40.

  23 *Census of population of Ireland, 1956, I: population, area and valuation ...*, p. xxii.

  24 Cormac Ó Grada and Brendan Walsh, 'The economic effects of emigration: Ireland', in *Emigration and its effects on the sending country*, ed. Beth J. Asch, Santa Monica, 1994, p. 101.

  25 Commission on Emigration, *Reports*. Without doubt, R. C. Geary prepared much, if not all, of this statistical material.

  26 Pauric Travers is the only Irish historian to have consulted *some* of this documentation, but he made relatively little use of it (see Pauric Travers, ' "There was nothing for me there": Irish female emigration, 1922–71', in *Irish women and Irish migration*, ed. Patrick O'Sullivan, part IV of the seres, *The Irish worldwide, history, heritage and identity*, London, 1995, pp. 146–67).

  27 Commission on Emigration, *Reports*, p. 2.

  28 Issac, *British postwar migration*, p. 194.

  29 TCD, MS 8306, S.2, rural survey: Kilkenny, conducted by J. J. Byrne and F. O'Leary, n.d. [Oct. 1948], p. 1.

  30 Ibid.

  31 Ibid.

  32 TCD, MS 8306, S.1, rural survey: Mayo and Sligo, conducted by J. P. Beddy, n.d. [Oct. 1948], p. 3.

  33 Ibid., p. 4.

  34 Ibid.

  35 Ibid.

  36 Ibid.

  37 TCD, MS 8301, summaries of evidence: reports from employment exchange managers, R.24 Carrick-on-Shannon, n.d., p. 33.

  38 TCD, MS 8306, S.2, rural survey: Leitrim and Donegal, conducted by R. C. Geary and F. O'Leary, 23–25 Sept. 1948, p. 1.

  39 Ibid.

  40 TCD, MS 8301, summaries of evidence: M.36 County Leitrim Vocational Educational Committee, n.d., pp. 3–4.

  41 TCD, MS 8306, S.2, rural survey: Leitrim and Donegal, p. 3.

  42 Ibid.

  43 Ibid.

  44 TCD, MS 8301, summaries of evidence: reports from employment exchange

managers, R.20 Letterkenny, n.d., p. 32.

45 TCD, MS 8306, S.2, rural survey: Leitrim and Donegal, p. 3.

46 Ibid., p. 4.

47 TCD, MS 8306, S.11, Tuam, conducted by John McElhinney, n.d., p. 1.

48 Ibid.

49 TCD, MS 8306, S.11, Galway, conducted by John McElhinney, n.d., p. 1.

50 Ibid.

51 TCD, MS 8306, rural surveys: S.7, Loughrea and Birr, conduced by Cornelius Lucey, n.d., p. 1.

52 Damian Hannan, 'Irish emigration since the war', typescript of unpublished RTE Thomas Davis lecture, [1973], p. 9.

53 TCD, MS 8306, rural surveys: S.22, Clare, conducted by Thomas Counihan, SJ, Oct. 1948, pp. 1–2.

54 Commission on Emigration, *Reports*, p. 130.

55 TCD, MS 8306, rural surveys: S.10, county Cork employment exchanges, conducted by Cornelius Lucey and M. D. McCarthy, n.d. [Oct. 1948], p. 10.

56 Ibid., p. 9.

57 Ibid., p.5.

58 TCD, MS 8301, summaries of evidence: reports from employment exchange managers, R.27 Cahirciveen, n.d., p. 35.

59 Ibid.

60 TCD, MS 8306, rural surveys: S.6, Killarney and Tralee, conducted by W. A. Honohan, p. 3.

61 TCD, MS 8307/1, transcripts of evidence: D. Kennedy, Chairman, Tipperary County Council (South Riding), 29 Oct. 1948, p. 1.

62 Ibid., p. 170.

63 TCD, MS 8306, rural surveys: S.18, Newbridge, conducted by F. O'Leary, n.d. [Oct. 1948], p. 3.

64 Ibid., pp. 2–3.

65 TCD, MS 8306, rural surveys: S.9, Edenderry and neighbourhood, conducted by Arnold Marsh, n.d., p. 1.

66 TCD, MS 8306, rural surveys: S.16, Athlone, conducted by the secretariat, n.d., p. 1.

67 TCD, MS 8306, rural surveys: S.1, Mayo and Sligo, p. 4.

68 TCD, MS 8306, rural surveys: S.11, Tuam, p. 1

69 Commission on Emigration, *Reports*, p. 79.

70 Ibid.

71 For a lucid survey of twentieth-century Irish marriage patterns, see B. M. Walsh, 'Marriage in Ireland in the twentieth century', in *Marriage in Ireland*, ed. Art Cosgrove, Dublin, 1985, pp. 132–50.

72 See K. H. Connell, 'Catholicism and marriage in Ireland in the century after the famine', in Connell, ed., *Irish peasant society: four historical essays*, Oxford, 1968, pp. 113–61; for a recent reinterpretation, see Timothy W. Guinnane, *The vanishing Ireland: households, migration, and the rural economy in Ireland, 1850–1914*, Princeton, 1997, pp. 191–240.

73 TCD, MS 8306, rural surveys: S.15, Longford, conduced by J. J. Byrne and F. O'Leary, n.d., p.1.

74 TCD, MS 8306, rural surveys: S.4, Leitrim and Donegal, p. 2. Although the respondent was interviewed in Leitrim, she was actually from county Sligo.

75 Commission on Emigration, *Reports*, p. 175.

76 TCD, MS 8306, rural surveys: S.5, Clonmel, Arklow and Wexford, Sept. 1948, p. 9.

77 TCD, MS 8306, rural surveys: S.8, Waterford, Dungarvan, New Ross, Carrick-on-Suir, Enniscorthy, Carlow and Bagenalstown, n.d., p. 2.

78 NAI, DT S 11582 D, Department of Social Welfare, memorandum for the government: control on emigration to employment in Great Britain, 19 July 1952, p. 1.

79 Issac, *British postwar migration*, p. 194.

80 Damian Hannan, *Rural exodus: a study of the forces influencing the large-scale migration of Irish rural youth*, London, 1970.

81 Detailed data are available for only 208 cases.

82 Calculated from TCD, MS 8306, rural surveys.

83 TCD, MS 8306, rural surveys: S.19, Tullow, p. 2.

84 Monica Boyd, 'Family and personal networks in international migration: recent developments and new agendas', *IMR*, vol. 23, 1989, p. 639.

85 TCD, MS 8306, rural surveys: S.22, Clare, p. 6.

86 TCD, MS 8306, rural surveys: S.1, Mayo and Sligo, p. 9.

87 Calculated from TCD, MS 8306, rural surveys.

88 William Ashworth, *History of the British coalmining industry, V: 1946–82, the nationalised industry*, Oxford, 1986, pp. 163–64; on the European Volunteer Workers and other 'displaced persons', see Diana Kay and Robert Miles, *Refugees or migrant workers? European Volunteer Workers in Britain, 1946–51*, London, 1992 and Colin Holmes, *John Bull's Island: immigration and British society, 1871–1971*, Basingstoke, 1988, pp. 212–14.

89 Commission on Emigration, *Reports*, p. 172.

90 Edward Nevin, *Wages in Ireland, 1946–62*, ESRI paper no. 12, Dublin, 1963, pp. 10–11.

91 TCD, MS 8306, rural surveys: S.4, Leitrim and Donegal, p. 3.

92 TCD, MS 8306, rural surveys: S.19, Tullow, p. 2.

93 Commission on Emigration, *Reports*, p. 36.

94 Ibid.

95 TCD, MS 8306, rural surveys: S.20, returned female emigrants, p. 1.

96 TCD, MS 8306, rural surveys: S.11, Tuam, p. 1

97 TCD, MS 8306, rural surveys: S.8, Waterford, Dungarvan, New Ross, Carrick-on-Suir, Enniscorthy, Carlow and Bagenalstown, conducted by Stanley Lyon, n.d., p. 2.

98 Commission on Emigration, *Reports*, p. 138.

99 TCD, MS 8307/3, transcripts of evidence: Irish Housewives' Association, n.d. [Dec. 1948], p. 3.

100 TCD, MS 8307/8, transcripts of evidence: Irish Women Workers' Union, n.d. [Dec. 1948], p. 4.

101 Peter Moser, 'Rural economy and female emigration in the west of Ireland, 1936–1956', *UCG Women's Studies Review*, vol. 2, 1993, p. 44.

102 Travers, ' "There was nothing for me there" ', p. 151.

103 Ibid., p. 163.

104 Bronwen Walter, *Gender and Irish migration to Britain*, Geography Working Paper no. 4, School of Geography, Anglia Higher Education College, Cambridge, 1989, p. 20.

105 Hannan, 'Irish emigration since the war', p. 3.

106 Commission on Emigration, *Reports*, p. 142.

107 Mary Daly, *Women and work in Ireland*, Dublin, 1997, pp. 50–51.

108 Commission on Emigration, *Reports*, p. 171.

109 Mary E. Daly, 'Women in the Irish workforce from pre-industrial to modern times', *Saothar*, vol. 7, 1987, pp. 80–81.

110 For a fascinating comparative example of this pattern of female migration *mutatis mutandis*, see Jennifer Luby and Oded Stark, 'Individual migration as a family strategy: young women in the Philippines', *Population Studies*, Vol. 42, 1988, pp. 473–86.

111 NAI, DT S11582 B, Department of Social Welfare: memorandum on growth of emigration control, 22 July 1947, p. 1.

112 Issac, *British postwar migration*, p. 194.

113 Commission on Emigration, *Reports*, pp. 268–69.

114 NAI, DT S 11582 B, Department of Social Welfare: memorandum on restrictions on emigration to employment, 15 Dec. 1947, p. 1.

115 NAI, DT S 11582 B, Department of Social Welfare: memorandum on growth of emigration control, 22 July 1947, p. 2.

116 NAI, DT S 11582 B, Department of Social Welfare: memorandum on restrictions on emigration to employment, 15 Dec. 1947, p. 1.

117 NAI, DT S 11582 B, Department of External Affairs: memorandum for the government [on female emigration], 30 Aug. 1947, p. 8.

118 Ibid., pp. 4–5.

119 Ibid., p. 8.

120 NAI, DT S 11582 B, Department of External Affairs, memorandum on emigration, 30 Dec. 1947, pp. 20–21.

121 Ibid., pp. 21–22.

122 NAI, DT S 15398 A, copy of letter from Dr James Staunton to Eamon de Valera, 13 Oct. 1947.

123 NAI, DT S 15398 A, copy of a letter from de Valera to Staunton, 16 Feb. 1948.

124 Ibid.

125 *Irish Catholic Directory, 1948*, 7 Oct. 1947, p. 731.

126 Ibid., 16 Nov. 1947, p. 737.

127 The response of the Church of Ireland to the migration of its members will be examined in the following chapter.

128 The idea for such a commission was no doubt related to the fact that a Royal Commission on Population was established by the British government in 1944.

129 NAI, DT S 11582 C, extract from cabinet minutes, GC 5/2, 24 Feb. 1948.

130 Commission on Emigration, *Reports*, p. 1.

131 *Report of the Royal Commission on Population*, 1948–49, Cmd. 7695, XIX, 635, p. iii.

132 *Irish Times*, 25 Mar. 1948; *Irish Independent*, 24 Mar. 1948; *Irish Press*, 24 Apr. 1948; on the disquiet regarding the composition of the commission, see Pauric

Travers, ' "The dream gone bust": Irish responses to emigration, 1922–60', in *Irish-Australian studies: papers delivered at the fifth Irish Australian conference*, ed. Oliver Mac-Donagh and W. F. Mandle, Canberra, 1989, pp. 329–30. De Blacam died in January 1951.

133 For biographical details, see the following works: on Geary, J. E. Spencer, 'Aspects of the life and personality of R. C. Geary', *Econ. Soc. Rev.*, vol. 24, 1993, pp. 215–24; on the others, see Henry A. Boylan, ed., *A dictionary of Irish biography*, 2nd edn, Dublin, 1988.

134 NAI, DFA 402/218/4, copy of letter from Secretary, Department of External Affairs to Secretary, Department of Social Welfare, 27 Oct. 1948.

135 NAI, DFA Secretary's files, P.15 (ii), memorandum on emigration ban prepared by unnamed member of the commission, n.d. [Nov. 1948], p. 1.

136 Ibid., p. 3.

137 Ibid., p. 4.

138 NAI, DFA 402/218/4, memorandum for the government: emigration of Irish girls for employment in Britain, 30 Sept. 1948, p. 4.

139 See, for example, NAI, DFA Secretary's files, P.15 (ii), Archbishop McQuaid to Seán MacBride, 22 Nov. 1948.

140 For an analysis of Clann na Poblachta, see Michael Gallagher *Electoral support for Irish political parties, 1927–1973*, London, 1976, pp. 55–58; see also Eithne Mac-Dermott, *Clann na Poblachta*, Cork, 1998; David McCullagh, *A makeshift majority: the first inter-party government, 1948–51*, Dublin, 1998; Kevin Rafter, *The Clann: the story of Clann na Poblachta* Cork, 1996.

141 NAI, DFA 402/218/4, copy of letter from Seán MacBride to the Rev. T. J. Counihan, S.J., Feb. 1949 [exact date not on copy].

142 The reservations of the government departments are outlined in NAI, DFA 402/218/4, copy of a letter from Secretary, Department of External Affairs to Secretary, Department of Social Welfare, 27 Oct. 1948, pp. 1–2.

143 'Notes and queries: the morality of a state ban on the emigration of minors', *Irish Ecclesiastical Record*, 5th series, vol. 71, 1949, pp. 269–72.

144 Commission on Emigration, *Reports*, p. 142.

145 *Irish Times*, 9 Dec. 1949.

146 Ruth Barrington, *Health, medicine and politics in Ireland, 1900–1970*, Dublin, 1987, pp. 200–01; for the programme of house building, see Mary Daly, *The buffer state: the historical roots of the Department of the Environment*, Dublin, 1997, pp. 337–79.

147 Departments of Health and Local Government, *Ireland is building*, Dublin, n.d. [1949], p. 2.

148 NAI, DFA 366/118, teleprinter message from J. G. Molloy (London) to C. C. O'Brien (Dublin), 8 Feb. 1950.

149 *Irish Times*, 2 Jan. 1950; *Irish Independent*, 2 Jan. 1950; *The Standard*, 6 Jan. 1950.

150 NAI, DFA 366/118, script of a talk given by M. J. Keyes, minister for local government, in the Radio Éireann series, 'Ireland is building', 29 Jan. 1950.

151 *Daily Express*, 16 Jan. 1950.

152 *Irish Independent*, 10 Jan. 1950; *Irish Press*, 18 Jan. 1950; *Irish Times*, 11 Jan. 1950.

153 NAI, DFA 366/118, teleprinter message from J. G. Molloy (London) to

B. Durnin (Dublin), with comments by C. C. O'Brien, 16 Jan. 1950.

154 *Irish Press*, 6 July 1950.

155 For more details on his ministerial career, see E. J. B. Rose and Nicholas Deakin, with others, *Colour and citizenship: a report on British race relations*, London, 1969, pp. 511–12.

156 NAI, DFA 402/222, some notes on the situation of Irish workers in Birmingham, prepared by Maurice Foley, n.d [July 1951], p. 2.

157 Ibid.

158 Ibid., p. 3.

159 Ibid., p. 5.

160 Ibid.

161 NAI, DFA 402/222, F. H. Boland (Irish ambassador to Britain) to Secretary, Department of External Affairs, 23 July 1951, p. 1.

162 NAI, DFA 402/222, text issued to the press of the taoiseach's statement at Galway, 30 Aug. 1951.

163 NAI, DFA 402/222, Boland to Secretary, Department of External Affairs, 23 July 1951, p. 4.

164 *Irish Times*, 31 Aug. 1951; *Irish Press*, 31 Aug. 1951; *Irish Independent*, 31 Aug. 1951; *Evening Herald*, 30 Aug. 1951; *Daily Mail*, 30 Aug. 1951; *Daily Telegraph*, 30 Aug. 1951; *Daily Herald*, 30 Aug. 1951; *The Times*, 30 Aug. 1951.

165 NAI, DFA 402/222, text issued to the press of the taoiseach's statement at Galway, 30 Aug. 1951, p. 2.

166 Kevin O'Rourke, 'Did labour flow uphill?: International migration and wage rates in twentieth-century Ireland', in *Labour market evolution: the economic history of market integration, wage flexibility and the employment relation*, ed. George Grantham and Mary MacKinnon, London, 1994, pp. 142–47.

167 PRO, DO 35/3917, G. W. Tory (British Embassy, Dublin) to N. E. Costar (Commonwealth Relations Office), 31 Aug. 1951.

168 Ibid., p. 3.

169 PRO, DO 35/3917, comment upon memorandum submitted by Irish Republican [*sic*] Chargé d'Affaires . . ., n.d. [Sept. 1951], pp. 2–3.

170 Ibid.

171 PRO, DO 35/3917, telegram no. 85, HM Chargé d'Affaires for UK in Dublin to Commonwealth Relations Office, 5 Sept. 1951.

172 PRO, DO 35/3917, memorandum on living conditions of Irish employees in midland cities, 5 Nov. 1951, p. 3.

173 PRO, DO 35/3917, extract from note by Mr Harris-Green (the United Kingdom Officer for Labour in Dublin), 5 Oct. 1951.

174 PRO, DO 35/3917, memorandum on living conditions of Irish employees . . ., p. 3.

175 NAI, DFA 402/218/4, memorandum: problems arising in connection with Irish workers in Britain, Nov. 1953, p. 2.

176 Ibid.

177 Ibid.

178 NAI, DT S 11582 F, draft statement on emigration and the flight from the land, 15 Apr. 1954, p. 1.

179 *Dáil Éireann deb.*, CXXXV (4 Dec. 1952), col. 736. *Dáil Éireann deb.*, CXXXVI

(4 Feb. 1953), col. 13; *Dáil Éireann deb.*, CXXXVI (11 Feb. 1953), cols 702–04.

180 *Dáil Éireann deb.*, LXXXVI (11 Feb. 1953), col. 701. Some of this increase can be explained by the fact that unemployment is generally higher in January than other months and also the coming into operation of the Social Welfare Act, 1952, which extended unemployment coverage to male agricultural workers and domestic servants; for further details, see Adrian Kelly, 'Social security in independent Ireland, 1922–52', unpub. PhD thesis, National University of Ireland, Maynooth, 1996, pp. 249–54.

181 NAI, DT S 11582 D, M. Ó Muimhneachain (Secretary, Department of the Taoiseach) to R. C. Geary (Director, Central Statistics Office), 23 Feb. 1953.

182 NAI, DT S 11582 D, memorandum for the government: methods of compilation of emigration statistics, 5 May 1953, p. 4.

183 Ibid., p. 5.

184 Ibid.

185 Cornelius Lucey's minority report was received in July 1954, hence the delay with the circulation of the reports in stencilled form. A printed version of the reports was published in October 1955 (*Dáil Éireann deb.*, CLIX (25 July 1956), col. 1708).

186 *Irish Independent*, 13–31 July 1954.

187 *The Leader*, 31 July 1954, p. 7, 4 Aug. 1954, p. 4, 28 Aug. 1954, pp. 18–19.

188 NAI, DT S 14249 A/2, extract from cabinet minutes, GC 7/16, 9 Aug. 1954.

189 For a very useful review of the findings of the commission, see W. J. L. Ryan, 'Some Irish population problems', *Population Studies*, vol. 9, 1955, pp. 185–88.

190 Commission on Emigration, *Reports*, p. 135.

191 Ibid., p. 137.

192 Ibid., p. 139.

193 Ibid.

194 Ibid., p. 141.

195 'Symposium on the Report of the Commision on Emigration and other Population Problems', *JSSISI*, vol. 19, 109th session, 1955–56, p. 108. Duncan had resigned from the commission in December 1948.

196 For a list of the detailed recommendations, see Commission on Emigration, *Reports*, pp. 189–90.

197 Ibid., pp. 14–15.

198 Ibid., p. 170.

199 Ibid., p. 142.

200 Ibid., p. 185.

201 NAI, D. Ind. & Comm., E 26/1/14/A, Office of the minister for agriculture, memorandum for the government: report of the Commission on Emigration and other Population Problems, 3 July 1956, p. 4.

202 Lucey was installed as the bishop of Cork in August 1952.

203 For details, see J. J. Lee, *Ireland, 1912–1985: politics and society*, Cambridge, 1989, pp. 564–66.

204 Commission on Emigration, *Reports*, p. 347.

205 NAI, DT S 14249 B, Land Commission, memorandum for the government: reports of Commission on Emigration, 20 May 1956, p. 16.

206 NAI, DT S 14249 B, Department of Defence, memorandum for the government: Commission on Emigration and other Population Problems, 30 June 1956, p. 2.

222   Demography, State and Society

207 NAI, D. Ind. & Comm., E 26/1/14/A, Commission on Emigration and other Population Problems: summary of memorandum, p. 1.

208 Ibid., p. 2.

209 NAI, D. Ind. & Comm., E 26/1/14/A memorandum on the report of the Commission on Emigration and other Population Problems, 26 Sept. 1956.

210 Ibid.

211 Ibid.

212 For the workings and operation of the commission, see Commission on Emigration, *Reports*, pp. 1–2.

213 NAI, DFA 412/9, memorandum for the government: reports of the Commission on Emigration and other Population Problems, 22 July 1956, pp. 4–5 (this document outlines the provision made by the Department of External Affairs for the welfare of Irish migrants in response to the commission's suggestions on this matter).

214 Kieran O'Shea, *The Irish emigrant chaplaincy scheme in Britain, 1957–82*, Naas, 1985, p. 12.

215 NAI, DT S 11582 F, copy of letter from F. H. Boland (London) to W. P. Fay (Dublin), 9 June 1954. Boland made this statement on the basis of 'confidential information'.

216 Ibid., pp. 14–15.

217 *Sunday Press*, 5 June 1955; *Irish Independent*, 6 June 1955; *Irish Times*, 6 June 1955; *Manchester Guardian*, 6 June 1955.

218 *Irish Catholic Directory, 1956*, 10 July 1955, p. 651; *Irish Independent*, 11 July 1955.

219 O'Shea, *The Irish emigrant chaplaincy scheme in Britain*, pp. 18–35.

220 Travers, 'The dream gone bust', pp. 326–27.

221 Ibid., p. 326.

222 Richard Dunphy, *The making of Fianna Fáil power in Ireland, 1923–1948*, Oxford, 1995, p. 299.

223 Quoted in Rafter, *The Clann*, p. 78.

224 See, for example, *Dáil Éireann deb.*, CXIX (15 Feb. 1950), col. 9; *Dáil Éireann deb.*, CXXI (13 May 1950), col. 902; *Dáil Éireann deb.*, CXXIII (25 Oct. 1950), col. 4.

225 *Dáil Éireann deb.*, CXXV (19 Apr. 1951), col. 1114.

226 *Dáil Éireann deb.*, CXXVII (31 Oct. 1951), col. 4.

227 Kieran A. Kennedy, Thomas Giblin and Deirdre McHugh, *The economic development of Ireland in the twentieth century*, London, 1988, p. 55; see also Patrick Lynch, 'The Irish economy since the war, 1946–51', in *Ireland in the war years and after, 1939–51*, ed. K. B. Nowlan and T. D. Williams, Dublin, 1969, p. 193.

228 Kieran A. Kennedy and Brendan R. Dowling, *Economic growth in Ireland: the experience since 1947*, Dublin, 1975, p. 215.

229 Brian Girvin, *Between two worlds: politics and economy in independent Ireland*, Dublin, 1989, pp. 185–86.

230 Evanne Kilmurray, *Fight, starve or emigrate: a history of the unemployed associations in the 1950s*, Dublin, [1989], p. 9; *Dáil Éireann deb.*, CXXXVI (4 Feb. 1953), cols 10–14; *Dáil Éireann deb.*, CXL (2 July 1953), cols 529–32.

231 Liam Kennedy, *The modern industrialisation of Ireland, 1940–1988*, Dublin, 1989, p. 9.

232 John A. O'Brien, ed., *The vanishing Irish*, New York, 1953.

233 John A. O'Brien, 'The Irish enigma', in *The vanishing Irish*, ed. O'Brien, p. 3.

234 R. C. Geary, 'Are the Irish vanishing?', *Éire-Ireland: weekly bulletin of the Department of External Affairs*, no. 227, March 1954, p. 9.

235 Patrick Noonan, 'Why few Irish marry', in *The vanishing Irish*, ed. O'Brien, p. 43.

236 Geary, 'Are the Irish vanishing?', p. 5.

237 Ibid., p. 6.

238 Ibid., p. 7.

239 Ibid., p. 6.

240 R. C. Geary, 'Some reflections on Irish population problems', *Studies*, vol. 43, 1954, p. 173. This was the text of Geary's contribution to a symposium on 'The Irish population problem' held in the Gresham Hotel, Dublin, on 9 May 1954.

241 Ibid., p. 172.

242 *Irish Times*, 10 May 1954; *Irish Independent*, 20 May 1954; *Irish Press*, 10 May 1954; see, for editorial comment, *Irish Times*, 11 May 1954.

243 *Dáil Éireann deb.*, CLII (14 July 1955), col. 1106.

244 *Irish Times*, 2, 12 20 and 25 June 1956; *Irish Press*, 2 June 1956; *Irish Independent*, 2 and 8 June 1956.

245 *Irish Times*, 25 June 1956.

246 Ibid.

247 *Dáil Éireann deb.*, CLIX (25 July 1956), cols 1694–98.

248 Ibid., col. 1705.

249 Nicholas R. Burnett, 'Emigration and modern Ireland', unpub. PhD thesis, The Johns Hopkins University, 1976, pp. 209–10.

250 Holmes, *John Bull's island*, pp. 210, 373 n. 5; K. O. Morgan, *Labour in power, 1945–51*, paperback edn, Oxford, 1985, p. 132.

251 Robert Miles, 'Nationality, citizenship, and migration to Britain, 1945–51', *Journal of Law and Society*, vol. 16, 1989, pp. 429–31. Other useful accounts of the policy of the Labour government include Kathleen Paul, *Whitewashing Britain: race and citizenship in the postwar era*, Ithaca, 1997, pp. 111–30; Kenneth Lunn, 'The British state and immigration, 1945–51: new light on the *Empire Windrush*', in *The politics of marginality: race, the radical right and minorities in twentieth-century Britain*, ed. Tony Kushner and Kenneth Lunn, London, 1990, pp. 161–74; D. W. Dean, 'Coping with colonial immigration, the Cold War and colonial policy: the Labour government and black communities in Britain, 1945–51', *Immigrants and Minorities*, vol. 6, 1987, pp. 305–33; Shirley Joshi and Bob Carter, 'The role of Labour in the creation of a racist Britain', *Race and Class*, vol. 25, 1984, pp. 53–70; Bob Carter, Marci Green and Rick Halpern, 'Immigration policy and the racialisation of migrant labour: the construction of national identities in the USA and Britain', *Ethnic and Racial Studies*, vol. 19, 1996, pp. 133–57.

252 *Report of the Royal Commission on Population*, p. 124.

253 John A. Jackson, *The Irish in Britain*, London, 1963, table II, p. 187.

254 Commission on Emigration, *Reports*, table 87, p. 116.

255 John A. Jackson, 'The Irish in Britain', in *Ireland and Britain since 1922*, ed. P. J. Drudy, Irish studies 5, Cambridge, 1986, p. 127.

256 Ibid.

257 Jackson, *The Irish in Britain*, p. 19.

258 Ibid., p. 105.

259 Ibid., p. 106.

260 Ibid. A special inquiry undertaken by the Wood Committee which examined nurse recruitment and training found that in 1946 12 per cent of hospital nursing staff in Britain were born in Ireland (Brian Abel-Smith, *A history of the nursing profession*, London, 1960, p. 215).

261 PRO, LAB 9/1483, Leopold to Rouse, 13 January 1947.

262 Jackson, *The Irish in Britain*, p. 106.

263 For background, see Ronan Fanning, *Independent Ireland*, Dublin, 1983, pp. 172–80.

264 PRO, CAB 1/46, cabinet committee on preparations for the meeting of Commonwealth prime ministers: the practical consequences of the termination of Éire's membership of the Commonwealth, note by secretary, app. I, pp. 5–9.

265 Fanning, *Independent Ireland*, p. 191.

266 Ibid.

267 Paul, *Whitewashing Britain*, p. 105.

268 Ibid., pp. 90–91. For a discussion of these rather complex and involved issues, see R. F. V. Heuston, 'British nationality and Irish citizenship', *International Affairs*, vol. 26, 1950, pp. 77–90 and John Megaw, 'British subjects and Éire citizens', *Northern Ireland Legal Quarterly*, vol. 8, 1949, pp. 129–39.

269 Robert Miles, 'Migration to Britain: the significance of a historical approach', *International Migration*, vol. 29, 1991, p. 531.

270 Zig Layton-Henry, *The politics of immigration: immigration, 'race' and 'race' relations in postwar Britain*, Oxford, 1992, p. 30.

271 Lunn, 'The British state and immigration, 1945–51', pp. 165–72.

272 Layton-Henry, *The politics of immigration*, p. 32.

273 PRO, CAB 129/77, CP 102, report of the committee on the social and economic problems arising from the growing influx into the United Kingdom of coloured workers from other Commonwealth countries, 3 Aug. 1955, p. 1.

274 Ibid., pp. 1–2.

275 This information was given by Michael Banton to Colin Holmes (Holmes, *John Bull's island*, p. 393 n. 325).

276 NAI, DFA 402/218/4, F. H. Boland to Sean Nunan, 26 Jan. 1955, p. 5.

277 PRO, CAB 129/77, CP 102, report of the committee on the social and economic problems . . ., p. 4.

278 Layton-Henry, *The politics of immigration*, p. 33.

279 Ibid., p. 32.

280 PRO, CAB 129/81, CP 145, colonial immigrants: report of the committee of ministers, 22 June 1956, p. 1.

281 Ibid., p. 7. The dissenting member was Lord Salisbury, the lord president, who argued that 'the longer we delay the worse the position is bound to become' (ibid., p. 7). For an assessment of Salisbury's views, see D. W. Dean, 'Conservative governments and the restriction of Commonwealth immigration in the 1950s: the problem of constraint', *Hist. J.*, vol. 35, 1992, pp. 183–84.

282 PRO, CAB 129/81, CP 145, colonial immigrants: report of the committee of ministers, 22 June 1956, p. 5.

283 PRO, CAB 129/84, CP 263, colonial immigrants: supplementary report of the committee of ministers, 14 Nov. 1956, p. 1.

284 Ibid., p. 2.

285 Ibid.

286 NAI, DFA 402/218/3, copy of 'The problems of coloured peoples in Britain' prepared by the Birmingham Young Conservatives, Oct. 1956, p. 2.

287 NAI, DFA 402/222, report on the Irish in Birmingham, prepared by Valentin Iremonger, [7] Aug. 1956, p. 4.

288 TCD, MS 8306, S.24 (b): report on survey covering the employment, social and living conditions of Irish emigrants (first generation) in Great Britain, prepared by Stanley Lyon, n.d. [Nov. 1948].

289 TCD, MS 8306, S.24 (c): the Irish emigrant in England: general report, prepared by Stanley Lyon, n.d. [Nov. 1948], p. 2.

290 Ibid.

291 Ibid., p. 3.

292 Anne O'Grady, *Irish migration to London in the 1940s and 1950s*, London, 1988, p. 14. See also the following accounts based on oral history: Mary Lennon, Marie McAdam and Joanne O'Brien, *Across the water: Irish women's lives in Britain*, London, 1988; Schweitzer, ed., *'Across the Irish sea'*.

5

Migration and return, 1958–1971

Most European states experienced large-scale migration in the late 1950s and throughout the 1960s, be it as sending or receiving societies. Roughly ten million people migrated from southern Europe to the industrialised economies of western Europe between the 1945 and the early 1970s, much of this movement occurring in the period after 1960, with the exception of Italy where the migrant flow developed in the late 1940s.[1] Migration from Greece, Portugal and Spain to West Germany, the Netherlands, France and other countries reached its peak in the 1960s.[2] As was the case with Irish migration to Britain, virtually all this population movement was within Europe rather than transatlantic in direction. A network of bilateral labour agreements between sending and receiving states regulated and controlled this migrant flow. In sharp contrast with Irish migrants who travelled to Britain, southern European migrants were 'guestworkers', subject to residence restrictions and liable to be sent home at some future date.[3]

Therefore, the Irish Republic was not unique in having a substantial proportion of its population living in another country. What was relatively unusual was that, in an era when restricting entry was the overriding characteristic of state policy on immigration throughout Europe, Irish migrants could enter Britain freely, work without a permit and stay for an unspecified length of time. The unrestricted access to the British labour market, which reflected both the demand for labour and the 'special' privileges which Irish citizens enjoyed, ensured that migration from the Irish Republic not only continued at its previous rate, but also substantially increased in volume in the late 1950s. The rise in the rate of emigration over the course of the 1950s was a stark manifestation of the crisis in the Irish economy at this time, both in real terms and in terms of confidence. Girvin observes that the 1950s were probably the 'worst decade since the famine'.[4]

The year 1958 marked the publication of *Economic Development*, the first serious attempt at economic planning in the Irish Republic, penned by T.K. Whitaker, the secretary of the Department of Finance.[5] A number of economists and historians have alluded to the effect that the publication of the depressing results of the 1956 census had on Whitaker, although it was one of the many factors that epitomised the economic situation during this period.[6] In fact, the opening section of *Economic Development* refers specifically to emigration:

> After 35 years of native government people are asking whether we can achieve an acceptable degree of economic progress. The common talk among people in the towns, as in rural Ireland, is of their children having to emigrate at as soon as their education is completed in order to be sure of a reasonable livelihood. To the children themselves and to many already in employment the jobs available at home look unattractive by comparison with those obtained in such variety and so readily elsewhere. All this seems to be setting up a vicious circle – of increasing emigration, resulting in a smaller domestic market depleted of initiative and skill, and a reduced incentive, whether for Irishmen or foreigners, to undertake and organise the productive enterprises which alone can provide increased employment opportunities and higher living standards.[7]

It is, however, important to note here that, quite apart from domestic economic planning initiatives which may have affected the rate and level of migration in the 1960s by creating additional non-agricultural employment, developments in the international economy also facilitated the growth of the Irish economy, and consequently reduced the rate of migration. The international economy in the 1960s had a favourable impact on the Irish economy and, whilst internal initiatives may have facilitated the resultant economic prosperity, it is worth bearing in mind that, in the absence of the wider developments in terms of international trade, the overall picture may well have been somewhat different.[8]

I

The period in Irish population history from 1958 until the early 1970s has been labelled as a 'demographic transformation'.[9] The principal elements of the 'transformation' have been examined by Walsh in a series of connected papers.[10] In short, he illustrates in some detail how the increased rate of marriage evident since 1958 (and more particularly from 1966 onwards) coupled with a lower age of marriage and the 'baby boom' of the 1960s constituted a radical departure from the rather peculiar Irish pattern of late and infrequent marriage and high levels of marital fertility.[11] A further key aspect of this demographic transformation was the changes in the rate and level of migration from Ireland in the 1960s, which will be described in more detail later. The total population of the Irish Republic decreased by nearly 3 per cent between 1956 and 1961.[12] This was the lowest figure for the total population since censuses were first taken by an independent Irish state in 1926. On the other hand, in the following five years (1961–66), the total population increased by 2 per cent and continued to grow, resulting in a 3.3 per cent gain by 1971.[13] This increase in the Irish population was the first trend of sustained population growth since the Great Irish Famine (1845–50) and is explained by the higher rate of natural increase and reduced rate of net migration.

In regional terms, the population growth was recorded for Leinster and Munster in the 1960s. However, the provinces of Connacht and Ulster continued to experience population decline, although this was of limited consequence for the three counties of Ulster between 1966 and 1971 (see appendix 13). For the first intercensal period (1956–61), Dublin was the only area to gain in population, while the western and north-western counties of Leitrim, Monaghan, Cavan, Mayo, Longford and Donegal experienced significant population losses. For the following five years from 1961 until 1966, gains in population were recorded in all counties in Leinster except Kilkenny, Laois and Longford. The population of Dublin grew quite significantly as did that of other cities such as Cork and Limerick. All counties in the provinces of Ulster and Connacht experienced population decline, although the actual level of decline was substantially lower in most counties than was the case in the previous two intercensal periods. The population of some counties, however, such as Leitrim and Mayo, continued to decline at a similar rate to before. Lastly, in the last five years covered by this study (1966–71), gains in population were recorded in Leinster and Munster, with two exceptions, namely counties Longford and Kerry (see appendix 13). The growth of the suburban areas of Dublin is well illustrated by the increase of over 30 per cent or some 55,000 people.[14] Again, apart from the marginal increases in counties Monaghan and Galway, population decline was concentrated in the province of Connacht and the north-west, albeit at lower levels than was hitherto the case. The general trends that can be observed therefore include population growth in the eastern part of the Irish Republic, which was particularly reflected in the increase in the population of Dublin and its suburbs. From 1961 onwards the decline of population in Munster was reversed in the main and by 1971 this process was more or less complete. Connacht and Ulster fared badly in terms of population decreases, but for the latter part of the period these losses were at a much lower level than the 1950s. Thus, in the 1960s, the Irish population continued to grow, but the gains were concentrated within particular regions.

In previous chapters, comment on the level of internal migration within Ireland was to some extent constrained by the fact that little research had been completed on this important aspect of population change. For this period, it is possible to be more conclusive about the matter. A detailed study of internal migration in the Irish Republic between 1946 and 1961 based on the data available in the censuses found that internal mobility within the state was of limited consequence when compared with external mobility or migration to places outside the state.[15] For the most, movement tended to be between contiguous counties and across short distances. Geary and Hughes's conclusions shed some interesting light on this pattern of internal migration:

> Compared with the period after 1961, 1946–61 was a period of economic stagnation during which internal mobility was small, its main features being in the positive side, movement of children and of brides, with subsequent attrition, mainly external, i.e. emigration. Furthermore, internal migration was short-distance, mainly cross-boundary. In reference to each county, internal migration was but a small factor of total migration, i.e. emigration predominated[16]

However, since the 1966 census did not include a question on birthplaces, it was difficult to be certain of the scale of internal migration in this period, but Geary and Hughes concluded that 'there has been a substantial increase in internal migration since 1961'.[17] A later study, which used the 1971 census data on 'usual residence one year previously', underlined the importance of the flow to Dublin from other areas in the 1960s.[18] The level of internal migration increased in this decade, but relative to the flow to places outside the state, migrants opting to live within the Irish Republic were by far in the minority. About one in five of those leaving provincial Ireland moved to Dublin; the remainder travelled to Britain and elsewhere.[19] In general terms, Hughes and Walsh noted the low overall level of internal migration and postulated that the high rate of external mobility was a determinant.[20] Migrants from rural and small town Ireland opted to live in British rather than Irish cities.

II

The late 1950s and the 1960s marked an important watershed in the history of Irish migration since this period encompassed both a significant increase in net migration in the late 1950s and a decrease throughout the 1960s. An overview of migration patterns between 1958 and 1971 is, however, complicated by the fact that it covers three intercensal periods. Nevertheless, what emerges clearly from an analysis of the census data is that two distinct phases can be demarcated. The first phase, from 1956 to 1961, marks the nadir of migration from independent Ireland: the average annual net migration from the Irish Republic during this period was over –40,000 people (see Table 5.1a). In the late 1950s, migration peaked with an average annual rate of –14.8 persons per 1,000 of the population (see Table 5.1b). On the other hand, in the following two periods (1961–66 and 1966–71), there was a marked decrease in the level of net migration. In 1961–66 net migration was less than half that in the period 1956–61 and considerably lower than for all the other intercensal periods since 1936. Between 1966 and 1971 average annual net migration dropped to –10,781 persons, just over a quarter of the number for the previous five years. The average annual rate of net migration per 1,000 decreased to –3.7 persons, the lowest figure since censuses were taken under the auspices of the Irish state (see Table 5.1b). In essence, this was a period of transition from the large-scale migration of the 1950s to the much lower levels that were evident in the 1960s.

The actual timing of this transition may be estimated on the basis of calculations of the average annual rate of net migration which Ó Gráda and Walsh obtained from the Irish Central Statistics Office. These estimates were presumably based on net passenger movement statistics used in conjunction with births and deaths data.[21] It can be seen that the year 1961 marks the beginning of a shift to a lower flow of net migration, though the rate does increase in the mid-1960s and thereafter declines (see Table 5.2). A further complication enters the already complex equation for the late 1960s and early 1970s in that substantial return migration occurred, resulting in a net inflow in 1971.

In gender terms, in the first period (1956–61) slightly more males than females migrated, but over the following decade the opposite was the case (see Table 5.1a). Nevertheless, the general observation that can be drawn from these data is the relative parity in the sexes. And,

Table 5.1a Average annual net Irish migration, 1956–71

Period	Males	Females	Total	Number of females per 1,000 males
1956–61	−21,914	−20,486	−42,400	935
1961–66	−7,523	−8,598	−16,121	1,143
1966–71	−4,950	−5,831	−10,781	1,178

Source: Census of population of Ireland, 1971: I, population of district electoral divisions, towns and larger units of area, Dublin, 1972, Prl. 2564, table x, p. xxi.

Table 5.1b Average annual rate of net Irish migration per 1,000 of the average population, 1956–71

Period	Males	Females	Total
1956–61	−15.2	−14.5	−14.8
1961–66	−5.4	−6.0	−5.7
1966–71	−3.4	−4.0	−3.7

Source: Census of population of Ireland, 1971: I, population of district electoral divisions ... table x, p. xxi.

Table 5.2 Estimated annual rate of net Irish external migration per 1,000 of the average population, 1958–71

Year	Rate	Year	Rate
1958	−11.2	1965	−7.3
1959	−14.4	1966	−4.5
1960	−14.1	1967	−5.5
1961	−5.3	1968	−5.1
1962	−2.8	1969	−1.7
1963	−6.0	1970	−1.7
1964	−7.0	1971	3.7

Source: After Cormac Ó Gráda and Brendan Walsh, 'The economic effects of emigration: Ireland', *Emigration and its effects on the sending country* ed. Beth J. Asch, Santa Monica, 1994, table 4.2, p. 99.

as noted in the commentary accompanying the 1971 census, despite the fact that the sex ratio of migrants had fluctuated since 1926, the difference over a long period of time was deemed 'not very great'.[22] It does not seem unreasonable to suggest on the basis of the detailed evidence presented in previous chapters that the majority of migrants were under 30 years of age. Unfortunately, data on the age profile, such as those derived from the statistics relating to the issuing of travel identity cards until 1952, are not available. Ó Gráda and Walsh's tabulations of cohort depletion, which were discussed in the previous chapter, shed light on the age profile of the migrant flow. The selective impact of migration on the younger age cohorts is illustrated in these data and more specifically in the case of those aged 20–24 years at the end of the intercensal periods (see Table 5.3). On the basis of estimates constructed by Garvey, it can be deduced that approximately 40 per cent of those aged 0–4 years, 5–9 years and 10–14 years in 1946, both male and female, had left the Irish Republic by 1971.[23] In other words, roughly one in three of those aged under 30 years in 1946 had migrated by 1971.[24] Despite the fact that the total level of net migration from the Irish Republic was falling during the 1960s, it was still predominantly young people who left the country.[25]

Table 5.3 Net Irish external migration by age group (gain or loss of population over intercensal period as a percentage of initial cohort), 1956–71

Period	Age at end of intercensal period							
	0–14	15–19	20–24	25–29	30–34	35–39	40–64	65+
1956–61	−0.8	−15.3	−31.7	−18.4	−9.4	−3.9	−4.7	+2.0
1961–66	+0.8	−10.0	−20.4	−5.1	+1.4	−1.8	−1.3	+0.7
1966–71	+1.3	−6.0	−16.7	−6.3	+1.8	+2.2	−0.9	+2.2

Source: After Cormac Ó Gráda and Brendan Walsh, 'The economic effects of emigration: Ireland', in Emigration and its effects on the sending country, ed. Beth J. Asch, Santa Monica, 1994, table 4.3, p. 99.

The conjugal status of these migrants is to some extent a matter for conjecture, although Garvey has devised estimates for the intercensal period 1961–71, using census of population and vital statistics data (see Table 5.4).[26] The majority of migrants were single, yet a small though significant proportion were married. Information collected when marriages were registered in the Irish Republic demonstrates that between the years 1961 and 1965, only 13 per cent of newly-wed couples stated that their intended future residence was outside the state, and this figure was only marginally different (12 per cent) over the following five years.[27] Notwithstanding this flow of married persons, it would be incorrect to imply otherwise than that the majority of migrants at this time were single.

Table 5.4 Estimates of net Irish migratory flows classified by marital status, 1961–71

	Single	Married	Widowed	Total
Male	–60,700	+3,100	–3,700	–61,300
Female	–61,400	–3,400	–5,800	–70,600

Source: Donal Garvey, 'The history of migration flows in the Republic of Ireland', *Population Trends*, No. 39, 1985, p. 25.

The regional impact of migration is clearly illustrated by the county level data on net migration (see appendix 14). In the first period (1956–61), every county was affected by migration to some degree, although of course these data included movements within the boundaries of the Irish state. The southern border counties and the complete province of Connacht were especially subject to outward flows, with counties Monaghan, Leitrim, Mayo and Cavan faring particularly badly. No county had an average rate of net migration lower than –10.0 persons per 1,000 of the population. During the 1960s, the effect of the overall pattern of decreased net migration is reflected in the county level data. For this decade, the majority of counties were still areas of net migration, but with lower rates than was previously the case. In a small number of counties net immigration occurred, although in the case of Wicklow, contiguous to Dublin, this had to do with the process of the suburbanisation of the capital's population rather than any other factor. Net migration decreased significantly in counties Cork, Clare and Kerry, a reversal of a long-standing pattern. In general terms, the rates for the migration-prone counties of the north-west (Cavan, Leitrim, Mayo and Roscommon) remained relatively high in comparison with those of the more prosperous regions along the eastern seaboard. One exception was the county of Monaghan, a border area with little by way of industrialisation: the average annual rate of net migration per 1,000 in 1956–61 was –26.5 persons, –12.9 per 1,000 in 1961–66 and this dropped to –4.4 per 1,000 in 1966–71.

Using birthplace data in conjunction with statistics on births and deaths, it is possible to construct estimates of net external migration for each county, i.e. out of the state. Hughes and Walsh have calculated estimates of rates of net external migration by county for the 1960s (see appendix 15). However, since the question asked in the 1971 census related to usual residence one year previously, there is an assumption that the data on internal migration for one year can be applied retrospectively to the complete intercensal period. The figure for internal migration is then deducted from the total net migration figure to arrive at the estimate of net external migration. Whilst mindful of the inherent dangers involved in such a procedure, these estimates do illustrate starkly the regional variation in the impact of net external migration. For example, the net external migration rate per 1,000 for males in Mayo aged 15–29 years in 1971 was –379.3, yet in Dublin the figure was –78.0. In Leitrim the figure for females of –367.5 per 1,000 contrasts sharply with that of –50.7 for Louth (see appendix 15). A general observation which may be made on the basis of these estimates is that, in the case of 18 of the 26 counties which constituted the Irish Republic, no less than 20 per cent of the cohort of the population mostly likely to emigrate (15–29 years) left the state during the 1960s.

It has been estimated that roughly four-fifths of the Irish migrant flow in the postwar period from 1951 to 1971 was to Britain.[28] Migrants did, however, travel to other countries. It is difficult to ascertain the actual numbers involved owing to the lack of detailed data. The only source of information available is the number of new passports issued to those who intended to live abroad permanently. Between 1951 and 1971 roughly 120,000 persons were in receipt of passports for this purpose.[29] Without doubt a substantial proportion travelled to the United States, but Australia also became an increasingly popular choice of destination in the late 1960s. The years 1967–72 marked the peak period in postwar Irish migration to Australia.[30]

III

On the basis of detailed studies undertaken in the 1960s and 1970s it is possible to examine in some detail the impact of migration on selected communities.[31] In addition, in many of these contemporary studies the motives for migration are analysed, which allows for comparison with the data collected by the Commission on Emigration and

Other Population Problems in 1948. In the late 1960s and early 1970s
the problems facing rural Ireland, particularly the agricultural community, were investigated in a plethora of rural or 'resource' surveys.[32]
A number of these reports were loosely based on the Limerick Rural
Survey, 1958–64, a pioneering attempt to assess the economic and
social structure of one county sponsored by the rural development
organisation, Muintir na Tíre.[33] The evidence that can be indirectly
gleaned from these studies relating to migration is of particular significance. Firstly, however, it would be useful to assess the changes in
the Irish agricultural labour force which bear directly on the level of
migration.

Undoubtedly, the majority of Irish migrants to Britain were from
an agricultural background. The total size of the agricultural labour
force declined by roughly a quarter in the period from 1951 to 1961
and by 27 per cent in the following decade.[34] Three-quarters of the
decline in the 1960s may be accounted for by natural wastage, but the
remainder can be attributed to the fact that twice as many people left
the agricultural labour force as entered it.[35] It can be seen that the
grouping most affected by this decline in the period 1951–71 was that
comprising relatives assisting on family farms, although paid agricultural labourers suffered a loss of fairly similar magnitude (see Table
5.5).

On closer inspection, as Walsh has demonstrated, it can be seen
that this decline was concentrated within specific categories of the
agricultural labour force. For instance, the decline between 1951 and

Table 5.5 Irish agricultural labour force in 1951 and 1971

	1951		1971		
	Number	Percentage of total	Number	Percentage of total	Percentage change 1951–71
Farmers	235,331	46.3	181,627	64.6	−22.8
Relatives assisting	171,085	33.6	52,921	18.8	−69.1
Agricultural labourers	84,657	16.6	35,569	12.6	−58.0
Others	17,686	3.5	11,294	4.0	−36.1
Total	508,759		281,411		−44.7

Source: After D. A. Gillmor, *Agriculture in the Republic of Ireland*, Budapest, 1977, p. 35.

1966 of relatives assisting on the family farm, such as farmers' sons, sons-in-law and daughters, was particularly high.[36] Using cohort depletion techniques, Walsh has calculated estimates of net mobility which reinforce impressionistic observations regarding the migrant flow that originated from the agricultural labour force: 'The net out-flow from agricultural occupations at the younger age groups may be partly an outflow from agricultural to non-agricultural occupations in Ireland, but no doubt the bulk of those leaving agriculture emigrate.'[37]

Migration not only involves individual 'decisions' to leave a region or country but also structural factors. Rural Ireland at this time was undergoing a silent but very significant process of economic and social change.[38] Hannan's seminal sociological work outlines the extent of this change. Coupled with the demographic trends already discussed, a number of other elements of change are evident: farm mechanisa-tion; developments in transport and mass media communications; a switch to pastoral farming away from tillage and other types of pro-duction which required a high labour input; and finally, the more elu-sive socio-cultural changes in people's attitudes, beliefs and values.[39] The world-view was no longer a local one: 'Thus a relatively closed cultural system whose reference groups were highly localised was gradually replaced by one where a number of families gradually started to identify with and take on the values exemplified by the urban middle class.'[40] From the viewpoint of young migrants, the stan-dard of living which was presented as the norm in the media and else-where could rarely be achieved within the local area. What is perhaps most striking is that the acquiescence with low income employment (and in the case of relatives assisting, no income employment) was replaced by a desire to maximise earning potential. In fact, some of these cultural changes were brought about as a result of contact with migrants living in Britain.[41]

More specific evidence which illustrates these general observa-tions can be found in a number of contemporary investigations of migration in the 1960s. A study conducted by Hannan entitled *Rural exodus* was based on interviews with 556 young people from county Cavan, the majority of whom were aged between 15 and 18 years of age. It should be remembered that Cavan was a county with a long-standing tradition of migration and the rate of net migration was con-siderably higher than the rate for most other counties during this period (see appendix 14). Nearly two-thirds of the population of this county were dependent on agriculture for employment and many of the holdings were of a small to medium size.[42] The fieldwork was completed in 1965, but in 1968 the author conducted a valuable follow-up study using a smaller sample.[43] Hannan's primary concern was with migration intentions in the first study and with subsequent behaviour in so far as it could be measured in the later fieldwork. However, it should be said that he is concerned with all types of migration – both internal and international – and not solely with those leaving for work in Britain. One of the deficiencies of his study is that the actual destinations of the migrants are not discussed at any length in either the original fieldwork or the follow-up study.

It is difficult to summarise within the confines of this volume the many findings that emerge from Hannan's important study. However, the principal finding is that 36 per cent of the sample definitely intended to migrate, 24 per cent intended to remain in the local community, and 40 per cent were unsure whether they would migrate or not.[44] The main motive for migration was occupational and income frustration or to quote Hannan, 'beliefs about one's ability to fulfil occupational and income aspirations were, by far, the most predictive of migration intentions'.[45] Levels of satisfaction with the local community and family work obligations were also determinants, but of less significance in the migration 'decision'.[46] The relative importance of the economic motive in migration was underlined by the fact that, of those who were planning to migrate or were unsure of their future intentions (76 per cent of the total sample), 72 per cent stated that they would remain in the local community if they could fulfil their occupational and income aspirations at home.[47] The perception that it would be extremely difficult to obtain a suitable job in the area ensured that many of these young people were planning to leave. Income and occupational aspirations varied by level of educational attainment and by sex. What emerges from an analysis of the data is that those with a lower level of education were more content to stay at home: 38 per cent of the sample who had completed only primary education and 25 per cent of the vocationally educated expressed an intention to remain in the local community.[48] However, only 12 per cent of those with secondary education stated that they would definitely stay at home.[49] Therefore, the relationship between educational attainment and migration was a direct one: in short, those who achieved a higher level of education exhibited more ambitious income and occupational aspirations which could only be satisfied by leaving the local community and in many cases, the country also.

Hannan's results on the sex differentials are particularly interest-ing, especially in the light of the findings presented thus far. When respondents were asked if they definitely intended to remain in the local community, 17 per cent more males than females replied in the affirmative.[50] When occupational background was controlled for, it emerged that the existence of a farming background explained much of this difference. The reason why females living on a family farm were more prone to migration was the obvious one – that farming is a pre-dominantly male occupation. This factor ensured that 'there is always a much greater number of females than males looking for non-farm jobs within rural communities', and if more opportunities for female non-farm employment did not exist, this helps explain the sex differ-ential in migration.[51] But levels of educational attainment were found to be of equal consequence: females from farming backgrounds tended to stay in education longer than their male counterparts, and hence a desire was evident to obtain better jobs which could not be found locally.[52]

In the previous chapter it was observed that a substantial propor-tion of the Commission on Emigration sample had relatives, particu-larly siblings, living in Britain and these networks both facilitated and aided migration. A similar finding emerges from Hannan's study, although he observes that it was siblings living in Britain or in other places within Ireland, rather than relatives more broadly, which appeared to be a significant determinant: 'Those with a higher pro-portion of migration sib[ling]s had higher levels of occupational and income frustration and showed greater tendencies to migrate than others. Such family influences appeared to play an independent role in migration.'[53] Migrants' perceptions of how the limited economic opportunities available in the locality compared with those available elsewhere were derived from information conveyed by brothers and sisters. This factor, which to some extent defies classification, was without doubt a very significant element in the formulation and sub-sequent realisation of migration plans. These networks ensured that the wage levels and standards of living in postwar Britain were trans-posed into rural Ireland. Inevitably, the level of remuneration and opportunities available locally did not fare well in such comparisons.

Three years after the original fieldwork was completed in 1965, Hannan conducted a follow-up study using a smaller sample (279 per-sons) which aimed to assess the relationship between migration inten-tions and actual behaviour. It may be remembered that 36 per cent of the original sample had stated that they definitely intended to migrate; by 1968 over 46 per cent of the smaller sample had migrated.[54] However, what is particularly interesting is that a substantial number of those who intended to stay in 1965 did in fact migrate and vice versa. Those with primary education alone who in 1965 had definitely intended to stay in the locality were 'generally more migratory than was expected or indeed than they expected themselves'.[55] People had changed their minds for a range of reasons including the availability of suitable employment, family obligations and educational opportunities elsewhere.[56] Information derived from interviews with the mothers of individuals who had actually migrated indicated that four-fifths of the migrants had left owing to a perceived lack of appropriate employment in the area which would enable them to secure the level of income and status to which they aspired.[57] In addition, Hannan's findings in the follow-up study underline the role of networks in facilitating migration: friends and close relatives provided valuable advice and, in some cases, practical assistance in terms of jobs and accommodation when it actually came to leaving the locality.[58]

The second study that deserves special consideration is Jackson's detailed report completed in 1964 on the town of Skibbereen in west Cork. Skibbereen was a market town with a population, including the immediate rural hinterland, of nearly 3,000 people in 1961.[59] That hinterland was predominantly an area of pastoral farming with small to medium-sized farms of between 30 and 50 acres.[60] This investigation by a distinguished sociologist with a particular expertise in Irish migration contains much that is of value relating to migration, coupled with a survey undertaken in 1965 of migrants from the town living in Britain.[61] Jackson's sample was divided into a number of groupings: 'urban'; 'rural'; 'shopkeepers'; 'old' school leavers (people born in 1924, 1934 and 1944); 'young' school leavers (i.e. those aged 15 in 1964); and lastly, 'emigrants' drawn from the above samples and relatives of respondents living in Britain and Northern Ireland. The impact of migration on this small community is illustrated by the fact that roughly three-quarters of the first three samples had relatives who had left the area, with approximately 60 per cent with one or more migrant sibling or child.[62] Perhaps of equal interest are the migration intentions of the sample of 'young' school leavers: of the 56 male and female respondents, roughly 30 per cent expected to leave the country. This finding was in line with that of the 'old' school leavers' sample as 28 per cent were no longer living in the country.[63] However, what emerged was that, whilst the majority of the respondents intended to leave the area, many saw their future as being in the cities of Dublin and Cork rather than Britain.[64] In an effort to ascertain the factors which lay behind migration, all the various samples, apart that is from the 'emigrants' themselves, were asked to suggest reasons why people might leave the local area. The explanation most commonly advanced was the attraction of better jobs and greater opportunities elsewhere.[65] Therefore, the economic motive underlined in Hannan's study of school leavers in Cavan was confirmed in Jackson's findings for Skibbereen, although it must be said that the data for the latter study are more revealing on the perceptions of why people left rather than actual migration intentions of a specific grouping.

The findings of the Skibbereen social survey in relation to those who had actually migrated to Britain provide a rare insight into the attitudes of migrants. The total sample consisted of 111 people from Skibbereen who were living in areas throughout the United Kingdom. The method of selection was, as Jackson acknowledged, somewhat 'unrepresentative of the population' as the names and addresses of migrants were collected from relatives still living in Skibbereen.[66] In addition, the age profile of the sample was skewed towards older people with only 20.7 per cent of the population under 29 years and 42.3 per cent between the ages of 40 and 64 years.[67] Notwithstanding these difficulties, several interesting points emerge, such as the fact that four-fifths of the sample had been employed in up to five jobs, suggesting a high degree of occupational and physical mobility since the original move to Britain. However, this apparent occupational mobility did not in turn lead to social mobility as there was relatively little transfer between manual and non-manual occupations.[68] The adaptation of the migrants from Skibbereen to their circumstances in Britain was a gradual process, but in the main a pragmatic outlook was adopted by those interviewed in their comparisons between living in Britain and life at home in Ireland:

> The majority lie somewhere between the two extremes, with their feet in both camps, able to return home and to slip on the old ways as easily as they slip on an old coat, but when in England exhibiting an ability and a practical accommodation which might contrast markedly with the role they play at home.[69]

When asked if they would like to return to the Irish Republic, 62 per cent expressed a desire to return at some future date, but 27 per cent stated that they would not like to return home. While the desire to return may have been strong, in reality 44 per cent expected to stay in Britain owing to the higher wage levels and better opportunities for employment. Equally significant is the fact that 13 per cent of the sample considered themselves more British than Irish.[70]

The role of family and kin networks in facilitating migration is illustrated by the proportion of the sample who had siblings living in Britain: over two-thirds had at least one brother also living in Britain, and 83 per cent had at least one migrant sister. Friends and relatives also played an important role in securing the first job. It is also perhaps worth noting that only 11 per cent stated that they had experienced any difficulty as a result of their being Irish.[71] The general finding that emerges from Jackson's research is that by the mid-1960s, the wave of migrants who left Ireland in the 1940s and 1950s were settling down to life in Britain. Nevertheless, many wished to return home eventually, which is not an unnatural aspiration for migrants, especially when frequent contact was maintained through letters and visits home. The close proximity of the two countries ensured that travelling home for holidays was a frequent occurrence: over 66 per cent of the sample had been home within the previous 12 months and 63 per cent claimed they wrote at least one letter to their family back in Ireland every month.[72] In many ways, these migrants were 'between two worlds', with regular contact and return trips. Undoubtedly, this resulted in migration to Britain being a less traumatic move than transatlantic movement to the United States.

Whilst Hannan's and Jackson's studies were specifically concerned with migration from a region or county, a number of other reports which aimed to investigate the wider economic environment complement these examinations of Irish migration. The first detailed attempt to evaluate the economic and social structure of a particular county was the wide-ranging Limerick Rural Survey, 1958–64. Limerick was an agricultural county with farmers engaged in dairying for the most part. Within the wider remit of the study, a detailed survey of the impact of migration was undertaken, including the reasons underlying the 'decision' to leave. Using cohort depletion techniques, McNabb found that females tended to migrate at an earlier age than males, with the greatest loss of females being in the 10–24 years age group compared with 20–29 years for males.[73] A decision was taken to confine the study to the eastern area of the county where the larger farms employed hired labour.[74] Of a total of 117 migrants who had left the four selected parishes between 1951 and 1956, 48 people had moved elsewhere within the country, 61 had travelled to Britain and 6 to the United States, while 2 had left for further afield.[75] It is perhaps noteworthy that over half of the migrants had gone to Britain, with roughly 5 per cent leaving for the United States.

In this area, daughters of farm labourers could only expect to be employed locally as domestic servants, a low-status arduous occupation; for males paid work on the larger farms was the principal source of employment, yet labourers tended 'to consider work on the farms as a purely temporary job prior to migration'.[76] However, farmers were becoming increasingly reluctant to employ hired labour, not only because of the changes brought about by farm mechanisation, but also because of the requirement for standard hours of work and fixed remuneration. Many of these males who were generically labelled 'farm labourers' were also employed on local authority road work or at other unskilled work for part of the year.[77] But in the face of a decreasing demand for farm labour and given their unwillingness to eke out a living on the basis of intermittent public work, migration to Britain was a viable means by which to secure steady employment: 'Migration among farm workers is due to contracting opportunities for employment on the land and lack of alternative sources of employment, allied to problems of status and changing attitudes to the class structure.'[78]

An examination of attitudes of parents sheds interesting light on the aspirations of their children and may explain their desire to leave the area. On the basis of detailed data on migrants from four parishes, McNabb found that farmers' daughters were the best educated, although 'their education places them at variance with their environment and poor opportunities for marriage are a source of dissatisfaction'.[79] Farmers' sons were not as well educated and roughly half of these migrants had a low level of basic education.[80] In general, farm labourers' sons and daughters received basic primary schooling as parents could only provide for this level of education, despite the fact they clearly viewed education as the best possible means for their children to secure steady non-agricultural employment.[81] Such employment was associated with greater status and did not have the stigma attached to being a farm labourer: one parent stated in a pithy manner that 'one can get a job on one's merits in England. Employers don't ask who you are, but what you can do.'[82] Whilst the question of status is very much a subjective matter, it is clear that parents at least viewed migration as an avenue whereby their children could escape from the rigid social structure in this area. In this community a farm labourer was always viewed as inferior and the only way to achieve any status was to move away. It is also worth noting that farm labourers' children after migration were working in semi-skilled and unskilled employment as builders' labourers, factory workers and domestic servants, but a crucial difference existed. When it was pointed out to the wife of a farm labourer that after leaving the area females seemed to take up domestic employment, a job which had a distinct stigma attached to it at home, the response was telling: 'It is different in England: there they respect you for your work.'[83] It was the low status (and low pay) associated with unskilled work in this area of rural Ireland which spurred on the children of farm labourers to take up similar employment in terms of skill level, albeit better paid, in Britain. The rigidity of the social structure and the changing attitudes and values regarding the desirability of securing unskilled farm work both as a labourer and farm servant were key determinants of migration from these parishes in east Limerick.

One last observation may be made in relation to the findings of the Limerick Rural Survey. In the two studies discussed above, and the earlier Commission on Emigration sample, contact with migrant relatives was underlined as a significant factor, in facilitating those wishing to leave the local community. In addition, a study based on fieldwork in the early 1970s found that, in contrast to what one would imagine, contact with migrant siblings tended to be more frequent between those living in Ireland and their sisters and brothers in Britain, than between siblings all based in Ireland.[84] This may be partly explained by return visits home for holidays. In Limerick a similar situation was found to be in evidence, with migrant relatives and friends providing the essential contacts for the children of farm labourers and farmers alike. In fact, close relatives tended to determine the choice of destination:

> According to the parents, with the exception of those going to religious or nursing establishments, a boy or girl would not normally emigrate unless he or she had contacts abroad. The emigrants from farm families also tended to attract other relatives and friends to join them. Parents themselves believed that family contacts determined the choice of residence.[85]

Therefore migrant siblings in particular played an important role in providing information regarding conditions in Britain together with practical assistance, especially in terms of accommodation, when it came to leaving Ireland.

The late 1960s in particular witnessed an unprecedented concern with the fate of rural Ireland. John Healy, a distinguished journalist with the *Irish Times*, penned a series of influential articles which were later published as *The death of an Irish town*.[86] Based on his intimate knowledge of the fate of his home town, Charlestown, county Mayo, this account of the sense of malaise associated with areas of rural Ireland is a poignant indication of contemporary anxiety regarding the future of underdeveloped regions which failed to attract industrial and manufacturing employment. But the problems of rural Ireland, especially the western counties, were also the subject of official inquiry by a government-appointed committee.[87] By far the most determined attempt to grapple with these issues was written by an official of the Department of Agriculture, J. J. Scully, who was specifically concerned with the state of small farms in western Ireland.[88] What emerges from these reports is the commonly cited range of factors that influenced the economic environment and consequently migration. Poor land, few sources of non-agricultural employment and the small size of agricultural holdings all resulted in a long-standing tradition of migration to other areas within Ireland, Britain and prior to the Second World War, the United States. For example, in the Glenties district of west Donegal, it was found that 'over two-thirds of the children had migrated from the area by the time they reach their thirties'.[89] The evidence indicated that the majority of these migrants left the country by the age of 25 years which naturally resulted in structural imbalances within the population.[90] An even more extreme case was county Leitrim. Between 1951 and 1971, it was estimated that over half of the county's males aged 0–4 years in 1951 had left there by 1971; for females of the same age in 1951, a staggering 68.4 per cent had migrated by 1971.[91] Unlike other counties, Leitrim had few large towns, which usually had a stable population, and therefore decline in the rural community inevitably resulted in a high rate of population decrease for the county as a whole.[92] Such a massive exodus had many effects including an unbalanced age structure in the population, a contraction in the economically active population, a low marriage rate, a high level of permanent male celibacy and finally, a larger than average proportion of single-person households (18.3 per cent), the highest percentage for any county in the state.[93] Curry's general comments with regard to county Leitrim could apply to any of the areas under discussion:

The creation of additional job opportunities in the non-farming sector, especially in manufacturing industry, appears to offer the best possible brake on population decline in a county with a high dependency on agriculture. Rapid expansion of manufacturing jobs cannot be expected to stabilise population in the near future but could lead to stability of population in the long term.[94]

An analogous picture emerges for county Kerry with the decline of the agricultural labour force and high levels of migration from the county.[95] Between 1951 and 1966 the total number of farm relatives decreased by 53 per cent. Similarly, the number of farm labourers decreased by 40 per cent in the same period.[96] As was the case in the other surveys, migration particularly affected young people aged between 20 and 44 years.[97] The result was a declining and ageing farm population in county Kerry which 'seriously inhibited' the development of agriculture within the county.[98]

West Cork was also the subject of a detailed 'resource' survey compiled by An Foras Talúntais (Agricultural Institute) between 1960 and 1963.[99] A comparable process of population decline and rural depopulation was evident: in the 1960s the total population of the survey area had decreased by 13 per cent.[100] In order to assess the impact of migration on west Cork, data were collected relating to 303 people who had migrated from the area: 178 householders within the survey area provided the relevant information.[101] Of the total number, 84 per cent, equally divided by sex, were living in Britain or North America, and the remainder lived elsewhere within Ireland.[102] The date of departure is of particular interest in terms of the eventual destination and the results are presented in Table 5.6. The shift towards Britain prior to and during the Second World War is clearly illustrated by these migration histories. A significant difference existed between the sexes in the actual timing of migration: 'Approximately 50 per cent of the females and 25 per cent of the males left home before 21 years. By the age of 25 the majority of females had gone, whereas about 40 per cent of the males still had to leave.'[103] Females tended to migrate at an earlier age than males. This was related to the difficulty females experienced in securing suitable employment within the locality, especially in this area where 'opportunities for women were few'.[104] The low incomes in the vicinity also militated against marriage and 'female migration is thus aggravated by lessening suitable marriage prospects for these women who might otherwise be in a position to stay at home'.[105] The higher rate of female migration from the district was explained by the fact that a greater proportion of males remained in the community

Table 5.6 West Cork resource survey: migrants classified by sex, period of departure and location, 1963[a]

Period of departure	Male		Female		Total	
	United States	Britain	United States	Britain	United States	Britain
pre-1929	43	1	22	11	65	12
1930–45	5	29	24	38	29	67
1946–55	3	20	4	13	7	33
1956–62	–	27	2	14	2	41
Total	51	77	52	76	103	153

Note:[a] The information was provided by 178 householders in the survey area.
Source: After Patrick Commins, 'Demographic and sociological aspects of west Cork', in An Foras Talúntais, West Cork resource survey, Dublin, 1963, section c, table xxi, p. 90.

since they could secure farmwork or other forms of casual employment, albeit at a low level of remuneration.[106]

When informants were asked to suggest reasons for migration, the economic motive was underlined by the majority of respondents. The lack of employment opportunities in the locality was cited frequently, although in many of the comments implicit references were made to 'social and psychological factors'.[107] Commins does not specify what exactly constituted 'social and psychological factors', although it may be assumed these would include dissatisfaction with rural life and a desire to travel or take advantage of training not available in the locality. Interestingly, few informants attached much weight to the influence of relatives abroad. However, as Commins remarked, the destination of migrants from the area seemed to contradict these assertions:

> Even where economic factors were mentioned as causes for migration, relatives had speeded the departure of many by securing employment for them or by paying their fares. At present, prospective migrants from the survey area tend to join relatives and friends working in London, Manchester or Birmingham.[108]

It is clear that whilst relatives may not have directly encouraged migration with exhortations to travel, information on wage levels, employment opportunities and the general standard of living which percolated back to those living in Ireland was none the less a determinant in the migration of family members and friends. Lastly, it may be remembered that members of the Commission on Emigration and Other Population Problems remarked that in certain areas of the country a worrying trend was evident whereby no prospective heir was living in the country or was willing to return to inherit the family farm. Hannan has observed that 'whereas in the 1920s brothers had competed for the inheritance, in the 1960s they vied to escape it'.[109] This general observation would seem to be confirmed by the data derived from a study of over 8,000 farms in the west of Ireland. Scully found that 8.3 per cent of a total of 4,484 farmers aged over 50 years had no heirs living in the region.[110] He concluded that, given the economic environment in the west of Ireland and despite the fact that the parents were optimistic that a family member would return to succeed the title, this was unlikely to be the case.[111] As Kennedy has noted, the British labour market 'offered the youth of rural Ireland effective economic alternatives, in the process devaluing the benefits of land inheritance and squeezing the supply of heirs'.[112]

The studies and reports which were discussed in some detail illustrate the reasons and explanations for migration on a local or regional level, emphasising the lack of non-agricultural employment as a key determinant in the incidence of migration. Of course, it should be said that these reports or surveys tend to highlight what is wrong or deficient in a district, and the choice of study area is determined by the fact that it was perceived to be an 'underdeveloped region'. What is particularly interesting about Hannan's study of the migration intentions of young persons in Cavan is the fact that educational attainment was positively correlated with migration, with the most migratory grouping being those with secondary education. To realise occupational and income aspirations, young people believed that they had to leave the local area. This was also found to be the case in the Drogheda Manpower Survey in 1967: 80 per cent of boys completing the Leaving Certificate intended to leave the area, with one-quarter of this grouping planning to go to Britain.[113] Of the young women taking the Leaving Certificate, 66 per cent intended to leave the area, with half of them planning to leave Ireland: of this grouping 50 per cent intended to travel to Britain.[114] It is also noteworthy that agriculture as a way of life was rejected by many migrants. It has been observed that economic expectations were a key factor in the migration 'decision'. The local 'resource' surveys demonstrate that in the poorer regions of western and north-western Ireland, livelihoods other than farming were perceived to present better opportunities. The rejection of the family holding by the prospective heir is the most extreme example of this phenomenon.

IV

In the interwar years, the rate of migration for Irish Protestants was higher than that for Irish Catholics, as was demonstrated in chapter 2. In this section whether this pattern continued throughout the postwar period will be assessed. Between 1946 and 1971, the population of the main Protestant denominations in the Irish Republic declined by roughly a quarter.[115] The percentage of each religious denomination in the total population for the three censuses of 1946, 1961 and 1971 is set out in Table 5.7, and it can be seen that each Protestant denomination decreased in numbers relative to the total population. In 1961, Protestants formed roughly five per cent of the total population, hence the title of Viney's famous pamphlet, *The five per cent*, published in 1965.[116] By 1971, at the close of our period, Protestants constituted approximately four per cent of the population of the Republic. How this state of affairs came about has attracted a good deal of scholarly attention, particularly from demographers, and a range of explanations have been advanced focusing on the rate of natural increase, or more accurately natural decrease, and the impact of migration on the main Protestant denominations.

Walsh has estimated that the 'other denominations', mostly

Table 5.7 Population of the Irish Republic by religion, 1946–71 (%)[a]

Period	1946	1961	1971
Roman Catholic	94.3	94.9	93.9
Church of Ireland	4.2	3.7	3.3
Presbyterians	0.8	0.7	0.5
Methodists	0.3	0.2	0.2
Jewish	0.1	0.1	0.1
Other	–	0.2	0.2
No religion	–	–	0.3
No statement	–	0.2	1.6

Note:[a] The census in 1946 provides no details of the 'other' (including 'no statement') category.
Source: B. M. Walsh, 'Trends in the religious composition of the population in the Republic of Ireland, 1946–71', *Econ. Soc. Rev.*, Vol. 6, 1975, table 1, p. 544.

Protestants, experienced a 'substantial' natural decrease in the inter-censal period, 1946–61.[117] The reasons for this parlous state of affairs for any population were related to both the fertility and nuptiality of Irish Protestants: 'The natural decrease reflects a low marriage rate, moderately low marriage fertility, an abnormally old population age structure (the consequence of a falling population in previous decades), and the impact of mixed marriages in which all the offspring are raised as Catholics.'[118] In the 1960s these trends continued to affect the Protestant community and it has been estimated that the average annual rate of natural decrease for 'other denominations' (mostly Protestants) was –3.0 per 1,000 in the decade 1961–71.[119] The issue of mixed marriages between Protestants and Catholics which, under Roman Catholic teaching, resulted in the children being raised as Catholics, has been the subject of some controversy. This is not the place for a full discussion of this vexed aspect of the demographic decline of the Protestant community in the Irish Republic, but suffice it to say that in the 1960s the number of Protestants who married Catholics in a Roman Catholic ceremony increased. Walsh concluded that 'mixed marriages have been an important phenomenon for the non-Roman Catholic population of the Republic between 1961 and 1971, and probably at earlier dates'.[120] A recent detailed analysis con-duced by Sexton and O'Leary found further corroborative evidence that the impact of mixed marriages was a 'significant factor' in the decline of the Protestant community:

> Mixed marriages are therefore very relevant to numerical loss in so far as the minority religious communities are concerned as the children of these mar-riages are disproportionally brought up as Catholics. These losses assume even greater significance if cumulative or intergenerational effects are taken into account. The evidence suggests therefore, that mixed marriages were a signif-icant factor in contributing to the decline in the minority religious communi-ties in the period since the Second World War.[121]

Our particular interest is in the rates of net migration that were experienced by the main Protestant denominations. Several estimates of net migration from the Irish Republic by religious denomination have been calculated by demographers. Whereas in the interwar period the rates of net migration were higher for Protestants than Catholics, for the postwar years the situation was reversed. Using the cohort depletion methods discussed in chapter 2, Sexton and O'Leary calculated net migration rates distinguishing between Catholics and other religious denominations (see Table 5.8). These estimates

Table 5.8 Average annual rate of net Irish migration per 1,000 of the average population by religion, 1946–71

Period	Rate of net migration		
	Roman Catholic	Other denominations	Total
1946–61	−12.4	−8.8	−12.2
1961–71	−4.7	−4.4	−4.6

Source: After J.J. Sexton and Richard O'Leary, 'Factors affecting population decline in minority religious communities in the Republic of Ireland', in *Building trust in Ireland: studies commissioned by the Forum for Peace and Reconciliation*, Belfast, 1996, table 9, p. 302.

demonstrate that in the first intercensal period for which comparable data are available, between 1946 and 1961, the rate for 'other denominations' is considerably lower than for Catholics. In the following decade, the net migration rates are roughly comparable across all religious denominations. These estimates conform broadly with Walsh's two earlier studies. In the intercensal period 1946–61, the rates were higher for Roman Catholics (–7.6 per 1,000) than for 'other denominations' (–12.5 per 1,000).[122] Walsh disaggregated the broad category of 'other religious denominations' in his cohort depletion estimates in the later study and his results are presented in Table 5.9. What emerges clearly is that the migration rate for members of the Church of Ireland is about one-third the Roman Catholic rate in the 1960s. However, this contrasts sharply with the rate for other Protestant denominations such as the Presbyterians and Methodists with their respective average annual rates of net migration of –13.9 and –13.4 per 1,000 of the population. Even when the three main Protestant denominations are grouped together, the rate is still considerably lower than that for Catholics. Therefore the impact of migration on the Protestant community was of less significance in comparison with that on Catholics in the postwar period. Without doubt, migration accelerated the decline of the Protestant community, although clearly the main factors that account for this diminution in numbers over time are the negative rate of natural increase and the impact of mixed marriages. In fact, as Walsh notes, 'the migration experience of the Protestant community has been much more favourable than that of the Roman Catholic community in the 1960s'.[123]

Table 5.9 Average annual rate of net Irish migration per 1,000 of the population
by religious denomination, 1961–71

Period	Roman Catholic	Church of Ireland	Presbyterians	Methodists	Three major Protestant denominations
1961–71	–6.5	–2.5	–13.9	–13.4	–4.7

Source: Walsh, 'Trends in the religious composition', table 2, p. 547.

The explanations for migration of Protestants would be comparable to the range of factors that were outlined for all religious denominations. There is much of value in Bowen's suggestion that the
economic pressures which resulted in the migration of Catholics were
similar to those that affected Protestants.[124] The cultural and political
factors that accelerated migration during the interwar period seem to
have been of far less consequence in the 1950s and 1960s. However, the
tradition of migration that had been established in previous decades
was still of some significance. One study of the postwar Church of Ireland population of the diocese of Ferns in county Wexford found the
general move away from agriculture and the lack of alternative
employment for both sexes (a problem experienced by all religious
denominations) explained why so few young Protestants remained in
the diocese and instead sought better opportunities either in Dublin
or abroad.[125] A similar study of Ardfert in county Kerry arrived at the
same conclusion, but also noted that females who had not married by
the age of 25 years tended to migrate, obviously reflecting a desire to
seek better career and marriage opportunities.[126]

For the Church of Ireland community in Ireland during the postwar period, the level of public comment with regard to migration is
not as high as it was in the interwar period. However, at the General
Synod of the Church of Ireland in 1956 a Commission for Sparsely
Populated Areas was instituted to inquire into the question of
parochial reorganisation.[127] During the course of its inquiries conducted over a period of nine years, the commission found that one of
the main problems facing the Church of Ireland was migration. In
many parishes, the number of people aged between 16 and 24 years
was low in proportion to the number of children below this age.[128] The
commission also noted a serious lack of information concerning the
opportunities for employment in the Irish Republic, and with a view

to alleviating this problem it published a pamphlet for distribution to all those of school-leaving age to brief them on possible career opportunities in Ireland.[129] Some 12,000 copies of this pamphlet were printed in 1959 and distributed to teachers, clergymen and parents. As George Simms, the archbishop of Dublin, noted in the foreword, the objective was to dispel the commonly held belief among Protestants that no opportunities for employment existed at home for the young members of their families. According to Simms, 'psychologically, too many people, by their attitudes and presuppositions, had become emigrants. Emigration was the word uppermost in their minds as a quick and ready expedient when the question of choosing a career for their children arose.'[130] The success or otherwise of the pamphlet is difficult to gauge but as already noted, the rate of migration for Protestants did decline in the 1960s, although this undoubtedly had more to do with improvements in the Irish economy at this time than any other factor.

In short, the decline of the total number of Protestants in the Irish Republic in the postwar period can be attributed to three interrelated factors: firstly, a negative rate of natural increase owing to the high death rates, a low rate of nuptiality and low rates of marital fertility; secondly, the impact of mixed marriages with Catholics and the concomitant obligation to raise the children as Catholics; and lastly, migration. Migration rates for Protestants were somewhat lower than those experienced by Catholics, although within the Protestant community, denominations such as Presbyterians and Methodists had a higher rate of migration than members of the Church of Ireland. Protestants migrated for a similar range of reasons to those advanced for Catholics, and there is no evidence to suggest that the cultural and political factors which accelerated migration in the interwar years continued to be of significance in the postwar period.

V

Whilst migration to Britain was the subject of much discussion in this period, the hue and cry associated with this issue in the 1940s and early 1950s was conspicuous by its absence in the late 1950s and throughout the 1960s. During the period under consideration, the Fianna Fáil party held power for four successive administrations (1957–61, 1961–65, 1965–69, 1969–73) with de Valera as taoiseach for a short period (1957–59), Lemass for a much longer tenure (1959–66) and finally, Jack Lynch, who held office for eight years (1966–73). However, at least in the popular historical consciousness, the 1960s in the Irish Republic are usually associated with the 'Lemass era'.

Inevitably, the availability and veracity of statistics that purported to gauge the extent of migration were a matter of debate. When in February 1959 the taoiseach, Seán Lemass, was asked to provide estimates of emigration for the previous year, the problems with regard to annual migration statistics were outlined for the benefit of Dr Noël Browne.[131] As Lemass remarked in the reply to a supplementary parliamentary question, no method of estimating annual migration figures had been devised, despite several investigations by the Central Statistics Office. He noted that the only satisfactory estimates were those of net migration based on census returns.[132] Lemass was again questioned on the matter in November 1960 and he stated that it was not possible to devise a scheme without causing great inconvenience to the travelling public.[133] Regardless of the obvious difficulties in the institution of such a check on migration, it is a matter for conjecture whether the government actually desired the production of such migration estimates, especially considering the political capital that the opposition parties could derive from the publication of embarrassing annual migration figures. In another context, that of the publication of unemployment statistics, Lemass displayed a revealing indication of his views regarding the publicity generated following the dissemination of statistics:

> The publication of depressing statistics, whatever justification there may be for it on the grounds of bringing the facts of the national economic situation to public attention, can have in itself economic effects. It is so important to sustain public confidence in the capacity of the country to achieve economic expansion that this must be the overriding consideration when deciding both the timing of publication and the method of presentation of the data.[135]

Sometime later, in April 1964, Seán MacEntee, the tánaiste, stated at a public meeting in Blessington, county Wicklow, that an estimate of 12,500 people produced by the Central Statistics Office for migration for the year ending 1963 was a miscalculation by the statisticians.[135] These estimates were not in fact of net migration, but rather net passenger movement which Lemass observed 'agreed reasonably closely with the estimates of net emigration derived from the censuses'.[136] The background of this allegation was that estimates of net passenger balance of 25,000 people for the following year (1964) had been produced by the Central Statistics Office, thereby suggesting that the number of people leaving the country had doubled. MacEntee's comments were reported in the press.[137] He was requested by the taoiseach to write a report on his statement, presumably since MacEntee seemed to be suggesting that the government was interfering with the independence of the Central Statistics Office.[138] His report makes for interesting reading, not only for what it reveals about the attitude of a leading politician to statistics, but also because of the political fall-out associated with estimates of net migration. In the first instance, as Lemass stated in the Dáil, the figure for net outward passenger movement for the year ending February 1963 was 12,200 people, and for the following year this rose to 25,000 people.[139] This was where the problem arose, as these estimates seemed to suggest, in the minds of opposition politicians at least, that net migration had doubled. Lemass pointed out that the Central Statistics Office had not amended or cancelled any statistics. This was in effect a refutation of MacEntee's original statement. Secondly, and perhaps fairly, he observed that the figures for the year ending February 1963 were not a reliable guide to the general trends in net migration as adverse weather conditions in Britain at the beginning of the year had created 'an abnormal employment situation' and decreased the level of migration.[140] Lemass, however, made a telling comment regarding estimates produced by the Central Statistics Office in reply to a supplementary question concerning the independence of the office:

> The deputy may be assured that the information published by the Central Statistics Office is what they believe to be correct but I am certainly not going to preclude myself from discussing with the Director of the Central Statistics Office the method of compilation of estimates if, in my opinion, they require to be revised.[141]

His qualifications in the statistical sciences which would enable him to arrive at such an assessment were not alluded to.

Political discourse in relation to the level of migration was invariably centred on the success or otherwise of Irish economic policy. In the late 1950s and throughout the 1960s, successive Fianna Fáil administrations could point to the institution of a series of national economic programmes as evidence of their commitment to creating the circumstances whereby migration would be reduced. Lemass in particular viewed the reduction of emigration as the 'acid test' for government policy, and 'the inability of many governments with which he was associated to effect any more than a temporary reduction [in emigration] was a permanent reminder of an uncompleted task'.[142] Lemass stated in November 1960, in response to criticism of the government's record with regard to migration, that 'we have set ourselves the task of removing the economic causes of emigration by the promotion of a major programme of economic expansion'.[143] In 1961 Lemass identified emigration as being 'the central problem so far as national policy is concerned'.[144] In fact, the *Programme for economic expansion*, the white paper published in 1958 based on Whitaker's *Economic Development* of the same year, specifically identified the reduction of migration as a key objective of increased national output.[145] Similarly, the *Second programme for economic expansion*, published in 1963 and covering the period from 1964 until 1970, referred to the reduction of net migration in the early 1960s and by implication attributed this decrease to the achievements of the earlier white paper.[146] More optimistically, the *Second programme* (which was later abandoned in 1967 when it became apparent that its targets would not be met) had the reduction of net migration as 'one of its basic aims', and set out to achieve the reduction of the level of net migration by 1970 to '10,000 at most'.[147] By 1968, a detailed review of progress of the programme acknowledged that achieving this reduction in net migration was proving elusive in practice.[148]

There is to some degree an element of *post hoc, ergo propter hoc* reasoning among historians and other commentators in attributing the reduction of net migration in the 1960s simply to these elements of economic planning.[149] For instance, Tobin seems to suggest a direct relationship between Irish economic policy and levels of emigration.[150] On the other hand, Kennedy has suggested that the initiatives undertaken by the Irish state, including a broad range of measures encompassing other elements of economic policy rather than solely the first programme for economic expansion (1959–63), in conjunction with developments in the international economy, are also crucial factors in any understanding of the relative prosperity of the Irish economy in the 1960s: 'What is most significant about domestic policy, as it evolved over time, was that it was well positioned to take advantage of opportunities in the international economy, since the key for industrial growth for a small, relatively open economy ultimately lay outside Ireland.'[151] It is therefore somewhat facile to argue that the reduction in Irish net migration in the 1960s was brought about solely as a result of Irish economic policy since clearly exogenous factors beyond the direct control of Irish policy makers contributed significantly to this economic prosperity, which in turn resulted in a lower rate of migration to Britain.

It was also acknowledged by some politicians that migration was additionally influenced by non-economic factors. When addressing the Dublin Chamber of Commerce in October 1960, Seán Lemass stated that there were 'social and psychological forces at work which were as potent as, if not more potent than, economic factors'.[152] He was referring to the attitude whereby migration was viewed as inevitable for young Irish people and suggested that school children should be conditioned to think about the opportunities available at home from an early age.[153] In addition, a more widespread change of attitudes towards migration was required in order 'to get public acceptance of the idea that excessive emigration can be brought to an end' and that 'its persistence was not inevitable'.[154] His analysis of the place of migration in the Irish national psyche is worthy of quotation:

> It would be a very foolish man indeed who would suggest that the factors affecting and sustaining Irish emigration are simple and capable of a simple remedy. It is time, however, that we began to think deeply about it and not merely as a political catch-cry or as a measure of our economic expansion needs. It would help, also, if we could encourage more objective thinking about it without allowing judgements to be swamped by emotionalism, although that is not easy in view of our national history and the personal problems which are often involved.[155]

In another speech the following year, Lemass noted that, although the primary responsibility for economic development lay with the state, 'eliminating the causes of excessive emigration is everybody's business'.[156] In 1959, James Dillon, the future leader of Fine Gael, observed that basically people did not leave the country because of economic want but rather to increase their earning potential.[157] What he did not seem to understand was that those from the poorer parts of rural Ireland, or at the bottom of the hierarchical social structure, were no longer content to simply survive at a virtual subsistence level since they had the option of earning a much higher wage in Britain. The point which should be emphasised perhaps is that attitudes towards migration were slowly and gradually changing among some members of the body politic. Gone for the most part was the condemnatory rhetoric which characterised much of the discourse in the late 1940s and early 1950s. The reasons underlying this subtle change in the attitudes and views of politicians are worthy of attention. Firstly, after nearly 40 years of self-government it became acutely obvious that even with relative economic prosperity, people would still leave the Irish Republic to seek a livelihood in another country and the state could not actually do very much to prevent this flow which emanated mostly from the agricultural labour force. In response to the debate in Britain surrounding possible immigration restrictions in November 1961 and the possibility that controls would be introduced on the entry of Irish citizens, Lemass asserted that 'there is in Ireland a desire to minimise and eventually eliminate emigration, and the government's economic development plans envisage this *possibility*' (my emphasis).[158] He further reflected on the ease of movement between the two countries and ruled out some form of bilateral labour agreement with the British authorities:

> While the Irish government would see some advantages in an arrangement by which Irish workers, before going to Britain, could have an offer of employment, certified as suitable and bona fide by a British government authority, it could not agree to participate in any scheme by which such offers would be made in Ireland, and which might be regarded – or in effect so operate – as to be an encouragement to emigration.[159]

Secondly, even though there was a reluctance on the part of the Irish state to institute a formal labour agreement with the British authorities, there was an implicit acceptance that the long-standing association in Irish nationalist thinking between emigration and the ill-effects of British rule could no longer apply some 40 years after independence. Lastly, a distinction – albeit a fairly nebulous one – was made by some politicians between 'necessary' and 'unnecessary' migration for employment in Britain. This was a significant nuance in official thinking in relation to emigration. Lemass made such a distinction in a number of speeches and another minister, Donogh O'Malley, stated in 1966 that the aim of the policy of the Irish state was not to 'eliminate emigration' since people would still wish to leave the country for a variety of reasons:

> The provision of sufficient job opportunities so that no one is compelled to go abroad in search of a fair or acceptable standard of living is still an important national objective. In a world of jet travel, and movement it would be rash to expect emigration to be completely terminated. But our goal is to reach the point where emigration is 'optional' – where people emigrate not because they have to, but because they want to. Then we would have provided our citizens with the choice which they are entitled to, as citizens of the world.[160]

Whatever the more nuanced views expressed in relation to migration itself, the Irish state continued to retain a close interest in the welfare of Irish persons living in Britain│ However, the Irish state was very reluctant to provide financial assistance despite numerous requests to do so.[161] The issue arose in relation to the Irish centres that were set up in the late 1950s and 1960s by the Roman Catholic church in cities throughout Britain including London, Liverpool, Manchester and Birmingham.[16]│ The position of the government was outlined in some detail in 1964 by Frank Aiken, the minister for external affairs. According to Aiken, it was not feasible for the state to offer assistance to Irish citizens living outside the country:

> The government is of course willing and anxious to help all Irish citizens in need, but distribution of state funds on an *ad hoc* basis to various individuals, organisations and areas in Britain could not be effectively and equitably administered. Equity and reasonable control of the expenditure of the taxpayers' money require that the distribution of state funds to groups of Irish citizens claiming assistance should take place here in Ireland in accordance with the rules which govern our non-contributory social services.[163]

The long-established (and convenient) policy of the Irish state was that such welfare work was more properly the remit of voluntary agencies, particularly the range of Catholic organisations involved in assisting Irish migrants. Quite apart from the question of financial responsibility, civil servants and ministers argued that the Catholic church would 'be far more effective than anything that can usefully be done by state interference', to quote the Irish ambassador to Britain, H. J. McCann, writing in 1958.[164] These sentiments are reminiscent of the stand adopted in the early to mid-1950s when the Irish state was requested to become actively involved in the provision of resources for welfare work with Irish migrants. Then, it was stated by government ministers that the needs of migrants were the concern of the Catholic clergy rather than Irish officials.

Sometime later, this point was underlined in contacts between the hierarchy of the Roman Catholic church in Ireland and the Irish government in 1965. The joint secretaries of the hierarchy wrote to Lemass in February 1965 to express their 'grave concern' on the matter of the migration of young people under the age of 18 years to Britain with its inherent 'dangers'.[165] The Catholic hierarchy requested that the Irish state take action to control this movement across the Irish Sea. The reply from Lemass is particularly revealing. He acknowledged that the government 'have long been concerned' with the migration of young persons but he ruled out any form of restriction on moral, legal and practical grounds. In addition he noted that 'it should also be borne in mind that the great majority of young people who emigrate to Great Britain appear to do so with their parents' consent'.[166] The matter did not rest there and the hierarchy in July 1965 requested that the government provide financial assistance for the Irish centres in Britain, some of which were in dire straits.[167] The response from Lemass outlined the government's policy in relation to the question of the funding of Irish centres: 'the government remain of the opinion that the diversion of Irish state revenue to the support of the Irish centres in England would be unsound from the point of view of state finance and would, in practice, be incapable of being kept within fixed limits'.[168] He also reiterated the long-held view that it was more proper for such centres to be financed on a voluntary basis and suggested that a campaign to solicit donations be launched by the Irish hierarchy which would have the full support of members of the government.[169] Sometime later, in 1970, the Irish hierarchy did actually follow this course of action and sponsored a 'once only' collection for the Irish migrants living in Britain, this money being used to help fund Irish centres.[170] It should be said that the government's stance on the provision of funding for welfare work with Irish migrants was consistent with that outlined in response to similar requests in the late 1930s: the Irish state did not view such activities as falling within the remit of exchequer funding, perhaps realising that such a commitment could be setting a precedent which would place an unwelcome burden on Irish taxpayers. In a similar manner to the outcome of similar representations in the mid-1950s, the Catholic church was given no other option but to draw on the generosity of its flock living in Ireland.

A common feature of migration discourse in other sending societies during the postwar period was a concern about the skilled nature of the migrant flow. In the Irish Republic such anxiety was somewhat muted since it was realised that it was impossible to accommodate all skilled workers within the home economy. The Commission on Higher Education, 1960–67, noted within the broader context of the provision of medical education that the migration of doctors trained in Ireland was a well-established trend, although it was 'particularly difficult to place a figure on the rate of emigration of Irish doctors'.[171] It was estimated that roughly 25 per cent of Irish medical graduates migrated for employment in other countries, the majority going to Britain.[172] However, a survey of medical graduates from University College, Cork, in the decade 1945–54, found that over half of the 408 respondents were living in the United Kingdom.[173] Nevertheless, the commission was not convinced that this survey was wholly representative and suggested that the lower figure of 25 per cent was probably a more accurate estimate. For one member, the redoubtable former secretary of the Department of Finance and ex-governor of the Central Bank of Ireland, J. J. McElligott, the data from the Cork survey were hard evidence that third-level educational provision for doctors in Ireland not only was adequate but could also produce a surplus: 'These various figures go some way towards refuting charges of lack of university openings and facilities in this country and show that, in addition to meeting our home requirements, we produce substantial numbers for export.'[174]

Migration did not affect solely medical graduates, as illustrated by the results of a survey of the future intentions of 'several hundred' male commerce, engineering and science students in Irish universities in the mid-1960s.[175] Roughly half of the students interviewed intended to emigrate soon after graduation, although many expressed a desire to return home after a period of three to five years abroad.[176] A comprehensive investigation of the Irish 'brain drain' phenomenon was undertaken by Lynn in the late 1960s. He estimated that 'somewhere over half of Irish graduates are permanently lost to Ireland', and he also found that in a survey of male students across all subjects in University College, Dublin, approximately 79 per cent intended to migrate.[177] It is also noteworthy that Lynn did not deem it appropriate to include female graduates in his research. Notwithstanding the large percentage of males who intended to migrate after graduating from university, by tracing a cohort who actually left University College, Dublin, in 1952, it was possible to state more definitely the extent of the 'brain drain'. Of 223 males who left this university in 1952, 187 were traceable; 27 per cent were employed abroad but, as Lynn observed, it is likely that a high proportion of those whom he was unable to trace were living outside the state.[178] The general conclusion that can be drawn from Lynn's study is that high levels of graduate migration were evident in the 1960s. As regards possible explanations, Lynn remarked that the nature of third-level education in Ireland was to some extent a factor in this 'brain drain': 'The brain drain appears to be due partly to our producing more graduates than there is demand for in Ireland and partly to producing graduates of the wrong kind.'[179]

As a result of the emphasis in Irish university education on the traditional professions such as medicine and engineering and the consequent neglect of subjects such as business studies, Irish universities were 'in some way orientating students towards employment abroad' or in other words, training students for export.[180] However, Lynn also acknowledged that, in order to encourage young people to remain in Ireland and those abroad to return, the level of taxation would need to be in line with that prevailing elsewhere.[181]

Lynn's study is a good example of the more informed discussion of the issue of migration which characterised the close of the period under study. With economic planning came an attempt to place the study of the economic and social issues that confronted the Irish Republic on a firm empirical footing.[182] The establishment of the Economic Research Institute in 1960 in particular supported empirical research which enabled policy makers to draw upon professionally conducted studies. By the late 1960s the institute had added social research to its general brief.[183] Hannan's work, *Rural exodus*, was completed with assistance from the Economic and Social Research Institute and Lynn's study was undertaken whilst he was a member of staff at the institute. The flow of research papers throughout the 1960s points to the fact that the philosophy underlying much of the research endeavour was that of applied research. An Foras Talúntais was founded in 1958 to assist and undertake agricultural research and, as was illustrated by the reports discussed earlier in this chapter, this organisation did much to actually investigate the problems facing rural Ireland.[184]

Periodicals and journals such as *Christus Rex*, which previously contained articles that were good on opinion and pitched at a general level, increasingly became forums for the presentation of detailed research findings. For example, in January 1961 a number of the journal *Christus Rex* was devoted to the 'emigration issue' and contained articles penned by those with special knowledge of migration trends. One author noted that there seemed to be a recognition that there was a 'new policy of adjustment to the stubborn fact of emigration'.[185] In some senses this was quite an acute observation. Migration was a permanent feature of postwar Irish society and neither exhortation nor condemnation had stemmed the flow. In tandem with the surveys conducted under the auspices of An Foras Talúntais, other detailed examinations of regions of western Ireland which seemed to be in a process of irreversible decline appeared in journals such as *Christus Rex* in the 1960s.[186]

By the close of our period, migration was viewed with a certain degree of ambivalence. Nearly 50 years after the foundation of the Irish state and with a perception that fewer people were leaving the Irish Republic in the late 1960s, rhetoric denouncing emigration was a rarity. Instead attitudes among the élite levels of Irish society acknowledged that some level of migration to Britain was inevitable given the employment opportunities and high wages in Britain, and the challenge was to reduce this level even further. On the part of politicians and other commentators, there was also a distinction made between those who migrated because of sheer economic necessity and those who left for better jobs at a higher level of remuneration. By the mid-1960s the emotion that was associated with this subject dissipated, and as Jackson noted in 1966, 'many of the ideological issues which have clouded the emigration question are now being resolved'.[187] That the ideological and political aspects of migration had altered was evident from the comments of the former director of the Central Statistics Office, M. D. McCarthy, who challenged the traditional consensus in 1967 on the place of migration within the Irish national consciousness.

> When Irishmen [sic] discuss emigration they are apt to give expression to value judgements and to base these rather indiscriminately on moral, sociological, economic and sentimental considerations. Indubitably the individual emigrant Irishman, on average, benefits materially from emigration, in that he enjoys a higher material standard of living in the country to which he goes than he would enjoy if he stayed at home.[188]

McCarthy also maintained the right of the individual to leave the country for economic betterment and concluded that value judgements in relation to this subject were of little worth, but that practical policies which might reduce the incidence of migration should be of paramount concern: 'At any rate many of the credits and debits of this type are incommensurable and one simply cannot say that emigration is "good" or "bad". It is a fact of Irish life and our task is to try to reduce its magnitude and mitigate its undesirable effects.'[189]

Notwithstanding the more nuanced views which were expressed vis-á-vis Irish migration in the 1960s, deeply engrained attitudes still persisted in official circles. The Department of Labour under the then minister, Patrick Hillery, proposed a radical rethink of the policy of the Irish state on migration to Britain in November 1968. The logic underpinning this reappraisal of official policy was that migration to Britain would continue 'despite sustained economic growth and rising living standards' and 'a more realistic and positive attitude towards the welfare of migrants' was required.[190] In short, the Department of Labour proposed that migrants wishing to travel abroad would be made aware of opportunities for employment in Britain through local employment exchanges, state aid would be provided to voluntary organisations that catered for Irish migrants, both in the Irish Republic and Britain, and lastly, arrangements should be made with the British authorities for mutual recognition of educational qualifications.[191] The dangers of such a policy were anticipated, in particular the perception that the Irish state was encouraging migration to Britain; according to the Department of Labour, 'it would be reasonable ... to point out that the extension of facilities as now envisaged represents a recognition of basic facts'.[192] The proposed measures constituted a extremely significant departure in the policy of the Irish state on migration to Britain. In essence, the Department of Labour envisaged a system which would be similar in content and purpose to the bilateral labour agreements that regulated the flow of workers from southern European countries to the western industrialised economies. However, considerable opposition to these measures emanated from the Department of External Affairs and the Department of Finance. For the Department of External Affairs, the proposed liaison between the Irish and British employment services would be an injudicious move because of 'the danger that such arrangements would give them [the British government] the possibility of exerting a control over Irish emigration to Britain which they would not hesitate to use to their own advantage if necessary'.[193] Equally important was the atmosphere in relation to migration to Britain:

> In Britain there is a growing volume of unease about immigration into that country, and while the anxiety at present relates primarily to coloured immigration it could well develop into a campaign against all immigration so as to avoid charges of colour prejudice. The liaison proposed between the Irish and British services concerned with Irish immigration to Britain could be the thin end of a wedge by means of which the British might ultimately try to establish a control over Irish immigration enabling them to tailor it to meet their own needs, if any.[194]

There was clearly an element of exaggeration in this suggestion that the British state would impose some form of restriction on Irish immigration, but perhaps the principal point which the Department of External Affairs wished to underline was that it was inadvisable to grant the British authorities any element of control over the migrant flow from the Irish Republic, in case it was decided at a later date to apply some form of restriction on entry. In addition, it was regarded as 'inadvisable' to provide financial assistance to voluntary agencies working with Irish migrants in Britain. Not surprisingly, officials from the Department of Finance concurred with this view on the provision of financial aid, arguing that this would 'reduce the scope for voluntary effort'.[195] Both departments emphasised the possible adverse criticism which would result from such measures, and the role that the educational system already played in preparing migrants for employment both at home and abroad. These proposals were postponed from the agenda of the cabinet throughout 1968 and ultimately the cabinet agreed in March 1969 only to pursue the issues of mutual recognition of educational qualifications and limited financial aid for advisory services for migrants.[196] The chief significance of this policy proposal lies in the fact that by the late 1960s certain elements within official circles were urging that a more pragmatic stance be adopted in relation to Irish migration to Britain which, it was believed, would benefit prospective migrants and those already living in Britain. That these measures were not fully implemented, presumably on the basis that they would be seen to encourage migration, is indicative of the political significance still attached to emigration in the late 1960s. The government of the Irish Republic would not be a party to any agreement with the British authorities which could be interpreted as either aiding or encouraging migration, notwithstanding the obvious benefits that could be accrued from the point of view of migrants.

VI

Contrary to popular perception, the Irish were by far the largest ethnic minority in Britain in 1971.[197] The impact of the 'second wave' of Irish migration to Britain was illustrated by the results of the 1971 census. By that year, the Irish-born population in Great Britain numbered 709,235 people, a decrease of roughly 70,000 since the 1961 census.[198] The Irish-born population was concentrated in the large urban settlements of Britain, particularly in the Greater London area.[199] In occupational terms, Irish migrants were heavily represented in the skilled and unskilled manual categories, but as Jackson has noted, 'they penetrated deeply into the occupational and social structure at all levels' (see Table 5.10).[200] Irish migrants were clustered within

Table 5.10 Occupational categories of Irish-born population in Britain in 1971 (%)[a]

Occupational category	Male	Female
Professional	3.0	2.0
Intermediate	9.0	16.0
Skilled non-manual	7.0	15.0
Skilled manual	34.0	23.0
Partly skilled manual	20.0	24.0
Unskilled manual	20.0	11.0
Unclassified	5.0	9.0
	100.0	100.0

Note: [a]Rounding errors result in discrepancies in percentage totals.
Source: After J. A. Jackson, 'The Irish in Britain', in *Ireland and Britain since 1922*, ed. P. J. Drudy, Irish studies 5, Cambridge, 1986, table. 7.2, p. 130.

particular occupational groupings: for instance, of all immigrant males employed in the construction industry, roughly two-thirds were born in the Irish Republic, and of all female immigrant workers in the distributive trades, one-third were Irish-born.[201]

As was noted earlier, Irish citizens retained the right to enter Britain freely under the British Nationality Act of 1948; in addition, they could vote in local and national elections, apply for naturalisation after five years' residence and were entitled to claim British social security benefits.[202] Throughout the 1960s and culminating in the 1971 Immigration Act, the British state introduced several pieces of legislation which aimed to control immigration from the 'New Commonwealth'.[203] However, this corpus of legislation did not affect the 'special position' afforded Irish citizens, although it did appear likely in 1961 that some degree of control would be applied to Irish immigrants. As a precursor to the announcement of the official government policy on immigration in September 1961, it was suggested that entry controls would apply to all immigrants, including the Irish.[204] When the Irish government approached the British authorities on the matter, fears that Irish immigration would be restricted were alleviated. One Irish official recounted a conversation that a member of the London embassy staff had with an official from the Commonwealth Relations Office which is revealing on the 'special position' of Irish migrants:

> … he thought that in their [Irish citizens] regard a certain amount of administrative 'winking' would have to go on and that emigration from Ireland to Great Britain was unlikely to be radically affected. He thought that the

imposition of a control on movement across the Irish Sea would be extremely difficult short of instituting an expensive administrative machinery to operate such a control.[205]

None the less, others were not so convinced regarding the merits of excluding Irish citizens from any prospective legislation to control immigration. Cyril Osborne, a Conservative member of parliament and notorious campaigner against black immigration, suggested in February 1961 that the solution to Irish immigration was for wealthy Irish-American families such as the Kennedys to invest their money in Ireland and create jobs so that the Irish could remain there.[206] The Commonwealth Immigrants Act which passed through the House of Commons in July 1962 restricted the entry of British subjects coming to employment in Britain by means of a voucher system and was primarily intended to limit the immigration from the 'New Commonwealth'.[207] No control on Irish immigration was introduced, but it is worth noting that some members of parliament suggested during the debates on this bill that Irish people were a 'social liability'.[208] Similarly, the other legislative measures such as the Commonwealth Immigrants Act of 1968 did not impose any restrictions on Irish citizens entering Britain. In 1971 the Immigration Act, which drew together much of the earlier legislation and introduced the notion of 'partial status' for Commonwealth citizens (proof of a close connection with the United Kingdom by birth, descent or settlement), did not affect the free entry of Irish citizens, although they could still be liable to deportation.[209]

Notwithstanding the special legal provisions which related to the entry of Irish citizens, it would be misleading to imply that Irish migrants in Britain were subject to no overt hostility. An opinion survey conducted in October 1967, which posed the question as to whether Britain had 'benefited or been harmed' as a result of Irish immigration, found that 16 per cent believed that the country had benefited from Irish immigration, 22 per cent thought that Britain had been harmed, 46 per cent felt it made no difference and the 'don't knows' accounted for 16 per cent.[210] However, hostility towards Irish people living in Britain tended to be focused around distinct issues, especially crime. In particular, there was a perception that the Irish were more prone to criminality. Such a viewpoint underlies the comments of the recorder of Nottingham who asked a defendant in November 1961 the following question: 'You are not a member of the IRA, I suppose? Or an Irishman, or a Catholic?'.[211] In fact, the person concerned was none of these things. The recorder, Christopher

Shawcross, later apologised for this remark.[212] Back in May 1957, the chairman of the London sessions had observed that 'this court is infested with Irishmen who come here to commit offences and the more that can be persuaded to go back the better'.[213] Under the Commonwealth Immigrants Act, 1962, Irish citizens (and Commonwealth immigrants) not resident in the United Kingdom for five years prior to committing an offence were liable to deportation, and a substantial number of Irish citizens were sent back to Ireland after being found guilty of criminal offences. According to Jackson, these people were sent home mostly for petty crimes, but it also illustrates a more general view of Irish migrants:

> The excessive number of recommendations for deportation of Irish immigrants for petty offences since the implementation of the Commonwealth Immigrants Act [1962] further reflects a view of the Irish as 'undesirables', unwanted and even categorically excluded in advertisements for accommodation or employment – 'No coloured or Irish need apply.'[214]

There is, however, some evidence to suggest that in this case the perception was not entirely divorced from the reality. Two contemporary assessments of the available crime statistics found that Irish people were disproportionately represented among offenders, relative to the total size of the Irish-born population in Britain, although the age profile of Irish migrants was skewed towards young people who were more prone to committing crime.[215] After reviewing sets of data from a number of locations in England, Bottoms concluded that, 'it seems likely . . . that general Irish crime rates in England are relatively high even after allowing for the age bias of the Irish population'.[216] Russell observed that a number of statistics, including those on crime, deportations and the prison population, allowed for only one conclusion: 'having made all possible allowances, we find ourselves faced with the inescapable fact that the state of affairs existing among the Irish in England is not a happy one, and must be the subject of concern and self-questioning for all of us in this country [Irish Republic].'[217]

The reasons that were posited for the greater propensity of Irish migrants to commit crime were numerous, but it seems the upheaval involved in moving from rural Ireland to urban Britain was judged by contemporaries to be a significant factor. Gibbens and Ahrenfeldt described the process in 1966 in general, if impressionistic, terms:

> Irish society, it is argued, has strong external controls in the form of the church's dominant social interest and also in the form of the over-protective

and dominant Irish mother. The individual Irishman [*sic*] internalises these controls, but on leaving a society with such strong external controls for a more flexible and fluid society, delinquency develops. However, the delinquent is still left with inner controls, and this causes him to increase certain types of conflict behaviour such as heavy drinking, and to feel sexual guilt.[218]

Whilst this general theory may well appear attractive, even if it is based for the most part on stereotypical views of the Irish mother and the firm grip of the Irish Catholic church on its flock, when it comes to explaining the higher rate of criminality amongst Irish migrants, it would be difficult to assess its applicability on the basis of detailed evidence. The fact that Irish migrant males were, for the most part, young and single may also account for this propensity towards crime, albeit petty offences such as theft and drunken and disorderly behaviour. The impact of the changes involved in moving from a homogenous stratified rural society to a diverse urban society with its associated problems and freedom may also have been a factor in the high rates of mental illness of the Irish in Britain, although there is some evidence to suggest that this was not peculiar to migrants but also existed among those who were left behind.[219] More importantly, as a detailed study of crime in Birmingham in 1966–67 demonstrates, Irish migrants were 'over-represented among the urban poor and so over-represented among the ranks of offenders'.[220]

Throughout the 1960s, the Institute of Race Relations, which was established in 1958 to facilitate the study of ethnic relations, commissioned a number of studies of the issues relating to immigrants in Britain. A plethora of books, reports and surveys were produced under the auspices of the institute, some of which examined the position of Irish migrants, mainly for comparison purposes with other immigrant groupings. The most famous study, Rex and Moore's *Race, community, and conflict*, contains much of interest relating to Irish migrants in Birmingham. Sparkbrook was in the inner-city area of Birmingham and was associated with poor-quality housing which was predominantly inhabited by immigrants: 55 per cent of the population were immigrants and the Irish were by far the largest immigrant grouping.[221] The Irish population in Birmingham, and specifically in this area, was somewhat transitory, and many wished to move out of the area, although in some senses a permanent Irish 'colony' had developed over time.[222] What emerges clearly from Rex and Moore's study is the distinct Irishness of the migrants in Britain. The key institutions in the daily lives of the Irish in Sparkbrook were the public houses, cafes and shops, but 'the Roman Catholic church is the biggest Irish migrant organisation of all'.[223] Mass attendance rates were high, with nearly three-fifths of the Irish respondents attending mass on a weekly basis.[224] Rex and Moore's comments about the role of the priest, who in this instance was on secondment in Birmingham from county Clare, are of particular interest:

> What the priest saw was a vast mass of Irishmen [*sic*], many of whom would be lost to the church through drink and sex. Against this he saw his role as helping individuals to fight the temptations to which they were subject and to achieve a stable marriage, sound family life, and good housing conditions. The pubs and unsupervised mixed-sex lodging houses stood in the way of this ideal. One prevented saving and the other encouraged extra-marital sex.[225]

The special circumstances in Sparkbrook may account for this crusading zeal in that it was a first step for many of the Irish migrants living there and hence they would be more likely to succumb to the 'evils' of drink and sex. It is difficult to generalise about the Irish population since there was an element of social stratification as might be expected in any 'colony' type structure:

> It should be remembered in all that has been said that there are many different kinds of Irish of varying degrees of respectability and status. The 'respectable' ones tend to assimilate easily into the English working class and eventually to migrate to the suburbs, where their children become absorbed into English society. But there remains a pool of less settled people with slender family ties or perhaps with large families and these loom large in the problems of Sparkbrook's lodging-house area. None the less, there is no Irish-interest organisation which fights for the interests of Irishmen as such. There appears to be no need for one because the opportunities of assimilation are there. What does exist is a colony structure in which people may live before they finally become assimilated.[226]

An earlier study of immigrant communities undertaken by Jones illustrated how this process of dispersal of 'respectable' Irish people occurred in Birmingham, with Irish migrants who were disproportionately clustered in the poorer housing areas moving to the suburban areas to be in turn replaced by 'New Commonwealth' immigrants.[227]

Rose and others argued in their massive survey of British 'race relations' that by 1945 Irish migrants were 'largely accepted' in Britain.[228] In the 1960s and 1970s 'assimilation' was the dominant concern for scholars investigating the position of ethnic minority groupings. More recent studies, however, informed by developments in ethnic studies, point to the fact that Irish migrants developed and maintained a distinctive and enduring ethnic identity in Britain'.[229] Local case studies shed some light on this issue. Walter's research on Bolton, an area of long-standing Irish settlement which had experienced a decrease in the Irish-born population from 7.9 per cent in 1861 to 1.7 per cent in 1971, and Luton, which experienced significant Irish settlement in the postwar period with 5.8 per cent of the population being Irish-born in 1971, emphasises the extent to which the period of time during which settlement had occurred was a key determinant in Irish ethnic identity.[230] Her research, which was based on interviews conducted between 1973 and 1975, found that in Luton the Irish migrants had developed few social contacts with the host community in comparison with the situation in Bolton where 'social networks were well developed and included a majority of non-Irish members'.[231] In Luton, the wave of Irish migrants who came to the town in the postwar period ensured that Irish ethnicity was expressed through the medium of specifically Irish institutions, such as a large Irish club, Gaelic sporting teams and Irish dancing groups. By way of contrast, Bolton had no such institutions which ensured that contact was across a broader community. This point is further illustrated by the marriage patterns of Irish migrants living in Bolton, with 33 per cent of the spouses having no Irish connection compared with only 8 per cent in Luton.[232]

Irish ethnic identity was closely associated with the Roman Catholic church. Hickey has argued that the Catholic Irish immigrant identity was based on the sense of being distinctive and different and that this was reflected in the exhortations of the church authorities to send children to Catholic schools. His comments on Catholics in urban society in the mid-1960s are particularly revealing:

> The positive motive to assimilate is one feature which is conspicuously lacking amongst immigrant Catholics in England. The whole weight of this study has indicated that urban Catholics did not want to 'become English' in the sense of adopting the standards, customs and political outlook and aspirations of the host society. As has been demonstrated, the opposite in fact was true; it was considered disloyalty to Ireland to 'become English' and dangerous to the individual's Catholic faith to come into close contact with non-Catholics. Isolation, then, was not only endured but deliberately encouraged.[233]

Therefore, Hickey identified Catholicism as a defining feature of Irish ethnic identity in Britain. Whilst the Catholic church may have implicitly advocated isolation from the host community in terms of educational provision and its distaste for mixed marriages, the ethnicity of Irish migrants should be viewed within the broader context of the society in which they lived. Ryan, who completed a detailed study on Irish migrants in Britain based on the results of a survey of over 1,400 postwar migrants living in the London area in the early 1970s, observed that a distinctive Irish ethnicity could be discerned:

> a majority of Irish immigrants in Britain have successfully integrated with the host society . . . a sizeable minority have reached the further stage of assimilation . . . [one]-third are at various levels of accommodation, that is they established themselves economically and residentially and conform to the basic social norms of Britain without becoming fully part of the new society and without losing their Irish identity and Irish cultural traits; . . . a further third have achieved integration into British society in that they are involved in the full social, civic, political, religious and economic life of Britain, have achieved some degree of occupational and residential mobility, but without developing any allegiance to Britain and without loss of Irish cultural identity; a final third are well on the way toward identificational and cultural assimilation with their adopted country.[234]

On the basis on Ryan's evidence, it can be seen that by the close of our period, Irish migrants in Britain were not a monolithic grouping who had 'assimilated' within the host society. Geographical concentration, the length of time spent in Britain and the future intentions of migrants to return to Ireland were all significant determinants of Irish migrant identity. For many who viewed their future in Britain some level of integration was evident, although Irish cultural activities still formed a central part of their social life. However, for others involvement in specifically Irish activities and not conforming to British mores or customs proved a defining feature of their ethnicity.

VII

Migration to Britain was rarely viewed as a permanent or lifelong move: for example, the *Report of the Skibbereen social survey* (1967) indicated that over two-thirds of the sample of migrants from the area living in Britain expressed a desire to return to Ireland.[235] Of 110 Irish migrants interviewed in the St Paul's areas of Bristol in 1965, nearly half stated that when they originally left Ireland they had intended to return home at a later date.[236] However, by the time of the survey over two-thirds of the respondents declared their intention to stay in Britain, with one-fifth still hoping to return home.[237] Admittedly surveys of this nature are very sensitive to the point in time when the interviews were completed. A survey of return migration intentions taken in the midst of an economic recession in either the sending or receiving society will produce quite different results. Invariably, migrants, whilst living abroad, do express a desire to return, although whether this aspiration is realised is another matter.[238] Throughout the period under consideration, estimates of net migration do not take account of the fact that a substantial number of people may have left the Irish Republic and subsequently returned during the intervening time between the two enumerations. In addition, with the expansion of inexpensive travel facilities across the Irish Sea, the distinction between permanent return migration and temporary return migration becomes somewhat obscured.[239] Therefore, the scale of return migration within intercensal periods is to some extent a matter for conjecture owing to the absence of frontier controls. However, what is clear is that migration to Britain was not an irrevocable step, unlike previous migration to the United States prior to the Second World War which was almost invariably on a permanent basis. Bovenkerk found in fieldwork conducted in county Kerry in the late 1960s that one-third of the sample had lived or worked overseas, although admittedly the sample was a small one of only 43 people.[240] These estimates are broadly in line with the data from Skibbereen: 24 per cent of the population of this town and 32 per cent of the population of the rural area had spent time outside the country, the majority having been in Britain, according to the results of Jackson's survey taken in 1964.[241] Jackson was to estimate later, in 1966, that 'something in the region of one quarter of the Irish population has at some time lived and worked outside Ireland', although he acknowledges that it is difficult to be conclusive about this matter.[242]

Garvey's examination of net migration data by age and country of birth indicates that, between 1961 and 1971, a trend developed whereby migrants returned from Britain with their families, a conclusion borne out by the finding that there was a net gain of roughly 32,000 children aged under 15 years who had been born in Britain.[243] Using birthplace data from the Irish census taken in 1971, some evidence of the scale and profile of return flow in the period 1970–71 can also be gleaned. Hughes and Walsh have concluded that there was 'an estimated net immigration of nearly 3,000 persons into Ireland in 1970–71'; the gross flows both inwards and outwards were calculated as being eight times as large as the net flow.[244] The vast majority of these immigrants were born in Ireland or were the children of Irish-born parents, and three-quarters of the inflow were resident in the United Kingdom one year previously.[245] Of particular interest are the occupational categories represented in the return migrant flow. For males, 'engineering and related trades', and 'professional and technical workers' were over-represented compared with the proportion of similar categories in the Irish labour force. In the case of females, nearly 45 per cent of one-year immigrants were recorded as 'professional and technical workers', with nurses who had been trained in Britain undoubtedly forming a substantial proportion of this grouping. Walsh and Hughes conclude that these skilled workers played a vital role in the development of the Irish economy.[246] A little-known survey of over 500 returned migrants drawn from counties Dublin, Mayo and Clare completed by the Economic and Social Research Institute (ESRI) in 1975 provides some evidence to support this observation. Three-quarters of those interviewed left with no skill and nearly two-fifths returned with skills acquired in Britain.[247]

Why were migrants returning to the Irish Republic during the late 1960s and early 1970s? Without doubt the relative prosperity experienced at this time was one determining factor as an outward, export-orientated approach was adopted as a key element in Irish economic planning, which together with developments in the international economy resulted in an increase in employment opportunities.[248] Employment in the service and manufacturing industries rose, which provided attractive job opportunities for returned migrants: between 1960 and 1973 manufacturing employment grew by one-third, and service employment increased by over 14 per cent.[249] A study of rural industrialisation completed by Lucey and Kaldor in two areas where new industrial plants were located in counties Sligo and Clare illustrates this point. Roughly two-fifths of the plant employees in Tubercurry, county Sligo, had worked in Britain, with 27 per cent having lived in Britain immediately prior to taking up employment in the plant.[250] For the other plant in Scarriff, county Clare, the figure was 21 per cent, with 13 per cent having worked in Britain just prior to obtaining a job in the plant.[251] Nevertheless, it was concluded that rural industrialisation did not lead to large-scale return migration, although it may have prevented people leaving the area in the first instance:

> This evidence indicates that the new plants did attract back some employees who had left those areas in search of employment in England, but that the major employment effects of the new plants operated through increasing

employment in the two areas by providing employment opportunities for people who would probably have otherwise left the two areas rather than by
attracting back former residents of the areas to work in the new plants.[252]

One factor that facilitated the return of workers from Britain was
the reciprocal social security arrangements between the two countries.
National insurance contributions paid when employed in Britain were
counted for benefits in the Irish Republic, including unemployment
benefit, and provided that a minimum amount of contributions was
paid on return, a claimant could receive the full level of social security
payment.[253] From April 1966 onwards, persons who had paid sufficient
British contributions were entitled to receive a full pension in Ireland
at the British rate.[254] These developments in reciprocal pension payments facilitated the return of persons aged 65 years and over, a trend
that can be noted in Table 5.3. This pattern of elderly return migration
would become a permanent feature of the inflow into the Irish Republic in subsequent decades.[255]

In the 1970s and 1980s a number of scholars examined this movement of people back to Ireland.[256] Whilst taking account of the fact that
differences over time may well hinder the applicability of these findings to the late 1960s and early 1970s, several observations can be
made. Foeken's study of return migration to the regions of Carrick-on-
Shannon and Boyle in counties Leitrim and Roscommon based on
fieldwork conducted in 1975 found that return migrants were living in
roughly a quarter of the sample households, although considering the
rates of migration from this area, this is not altogether surprising.[257]
The highest rate of return migration was amongst migrants who had
travelled to Britain, as might be expected.[258] When asked the principal
motive for returning, a range of answers were given (see Table 5.11). It
appears that males had a tendency to underline economic and altruis-
tic motives, whereas females returned because they found it difficult
to adjust to life elsewhere or to marry. For females, marriage was one
of the principal motives which in effect involved the termination of
their career as paid workers since 'the chances to find an occupation
after return were non-existent' in the area.[259] Without doubt these
responses should be viewed with some degree of caution as returnees
may have rationalised their decision to return at a later date.

Foeken, however, does not examine to any degree the reintegration
of returned migrants. Gmelch's anthropological work on this issue is
particularly valuable. Drawing on data collected by interviews in the
1970s and 1980s, Gmelch found that the 'pull factors, or attractions of

Table 5.11 Principal motives for return: Carrick-on-Shannon and Boyle sample, 1975 (%)

	Males	Females
Could inherit farm/shop	26.4	15.4
To assist family	26.4	15.4
To marry	–	30.8
Could get a job here	18.9	7.7
Bought farm/land	9.4	–
Could not grow accustomed	5.7	23.1
Other reasons	13.2	7.7

n = 53 males, 26 females
Source: Dick Foeken, 'Return migration to a marginal rural area in north-western Ireland', *Tijdschrift voor Economische en Sociale Geografie*, vol. 71, 1980, table 6, p. 116.

the homeland' were cited as reasons for their return home by over 55 per cent of a sample of 606 return migrants in areas of western Ireland.[260] The desire to live near friends and relatives was an equally significant factor with two-fifths citing this reason, whereas employment or occupational 'pull' factors were of less significance.[261] A particularly interesting observation relates to the primacy of economic factors in the original decision to migrate, while strangely they seemed to be of little consequence for return migrants:

> Overall, economic factors were found to be less important in return decisions than were other categories. This contrasts sharply with the overriding importance of economic concerns in out-migration: 71 per cent of the respondents cited either lack of employment or desire for a better job as the primary reason for migrating. For migrants to return to their homelands while there is still higher unemployment than in the host societies attests to the importance of the non-economic motives in Irish return migration.[262]

This would certainly appear to cast doubt on the explanations which view return migration as solely a response to improved economic conditions, although whether this finding would apply to other areas of Ireland is debatable. It would also be informative to ascertain how many return migrants from this area were settled in urban centres such as Dublin and Cork.

In terms of the readjustment of return migrants, the data collected by Gmelch are most revealing. Over half (51 per cent) of the sample stated that during their first year back home they were not satisfied with life and 'would have been happier had they stayed abroad'.[263] The reasons for their dissatisfaction were the lethargic pace of life in rural Ireland, the perceived 'narrow-minded' attitudes of the local people and the problems in re-establishing former relationships with friends and relatives.[264] However, as time passed, returnees became more satisfied with their situation: of those who had been back more than five years, 17 per cent expressed dissatisfaction, although this does not include an estimated 5 to 10 per cent who had re-emigrated.[265] As Gmelch astutely observes, it was the size of the communities to which migrants returned that created many of the problems in terms of readjustment:

> To a large extent, the problems return emigrants experience can be attributed to differences in the scale of the communities they have returned to. Nearly three-quarters of the sample had left large cities in Britain and America and returned to small villages and towns in western Ireland. Their complaints that neighbours seem narrow-minded and provincial would probably be the same had they moved to rural areas within North America or Britain. In other words, many of the complaints about life in small communities in rural Ireland are true of small communities elsewhere.[266]

This is somewhat ironic as one of the principal problems identified with Irish migration to Britain throughout the postwar period was that young people from rural Ireland had difficulty adapting to life in a large urban centre such as London or Birmingham; yet on their return after perhaps a few years in Britain, it appears they found it difficult to readjust to life in rural and small-town Ireland. Census data indicate that many return migrants in the 1960s settled in large centres of population such as Dublin and Cork, reflecting the more attractive employment opportunities available in these cities, particularly in the service sector.[267] In addition, there were also the migrants originally from urban centres who left for Britain and subsequently came back. It is a significant deficiency in the published work on Irish return migration that as yet a study of migrants returning to an urban area rather than a rural community has not been undertaken to date.[268]

Finally, Gmelch touches on one aspect of return migration which has been examined in the course of this study: the impact of returnees on migration patterns from the local area. The majority of respondents believed that migration was on the whole a positive experience: in fact, nearly two-thirds of Gmelch's sample stated that they would encourage young people to migrate.[269] But, as he notes, it was not so much the direct impact but the impression conveyed that was of more import: 'their presence in the local community – more prosperous and more "worldly" than local people – presents an attractive role model for the young.'[270] In some senses, returnees perpetuated the belief that to prosper one must migrate and then later come back home having reaped the benefits of material success elsewhere.

The ESRI survey of returned migrants discussed earlier also investigated the factors underpinning the return 'decision' and a similar range of reasons were offered by respondents. Family ties, a preference for living in Ireland, a desire to raise children and the availability of employment were significant determinants (see Table 5.12). It is noteworthy that the reasons cited for return varied with age. For those migrants who had left before 1950, family ties and caring for relatives were the overriding considerations in the decision to return.[271] On the other hand, migrants who travelled to Britain during the 1950s and 1960s returned home to raise children or to marry. The stage in the life cycle of the migrant therefore determined return migration.[272] When it came to employment, 56 per cent of the respondents sought and secured employment, 11 per cent were unable to find work and roughly a quarter either retired or worked within the family home. It is of particular interest that the average time elapsing before migrants secured employment on their return from Britain was three weeks for those who opted to stay in Ireland.[273] Presumably for many of those who did not find employment, migration again became a realistic option.

Table 5.12 Reasons for return: ESRI sample, 1975 (%)

Family ties	19.9
Preference for Ireland	13.4
To care for relatives	13.2
To bring up children	11.5
Jobs in Ireland	11.5
To marry	5.7
No jobs in Britain	5.0
Better housing	3.6
Hostility to the Irish in Britain	1.3
Less pressure in Ireland	1.1
Living in Britain unpleasant	0.8
Don't know, no answer	13.0

n = 523

Source: B. J. Whelan and J. G. Hughes, *A survey of returned and intending emigrants in Ireland*, Dublin, 1976, p. 45.

VIII

In sharp contrast with the late 1940s and early 1950s, the 1960s witnessed a decrease in the number of people migrating to Britain. By the
early 1970s a substantial return migrant flow is evident which is a
novel development in modern Irish demographic history. Emigration
was seen not as the irreversible and final decision that was associated
with nineteenth-century transatlantic movement, but rather as a temporary period 'across the water'. This no doubt had a significant effect
on views towards migration since for many people it involved only a
relatively brief sojourn abroad. The fact that migrants returned in
such numbers is evidence that, for many, their stay in Britain was
viewed as a stage in the life cycle, rather than an end in itself. For
many others, however, what had originally been intended as a short
stay resulted in permanent settlement in Britain.

NOTES

1 Anthony Fielding, 'Migrations, institutions and politics: the evolution of
European migration policies', in *Mass migration in Europe: the legacy and the future*, ed.
Russell King, London, 1993, p. 43; Enda Delaney, 'Placing postwar Irish migration to
Britain in a comparative European perspective, 1945–81', in *The Irish diaspora*, ed.
Andy Bielenberg, London, pp. 331–56.

2 Russell King, 'European international migration, 1945–90: a statistical and
geographical overview', in *Mass migration in Europe*, ed. King, pp. 22–23.

3 John Salt, 'International labour migration: the geographical pattern of
demand', in *Migration in postwar Europe: geographical essays*, ed. John Salt and Hugh
Clout, London, 1976, p. 98.

4 Brian Girvin, 'Political culture, political independence and economic success
in Ireland', *Irish Political Studies*, Vol. 12, 1997, p. 61.

5 Department of Finance, *Economic development*, Dublin, 1958, Pr. 4803.

6 Ronan Fanning, 'The genesis of *Economic Development*', in *Planning Ireland's
future: the legacy of T. K. Whitaker*, ed. John F. McCarthy, Dublin, 1990, p. 32, and
Ronan Fanning, *The Irish Department of Finance, 1922–58*, Dublin, 1978, pp. 515–16;
B. M. Walsh, 'Economic growth and development', in *Ireland, 1945–70*, ed. J. J. Lee,
Dublin, 1979, pp. 28–29. The preliminary results of the 1956 census were published
in June of the same year.

7 Department of Finance, *Economic development*, p. 5.

8 On this point, see Liam Kennedy, *The modern industrialisation of Ireland,
1940–1988*, Dublin, 1989, p. 15.

9 B. M. Walsh, 'Ireland's demographic transformation, 1958–70', *Econ. Soc. Rev.*, Vol 3, 1972, pp. 251–75; for a comparative overview, see D. C. Coleman, 'The demographic transition in Ireland in international context', in *The development of industrial society in Ireland*, ed. J. H. Goldthorpe and C. T. Whelan, Oxford, 1992, pp. 53–78.

10 B. M. Walsh, *Some Irish population problems reconsidered*, ESRI paper no. 42, Dublin, 1968; 'A study of Irish county marriage rates, 1961–1966', *Population Studies*, Vol. 24, 1970, pp. 205–16; 'Ireland's demographic transformation'; 'Trends in age at marriage in postwar Ireland', *Demography*, Vol. 9, 1972, pp. 187–202.

11 Walsh, 'Ireland's demographic transformation', p. 268.

12 *Census of population of Ireland, 1966, I: population of district electoral divisions, towns and larger units of area*, Dublin, 1967, Pr. 9513, table 1, p. x.

13 *Census of population of Ireland, 1971, I: population of district electoral divisions, towns and larger units of area*, Dublin, 1972, Prl. 2564, table 1, p. xii.

14 Ibid., p. xiv.

15 R. C. Geary and J. G. Hughes, *Internal migration in Ireland*, ESRI paper no. 54, Dublin, 1970, p. 63.

16 Ibid.

17 Ibid.

18 J. G. Hughes and B. M. Walsh, *Internal migration flows in Ireland and their determinants*, ESRI paper no. 98, Dublin, 1980, pp. 54–55.

19 Ibid., p. 75.

20 Ibid.

21 These estimates are broadly in line with those of Hughes used in previous chapters; see J. G. Hughes, *Estimates of annual net migration and their relationship with series on annual net passenger movement: Ireland 1926–76*, ESRI memorandum no. 122, Dublin, 1977, p. 8.

22 *Census of population of Ireland, 1971, I*, table x, p. xxii.

23 Donal Garvey, 'The history of migration flows in the Republic of Ireland', *Population Trends*, No. 39, 1985, p. 25.

24 Ibid.

25 Cormac Ó Gráda and Brendan Walsh, 'The economic effects of emigration: Ireland', in *Emigration and its effects on the sending country*, ed. Beth J. Asch, Santa Monica, 1994, p. 98.

26 Garvey, 'History of migration flows', p. 25.

27 Ibid., table 5, p. 26.

28 B. M. Walsh, 'Expectations, information, and human migration: specifying an econometric model of Irish migration to Britain', *Journal of Regional Science*, Vol. 14, 1974, p. 108; Damian Hannan, 'Irish emigration since the war', typescript of RTE Thomas Davis Lecture, [1973], p. 1.

29 NESC report no. 90, *The economic and social implications of emigration*, Dublin, 1991, Pl. 7840, table 2.6, p. 58.

30 See Seamus Grimes, 'Postwar Irish immigration in Australia', in *Contemporary Irish migration* ed. Russell King, GSI special publications no. 6, Dublin, 1991 pp. 43–44.

31 Damian Hannan, *Rural exodus: a study of the forces influencing the large-scale migration of Irish rural youth*, London, 1970; J. A. Jackson, *Report on the Skibbereen social*

survey, Dublin, 1967.

32 Three of these studies were completed by An Foras Talúntais (Agricultural Institute).

33 Jeremiah Newman, ed., *The Limerick rural survey, 1958–64*, Tipperary, 1964.

34 D. A. Gillmor, *Agriculture in the Republic of Ireland*, Budapest, 1977, p. 35.

35 Ibid.

36 B. M. Walsh, 'Economic and demographic adjustment of the Irish agricultural labour force, 1961–66', *Ir. J. Agr. Econ. Rur. Soc.*, Vol. 3, 1970, pp. 114–15; see also his earlier study, 'Influences on mobility and employment in Irish family farming', *Ir. J. Agr. Econ. Rur. Soc.*, Vol. 2, 1969, pp. 13–24.

37 Walsh, 'Economic and demographic adjustment', p. 116.

38 Damian Hannan, 'Kinship, neighbourhood and social change in Irish rural communities', *Econ. Soc. Rev.*, Vol. 3, 1972, pp. 163–88.

39 Ibid., p. 178.

40 Ibid., p. 185.

41 Ibid., n. 34.

42 Hannan, *Rural exodus*, p. 35.

43 See ibid., pp. 29–64, 178–81, for full details of the area studied and the methods employed.

44 Hannan, *Rural exodus*, pp. 84–85.

45 Damian Hannan, 'Migration motives and migration differentials among Irish rural youth', *Sociologia Ruralis*, Vol. 9, 1969, p. 201.

46 Hannan, *Rural exodus*, pp. 166–67.

47 Ibid., pp. 167–68.

48 Ibid., p. 168.

49 Ibid.

50 Hannan, 'Migration motives and migration differentials', p. 209.

51 Ibid., p. 210.

52 Ibid.

53 Hannan, *Rural exodus*, p. 175.

54 Ibid., p. 183.

55 Ibid., p. 235.

56 Ibid., pp. 188–97.

57 Ibid., p. 199.

58 Ibid., p. 242.

59 Jackson, *Report on the Skibbereen social survey*, p. 4.

60 Ibid., p. 8.

61 Jackson's monograph on *The Irish in Britain*, London, 1963, remains one of the most valuable books on Irish migration.

62 Jackson, *Report on the Skibbereen social survey*, p. 14.

63 Ibid., pp. 15–16.

64 For an interesting study analysing the attitudes of farmers in west Cork towards migration to Dublin, see Gordan Streib, 'Migration and filial bonds: attitudes of Cork farmers and Dublin men', *Ir. J. Agr. Econ. Rur. Soc.*, Vol. 3, 1970, pp. 61–73.

65 Jackson, *Report on the Skibbereen social survey*, pp. 16–17.

66 Ibid., p. 34.

67 Ibid., p. 35.

68 Ibid, pp. 35–36, 38.

69 Ibid., p. 39.

70 Ibid., p. 40.

71 Ibid., p. 41.

72 Ibid., p. 40.

73 Patrick McNabb, 'Demography', in *The Limerick rural survey*, ed. Newman, p. 172.

74 Ibid., p. 165.

75 Ibid., p. 159. These last two migrants had travelled to Canada and Africa respectively.

76 Ibid., p. 173.

77 Ibid., p. 200.

78 Ibid., p. 188.

79 Ibid., p. 188.

80 Ibid., p. 187.

81 Ibid., p. 203.

82 Ibid., p. 206.

83 Ibid., p. 207.

84 Damian F. Hannan, *Displacement and development: class, kinship and social change in Irish rural communities*, ESRI paper no. 96, Dublin, 1979, p. 166.

85 McNabb, 'Demography', p. 217.

86 John Healy, *The death of an Irish town*, Cork, 1968; later reprinted as *No one shouted stop!*, Achill, 1988.

87 Department of Agriculture, *Report by the interdepartmental committee on the problems of small western farms*, Dublin, 1962, Pr. 6540, and *Report on pilot area development by the interdepartmental committee on the problems of small western farms*, Dublin, 1964, Pr. 7616.

88 J. J. Scully, *Agriculture in the west of Ireland: a study of the low farm income problem*, Dublin, 1971, Prl. 2017.

89 Patrick Commins, 'Demographic conditions', in An Foras Talúntais, *West Donegal resource survey*, pt. 3, Dublin, 1969, p. 40.

90 Ibid.

91 John Curry, 'Demographic features', in An Foras Talúntais, *County Leitrim resource survey*, pt. 3, Dublin, 1975, p. 15.

92 Ibid., p. 14.

93 Ibid., pp. 17–21.

94 Ibid., p. 28.

95 Kerry County Committee of Agriculture, *County Kerry Agricultural Resource Survey*, Tralee, 1972, p. 17.

96 Ibid., pp. 70–71.

97 Ibid., p. 62.

98 Ibid., p. 72.

99 For full details of the specific survey area, see An Foras Talúntais, *West Cork resource survey*, Dublin, 1963, section a, pp. 2–4.

100 Patrick Commins, 'Demographic and sociological aspects of west Cork', in An Foras Talúntais, *West Cork resource survey*, Dublin, 1963 section c, p. 58.

101 Ibid., p. 88.

102 A small number were also found to be in New Zealand and Australia but were excluded from the analysis, as was the case with members of religious orders living abroad.

103 Commins, 'Demographic and sociological aspects of west Cork', p. 90.

104 Ibid., p. 82.

105 Ibid.

106 Ibid. This pattern was confirmed by Scully in his study of the low farm income problem in the west of Ireland. He noted that 'females tended to migrate at a much earlier age than males' (Scully, *Agriculture in the west of Ireland*, p. 33).

107 Commins, 'Demographic and sociological aspects of west Cork', p. 93.

108 Ibid.

109 Hannan, *Displacement and development*, p. 159.

110 Scully, *Agriculture in the west of Ireland*, p. 37.

111 Ibid.

112 Liam Kennedy, 'Farm succession in modern Ireland: elements of a theory of inheritance', *Econ. Hist. Rev.*, 2nd series, Vol. 44, 1991, p. 494.

113 C. K. Ward, *Manpower in a developing community: a pilot survey in Drogheda (abridged report)*, Dublin, 1967, para. 20.34

114 Ibid., para. 20.35.

115 B. M. Walsh, 'Trends in the religious composition of the population in the Republic of Ireland, 1946–71', *Econ. Soc. Rev.*, Vol. 6, 1975, p. 544.

116 Michael Viney, *The five per cent: a survey of Protestants in the Republic*, Dublin, n.d. [1965], p. 5. This is a booklet of articles originally published in the *Irish Times*, 22–26 Mar. 1965.

117 B. M. Walsh, *Religion and demographic behaviour in Ireland*, ESRI paper no. 55, Dublin, 1970 p. 34.

118 Ibid., p. 35.

119 J. J. Sexton and Richard O'Leary, 'Factors affecting population decline in minority religious communities in the Republic of Ireland', in *Building trust in Ireland: studies commissioned by the Forum for Peace and Reconciliation*, Belfast, 1996, table 8, p. 296; see also Walsh, 'Trends in the religious composition', pp. 547–48 and Cormac Ó Gráda and Brendan Walsh, 'Fertility and population in Ireland, north and south', *Population Studies*, Vol. 49, 1995, pp. 263–64.

120 Walsh, 'Trends in the religious composition', p. 553.

121 Sexton and O'Leary, 'Factors affecting population decline', p. 293.

122 Walsh, *Religion and demographic behaviour*, table 11, p. 19.

123 Walsh, 'Trends in the religious composition', p. 546.

124 Kurt Bowen, *Protestants in a Catholic state: Ireland's privileged minority*, Dublin, 1983, p. 39.

125 H. W. Robinson, *A study of the Church of Ireland population of Ferns diocese, 1973*, Dublin, n.d. [1974], p. 14.

126 H. W. Robinson, 'A study of the Church of Ireland population of Ardfert, county Kerry, 1971', *Econ. Soc. Rev.*, Vol. 4, 1974, p. 114.

127 J. L. B. Deane, *Church of Ireland handbook: a guide to the general organisation of the church*, Dublin, 1962, p. 212.

128 *Journal of Proceedings of the General Synod of the Church of Ireland, 1959*, Dublin, 1960, p. 230.

129 Sparsely Populated Areas Commission of the Church of Ireland, *Careers in Ireland*, Dublin, [1959].

130 Ibid., foreword by George O. Simms [not paginated].

131 *Dáil Éireann deb.*, CLXXIII (25 Feb. 1959), col. 1.

132 Ibid., col. 3.

133 *Dáil Éireann deb.*, CLXXXIV (9 Nov. 1960), col. 677.

134 NAI, DT S 13101 F, memorandum from Seán Lemass to Secretary, 1 Apr. 1960.

135 NAI, DT S 13746 D, note prepared by an Tánaiste, Seán MacEntee, on the proceedings at the Tuairim symposium, 24 Apr. 1964.

136 *Dáil Éireann deb.*, CCIX (28 Apr. 1964), col. 456.

137 See *Irish Independent*, 20 Apr. 1964.

138 NAI, DT S 13746 D, note prepared by an Tánaiste ...

139 *Dáil Éireann deb.*, CCIX (28 Apr. 1964), col. 457.

140 Ibid.

141 Ibid., col. 459.

142 John Horgan, *Sean Lemass: the enigmatic patriot*, Dublin, 1997, p. 162.

143 *Dáil Éireann deb.*, CLXXXIV (2 Nov. 1960), col. 350; for a similar statement of Irish government policy see NAI, DT S 16325 B, emigration to Britain: brief statement of the policy of the government of Ireland, 7 Oct. 1960.

144 NAI, DT S 97/6/310, text of speech by Seán Lemass at the annual dinner of Galway Chamber of Commerce, 19 Jan. 1961, p. 1.

145 Department of Finance, *Programme for economic expansion*, Dublin, 1958, Pr. 4796, p. 7.

146 Department of Finance, *Second programme for economic expansion*, Part I, Dublin, 1963, Pr. 7239, p. 16.

147 Ibid., pp. 16–17.

148 Department of Finance, *Second programme for economic expansion: review of progress, 1964–67*, Dublin, 1968, Pr. 9949, p. 76; for more detail on these programmes, see Kieran A. Kennedy, Thomas Giblin and Deirdre McHugh, *The economic development of Ireland in the twentieth century*, London, 1988, p. 66.

149 For an example of this line of thinking see J. J. Lee, *Ireland, 1912–1985: politics and society*, Cambridge, 1989, pp. 359–60.

150 Fergal Tobin, *The best of decades: Ireland in the 1960s*, Dublin, 1984, p. 156.

151 Kennedy, *Modern industrialisation*, p. 15.

152 NAI, DT S 16325 B, text of speech by Seán Lemass at the annual dinner of the Dublin Chamber of Commerce, Gresham Hotel [Dublin], 25 Oct. 1960, p. 2. This speech was later reproduced in Sean Lemass, 'Social factors and emigration', *Christus Rex*, Vol. 15, 1961, pp. 16–20.

153 NAI, DT S 16325 B, text of speech by Seán Lemass at the annual dinner of the Dublin Chamber of Commerce, 25 Oct. 1960, p. 2.

154 Ibid., p. 4.

155 Ibid., p. 3.

156 NAI, DT S 97/6/310, text of speech by Seán Lemass at the annual dinner of Galway Chamber of Commerce, 19 Jan. 1961, p. 4.

157 *Dáil Éireann deb.*, CLXXV (2 June 1959), cols 775–77.

158 NAI, DT S 97/6/310, statement by Seán Lemass on proposed British legislation on immigration, 21 Nov. 1961, p. 1.

159 Ibid.

160 NAI, DT S 96/6/437, copy of address by Donogh O'Malley, minister for health, to the National University of Ireland Club, London, 17 Mar. 1966, p. 8. For the comments of Lemass, see NAI, DT S 16325 B, text of speech by Seán Lemass at the annual dinner of the Dublin Chamber of Commerce, 25 Oct. 1960, p. 2 and NAI, DT S 97/6/310, text of speech by Seán Lemass at the annual dinner of Galway Chamber of Commerce, 19 Jan. 1961, p. 2.

161 *Dáil Éireann deb.*, CXCI (11 July 1961), cols. 573–74, 671–72; *Dáil Éireann deb.*, CCVIII (5 Mar. 1964), cols 412–13; for a brief account of the postwar policy of the Irish state regarding the welfare of Irish migrants in Britain, see NAI, DT S 97/6/310, Department of External Affairs: memorandum on welfare work amongst the Irish workers in Britain, 15 Dec. 1961.

162 For more details, see Kevin O'Connor, *The Irish in Britain*, London, 1972, p. 141; Jackson, *The Irish in Britain*, p. 147.

163 *Dáil Éireann deb.*, CCVII (20 Feb. 1964), cols. 1366–67.

164 NAI, DFA 402/218/6, extract from report of the Irish ambassador in London, H. J. McCann, 9 June 1958, p. 2.

165 NAI, DT S 15398 B, Eugene O'Doherty and James Fergus, joint secretaries of the Irish hierarchy, to Lemass, 6 Feb. 1965.

166 NAI, DT S 15398 B, copy of letter from Lemass to O'Doherty and Fergus, 23 Mar. 1965.

167 NAI, DT S 15398 B, Fergus to Lemass, 31 July 1965.

168 NAI, DT S 15398 B, copy of a letter from Lemass to Fergus, secretary of the Irish hierarchy, 7 Sept. 1965.

169 Ibid.

170 O'Connor, *The Irish in Britain*, pp. 141–42.

171 *Commission on higher education, 1960–67: II Report*, Dublin, 1967, Vol. I, Pr. 9389, p. 246.

172 Ibid., p. 247.

173 Ibid., n. 14.

174 *Commission on higher education, 1960–67: II Report*, Dublin, 1967, Vol. II, Pr. 9588, p. 910.

175 The four universities were University College, Cork, University College, Dublin, University College, Galway and Trinity College, Dublin.

176 Cited in Richard Lynn, *The Irish brain drain*, ESRI paper no. 43, Dublin, 1968, p. 1.

177 Ibid., p. 2.

178 Ibid.

179 Ibid., p. 9.

180 Ibid., p. 19.

181 Ibid.

182 D. B. Rottman and P. J. O'Connell, 'The changing social structure', in *Unequal achievement: the Irish experience, 1957–1982*, ed. Frank Litton, Dublin, 1982, pp. 67–68.

183 K. A. Kennedy, 'R. C. Geary and the ESRI', *Econ. Soc. Rev.*, Vol. 24, 1993, pp. 239–41.

184 Rottman and O'Connell, 'The changing social structure', p. 68.

185 Daniel Duffy, 'The emigration issue', *Christus Rex*, Vol. 15, 1961, p. 7.

186 Thomas Breathnach, 'Social and economic problems of western Ireland', *Christus Rex*, Vol. 20, 1966, pp. 125–33; P. J. Drudy, 'An analysis of population decline and structure in a western county', *Christus Rex*, Vol. 23, 1969, pp. 39–48; John Healy, 'Problems and prospects of rural Ireland', *Christus Rex*, Vol. 22, 1968, pp. 302–16.

187 J. A. Jackson, 'Ireland', in OECD, *Emigrants workers returning to the home country: supplement to the final report*, Paris, 1967, p. 112.

188 M. D. McCarthy, 'Some Irish population problems', *Studies*, Vol. 56, 1967, p. 240.

189 Ibid.

190 NAI, DT S 99/1/287, Department of Labour: proposals in relation to official policy on emigration to Great Britain, 29 Nov. 1968, p. 1.

191 Ibid., pp. 25–26.

192 Ibid., p. 15.

193 NAI, DT S 99/1/287, Department of External Affairs, memorandum for the government: proposals of the Minister for Labour in relation to official policy on emigration to Britain, 16 Dec. 1968, p. 2.

194 Ibid., pp. 2–3.

195 NAI, DT S 99/1/287, Department of Labour: proposals in relation to official policy on emigration to Great Britain, 29 Nov. 1968, p. 3.

196 NAI, DT S 2000/6/561, extract from cabinet minutes, GC 12/171, 28 Mar. 1969.

197 Ceri Peach, 'The growth and distribution of the black population in Britain, 1945–1980', in *Demography of immigrants and minority groups in the United Kingdom*, ed. D. A. Coleman, Oxford, 1982, p. 24.

198 Ceri Peach, Vaughan Robinson, Julia Maxted and Judith Chance, 'Immigration and ethnicity', in *British social trends since 1900*, ed. A. H. Halsey, London, 1988, table 14.5, p. 573. This figure relates to those born in the Irish Republic and Ireland place not stated, and does not include Northern Ireland.

199 For more details, see Bronwen Walter, 'Time-space patterns of second-wave Irish immigration into British towns', *Trans. Inst. Brit. Geog.*, new series, Vol. 5, 1980, pp. 297–301.

200 J. A. Jackson, 'The Irish in Britain', in *Ireland and Britain since 1922*, ed. P. J. Drudy, Irish studies 5, Cambridge, 1986, p. 130.

201 Ibid., p. 131.

202 Ibid., p. 133.

203 For more details, see Colin Holmes, 'Immigration', in *Britain since 1945*, ed. Terry Gourvish and Alan O'Day, London, 1991, pp. 218–21.

204 *Sunday Times*, 5 Feb. 1961. On the detailed background to the Commonwealth Immigrants Bill, see Nicholas Deakin, 'The politics of the Commonwealth Immigrants Bill', *Political Quarterly*, Vol. 39, 1968, pp. 25–45 and Kathleen Paul, *Whitewashing Britain: race and citizenship in the postwar era*, Ithaca, 1997, pp. 151–69.

205 NAI, S 13746 D/61, C. C. Cremin (Secretary, Department of External Affairs) to Secretary, Department of the Taoiseach, 13 Feb. 1961.

206 *Irish Press*, 18 Feb. 1961.

207 Colin Holmes, *John Bull's island: immigration and British society, 1871–1971*, London, 1988, p. 253; Paul, *Whitewashing Britain*, pp. 166–69.

208 Holmes, *John Bull's island*, p. 260.

209 Holmes, 'Immigration', pp. 218–19; Paul, *Whitewashing Britain*, p. 181.

210 O'Connor, *The Irish in Britain*, p. 144.

211 *Irish Independent*, 3 Nov. 1959.

212 *Irish Press*, 13 Nov. 1959.

213 Quoted in Jackson, *The Irish in Britain*, p. 157.

214 Ibid.

215 A. E. Bottoms, 'Delinquency amongst immigrants', *Race*, Vol. 8, 1967, pp. 357–83; Matthew Russell, 'The Irish delinquent in England', *Studies*, Vol. 53, 1964, pp. 136–48.

216 Bottoms, 'Delinquency amongst immigrants', p. 364.

217 Russell, 'The Irish delinquent in England', p. 148.

218 T. C. N. Gibbens and R. H. Ahrenfeldt, eds, *Cultural factors in delinquency*, London, 1966, pp. 140–42 (summarised in Bottoms, 'Delinquency amongst immigrants', p. 365).

219 See Raymond Cochrane and Mary Stopes-Roe, 'Psychological disturbance in Ireland, in England and in Irish emigrants to England: a comparative study', *Econ. Soc. Rev.*, Vol. 10, 1979, pp. 301–20; Maggie Pearson, Moss Madden and Liam Greenslade, *Generations of an invisible minority: the health and well-being of the Irish in Britain*, Occasional papers in Irish studies no. 2, Liverpool, 1992: On mental illness in rural Ireland, see Nancy Scheper-Hughes, *Saints, scholars, and schizophrenics: mental illness in rural Ireland*, Berkeley, 1979. It should be added that Scheper-Hughes' work has been accorded severely critical reviews by other social scientists.

220 John R. Lambert, *Crime, police, and race relations: a study in Birmingham*, London, 1970, p. 127.

221 John Rex and Robert Moore, *Race, community, and conflict: a study of Sparkbrook*, London, 1967, p. 56.

222 Ibid., p. 92.

223 Ibid., p. 150.

224 Ibid., p. 96. Several surveys taken in the early 1970s found that approximately 90 per cent of Irish Catholic adults 'like to be thought to go regularly to mass' (J. H. Whyte, *Church and state in modern Ireland, 1923–1979*, 2nd edn, Dublin, 1980, p. 382.)

225 Rex and Moore, *Race, community and conflict*, p. 151.

226 Ibid., pp. 154–55.

227 Philip Jones, *The segregation of immigrant communities in the city of Birmingham, 1961*, University of Hull Occasional Papers in Geography no. 7, Hull, 1967, p. 44.

228 E. J. B. Rose et al., *Colour and citzenship: a report on British race relations*, London, 1969, p. 19.

229 Steven Fielding, *Class and ethnicity: Irish Catholics in England, 1880–1939*, Buckingham, 1993; Mary J. Hickman, *Religion, class and identity: the state, the Catholic church and education of the Irish in Britain*, London, 1995.

230 Bronwen Walter, 'Tradition and ethnic interaction: second-wave settlement in Luton and Bolton', in *Geography and ethnic pluralism*, ed. Colin Clarke, David Ley and Ceri Peach, London, 1984, p. 263.

231 Ibid., p. 270.

232 Ibid., p. 273.

233 John Hickey, *Urban Catholics: urban Catholicism in England and Wales from*

1829 to the present day, London, 1967, pp. 168–69.

234 W. J. L[iam]. Ryan, 'Assimilation of Irish immigrants to Britain', unpub. PhD thesis, St Louis University, 1973, pp. 231–32 (quoted in M. P. Hornsby-Smith, *Roman Catholics in England: studies in social structure since the Second World War*, Cambridge, 1987, pp. 128–29).

235 Jackson, *Report on the Skibbereen social survey*, p. 39.

236 Anthony H. Richmond, *Migration and race relations in an English city: a study of Bristol*, London, 1973, p. 244.

237 Ibid., p. 245.

238 For a comparative example of the 'myth of return', see Muhammad Anwar, *The myth of return: Pakistanis in Britain*, London, 1979.

239 For the extent of travel back and forth across the Irish Sea, see Micheál Ó Riain, 'Cross-channel passenger traffic, 1960–1980', *JSSISI*, Vol. 26, 1991/92, pp. 45–90.

240 Frank Bovenkerk, 'On the causes of Irish emigration', *Sociologia Ruralis*, Vol. 13, 1973, p. 272.

241 Jackson, *Report of the Skibbereen social survey*, pp. 13–14.

242 Jackson, 'Ireland', p. 4.

243 Garvey, 'History of migration flows', p. 25.

244 J. G. Hughes and B. M. Walsh, 'Migration flows between Ireland, the United Kingdom and the rest of the world, 1966–71', *European Demographic Information Bulletin*, Vol. 7, 1976, p. 127.

245 Ibid., p. 147.

246 Ibid., p. 149.

247 B. J. Whelan and J. G. Hughes, *A survey of returned and intending emigrants in Ireland*, Dublin, 1976, p. 45. My thanks to Kevin Dillon of the library in the Economic and Social Research Institute in Dublin for locating and making available to me a copy of this report.

248 For useful accounts of these developments, see Kennedy et al., *Economic development of Ireland in the twentieth century*, pp. 65–70; Lee, *Ireland, 1912–1985*, pp. 341–65; and Kennedy, *The modern industrialisation of Ireland*, pp. 14–20.

249 William Black, 'Industrial development and regional policy', in *Economic activity in Ireland: a study of two open economies*, ed. N. J. Gibson and J. E. Spencer, Dublin, 1977, pp. 50, 57.

250 D. I. F. Lucey and D. R. Kaldor, *Rural industrialisation: the impact of industrialisation on two rural communites in western Ireland*, London, 1969, table 27, p. 112.

251 Ibid.

252 Ibid., p. 115.

253 Jackson, 'Ireland', p. 10.

254 Ibid.

255 See Elizabeth Malcolm, *Elderly return migration from Britain to Ireland: a preliminary study*, Dublin, 1996.

256 For a brief assessment of the published work on Irish return migration, see Fiona McGrath, 'The economic, social and cultural impacts of return migration to Achill Island', in *Contemporary Irish migration*, ed. Russell King, GSI special publications no. 6, Dublin, 1991 p. 55.

257 Dick Foeken, 'Return migration to a marginal rural area in north-western

Ireland', *Tijdschrift voor Economische en Sociale Geografie*, Vol. 71, 1980, p. 116.

258 Ibid.

259 Ibid., p. 119.

260 George Gmelch, 'Return migration to rural Ireland', in *Migrants in Europe: the role of family, labor, and politics*, ed. Hans Christian Buechler and Judith-Maria Buechler, New York, 1987, p. 270.

261 Ibid.

262 Ibid., p. 271.

263 George Gmelch, 'The readjustment of returned migrants in the west of Ireland', in *Return migration and regional economic problems*, ed. Russell King, London, 1986, p. 156.

264 Ibid., pp. 156–58.

265 Ibid., p. 163.

266 Gmelch, 'Return migration to rural Ireland', p. 277.

267 J. A. Walsh, 'Immigration to the Republic of Ireland, 1946–71', *Ir. Geog.*, Vol. 12, 1979, pp. 109–10.

268 It should be noted that Gmelch actually discusses this point (Gmelch, 'Return migration to rural Ireland', p. 280).

269 Gmelch, 'The readjustment of returned migrants in the west of Ireland', p. 168.

270 Ibid.

271 Whelan and Hughes, *A survey of returned and intending emigrants in Ireland*, p. 45.

272 Ibid.

273 Ibid., p. 46.

Conclusion

Migration from rural to urban areas was a feature of the development of most western societies. However, Irish migration was distinctive in that most Irish migrants left their local area for British rather than Irish cities and towns. The body of literature that can be loosely categorised as migration theory provides a number of useful vantage points from which to assess migration from independent Ireland. Inevitably, no single model or framework explains fully the patterns of Irish migration, although there is much of value which may be derived from the range of approaches from a number of disciplines. Mass migration, whether it is viewed as a conglomeration of actors optimising earning potential or as the result of structural features within a particular society, to some extent defies classification under one particular schema. In essence, there is a range of explanations for migration across time and geographical location. Nevertheless, the findings of this study would demonstrate that, while economic factors (broadly interpreted) were a key determinant of Irish migration patterns and trends, changing aspirations towards a higher standard of living, and not simply sheer economic necessity, also shaped the history of Irish migration between 1921 and 1971.

The patterns of Irish migration to Britain between 1921 and 1971 have been examined in detail in the course of this discussion. In general terms, a continuous flow of migrants from Ireland to Britain over the complete period is evident, although the numbers involved registered peaks in the mid-1930s, in the war years and the late 1940s, and throughout the 1950s. By the close of our period, a decreased level of migration and indeed substantial return flow from Britain were apparent. Irish migration to Britain continued in the 1970s, albeit at a lower level as a result of the depressed state of the British economy and 'a relatively stable Irish economy'.[1] In the 1980s large-scale migration returned, reflecting the sorry state of the Irish economy at this time. The United States again regained its importance as a destination for Irish migrants, although Britain was still the recipient of the majority of Irish migrants in this decade.[2] Other European countries also proved popular as a minor element of the 'third wave' of Irish migrants opted for other destinations apart from Britain and the United States, due in no small part to the provisions for the freedom of movement of labour within the European Union.[3]

Irish migration between 1921 and 1971 may be explained in general terms by reference to the same factor that influenced many other international migration patterns, namely economic underdevelopment. This absence of sustained economic development was reflected in the dearth of employment opportunities available which would provide otherwise prospective migrants with a steady income at home. There was also a change in social attitudes evident in the postwar period in relation to what was deemed to be an acceptable standard of living; the aspiration to achieve this desired standard of living could, in the minds of many migrants, only be realised by leaving Ireland. This study has demonstrated that rising expectations constituted one of the driving forces behind Irish migration, particularly in the postwar years. Notwithstanding the fact that the great majority of migrants were unskilled workers, a skilled and professional element was a continuing if minor component of the flow, a pattern which has remained a feature of Irish migration until the present day.[4] More broadly this study has examined the flow of labour from an underdeveloped economy to an industrialised one, or in other words, from the periphery to the core within the overall international economic system. In terms of wage levels what was available in Ireland always compared unfavourably with that on offer in Britain, especially for unskilled or semi-skilled employment. Migration to Britain was an avenue whereby expectations in terms of income and occupational status could be achieved, in theory at the very least. Frequent contact with relatives and friends in Britain ensured that there was widespread knowledge of the higher standard of living in Britain and well-developed migrant pathways made the decision to travel that bit easier.

Throughout this study it has been observed that migration to Britain was a qualitatively different experience from the transatlantic journey to the United States. Return trips home for holidays were possible and the available evidence suggests that there was a considerable volume of traffic back and forth across the Irish Sea, especially in the postwar period.[5] The decision to travel to Britain did not involve the traumatic break with home that characterised migration to North America, Australia and other far-away destinations. If anything transience was the leitmotiv of twentieth-century Irish migration to Britain. Migrants could work in Britain for a short time, return to Ireland and then, if so desired, travel back to Britain. Numerous contemporary studies pointed to the fact that many Irish migrants living in Britain expressed a desire to return home to live in the Irish Republic permanently. In the 1960s and 1970s this became a realistic option with the relatively prosperous state of the Irish economy, and one that was chosen by a substantial number of migrants. Reciprocal social security arrangements made the decision to return home easier to contemplate. For others, however, even though return was an aspiration and permanent settlement was not envisaged at the time of the original decision to travel, circumstances dictated otherwise.

The relationship between migration and demographic change has been illustrated throughout this study. Most Irish counties experienced population decline as a direct consequence of migration, both internal and international. This decline was concentrated in western and north-western counties, although almost every county decreased in population to a greater or lesser extent over time, with the exception of Dublin. In terms of the total population, any gains accruing from natural increase were negated by the high rate of migration. Only in the mid-1960s did the Irish population increase, due in no small part to the reduction in the level of migration and the higher rate of natural increase resulting from the rise in the rate of marriage. For the first time since the Great Irish Famine (1845–50), gains in the total Irish population were recorded in the 1960s and 1970s. As Kennedy has observed, this was 'a turnabout in the population experience of the Irish Republic'.[6] Our findings also demonstrate that prior to 1971 the low level of internal migration within the Irish state was directly related to the high rate of migration to Britain.

One overarching factor determined the level of Irish migration to Britain and this was the demand for labour in the British economy. From the mid-1930s onwards Irish migrants availed themselves of the numerous opportunities available in a number of sectors of the economy, for the most part unskilled occupations, although this would change over time. In the postwar years the range of occupations in which Irish migrants were represented grew steadily. Without this demand for labour, it is difficult to imagine the continuance of large-scale Irish migration to Britain. In the first instance, unless suitable employment opportunities were available, few migrants would have made the journey to Britain. Secondly, in the face of high unemployment and a constant flow of migrants from across the Irish Sea, it seems likely that the British state would have endeavoured to control the level of immigration from Ireland, regardless of the oft-cited 'special' historical relationship or geographical proximity. The demands of war and postwar reconstruction were perhaps the most significant external factors that influenced the level and rate of Irish migration to Britain.

The pivotal role of the state in facilitating or hindering migration has been emphasised in this study. Whilst restrictions were considered by both the Irish state in the late 1940s and the British state in the late 1920s and early 1930s, no limitation resulted. During the Second World War, the role of the state encompassed all aspects of labour migration, and a gamut of travel restrictions and controls were introduced by the British and Irish authorities. Most of these controls on migration were dismantled in the immediate postwar period. In some senses the Irish state facilitated migration in the war years, although it did nothing to encourage this movement of population. Owing to the exigencies of the war effort, the British state actively recruited Irish labour, although this was done with due deference to Irish sensitivities regarding neutrality. For the postwar period no state action aimed at limiting or hindering migration from Ireland is evident. For the majority of the period covered by this study, the British and Irish states ensured that the freedom of movement of persons was maintained.

An investigation of Irish and British state policy drawing on hitherto neglected unpublished official records formed a central element of this study. It has been clearly demonstrated that only on specific occasions were both states concerned with migration. During the interwar period, little interest was displayed in this issue by policy makers in Ireland. In Britain, successive governments were apprehensive about the level of Irish immigration and the concomitant social problems during the 1920s and 1930s, although after fairly exhaustive inquiries, it was found that this anxiety was to a certain extent misplaced. In the war years, both states were concerned with migration for a variety of reasons including the supply of labour, security considerations and concerns about Ireland's neutrality. The postwar years were marked by increasing uneasiness on the part of the Irish state in relation to the level and extent of migration to Britain, coupled with anxiety in relation to the welfare of Irish migrants living in Britain. Much of the impetus for this concern emanated from Catholic prelates and clerics who made representations to successive Irish governments on the difficulties faced by Irish migrants in Britain. The role of the Roman Catholic church in highlighting the plight of Irish migrants in Britain has been underlined in this study. By the mid-1950s, however, this concern had been translated into practical assistance in the form of the provision of clergy who catered for the spiritual and moral welfare of Irish migrants living in Britain. For consecutive postwar British governments, Irish migrants acted as a useful supplement to the home labour supply, particularly during the shortage in the immediate period after the end of the war in May 1945. Historical and practical concerns ensured that Irish citizens could freely enter Britain even after Ireland left the Commonwealth in 1949. The body of immigration legislation introduced in the 1960s and in 1971 was not applied to citizens of the Irish Republic who were viewed instead as having a 'special' status in Britain, although skin colour played no small part in these official considerations.

The policy of the Irish state *vis-à-vis* migration to Britain remained remarkably consistent over this period. Two statements separated in time by nearly 25 years are revealing on Irish state policy. The first is a statement by de Valera made in response to a question in the Dáil in February 1937; the second is an official document on the policy of the Irish government, prepared in October 1960:

> The aim of this Irish government is not to provide facilities for the emigration of our people to the states of the British Commonwealth or elsewhere. Its aim is to concentrate on utilising the resources of this country and so improving the conditions of life here that our people will not have to emigrate, but will be able to find a livelihood in their own country.[7]

> So far as the formulation of policy is concerned, Irish emigration to Britain is not distinguished from Irish emigration to other countries. Emigration is regarded as a serious problem and is not encouraged, although there are no official restrictions imposed. The objective aimed at by the policy of the Irish government is to remove the economic need for emigration by promoting increased economic activity at home. The lines along which that policy is directed are set out in the *Programme for economic expansion* adopted by the government at the end of 1958.[8]

In theory, the necessity for people to leave Ireland would be removed

by the creation of employment opportunities. The failure of this policy prior to the mid-1960s is starkly illustrated by the level of Irish
migration to Britain, particularly in the 1940s and 1950s.

Baines has argued, in the context of a discussion of European emigration between 1815 and 1930, that the 'big problem is to explain the
incidence of emigration'.[9] Some regions were more affected by migration from independent Ireland than others, as was the case for the
nineteenth and early twentieth centuries. The regional aspect of both
the incidence and impact of migration has been investigated by examining county-level data on the rates of net migration and drawing on
numerous detailed local studies, especially in the postwar period. The
information derived from the rural surveys prepared for the purposes
of the landmark Commission on Emigration and Other Population
Problems, 1948–54, was especially instructive on this aspect of Irish
migration patterns. It has been possible to examine the explanations
as to why some regions experienced high rates of migration by looking in particular at the decline of the Irish agricultural labour force
and the limited opportunities for non-agricultural employment.
Detailed survey data from the 1960s also proved valuable for investigating the reasons why migrants left a region or county. Higher
regional rates of migration may be attributed to an established tradition of migration, a low level of non-agricultural employment and
usually an underdeveloped agricultural economy with few opportunities to secure a reasonable standard of living in farming.

This leads us to the question of non-migration. In the face of such
an unappealing future how can we explain the decision to remain in
Ireland? In the first instance, family or personal commitments would
preclude the migration of many people, be it as a result of marriage or
of the need to remain to look after parents or children. Migration often
occurred at a particular stage in the life cycle between the late teens and
mid-twenties. If it were not feasible to leave at this stage, to opt to
migrate at a later date might well have proved problematic as a result
of these commitments. Of equal importance is the fact that many people had employment with which they were satisfied, and without doubt
non-migrants may well have been content to stay within their local
environment, even if this confined them to an impecunious existence.

The role of family and personal networks in shaping the history of
twentieth-century Irish migration has been emphasised in this study.
Migrant networks both accelerated and facilitated large-scale migration from twentieth-century Ireland. Friends, siblings and other

relatives already living in Britain played a crucial role in providing information on job opportunities, wage levels and accommodation, and equally significantly, in determining the choice of destination in Britain. The inherent risks involved in the move to Britain were considerably reduced by these migrant networks. The existence of these networks also goes some way towards explaining the differential impact of migration. Those who had access to information or practical assistance were more likely to migrate. In addition, family and friends ensured that prospective migrants were aware of the better opportunities available elsewhere.

We have also explored the relationship between religious denomination and patterns of twentieth-century Irish migration, focusing on the minority Protestant population. It was demonstrated that the long-term decline of the Protestant community, evident since at least the second half of the nineteenth century, was exacerbated to some degree by the end of the union with Britain in 1921. Quite apart from the withdrawal of the British army and its dependants and the migration of some former members of the Royal Irish Constabulary, the political upheaval of the revolutionary period (1919–23) was shown to have influenced the rate of Protestant migration. After political stability was restored in 1923, Protestants in the Irish Free State were subjected to hostile cultural pressures such as the introduction of the compulsory teaching of the Irish language in the state educational system from the 1920s. However, the decline of the Protestant community in the interwar period must also be viewed within the broader context of the long-term decline of Protestants in Ireland. In the postwar period, the unhealthy demographic structure of the Protestant community, with its high death rates and low marital fertility, resulted in a negative rate of natural increase. Associated in addition with the increasing frequency of mixed marriages, the demographic decline was also determined by migration. Nevertheless, Catholics had a higher rate of net migration than Protestants and there is no evidence to suggest that the migration of Protestants from postwar Ireland was due to any factors peculiar to this grouping. Protestants migrated from postwar Ireland for much the same reasons as Catholics.

Political discourse concerning demographic patterns or 'population politics' was not peculiar, as regards western Europe, to twentieth-century Ireland. Throughout the twentieth century, but more particularly in the fascist regimes of the interwar period, debates about demographic patterns occurred in many other countries, especially with regard to the level of fertility.[10] In the Irish Republic during the 1950s migration was intimately associated with political discourse relating to the crises in the economy and the associated sense of malaise and despondency. By the 1960s, however, as a result of the much reduced level of emigration, it declined in importance as a political issue. In the postwar period emigration was frequently debated by Irish politicians of different political hues. What is most revealing is that few discernible differences between the political parties are evident on this issue. Opposition politicians from all of the parties invariably attacked the government's record on emigration in parliamentary debates or election speeches, but offered nothing by way of innovative analyses of the high rates of emigration from postwar Ireland. Political parties when in power could do little more than defend their economic policy, which, it was argued, would reduce the level of emigration. With the decrease in emigration in the 1960s, political rhetoric denouncing emigration became a rarity. In general terms, therefore, despite the fact that emigration was a politically charged issue, no party developed a distinct policy on emigration but rather they anticipated that a reduction in emigration could be brought about by a successful economic policy.

A central theme throughout this study has been an examination of discourse on the subject of migration from a broad spectrum of opinion in Ireland. What emerges from the mass of views expressed is that, whilst migration attracted a good deal of attention, especially in the postwar period, much of the comment indicated that many regarded the state as the agency responsible for reducing the levels of migration. Yet few analyses attempted to explain what features of Irish society caused such a substantial outflow of young people, the *Reports* of the Commission on Emigration being a notable exception. Much of the academic or intellectual discourse implicitly assumed that some level of migration was inevitable. By the 1960s, this view had gained currency amongst the members of the body politic, due no doubt in part to the recognition that after 40 years of self-government, migration was an immutable aspect of Irish life. Notwithstanding this recognition of the persistence of migration even during periods of relative economic prosperity, the pragmatic suggestion by the Irish Department of Labour in 1968 that the Irish state establish mechanisms to facilitate migration was not taken up, presumably owing to the possibility of creating the perception that the Irish state was encouraging migration.

A last significant finding of this study is that, for the most part, Irish immigration attracted little attention in migration discourse in Britain. In the interwar period, owing to agitation on the part of the churches in Scotland and local figures in Liverpool, occurring as it did within the broader context of economic depression, Irish immigration was the subject of some interest, albeit relatively short-lived. Thus, during the war years and in the postwar period, Irish migrants were rarely the focus of public interest. In comparison with the attention and coverage devoted to 'New Commonwealth' immigration, reaction to the flow from the Irish Republic was negligible. By 1971 the Irish-born population was the largest migrant grouping in Britain, yet relatively little is known about the actual experience of these migrants. Further studies using oral testimony and documentary sources should begin the process of unravelling this complex and nuanced facet of the Irish migrant experience. Only when a number of such studies are completed can questions relating to the ethnicity of Irish migrants in Britain begin to be answered with any degree of certainty.

NOTES

1 F. X. Kirwan and A. G. Nairn, 'Migrant employment and the recession: the case of the Irish in Britain', *IMR*, Vol. 17, 1983, p. 680.

2 See Cormac Ó Gráda and Brendan Walsh, 'The economic effects of emigration: Ireland', in *Emigration and its effects on the sending country*, ed. Beth J. Asch, Santa Monica, 1994, pp. 103–05.

3 NESC, *The economic and social implications of emigration*, NESC report no. 90, Dublin, 1991, table A2.1, p. 277.

4 Ian Shuttleworth, 'Graduate emigration from Ireland: a symptom of peripherality', in *Contemporary Irish emigration*, GSI special publications no. 6 ed. Russell King, Dublin, 1991, pp. 83–95, and 'Irish graduate emigration: the mobility of qualified manpower in the context of peripherality', in *Mass migration in Europe: the legacy and the future*, ed. Russell King, London, 1993, pp. 310–26.

5 On the post-1960 period, see Micheál Ó Riain, 'Cross-channel passenger traffic, 1960–1980', *JSSISI*, Vol. 26, 1991/92, pp. 45–90.

6 Liam Kennedy, *People and population change: a comparative study of population change in Northern Ireland and the Republic of Ireland*, Dublin and Belfast, 1994, p. 4.

7 *Dáil Éireann deb.*, LXV, 17 Feb. 1937, col. 332.

8 NAI, DT S 16325 B, Emigration to Britain: brief statement of the policy of the government of Ireland, 7 Oct. 1960.

9 Dudley Baines, *Emigration from Europe, 1815–1930*, London, 1991, p. 74.

10 For a useful summary, see Maria Sophia Quine, *Population politics in twentieth-century Europe*, London, 1996; on the politics of migration, see Daniel Kubat, ed., *The politics of migration policies*, New York, 1979.

Appendices

Appendix 1 Percentage change of population of each Irish county, 1911–36

Province or county	1911–26	1926–36
Total	−5.3	−0.1
Leinster	−1.1	+6.2
Munster	−6.8	−2.3
Connacht	−9.5	−5.0
Ulster	−9.4	−6.6
LEINSTER		
Carlow	−4.9	−0.1
Dublin	+6.0	+16.1
Kildare	−12.9	−0.2
Kilkenny	−5.3	−3.4
Laois	−5.7	−2.8
Longford	−9.0	−5.0
Louth	−1.5	+2.6
Meath	−3.2	−2.5
Offaly	−7.5	−2.4
Westmeath	−5.3	−3.7
Wexford	−6.3	−1.7
Wicklow	−5.2	+1.7
MUNSTER		
Clare	−8.8	−5.5
Cork	−6.7	−2.7
Kerry	−6.6	−6.3
Limerick	−1.9	+0.6
Tipperary	−7.5	−2.3
Waterford	−6.4	−1.2
CONNACHT		
Galway	−7.1	−0.7
Leitrim	−12.1	−8.9
Mayo	−10.1	−6.6
Roscommon	−11.1	−7.2

Appendix 1 continued

Sligo	–9.7	–5.5
ULSTER		
Cavan	–9.6	–7.0
Donegal	–9.5	–6.7
Monaghan	–8.9	–5.9

Source: Census of population, 1936, I: population, table 4, p.7.

Appendix 2 Irish inter-county migration up to 1926 and 1936

County	1926		1936	
	Inward[a]	Outward[b]	Inward[a]	Outward[b]
LEINSTER				
Carlow	19.6	27.0	21.7	27.1
Dublin	22.1	7.8	21.7	7.4
Kildare	26.3	28.4	27.6	29.3
Kilkenny	12.9	17.8	13.5	19.4
Laois	16.3	23.0	17.3	24.4
Longford	10.8	15.1	11.8	15.9
Louth	12.6	14.0	13.2	14.2
Meath	17.3	24.8	18.6	25.4
Offaly	16.6	20.0	17.3	21.8
Westmeath	19.1	20.8	18.1	22.1
Wexford	7.8	15.0	8.0	15.4
Wicklow	23.2	30.5	25.4	30.1
MUNSTER				
Clare	6.2	10.7	6.4	12.2
Cork	6.1	6.5	6.8	7.3
Kerry	4.0	8.6	4.4	10.9
Limerick	11.8	13.6	12.1	14.6
Tipperary	11.3	17.2	12.3	18.1
Waterford	13.8	13.3	14.7	14.3
CONNACHT				
Galway	6.8	8.6	8.0	10.1
Leitrim	7.7	13.1	8.2	15.2
Mayo	4.3	6.7	4.9	8.6
Roscommon	9.8	12.6	11.0	15.0
Sligo	9.0	11.2	10.3	12.9
ULSTER				
Cavan	7.3	14.0	8.8	15.8
Donegal	2.3	2.8	2.1	4.0
Monaghan	7.3	9.6	8.3	11.4

Notes:[a] Migrants living in each county as a percentage of the total population of that county.
[b]Migrants from each county as a percentage of residents of Éire born in that county.
This table can be read as follows: for the 'inward' column, of every 1,000 persons residing in county Carlow in 1926, 196 were born elsewhere in the Irish Free State; for the 'outward' column, out of every 1,000 persons living in the Irish Free State who were born in county Carlow, 270 lived outside the county.
Source: Census of population, 1926, X: general report, p. 43; *Census of population, 1936, IX: general report,* p. 81.

Appendix 3 Irish emigration, 1901–21 (from the 26 counties)

Year	Males	Females	Total
1901	15,131	18,353	33,484
1902	15,288	18,289	33,577
1903	14,699	17,846	32,545
1904	13,008	16,366	29,374
1905	11,586	11,365	22,951
1906	13,767	12,145	25,912
1907	14,612	13,289	27,901
1908	7,146	9,736	16,882
1909	10,092	10,561	20,653
1910	11,961	11,071	23,032
1901–1910	**127,290**	**139,021**	**266,311**
1911	11,015	10,174	21,189
1912	10,083	10,069	20,152
1913	10,816	10,454	21,270
1914	8,065	7,394	15,459
1915	4,948	3,055	8,003
1916	933	4,248	5,181
1917	410	640	1,050
1918	324	382	706
1919	612	827	1439
1920	3,994	7,303	11,297
1921	3,764	6,450	10,214
1911–21	**54,964**	**60,996**	**115,960**

Source: Commission on Emigration, *Reports*, table 28, p. 319.

Appendix 4 Number of overseas migrants from the Irish Free State/Éire classified by destination, 1924–39[a]

Year	USA	Canada	Australia	Other	Total
1924	12,016	5,237	1,138	686	19,077
1925	26,431	1,858	1,076	815	30,180
1926	26,063	1,989	1,267	722	30,041
1927	23,793	1,814	1,036	505	27,148
1928	21,684	1,598	806	603	24,691
1929	18,035	1,766	497	504	20,802
1930	14,072	1,047	398	449	15,966
1931	801	145	164	352	1,462
1932	256	86	178	291	811
1933	355	62	187	299	903
1934	415	88	142	389	1,034
1935	379	78	207	367	1,031
1936	440	63	316	442	1,261
1937	493	68	209	458	1,228
1938	995	100	207	449	1,751
1939	826	34	68	188	1,116
Total	147,054	16,033	7,896	7,519	178,502

Note:[a] The data prior to 1924 refer to the island of Ireland and are therefore not comparable.
Source: Commission on Emigration, *Reports*, table 27, p. 317.

Appendix 5 Average annual rate of net migration per 1,000 from each Irish
county and province, 1926–36

Province or county	1926–36
Total	−5.6
Leinster	−0.4
Munster	−8.1
Connacht	−10.2
Ulster	−10.3
LEINSTER	
Carlow	−5.0
Dublin	+6.3
Kildare	−7.3
Kilkenny	−7.3
Laois	−6.3
Longford	−9.2
Louth	−2.4
Meath	−6.2
Offaly	−7.3
Westmeath	−8.9
Wexford	−5.0
Wicklow	−2.5
MUNSTER	
Clare	−10.2
Cork	−7.0
Kerry	−12.7
Limerick	−6.8
Tipperary	−7.4
Waterford	−6.4
CONNACHT	
Galway	−7.8
Leitrim	−11.7
Mayo	−12.5
Roscommon	−10.8
Sligo	−8.5
ULSTER	
Cavan	−10.4
Donegal	−10.7
Monaghan	−9.1

Source: Commission on Emigration, *Reports*, table 35, p. 326.

Appendix 6 Percentage change of Irish Protestant population by county, 1911–36[a]

Province or county	1911–26	1926–36
Total	–33.2	–11.6
Leinster	–33.7	–7.9
Munster	–44.8	–16.6
Connacht	–37.0	–16.3
Ulster	–22.4	–15.5
LEINSTER		
Carlow	–24.7	–6.5
Dublin	–31.0	+5.6
Kildare	–69.8	–14.7
Kilkenny	–31.3	–12.4
Laois	–23.6	–9.7
Longford	–31.2	–18.9
Louth	–42.4	–10.3
Meath	–29.1	–13.5
Offaly	–32.0	–13.7
Westmeath	–50.8	–14.6
Wexford	–28.3	–11.2
Wicklow	–22.5	–8.3
MUNSTER		
Clare	–53.3	–28.1
Cork	–43.5	–14.7
Kerry	–46.9	–21.4
Limerick	–45.0	–22.1
Tipperary	–48.9	–16.2
Waterford	–40.8	–22.5
CONNACHT		
Galway	–54.1	–11.1
Leitrim	–32.1	–19.3
Mayo	–40.5	–19.6
Roscommon	–40.3	–20.7
Sligo	–26.8	–13.1
ULSTER		
Cavan	–23.0	–14.4
Donegal	–21.9	–15.2
Monaghan	–22.8	–16.9

Note: [a] Protestants includes Anglicans, Presbyterians, Methodists and Baptists, excluding 'others'.
Source: *Census of population, 1936, III, pt. I: religions*, table 9, pp. 15–19.

Appendix 7 Percentage change of population of each Irish county, 1936–46

Province or county	
Total	−0.4
Leinster	+5.0
Munster	−2.6
Connacht	−6.2
Ulster	−5.8
LEINSTER	
Carlow	−1.1
Dublin	+8.4
Kildare	+12.0
Kilkenny	−2.8
Laois	−0.8
Longford	−4.3
Louth	+2.9
Meath	+7.9
Offaly	+4.6
Westmeath	+0.4
Wexford	−2.5
Wicklow	+3.2
MUNSTER	
Clare	−5.4
Cork	−3.5
Kerry	−4.2
Limerick	+1.0
Tipperary N.R.	−2.4
Tipperary S.R.	−0.5
Waterford	−1.9
CONNACHT	
Galway	−1.8
Leitrim	−12.4
Mayo	−8.2
Roscommon	−6.5
Sligo	−7.5
ULSTER	
Cavan	−8.2
Donegal	−4.2
Monaghan	−6.6

Source: *Censuses of population 1946 and 1951: general report*, table 3, p. 18.

Appendix 8 Irish inter-county migration up to 1946

County	Inward[a]	Outward[b]
LEINSTER		
Carlow	20.9	26.3
Dublin	21.2	8.3
Kildare	31.2	26.5
Kilkenny	14.0	20.6
Laois	28.7	24.3
Longford	31.2	17.9
Louth	14.3	14.5
Meath	23.6	24.6
Offaly	20.8	21.1
Westmeath	20.0	23.2
Wexford	8.5	16.2
Wicklow	28.7	28.2
MUNSTER		
Clare	7.7	14.5
Cork	7.3	8.5
Kerry	4.8	13.4
Limerick	12.6	15.7
Tipperary	12.8	18.9
Waterford	14.9	15.5
CONNACHT		
Galway	8.3	12.4
Leitrim	8.9	18.5
Mayo	5.5	11.2
Roscommon	12.6	16.9
Sligo	11.6	14.6
ULSTER		
Cavan	9.1	17.8
Donegal	3.1	5.3
Monaghan	9.1	13.1

Notes: [a] Migrants living in each county as a percentage of the total population of that county.
[b] Migrants from each county as a percentage of residents of Éire born in that county.
Source: *Censuses of population 1946 and 1951: general report*, table 161, p. 174.
See note below appendix 2 for details on how to read this table.

Appendix 9 Persons in receipt of Irish travel documents by county of last residence: rates per 1,000 per annum, 1940–45

County	Male	Female
LEINSTER		
Carlow	12.2	6.1
Dublin	22.3	6.7
Kildare	6.9	4.1
Kilkenny	7.8	5.3
Laois	6.4	4.1
Longford	7.7	5.9
Louth	17.6	4.8
Meath	7.7	5.3
Offaly	5.3	4.0
Westmeath	7.5	5.3
Wexford	11.9	5.4
Wicklow	15.6	6.5
MUNSTER		
Clare	9.8	7.9
Cork	15.2	6.9
Kerry	14.0	9.6
Limerick	14.3	7.9
Tipperary	8.6	5.2
Waterford	17.5	8.2
CONNACHT		
Galway	12.1	7.3
Leitrim	11.0	9.1
Mayo	36.1	14.8
Roscommon	11.0	9.3
Sligo	16.8	9.0
ULSTER		
Cavan	6.0	5.1
Donegal	19.4	6.7
Monaghan	5.5	3.7
IRELAND	15.3	9.1

Source: Irish Trade Journal and Statistical Bulletin, n.v., June 1946, p. 60.

Appendix 10 Numbers of conditionally landed Irish workers registered with the police, 1942–45

Defence region	21 September 1942			4 September 1943			1 July 1944			1 September 1945		
	Agricultural	Other	Total	Agricultural	Other	Total	Agricultural	Other	Total	Agricultural	Other	Total
London and SE	96	4,680	4,776	359	10,141	10,500	286	18,166	18,452	315	30,716	31,031
Eastern	510	5,249	5,759	1,062	10,556	11,618	822	8,162	8,984	1,080	6,183	7,263
Southern	263	3,746	4,009	750	5,647	6,397	582	7,834	8,416	500	5,508	6,008
South Western	156	7,414	7,570	474	6,176	6,650	617	6,337	6,954	448	5,025	5,473
Midland	130	10,329	10,459	135	18,897	19,032	154	22,854	23,008	164	20,313	20,477
North Midlands	1,296	6,276	7,572	1,886	10,651	12,537	1,900	7,123	9,023	3,089	5,594	8,683
North Eastern	454	914	1,368	722	2,002	2,724	393	2,914	3,307	727	2,810	3,537
North Western	702	3,422	4,124	888	5,264	6,152	1,214	8,217	9,431	1,361	9,273	10,634
Northern	179	334	513	261	473	734	294	825	1,119	414	805	1,219
Scotland	3,347	3,594	6,941	4,688	3,489	8,177	4,717	3,788	8,505	7,063	2,953	10,016
Wales	181	1,879	2,060	353	1,654	2,007	373	1,509	1,882	292	1,278	1,570
Great Britain	7,314	47,837	55,151	11,578	74,950	86,528	11,352	87,729	99,081	15,453	90,458	105,911

Source: PRO, LAB 8/1528, A. V. Judges, 'Irish labour in Great Britain, 1939–45', app. II, p. 86.

Appendix 11 Percentage change of population of each Irish county, 1946–56

Province or county	1946–51	1951–56
Total	+0.2	−2.1
Leinster	+4.3	+0.2
Munster	−2.0	−2.4
Connacht	−4.2	−5.4
Ulster	−4.0	−6.9
LEINSTER		
Carlow	+0.2	−0.8
Dublin	+8.9	+1.8
Kildare	+2.4	−0.8
Kilkenny	−2.2	−1.6
Laois	−2.5	−2.8
Longford	−4.6	−4.6
Louth	+3.9	+0.6
Meath	+0.2	+0.6
Offaly	−2.1	−1.1
Westmeath	−0.9	−0.6
Wexford	−2.0	−3.1
Wicklow	+3.5	−4.3
MUNSTER		
Clare	−4.4	−5.1
Cork	−0.7	−1.4
Kerry	−5.4	−3.6
Limerick	−0.9	−2.4
Tipperary	−2.0	−2.9
Waterford	−1.4	−1.5
CONNACHT		
Galway	−3.0	−2.9
Leitrim	−7.6	−10.1
Mayo	−4.2	−6.2
Roscommon	−6.1	−6.5
Sligo	−3.0	−6.0
ULSTER		
Cavan	−5.7	−7.0
Donegal	−3.5	−7.2
Monaghan	−3.3	−5.9

Source: Censuses of population 1946 and 1951: general report, table 3, p. 18; Census of population of Ireland, 1956, I: population, area and valuation ..., table 4, p. 7.

Appendix 12 Average annual rate of net migration per 1,000 from each Irish county and province, 1946–51 and 1951–56

Province or county	1946–51	1951–56
Total	−8.2	−13.4
Leinster	−2.1	−11.4
Munster	−11.7	−12.8
Connacht	−15.1	−17.4
Ulster	−14.6	−19.6
LEINSTER		
Carlow	−9.3	−12.9
Dublin	+5.5	−9.7
Kildare	−8.8	−15.5
Kilkenny	−13.1	−11.1
Laois	−12.2	−13.6
Longford	−16.8	−16.6
Louth	−3.3	−10.2
Meath	−8.6	−8.2
Offaly	−13.3	−12.3
Westmeath	−11.9	−13.3
Wexford	−12.3	−14.3
Wicklow	−2.1	−18.8
MUNSTER		
Clare	−15.9	−15.9
Cork	−7.9	−10.0
Kerry	−17.7	−14.0
Limerick	−12.7	−15.8
Tipperary N.R.	−12.6	−14.0
Tipperary S.R.	−13.5	−15.5
Waterford	−9.6	−10.6
CONNACHT		
Galway	−15.3	−15.2
Leitrim	−18.7	−23.1
Mayo	−15.3	−19.1
Roscommon	−15.9	−16.1
Sligo	−10.8	−17.1
ULSTER		
Cavan	−15.8	−18.2
Donegal	−14.6	−20.2
Monaghan	−13.2	−19.7

Source: *Census of population, 1956, I: population, area and valuation. . . .*, table XIII, p. xxii.

Appendix 13 Percentage change of population of each Irish county, 1956–71

Province or county	1956–61	1961–66	1966–71
Total	−2.8	+2.3	+3.3
Leinster	−0.5	+6.2	+5.9
Munster	−3.2	+1.2	+2.6
Connacht	−6.0	−4.2	−2.7
Ulster			
LEINSTER			
Carlow	−1.6	+0.8	+1.9
Dublin county borough	−0.4	+5.8	+0.0
Dun Laoghaire borough	+0.5	+8.3	+2.6
Dublin	+12.8	+31.1	+31.8
Kildare	−2.3	+3.1	+8.4
Kilkenny	−3.8	−2.0	+1.7
Laois	−4.3	−1.1	+1.5
Longford	−7.1	−5.4	−2.5
Louth	−2.6	+3.2	+7.8
Meath	−2.5	+3.4	+6.5
Offaly	−0.8	+0.4	+0.2
Westmeath	−2.3	+0.1	+1.3
Wexford	−4.5	+0.2	+3.5
Wicklow	−3.6	+3.3	+9.7
MUNSTER			
Clare	−4.5	−0.1	+1.9
Cork county borough	−2.5	+8.8	+5.3
Cork	−1.6	−0.3	+3.1
Kerry	−4.6	−3.2	−0.0
Limerick county borough	−0.2	+10.1	+2.2
Limerick	−5.1	−1.3	+2.3
Tipperary N.R.	−3.6	+0.3	+0.9
Tipperary S.R.	−4.9	−1.6	+0.4
Waterford county borough	−2.3	+5.4	+7.1
Waterford	−4.3	+0.2	+4.9
CONNACHT			
Galway	−3.6	−1.0	+0.6
Leitrim	−9.7	−8.7	−7.2
Mayo	−7.3	−6.3	−5.2
Roscommon	−7.1	−5.0	−4.8
Sligo	−5.8	−4.3	−1.9
ULSTER			
Cavan	−8.3	−4.5	−2.6
Donegal	−6.7	−4.6	−0.2
Monaghan	−9.6	−2.9	+1.1

Source: Census of population of Ireland, 1971, I: population of district electoral divisions ..., table III, p. xiv.

Appendix 14 Average annual rate of net migration per 1,000 from each Irish county and province, 1956–71

Province or county	1956–61	1961–66	1966–71
Total	−14.8	−5.7	−3.7
Leinster	−13.1	−1.5	−1.7
Munster	−14.2	−6.4	−3.5
Connacht	−18.3	−13.6	−10.0
Ulster	−20.7	−14.2	−6.6
LEINSTER			
Carlow	−16.1	−12.2	−8.9
Dublin	−10.1	+4.8	−0.7
Kildare	−18.4	−8.4	+0.9
Kilkenny	−15.6	−10.9	−4.2
Laois	−17.2	−12.6	−6.4
Longford	−20.8	−16.8	−11.3
Louth	−17.1	−6.8	+0.9
Meath	−14.7	−4.1	+1.3
Offaly	−13.2	−11.7	−11.6
Westmeath	−15.9	−12.3	−9.1
Wexford	−17.4	−9.5	−4.0
Wicklow	−17.2	−4.2	+7.5
MUNSTER			
Clare	−14.9	−6.3	−1.9
Cork	−11.2	−3.9	−1.9
Kerry	−15.2	−11.2	−4.7
Limerick	−17.0	−5.0	−6.5
Tipperary N.R.	−16.1	−8.3	−6.5
Tipperary S.R.	−18.6	−13.0	−8.2
Waterford	−14.8	−5.0	+1.6
CONNACHT			
Galway	−16.2	−10.6	−6.7
Leitrim	−22.7	−19.1	−14.7
Mayo	−20.3	−17.1	−14.0
Roscommon	−17.9	−11.7	−10.9
Sligo	−16.6	−12.7	−6.8
ULSTER			
Cavan	−21.3	−13.8	−9.1
Donegal	−17.9	−15.0	−6.3
Monaghan	−26.5	−12.9	−4.4

Source: Census of population, 1971, I: population of district electoral divisions . . ., table XII, p. xxiii.

Appendix 15 Net Irish external migration rates per 1,000 population by county, 1961–71, by age in 1971 and sex

County	15–29 years		15–64 years		All ages	
	Males	Females	Males	Females	Males	Females
LEINSTER						
Carlow	−207.2	−230.1	−98.7	−114.4	−92.0	−93.2
Dublin	−78.0	−58.5	−21.6	−33.6	−3.4	−8.1
Kildare	−150.4	−165.4	−72.0	−81.5	−93.7	−98.6
Kilkenny	−217.6	−233.4	−98.3	−117.6	−63.9	−59.1
Laois	−219.3	−256.0	−100.9	−124.0	−70.2	−69.6
Longford	−285.6	−294.0	−134.3	−147.0	−86.3	−95.4
Louth	−96.5	−50.7	−35.1	−38.0	+2.9	+1.0
Meath	−147.6	−177.3	−60.4	−77.1	−57.0	−72.9
Offaly	−228.6	−240.4	−112.3	−123.6	−78.9	−84.9
Westmeath	−228.2	−226.6	−118.9	−121.9	−103.0	−98.0
Wexford	−216.1	−222.6	−90.7	−107.7	−56.3	−62.4
Wicklow	−126.3	−155.4	−36.2	−67.4	−63.0	−77.5
MUNSTER						
Clare	−244.5	−258.4	−87.5	−104.1	−47.0	−49.9
Cork	−147.5	−131.1	−55.3	−61.8	−22.7	−25.3
Kerry	−259.8	−260.2	−110.0	−123.0	−55.3	−64.6
Limerick	−188.4	−182.6	−75.5	−89.2	−39.6	−47.1
Tipperary	−245.9	−247.9	−108.0	−118.7	−67.2	−74.4
Waterford	−134.7	−133.1	−44.9	−60.8	−13.6	−21.0
CONNACHT						
Galway	−254.8	−241.9	−112.0	−118.1	−41.3	−49.1
Leitrim	−344.1	−367.5	−167.8	−194.7	−100.0	−115.8
Mayo	−379.3	−356.8	−186.3	−180.5	−95.3	−100.3
Roscommon	−324.5	−329.1	−145.5	−150.3	−69.3	−76.2
Sligo	−278.5	−281.6	−128.3	−144.6	−67.9	−77.7
ULSTER						
Cavan	−294.8	−322.7	−138.4	−161.1	−90.2	−103.9
Donegal	−325.4	−300.8	−149.3	−158.1	−65.8	−75.4
Monaghan	−228.8	−232.2	−98.2	−120.0	−60.4	−77.1
TOTAL	−188.8	−179.9	−78.9	−87.0	−43.6	−46.9

Source: After J. G. Hughes and B. M. Walsh, *Internal migration flows in Ireland and their determinants*, ESRI paper no. 98, Dublin, 1980 table a.2, p. 83.

Bibliography

MANUSCRIPT SOURCES

A Government records

National Archives of Ireland, Dublin
Department of External Affairs
Department of Industry and Commerce
Department of the Taoiseach

Public Record Office, Kew
Cabinet Office
Dominions Office
Home Office
Ministry of Labour and National Service
Ministry of Supply

B Collections of private papers

National Archives of Ireland, Dublin
ICTU papers

National Library of Ireland, Dublin
Frank Gallagher papers

Public Record Office, Kew
Ramsay MacDonald papers

Trinity College, Dublin, Manuscripts Department
Arnold Marsh papers

University College, Dublin, Archives Department
Seán MacEntee papers
Patrick McGilligan papers

OFFICIAL PUBLICATIONS

International

International Labour Office, *International migration, 1945–57*, Geneva, 1959.
International Labour Office, 'The transfer of Irish workers to Great Britain', *International Labour Review*, Vol. 48, 1943, pp. 338–42.

Ireland

Guides and breviates

Ford, Percy and Ford, Grace, *A select list of reports and inquiries of the Irish Dáil and Senate, 1922–1974*, Shannon, 1974.
Maltby, Arthur and McKenna, Brian, *Irish official publications: a guide to the Republic of Ireland papers, with a breviate of reports, 1922–70*, Oxford, 1980.

Central Statistics Office

Census of Population of Ireland 1946.
Census of Population of Ireland 1951.
Census of Population of Ireland 1956.
Census of Population of Ireland 1961.
Census of Population of Ireland 1966.
Census of Population of Ireland 1971.

Department of Agriculture

Report by the interdepartmental committee on the problems of small western farms, 1962, Pr. 6540.
Report on pilot area development by the interdepartmental committee on the problems of small western farms, 1964, Pr. 7616.
J. J. Scully, *Agriculture in the west of Ireland: a study of the low farm income problem*, 1971, Prl. 2017.

Department of Education

Commission on higher education, 1960–67: I Presentation and summary of report, 1967, Pr. 9326; *II Report*, 2 vols, 1967, Pr. 9389 and Pr. 9588.
Investment in education: report of a survey team appointed by the Minister for Education in conjunction with the OECD, 2 vols, 1967, Pr. 8311.

Department of Finance

Economic Development, 1958, Pr. 4803.
Programmme for economic expansion, 1958, Pr. 4796.
Second programme for economic expansion – parts I and II, 1963–64, Pr. 7239 and Pr. 7670.
Third programme for economic and social development, 1969–72, 1969, Prl. 431.

Department of Health

'Ireland is building', 1950.

Department of Industry and Commerce
Census of Population of Ireland 1926.
Census of Population of Ireland 1936.
Same statistics of wages and hours of work in 1937, with comparative figures for certain previous years, 1938, P. 2904.

Parliamentary debates
Dáil Éireann debates.

Reports
Commission of inquiry into banking, currency and credit, 1938, reports, 1938, P. 2628.
Commission on Emigration and Other Population Problems, 1948–54, *Reports* [1955], Pr. 2541.
Gaeltacht commission, report, 1926.
Report of the Commission on Agriculture, 1923–4, 1924.
Report of the Commission on Vocational Organisation, 1943 [1944], Pr. 6743.
Report of the Commission on Youth Unemployment, 1951, Pr. 709.
Report of the Committee on Economic Statistics, 1925.
Reports of the Fiscal Inquiry Committee, 1923.
Report on the inter-departmental committee on seasonal migration to Great Britain, 1937–38, 1938, P. 3403.

United Kingdom

Guides and breviates
Butcher, David, *Official publications in Britain*, London, 1983.
Ford, Percy and Ford, Grace, *A breviate of parliamentary papers, 1917–1939*, Oxford, 1951.
Ford, Percy and Ford, Grace, *A breviate of parliamentary papers, 1940–54: war and reconstruction*, Oxford, 1961.
Pemberton, John E., *British official publications*, 2nd rev. edn, Oxford, 1973.

Ministry of Labour and National Service
Manpower: the story of Britain's mobilisation for war [1944].
Report on the postwar organization of private domestic employment, 1944–45, Cmd. 6650, V, 1.
Report of the working party on the recruitment and training of nurses, 1947 [Non-Parl.] [with Ministry of Health and Department of Health for Scotland].

Parliamentary debates
Hansard (Commons).

Parliamentary papers
Final report of the Royal Commission on Unemployment Insurance, 1930–32, 1931–32, Cmd. 4185, XIII, 393.
Oversea migration board, first annual report, July 1954, 1953–54, Cmd. 9261, XVIII, 1.
Oversea migration board, second annual report, Aug. 1956, 1955–56, Cmd. 9835, XVIII, 1003.

Oversea migration board, third annual report, Dec. 1957, 1957–58, Cmd. 336, XVI, 11.

Oversea migration board, fourth annual report, Dec. 1958, 1958–59, Cmd. 619, XVII, 305.

Oversea migration board, fifth annual report, Mar. 1960, 1959–60, Cmd. 975, XIX, 75.

Oversea migration board, sixth annual report, Dec. 1960, 1960–61, Cmd. 1243, IX, 35.

Oversea migration board, seventh annual report, Dec. 1961, 1961–62, Cmd. 1586, XVIII, 767.

Report of the Royal Commission on Population, 1948–49, Cmd. 7695, XIX, 635.

Report, to the Economic Advisory Council, of the committee on empire migration, 1931–32, Cmd. 4075, IX, 333.

Statement by His Majesty's Government in the United Kingdom on migration within the British Commonwealth, 1944–45, Cmd. 6658, X, 293.

CONTEMPORARY NEWSPAPERS, ANNUALS AND PERIODICALS

Administration
Catholic Bulletin
Christus Rex
Church of Ireland Gazette
Furrow
Ireland To-day
Irish Banking Review
Irish Catholic Directory
Irish Independent
Irish Press
Irish Statesman
Irish Times
Journal of the General Synod of the Church of Ireland
Journal of the Statistical and Social Inquiry Society of Ireland
Studies
The Bell
The Leader
The Times

CONTEMPORARY PUBLICATIONS

Articles in journals

Gair, G. R., 'The Irish immigration question', *Liverpool Review*, vol. 9, 1 Jan. 1934, pp. 11–13; 2 Feb. 1934, pp. 47–50; 3 Mar. 1934, pp. 86–88.

Gwynn, Stephen, 'Ireland since the Treaty', *Foreign Affairs*, vol. 12, 1933–34, pp. 319–30.

Hodson, H. V., 'Éire and the British Commonwealth', *Foreign Affairs*, vol. 16, 1937–38,

Bibliography 319

pp. 525–36.

Kelleher, John V., 'Ireland ... and where does she stand?', *Foreign Affairs*, Vol. 35, 1956–57, pp. 485–95.

Lucey, Cornelius, 'The problem of emigration', *University Review*, Vol. 1, 1957, pp. 3–10.

MacNeill, Eoin, 'Ten years of the Irish Free State', *Foreign Affairs*, Vol. 10, 1931–32, pp. 235–49.

O'Sullivan, M. D., 'Minorities in the Free State', *Quarterly Review*, Vol. 258, 1932, pp. 312–26.

Plunkett, Horace, 'Ireland's economic outlook', *Foreign Affairs*, Vol. 5, 1926–27, pp. 205–18.

Sjoestedt, M.-L, 'L'Irlande d'aujourd'hui: gens de la terre et de la côte', *Revue des Deux Mondes*, 15 June 1930, pp. 839–64, 1 July 1930, pp. 458–91.

Smyllie, R. M., 'Unneutral neutral Éire', *Foreign Affairs*, Vol. 24, 1946, pp. 317–26.

Spencer, A. E. C. W., 'Irish Catholics in England: recent immigration figures', *The Tablet*, 22 Aug. 1959.

Books and pamphlets

Babbington, Richard, *Mixed marriages*, Dublin, 1928.

Caradog Jones, David, ed., *The social survey of Merseyside*, 2 vols, London, 1934.

Cosgrave, William, *Policy of the Cumann na nGaedhael party*, Dublin, 1927.

Cumann na nGaedheal, *To the electorate of the Irish Free State*, Dublin, n.d. [1932].

Digby, J. P., *Emigration: the answer*, Dublin, 1951.

Fianna Fáil, *A national policy outlined by Eamon de Valera, delivered at the inaugural meeting of Fianna Fáil at La Scala Theatre, Dublin, May 1926*, Dublin, n.d. [1927].

Fianna Fáil, *Five years of policy and panic*, [Dublin], 1927.

Fianna Fáil, *The greatest failure in Irish history*, Dublin, n.d. [1932].

Fighting points for the Cumann na nGaedheal speakers and workers, general election, 1932, Dublin, 1932.

Fletcher, Dudley, *Rome and marriage: a warning*, Dublin, 1936.

Gaffney, Gertrude, *Emigration to England: what you should know about it, advice to Irish girls*, Dublin, n.d. [1937].

Gobán Saor [i.e. Arnold Marsh], *Economics for ourselves*, 2nd edn, Dublin, 1935.

Gregg, J. A. F., *The 'Ne Temere' Decree*, Dublin, 1943.

Irish Workers' League, *Emigration can be ended: a socialist view of Ireland's emigration problem*, Dublin, 1956.

League of Social Justice, *The Achill Ireland tragedy*, Dublin, 1937.

Marsh, Arnold, *Full employment in Ireland*, Dublin, 1945.

McDermott, R. P. and Webb, D. A., *Irish Protestantism: today and tomorrow, a demographic study*, Dublin, 1945.

Morrissey, Patrick, *Working conditions in Ireland and their effect on Irish emigration*, New York, 1957.

O'Brien, J. A., ed., *The vanishing Irish*, New York, 1953.

Pastoral letter of the archbishops and bishops of Ireland to the clergy on the emigrant problem, Dublin, 1967.

Sparsely Populated Areas Commission of the Church of Ireland, *Careers in Ireland,* *Dublin,* [1959].
Stanford, W. B., *A recognised church: the Church of Ireland in Éire,* Dublin, 1944.
Stevenson, R. L., *Shall I emigrate?,* Dublin, 1966.
Toner, Jerome, *Rural Ireland: some of its problems,* Dublin, 1955.
Ulster Unionist Council, *Southern Ireland's census returns: serious decline in Protestant* *population,* [Belfast, 1939].

MEMOIRS WRITTEN BY CONTEMPORARIES

Foley, Donal, *Three villages: an autobiography,* Dublin, 1977.
Inglis, Brian, *West Briton,* London, 1962.
Keane, John B., *Self-portrait,* Cork, 1964.
Keaney, Brian, *Don't hang about,* Oxford, 1985.
MacAmhlaigh, Donall, *An Irish navvy: the diary of an exile,* trans. from the Irish by Valentin Iremonger, London, 1964.
Moore, H. Kingsmill, *Reminiscences and reflections,* London, 1930.
Ó Ciaráin, Sean, *Farewell to Mayo: an emigrant's memoirs of Ireland and Scotland,* Dublin, 1991.
O'Donoghue, John, *In a strange land,* London, 1958.

OTHER PUBLISHED WORKS

Akenson, D. H., *The Irish diaspora: a primer,* Belfast, 1993.
Arensberg, C. M., *The Irish countryman,* New York, 1937.
Arensberg, C. M., and Kimball, S. T., *Family and community in Ireland,* 1st edn, Cambridge, Mass., 1940; 2nd edn, 1968.
Blake, J. W., *Northern Ireland in the Second World War,* Belfast, 1956.
Bovenkerk, Frank, 'On the causes of Irish emigration', *Sociologia Ruralis,* Vol. 13, 1973, pp. 263–75.
Bowen, Kurt, *Protestants in a Catholic state: Ireland's privileged minority,* Dublin, 1983.
Boyer, G. R., Hatton, T. J. and O'Rourke, Kevin, 'Emigration and real wages in Ireland 1850–1914', in *Migration and the international labour market, 1850–1939,* ed. T. J. Hatton and J. G. Williamson, London, 1994, pp. 221–39.
Breathnach, Proinnsias and Jackson, J. A., 'Ireland, emigration and the new international division of labour', in *Contemporary Irish migration,* ed. Russell King, GSI special publications no. 6, Dublin, 1991, pp. 1–10.
Breen, Richard, 'Farm servanthood in Ireland, 1900–40', *Econ. Hist. Rev.,* 2nd series, Vol. 36, 1983, pp. 87–103.
——'Population trends in late nineteenth and early twentieth century Ireland: a local study', *Econ. Soc. Rev.,* Vol. 15, 1984, pp. 95–108.
Brody, Hugh, *Inishkillane: change and decline in the west of Ireland,* London, 1973.
Brown, Stewart J., ' "Outside the Covenant": the Scottish Presbyterian churches and

Irish immigration, 1922–1938', *Innes Review*, Vol. 42, 1991, pp. 19–45.

Buckland, Patrick and Belchem, John, eds, *The Irish in British labour history*, Conference proceedings in Irish studies no. 1, Liverpool, 1992.

Canavan, Bernard, 'Story-tellers and writers: Irish identity in emigrant labourers' autobiographies, 1870–1970', in *The creative migrant*, ed. Patrick O'Sullivan, part III in *The Irish worldwide: history, heritage and identity*, London, 1993, pp. 154–69.

Chance, Judy, 'The Irish in London: an exploration of ethnic boundary maintenance', in *Race and racism: essays in social geography*, ed. Peter Jackson, London, 1987, pp. 142–60.

Coleman, D. A., 'The demographic transition in Ireland in international context', in *The development of industrial society in Ireland*, ed. J. H. Goldthorpe and C. T. Whelan, Oxford, 1992, pp. 53–78.

Collins, Brenda, 'Irish emigration to Dundee and Paisley during the first half of the nineteenth century', in *Irish population, economy and society: essays in honour of the late K. H. Connell*, ed. J. M. Goldstrom and L. A. Clarkson, Oxford, 1981, pp. 195–212.

——'Proto-industrialisation and pre-famine emigration', *Social History*, Vol. 7, 1982, pp. 127–46.

——'The Irish in Britain, 1780–1921', in *An historical geography of Ireland*, ed. B. J. Graham and L. J. Proudfoot, London, 1993, pp. 366–98.

——'The origins of Irish immigration to Scotland in the nineteenth and twentieth centuries', in *Irish immigrants and Scottish society in the nineteenth and twentieth centuries*, ed. T. M. Devine, Edinburgh, 1991, pp. 1–18.

Commins, Patrick, 'Demographic and sociological aspects of west Cork', in An Foras Talúntais, *West Cork resource survey*, section c, Dublin, 1963.

——'Demographic conditions', in An Foras Talúntais, *West Donegal resource survey*, pt. 3, Dublin, 1969.

——'Recent population changes analysed by community size', *Ir. J. Agr. Econ. Rur. Soc.*, Vol. 1, 1967–68, pp. 195–206.

Connell, K. H., *Irish peasant society: four historical essays*, Oxford, 1968.

Cousens, S. H., 'Population trends in Ireland at the beginning of the twentieth century', *Ir. Geog.*, Vol. 5, 1968, pp. 387–401.

Cullen, L. M., 'The Irish diaspora of the seventeenth and eighteenth centuries', in *Europeans on the move: studies on European migration*, ed. Nicholas Canny, Oxford, 1994.

Curry, John, 'Demographic features', in An Foras Talúntais, *County Leitrim resource survey*, pt. 3, Dublin, 1975.

Curtis, L. P., 'The Anglo-Irish predicament', *Twentieth-Century Studies*, Vol. 4, 1970, pp. 46–62.

Daniels, Mary, *Exile or opportunity? Irish nurses and midwives in Britain*, Occasional papers in Irish studies No. 5, Liverpool, 1993.

Davis, Graham, *The Irish in Britain, 1815–1914*, Dublin, 1991.

——'The Irish in nineteenth-century Britain', *Saothar*, Vol. 16, 1991, pp. 130–35 [essay in bibliography].

Dean, D. W., 'Conservative governments and the restriction of Commonwealth immigration in the 1950s: the problems of constraint', *Hist. J.*, Vol. 35, 1992, pp. 171–94.

——'Coping with colonial immigration, the Cold War and colonial policy: government and black communities in Britain, 1945–51', *Immigrants and Minorities*, Vol. 6, 1987, pp. 306–34.

Delaney, Enda, ' "Almost a class of helots in an alien land": the British state and Irish immigration, 1921–45', *Immigrants and Minorities*, Vol. 18, 1999, pp. 240–65.

——'Placing Irish migration to Britain in a comparative European perspective, 1945–81', in *The Irish diaspora*, ed. Andy Bielenberg, London, pp. 331–56.

—— 'State, politics and demography: the case of Irish emigration, 1921–71', *Irish Political Studies*, Vol. 13, 1998, pp. 25–49.

——'The churches and Irish emigration to Britain, 1921–60', *Archivium Hibernicum*, Vol. 52, 1998, pp. 98–114.

Devine, T. M., ed., *Irish immigrants and Scottish society in the nineteenth and twentieth century*, Edinburgh, 1991.

Divine, Robert A., *American immigration policy, 1924–1952*, New Haven, 1957.

Dooley, T. A. M., 'Monaghan Protestants in a time of crisis, 1919–22', in *Religion, conflict and coexistence in Ireland*, ed. R. V. Comerford, Mary Cullen, J. R. Hill and Colm Lennon, Dublin, 1990, pp. 235–51.

——*The decline of unionist politics in Monaghan, 1911–1923*, Maynooth, 1988.

Drudy, P. J., 'Irish population change and emigration since independence', in *The Irish in America: emigration, assimilation and impact*, ed. P. J. Drudy, Irish studies 4, Cambridge, 1985, pp. 63–86.

——ed., *Ireland and Britain since 1922*, Irish studies 5, Cambridge, 1986.

Duffy, Patrick, 'Literary reflections on Irish migration in the nineteenth and twentieth centuries', in *Writing across worlds: literature and migration*, ed. Russell King, John Connell and Paul White, London, 1996, pp. 20–38.

Emigrant experience: papers presented at the second annual Mary Murray weekend seminar, Galway, 1991.

Fedorowich, Kent, 'The problems of disbandment: the Royal Irish Constabulary and imperial migration, 1919–29', *IHS*, vol. 30, 1996, pp. 88–110.

Feldman, David, 'There was an Englishman, an Irishman and a Jew . . . Immigrants and minorities in Britain', *Hist. J.*, Vol. 26, 1983, pp. 185–99 [review article].

Fielding, Steven, *Class and ethnicity: Irish Catholics in England, 1880–1939*, Buckingham, 1993.

Fitzpatrick, David, ' "A peculiar tramping people": the Irish in Britain, 1801–70', in *A new history of Ireland, V: Ireland under the union, pt. I (1801–70)*, ed. W. E. Vaughan, Oxford, 1989, pp. 623–60.

——' "A share of the honeycomb": education, emigration and Irishwomen', *Continuity and Change*, Vol. 1, 1986, pp. 217–34.

——'Emigration, 1801–70', in *A new history of Ireland, V: Ireland under the union, pt. I (1801–70)*, ed. W. E. Vaughan, Oxford, 1989, pp. 562–622.

——'Emigration, 1871–1921', in *A new history of Ireland, VI: Ireland under the union, pt. II (1871–1921)*, ed. W. E. Vaughan, Oxford, 1996, pp. 606–52.

——*Irish emigration, 1801–1921*, Dublin, 1984.

——'Irish emigration in the later nineteenth century', *IHS*, Vol. 22, 1980, pp. 126–43.

——'Irish farming families before the First World War', *Comp. Stud. Soc. & Hist.*, Vol. 25, 1983, pp. 339–74.

——'Marriage in post-famine Ireland', in *Marriage in Ireland*, ed. Art Cosgrove,

Dublin, 1985, pp. 116–31.

——*Oceans of consolation: personal accounts of Irish migration to Australia*, Cork, 1994.

——'The Irish in Britain, 1871–1921', in *A new history of Ireland, VI: Ireland under the union, pt. II (1871–1921)*, ed. W. E. Vaughan, Oxford, 1996, pp. 653–98.

——'The modernisation of the Irish female', in *Rural Ireland, 1600–1900: modernisation and change*, ed. Patrick O'Flanagan, Paul Ferguson and Kevin Whelan, Cork, 1987, pp. 162–80.

Foeken, Dick, 'Return migration to a marginal rural area in north-western Ireland', *Tijdschrift voor Economische en Sociale Geografie*, Vol. 71, 1980, pp. 114–20.

Freeman, T. W., 'Emigration and rural Ireland', *JSSISI*, Vol. 17, 1944–45, pp. 404–22.

——*Ireland: its physical, historical, social and economic geography*, 1st edn, London, 1950.

——'The Irish emigration commission', *Geog. J.*, Vol. 122, 1956, pp. 281–82.

——'The Irish in Great Britain', *Geog. J.*, Vol. 123, 1957, pp. 274–76.

Garvey, Donal, 'The history of migration flows in the Republic of Ireland', *Population Trends*, no. 39, 1985, pp. 22–30.

Geary, P. T. and Ó Gráda, Cormac, 'Postwar migration between Ireland and the UK: models and estimates', in *European factor mobility: trends and consequences*, ed. Ian Gordon and A. P. Thirlwall, London, 1989, pp. 53–58.

Geary, R. C. and Hughes, J. G., *Internal migration in Ireland*, ESRI paper no. 54, Dublin, 1970.

Gibbon, Peter, 'Arensberg and Kimball revisited', *Economy & Society*, Vol. 2, 1973, pp. 479–98.

——and Chris Curtin, 'The stem family in Ireland', *Comp. Stud. Soc. & Hist.*, Vol. 20, 1978, pp. 429–53.

Gilley, Sheridan, 'English attitudes to the Irish in England, 1780–1900', in *Immigrants and minorities in British society*, ed. Colin Holmes, London, 1978, pp. 81–110.

——'Irish Catholicism in Britain', in *Religion, state and ethnic groups: comparative studies on governments and non-dominant ethnic groups in Europe, 1850–1940*, Vol. 2, ed. Donal A. Kerr, Aldershot, 1992, pp. 229–60.

——'The Catholic faith of the Irish slums: London, 1840–70', in *The Victorian city: images and reality*, ed. H. J. Dyos and Michael Wolff, 2 vols, London, 1973, Vol. II, pp. 837–53.

——'The Roman Catholic church and the nineteenth-century Irish diaspora', *Journal of Ecclesiastical History*, Vol. 35, 1984, pp. 188–207.

Girvin, Brian, *Between two worlds: politics and economy in independent Ireland*, Dublin, 1989.

Glenfield, Ferran, 'The Protestant population of south-east Leinster, 1834–1981', *Ir. Econ. & Soc. Hist.*, Vol. 20, 1993, pp. 82–83 [thesis abstract of unpub. MLitt. thesis, University of Dublin, 1990].

Glynn, Sean, 'Irish immigration to Britain, 1911–1951: patterns and policy', *Ir. Econ. & Soc. Hist.*, Vol. 8, 1981, pp. 50–69.

Gmelch, George, 'Return migration to rural Ireland', in *Migrants in Europe: the role of family, labour, and politics*, ed. Hans Christian Buechler and Judith-Maria Buechler, New York, 1987, pp. 265–81.

——'The readjustment of returned migrants in the west of Ireland', in *Return migration and regional economic problems*, ed. Russell King, London, 1986, pp. 152–70.

——'Who returns and why: return behaviour in two North Atlantic societies', *Human*

Organization, Vol. 42, 1983, pp. 46–54.

Gray, Henry, 'The extent, nature and circumstances of the emigration from Ireland and the work of the Catholic Social Welfare Bureau for Irish Catholic emigrants', *Social Compass*, Vol. 3, 1955, pp. 176–86.

Guinnane, T. W., 'Age of leaving home in rural Ireland, 1901–1911', *J. Econ. Hist.*, Vol. 52, 1992, pp. 651–74.

——'Coming of age in rural Ireland at the turn of the twentieth century', *Continuity and Change*, Vol. 5, 1990, pp. 443–72.

——'Economics, history, and the path of demographic adjustment: Ireland after the famine', *Research in Economic History*, Vol. 13, 1991, pp. 147–98.

——'Intergenerational transfers, emigration, and the rural Irish household system', *Exp. Econ. Hist.*, Vol. 29, 1992, pp. 156–76.

——'Rethinking the western European marriage pattern: the decision to marry in Ireland at the turn of the twentieth century', *Journal of Family History*, Vol. 16, 1991, pp. 47–64.

——*The vanishing Irish: households, migration and the rural economy in Ireland, 1850–1914*, Princeton, 1997.

Handley, J. E., *The Irish in modern Scotland*, Cork, 1947.

Hannan, D. F., *Displacement and development: class, kinship and social change in Irish rural communities*, ESRI paper no. 96, Dublin, 1979.

——'Irish emigration since the war', typescript of unpublished RTE Thomas Davis lecture, [1973].

——'Kinship, neighbourhood and social change in Irish rural communities', *Econ. Soc. Rev.*, Vol. 3, 1972, pp. 163–89.

——'Migration motives and migration differentials amongst Irish rural youths', *Sociologia Ruralis*, Vol. 9, 1969, pp. 195–200.

——'Peasant models and the understanding of social and cultural change in rural Ireland', in *Ireland: land, politics and people*, Irish studies 2, ed. P. J. Drudy, Cambridge, 1982, pp. 141–65.

——*Rural exodus: a study of the forces influencing the large-scale migration of Irish rural youth*, London, 1970.

Hannan, D. F. and Katsiaouni, Louise, *Traditional families? From culturally prescribed to negotiated roles in farm families*, ESRI paper no. 87, Dublin, 1977.

Hart, Peter, 'The Protestant experience of revolution in southern Ireland', in *Unionism in modern Ireland*, ed. Richard English and Graham Walker, Dublin, 1996, pp. 81–98.

Hatton, T. J. and Williamson, J. G., 'After the famine: emigration from Ireland, 1850–1913', *J. Econ. Hist.*, Vol. 53, 1993, pp. 575–600.

Healy, John, *The death of an Irish town*, Cork, 1968.

Heuston, R. F. V., 'British nationality and Irish citizenship', *International Affairs*, Vol. 26, 1950, pp. 77–90.

Hickey, J. V., *The Irish rural immigrant and British urban society*, London, 1960.

——*Urban Catholics: Urban Catholicism in England and Wales from 1829 to the present day*, London, 1967.

Hickman, Mary J., 'Reconstructing deconstructing "race": British political discourses about the Irish in Britain', *Ethnic and Racial Studies*, vol. 21, 1998, pp. 288–307.

——*Religion, class and identity: the state, the Catholic church and education of the Irish in*

Britain, Aldershot, 1995.

Hickman, Mary J. and Walter, Bronwen, 'Deconstructing whiteness: Irish women in Britain', *Feminist Review*, Vol. 50, 1995, pp. 5–19.

——*Discrimination and the Irish community in Britain*, London, 1997.

Holmes, Colin, 'Immigration', in *Britain since 1945*, ed. Terry Gourvish and Alan O'Day, London, 1991, pp. 209–31.

——*John Bull's island: immigration and British society, 1871–1971*, London, 1988.

——'The promised land? Immigration into Britain, 1870–1980', in *Demography of immigrants and minority groups in the United Kingdom*, ed. D. A. Coleman, London, 1982, pp. 1–21.

Hornsby-Smith, Michael, 'Irish Catholics in England: some sociological perspectives', *Social Studies*, Vol. 6, 1979, pp. 177–208.

——*Roman Catholics in England: studies in social structure since the Second World War*, Cambridge, 1987.

Hornsby-Smith, Michael and Dale, Angela, 'The assimilation of Irish immigrants in England', *British Journal of Sociology*, Vol. 39, 1988, pp. 519–43.

Hughes, J. G., *Estimates of annual net migration and their relationship with series on annual net passenger movement: Ireland 1926–1976*, ESRI memorandum series no. 122, Dublin, 1977.

Hughes, J. G. and Walsh, B. M. *Internal migration flows in Ireland and their determinants*, ESRI paper no. 98, Dublin, 1980.

——'Migration flows between Ireland, the United Kingdom and the rest of the world, 1966–1971', *European Demographic Information Bulletin*, Vol. 8, 1976, pp. 125–49.

Ince, Godfrey H., 'Mobilization of manpower in Great Britain for the Second World War', *Manchester School of Economic and Social Studies*, Vol. 14, 1946, pp. 17–52.

Inman, P[hylis], *Labour in the munitions industries*, London, 1957.

Issac, Julius, *British postwar migration*, Cambridge, 1954.

Jackson, J. A., 'Ireland', in OECD, *Emigrant workers returning to their home country: supplement to the final report*, Paris, 1967.

——*Report on the Skibbereen Social Survey*, Dublin, 1967.

——*The Irish in Britain*, London, 1963.

Jackson, Pauline, 'Women in nineteenth century Irish emigration', *IMR*, Vol. 18, 1984, pp. 1004–20.

Johnson, D. S., *The interwar economy in Ireland*, Dublin, 1985.

Johnson, J. H., 'Harvest migration from nineteenth century Ireland', *Trans. Inst. Brit. Geog.*, Vol. 41, 1967, pp. 97–112.

——'The context of migration: the example of Ireland in the nineteenth century', *Trans. Inst. Brit. Geog.*, new seres, Vol. 15, 1991, pp. 259–76.

Jones, Philip, *The segregation of immigrant communities in the city of Birmingham, 1961* University of Hull occasional papers in geography no. 7, Hull, 1967.

Joshi, Shirley and Carter, Bob, 'The role of Labour in the creation of a racist Britain', *Race and Class*, Vol. 25, 1984, pp. 53–70.

Keenan, J. G., 'Irish emigration: all or nothing resolved', *Econ. Soc. Rev.*, Vol. 12, 1981, pp. 169–86.

Keep, G. R. C., 'Official opinion on Irish emigration in the later nineteenth century', *Irish Ecclesiastical Record*, Vol. 81, 1954, pp. 412–21.

——'Some Irish opinion on population and emigration', *Irish Ecclesiastical Record*,

Vol. 84, 1955, pp. 377–86.

Kennedy, Kieran A., Giblin, Thomas and McHugh, Deirdre, *The economic development of Ireland in the twentieth century*, London, 1988.

Kennedy, Liam, 'Farm succession in modern Ireland: elements of a theory of inheritance', *Econ. Hist. Rev.*, 2nd series, Vol. 44, 1991, pp. 477–99.

——*People and population change: a comparative study of population change in Northern Ireland and the Republic of Ireland*, Dublin and Belfast, 1994.

——*The modern industrialisation of Ireland, 1940–1988*, Dublin, 1989.

Kennedy, Liam and Clarkson, L. A., 'Birth, death and exile: Irish population history, 1700–1921', in *An historical geography of Ireland*, ed. B. J. Graham, and L. J. Proudfoot, London, 1993, pp. 158–84.

Kennedy, Liam and Miller, Kerby A. with Mark Graham, 'The long retreat: Protestants, economy and society, 1660–1926', in *Longford: essays in county history*, ed. Raymond Gillespie and Gerard Moran, Dublin, 1991, pp. 31–61.

Kennedy, R. E., Jr., *The Irish: emigration, marriage and fertility*, Berkeley, 1973.

Keogh, Dermot, *Twentieth-century Ireland: nation and state*, Dublin, 1994.

Kerry County Committee of Agriculture, *County Kerry Agricultural Resource Survey*, Tralee, 1972.

King, Russell, ed., *Contemporary Irish migration*, GSI special publications no. 6, Dublin, 1991.

King, Russell and O'Connor, Henrietta, 'Migration and gender: Irish women in Leicester', *Geography*, Vol. 81, 1996, pp. 311–25.

King, Russell, Shuttleworth, Ian and Strachan, Alan, 'The Irish in Coventry: the social geography of a relic community', *Ir. Geog.*, Vol. 22, 1989, pp. 64–78.

Kirwan, F. X., 'Recent Anglo-Irish migration – the evidence of the British labour force surveys', *Econ. Soc. Rev.*, Vol. 13, 1982, pp. 191–203.

——'Recent Irish migration: a note on a neglected source data', *European Demographic Information Bulletin*, Vol. 12, 1981, pp. 56–62.

Kirwan, F. X. and Nairn, A. G., 'Migrant employment and the recession: the case of the Irish in Britain', *IMR*, Vol. 17, 1983, pp. 672–81.

Kushner, Tony, 'Immigration and "race relations" in postwar British society', in *Twentieth-century Britain*, ed. Paul Johnson, London, 1994, pp. 411–26.

Layton-Henry, Zig, *The politics of immigration: immigration, 'race' and 'race' relations in postwar Britain*, Oxford, 1992.

Lee, J. J., 'Emigration: a contemporary perspective', in *Migrations: the Irish at home and abroad*, ed. Richard Kearney, Dublin, 1990, pp. 33–44.

——*Ireland 1912–1985: politics and society*, Cambridge, 1989.

——ed., *Ireland, 1945–70*, Dublin, 1979.

Lennon, Mary, McAdam, Marie and O'Brien, Joanne, *Across the water: Irish women's lives in Britain*, London, 1988.

Lucey, Denis I. F. and Kaldor, Donald R., *Rural industrialisation: the impact of industrialisation on two rural communities in western Ireland*, London, 1969.

Lunn, Kenneth, ' "Good for a few hundred at least": Irish labour recruitment into Britain during the Second World War', in *The Irish in British labour history*, ed. Patrick Buckland and John Belchem, Liverpool, 1992, pp. 102–14.

——'The British state and immigration, 1945–51: new light on the *Empire Windrush*', in *The politics of marginality: race, the radical right and minorities in twentieth century*

Britain, ed. Tony Kushner and Kenneth Lunn, London, 1990, pp. 161–74.

Lynch, Anne, *The Irish in exile: stories of emigration*, London, [1988].

Lynn, Richard, *The Irish brain drain*, ESRI paper no. 43, Dublin, 1968.

MacLaughlin, Jim, 'Ireland: an "emigrant nursery" in the world economy', *International Migration*, Vol. 31, 1993, pp. 149–70.

——*Ireland: the emigrant nursery and the world economy*, Cork, 1994.

——ed., *Location and dislocation in contemporary Irish society: emigration and Irish identities*, Cork, 1997.

MacRaild, Donald M., *Irish migrants in modern Britain, 1750–1922*, Basingstoke, 1999.

Maguire, Martin, 'A socio-economic analysis of the Dublin Protestant working class, 1870–1926', *Ir. Econ. & Soc. Hist.*, Vol. 20, 1993, pp. 35–61.

Malcolm, Elizabeth, *Elderly return migration from Britain to Ireland: a preliminary study*, Dublin, 1996.

Marks, Lara, ' "The luckless waifs and strays of humanity": Irish and Jewish unwed mothers in London, 1870–1939', *Twentieth Century British History*, Vol. 3, 1992, pp. 113–37.

Meenan, James, 'Éire', in *Economics of international migration*, ed. Brinley Thomas, London, 1958, pp. 77–84.

——'Some features of Irish emigration', *International Labour Review*, Vol. 69, 1954, pp. 126–39.

——*The Irish economy since 1922*, Liverpool, 1970.

Megaw, John, 'British subjects and Éire citizens', *Northern Ireland Legal Quarterly*, Vol. 8, 1949, pp. 129–39.

Miles, Robert, 'Migration discourse in post-1945 British politics', *Migration*, Vol. 6, 1989, pp. 31–53.

——'Migration to Britain: the significance of a historical approach', *International Migration*, Vol. 29, 1991, pp. 527–43.

——'Nationality, citizenship, and migration to Britain, 1945–1951', *Journal of Law and Society*, Vol. 16, 1989, pp. 426–42.

——*Racism and migrant labour*, London, 1982.

——'Racism and nationalism in Britain', in *'Race' in Britain: continuity and change*, ed. Charles Husband, London, 1982, pp. 279–300.

——'The racialisation of British politics', *Political Studies*, Vol. 38, 1990, pp. 277–85.

Miles, Robert and Kay, Diana, *Refugees or migrant workers? European volunteer workers in Britain, 1946–51*, London, 1992.

Miller, Kerby A., *Emigrants and exiles: Ireland and the Irish exodus to North America*, New York, 1985.

——'Emigration, ideology, and identity in post-famine Ireland', *Studies*, Vol. 75, 1986, pp. 515–27.

Miller, Kerby A., Boling, Bruce and Doyle, D. N., 'Emigrants and exiles: Irish cultures and Irish emigration', *IHS*, Vol. 29, 1980, pp. 97–125.

Miller, Kerby A. with Doyle, D. N. and Kelleher, Patricia, ' "For love or liberty": Irish women, migration and domesticity in Ireland and America, 1815–1920', in *Irish women and Irish migration*, ed. Patrick O'Sullivan, part IV in *The Irish worldwide: history, heritage and identity*, London, 1995, pp. 41–65.

Moser, Peter, 'Rural economy and female emigration in the west of Ireland, 1936–1956', *UCG Women's Study Review*, Vol. 2, 1993, pp. 41–51.

Newman, Jeremiah, ed., *The Limerick rural survey, 1958–1964*, Tipperary, 1964.

Nolan, J. A., *Ourselves alone: emigration from Ireland, 1885–1920*, Lexington, 1989.

O'Carroll, Ide, *Models for movers: Irish women's emigration to America*, Dublin, 1991.

O'Connor, Kevin, *The Irish in Britain*, London, 1972; rev. edn, Dublin, 1974.

O'Dowd, Anne, *Spalpeens and tattie hokers: the history and folklore of the Irish migratory agricultural worker in Ireland and Britain*, Dublin, 1991.

Ó Gráda, Cormac, 'A note on nineteenth-century Irish emigration statistics', *Population Studies*, Vol. 29, 1975, pp. 143–49.

——'Across the briny ocean: some thoughts on Irish emigration to America, 1800–1850', in *Ireland and Scotland: parallels and contrasts in economic and social development*, ed. T. M. Devine and David Dickson, Edinburgh, 1983, pp. 118–30.

——'Determinants of Irish emigration: a note', *IMR*, Vol. 20, 1986, pp. 650–56.

——*Ireland before and after the famine: explorations in economic history, 1800–1925*, 2nd edn, Manchester, 1993.

——'New evidence on the fertility transition in Ireland 1880–1911', *Demography*, Vol. 28, 1991, pp. 535–48.

——'Primogeniture and ultimogeniture in rural Ireland', *Journal of Interdisciplinary History*, Vol. 10, 1980, pp. 491–97.

——'Seasonal migration and post-famine adjustment in the west of Ireland', *Studia Hibernica*, Vol. 13, 1973, pp. 48–76.

——'Some aspects of nineteenth-century Irish emigration', in *Comparative aspects of Scottish and Irish economic and social history, 1600–1900*, ed. L. M. Cullen and T. C. Smout, Edinburgh, 1977, pp. 65–73.

Ó Gráda, Cormac and O'Rourke, Kevin H., 'Migration as disaster relief: lessons from the Great Irish Famine', *European Review of Economic History*, Vol. 1, 1997, pp. 3–25.

Ó Gráda, Cormac and Walsh, B. M., 'Fertility and population in Ireland, north and south', *Population Studies*, Vol. 49, 1995, pp. 259–79.

——'The economic effects of emigration: Ireland', in Beth J. Asch, ed., *Emigration and its effects on the sending country* Santa Monica, 1994, pp. 97–152.

O'Grady, Anne, *Irish migration to London in the 1940s and 1950s*, Irish in Britain Research Forum paper no. 3, London, 1988.

Ó Riain, Micheál, 'Cross-channel passenger traffic, 1960–1990', *JSSISI*, Vol. 26, 1991–92, pp. 45–90.

O'Rourke, Desmond, 'A stocks and flows approach to a theory of human migration with examples from past Irish migration', *Demography*, Vol. 9, 1972, pp. 263–74.

O'Rourke, Kevin, 'Did labour flow uphill? International migration and wage rates in twentieth century Ireland', in *Labour market evolution: the economic history of market integration, wage flexibility and the employment relation*, ed. George Grantham and Mary MacKinnon, London, 1994, pp. 139–60

——'Emigration and living standards in Ireland since the famine', *Journal of Population Economics*, Vol. 8, 1995, pp. 407–21.

——'Why Ireland emigrated: a positive theory of factor flows', *Oxford Economic Papers*, Vol. 44, 1992, pp. 322–40.

O'Shea, Kieran, *The Irish emigrant chaplaincy scheme in Britain, 1957–82*, Naas, 1985.

O'Sullivan, Patrick, ed., *Patterns of migration*, part I in *The Irish worldwide: history, heritage, identity*, London, 1992.

——ed., *Irish women and Irish migration*, part IV in *The Irish worldwide: history, heritage, identity*, London, 1995.

——ed., *The creative migrant*, part III in *The Irish worldwide: history, heritage, identity*, London, 1993.

——ed., *The Irish in the new communities*, part II in *The Irish worldwide: history, heritage, identity*, London, 1992.

Ó Tuathaigh, M. A. G., 'The Irish in nineteenth-century Britain: problems of integration', *Transactions of the Royal Historical Society*, 5th series, Vol. 31, 1981, pp. 149–74.

Panayi, Panikos, 'The historiography of immigrants and ethnic minorities: Britain compared with the USA', *Ethnic and Racial Studies*, Vol. 19, 1996, pp. 823–40.

Parker, H. M. D., *Manpower: a study of war-time policy and administration*, London, 1957.

Patterson, Sheila, *Immigrants and race relations in Britain, 1960–67*, London, 1969.

Paul, Kathleen, *Whitewashing Britain: race and citizenship in the postwar era*, Ithaca, 1997.

Peillon, Michel, *Contemporary Irish society: an introduction*, Dublin, 1982.

Pooley, Colin G., 'The Irish in Liverpool, c. 1850–1940', in *Ethnic identity in urban Europe: comparative studies on governments and non-dominant ethnic groups in Europe, 1850–1940*, Vol. 8, ed. Max Engman, Aldershot, 1992, pp. 71–97.

Rex, John, and Moore, Robert, *Race, community, and conflict: a study of Sparkbrook*, London, 1967.

Richmond, Anthony H., *Migration and race relations in an English city: a study of Bristol*, London, 1973.

Robinson, H. W., 'A study of the Church of Ireland population of Ardfert, county Kerry, 1971', *Econ. Soc. Rev.*, Vol. 4, 1974, pp. 93–133.

——*A study of the Church of Ireland population of Ferns Diocese, 1973*, Dublin, n.d. [1974].

Rose, E. J. B. and Deakin, Nicholas, with others, *Colour and citizenship: a report on British race relations*, London, 1969.

Rossiter, Ann, 'Bringing the margins into the centre: a review of aspects of Irish women's emigration', in *Ireland's histories: aspects of state, society and ideology*, ed. Seán Hutton and Paul Stewart, London, 1991, pp. 223–42.

Rudd, Joy, 'Invisible exports: the emigration of Irish women this century', *Women's Studies International Forum*, Vol. 11, 1988, pp. 307–11.

——'The emigration of Irish women', *Social Studies*, Vol. 9, 1987, pp. 3–11.

Ryan, Liam, 'Irish emigration to Britain since World War II', in *Migrations: the Irish at home and abroad*, ed. Richard Kearney, Dublin, 1990, pp. 45–67.

——'Marriage patterns of Irish emigrants in Britain', *Social Studies*, Vol. 3, 1974, pp. 84–8.

——'Religious practise among Irish emigrants', *Social Studies*, Vol. 3, 1974, pp. 218–25.

Ryan, W. J. L., 'Some Irish population problems', *Population Studies*, Vol. 9, 1955, pp. 185–88.

Schrier, Arnold, *Ireland and the American emigration, 1850–1900*, Minneapolis, 1958.

Schweitzer, Pam, ed., *'Across the Irish sea'*, 2nd edn, London, 1991.

Sexton, J. J., Hannan, Damian, Walsh, Brendan M. and McMahon, Dorren, *The eco-*

nomic and social implications of emigration, NESC report no. 90, Dublin, 1991.

Sexton, J. J. and O'Leary, Richard, 'Factors affecting population decline in minority religious communities in the Republic of Ireland', in *Building trust in Ireland: studies commissioned by the Forum for Peace and Reconciliation*, Belfast, 1996, pp. 255–332.

Shuttleworth, Ian, 'Graduate emigration from Ireland: a symptom of peripherality', in *Contemporary Irish migration*, ed. Russell King, GSI special publications no. 6, Dublin, 1991, pp. 3–95.

——'Irish graduate emigration: the mobility of qualified manpower in the context of peripherality', in *Mass migration in Europe: the legacy and the future*, ed. Russell King, London, 1993, pp. 310–26.

Smyth, W. J., 'Irish emigration, 1700–1920', in *European expansion and migration*, ed. P. C. Emmer and Magnus Mörner, Oxford, 1992, pp. 49–78.

Spencer, A. E. C. W., 'Catholics in Britain and Ireland: regional contrasts', in *Demography of immigrants and minority groups in the United Kingdom*, ed. D. A. Coleman, London, 1982, pp. 213–43.

Streib, Gordon, 'Migration and filial bonds: attitudes of Cork farmers and Dublin men', *Ir. J. Agr. Econ. Rur. Soc.*, Vol. 3, 1970, pp. 61–73.

Swift, Roger, *The Irish in Britain, 1815–1914*, London, 1990.

——'The outcast Irish in the British Victorian city: problems and perspectives', *IHS*, Vol. 25, 1987, pp. 264–76.

Swift, Roger and Gilley, Sheridan, eds, *The Irish in Britain, 1815–1939*, London, 1989.

——eds, *The Irish in the Victorian city*, London, 1985.

Travers, Pauric, 'Emigration and gender: the case of Ireland, 1922–60', in *Chattel, servant or citizen: women's status in church, state and society*, ed. Mary O'Dowd and Sabine Wichert, Belfast, 1995, pp. 187–99.

——' "The dream gone bust": Irish responses to emigration, 1922–60', in *Irish-Australian Studies: papers delivered at the fifth Irish Australian conference*, ed. Oliver MacDonagh and W. F. Mandle, Canberra, 1989, pp. 318–42.

——' "There was nothing for me there": Irish female emigration, 1922–71', in *Irish women and Irish migration*, ed. Patrick O'Sullivan, part IV in *The Irish worldwide: history, heritage, identity*, London, 1995, pp. 146–67.

Vaughan, W. E. and Fitzpatrick, A. J., eds, *Irish historical statistics: population 1821–1971*, Dublin, 1978.

Viney, Michael, *The five per cent of Protestants in the Republic*, Dublin, n.d. [1965] [booklet of articles originally published in *Irish Times*, 22–26 March 1965].

Walker, W. W., 'Irish immigrants in Scotland: their priests, politics and parochial life', *Hist. J.*, Vol. 15, 1972, pp. 649–67.

Walsh, B. M., 'A perspective on Irish population patterns', *Éire-Ireland*, Vol. 4, 1969, pp. 3–21.

——'A study of Irish county marriage rates, 1961–1966', *Population Studies*, Vol. 24, 1970, pp. 205–16.

——'An empirical study of the age structure of the Irish population', *Econ. Soc. Rev.*, Vol. 1, 1970, pp. 259–79.

——'Economic and demographic adjustment of the Irish agricultural labour force, 1961–66', *Ir. J. Agr. Econ. Rur. Soc.*, Vol. 3, 1971, pp. 113–24.

——'Expectations, information, and human migration: specifying an econometric model of Irish migration to Britain', *Journal of Regional Science*, Vol. 14, 1974, pp. 107–20.

——*Ireland's changing demographic structure*, Dublin, 1989.

——'Ireland's demographic transformation, 1958–70', *Econ. Soc. Rev.*, Vol. 3, 1972, pp. 251–75.

——'Marriage in Ireland in the twentieth century', in *Marriage in Ireland*, ed. Art Cosgrove, Dublin, 1985, pp. 132–50.

——*Migration to the United Kingdom from Ireland, 1961–66*, ESRI memorandum series no. 70, Dublin, 1970.

——'Population policy in developed countries: Ireland', in *Population policy in developed countries*, ed. Bernard Berelson, New York, 1974, pp. 8–41.

——'Postwar demographic developments in the Republic of Ireland', *Social Studies*, Vol. 1, 1972, pp. 309–17.

——'Recent demographic changes in the Republic of Ireland', *Population Trends*, no. 21, 1980, pp. 3–9.

——*Religion and demographic behaviour in Ireland*, ESRI paper no. 55, Dublin, 1970.

——*Some Irish population problems reconsidered*, ESRI paper no. 42, Dublin, 1968.

——'Trends in the religious composition of the population in the Republic of Ireland, 1946–71', *Econ. Soc. Rev.*, Vol. 6, 1975, pp. 543–55.

Walshaw, R. S., *Migration to and from the British Isles: problems and policies*, London, 1941.

Walter, Bronwen, 'Ethnicity and Irish residential distribution', *Trans. Inst. Brit. Geog.*, new series, Vol. 11, 1986, pp. 131–46.

——*Gender and Irish migration to Britain*, Geography working paper no. 4, School of Geography, Anglia Higher Education College, Cambridge, 1989.

——'Irishness, gender and place', *Environment and planning, part D: society and space*, Vol. 13, 1995, pp. 35–50.

——'The geography of Irish migration to Britain since 1939', *Ir. Econ. & Soc. Hist.*, Vol. 8, 1981, pp. 110–112 [thesis abstract of D Phil. thesis, University of Oxford, 1979].

——'Time-space patterns of second-wave Irish immigration into British towns', *Trans. Inst. Brit. Geog.*, new series, Vol. 5, 1980, pp. 297–317.

——'Tradition and ethnic interaction: second-wave Irish settlement in Luton and Bolton', in *Geography and ethnic pluralism*, ed. Colin Clarke, David Ley and Ceri Peach, London, 1984, pp. 258–83.

Ward, C. K., *Manpower in a developing community: a pilot survey in Drogheda (abridged report)*, Dublin, 1967.

Whelan, B. J. and Hughes, J. G., *A survey of returned and intending emigrants in Ireland*, Dublin, 1976.

White, Jack, *Minority report: the protestant community in the Irish Republic*, Dublin, 1975.

THEORY AND METHODS

Baines, D. E., 'European emigration, 1815–1930: looking at the emigration decision again', *Econ. Hist. Rev.*, 2nd series, Vol. 47, 1994, pp. 525–44.

——'The use of published census data in migration studies', in *Nineteenth-century society: essays in the use of quantitative methods for the study of social data*, ed. E. A. Wrigley, Cambridge, 1972, pp. 311–35.

Barry, Brian, 'Review article: "Exit, voice and loyalty" ', *British Journal of Political Science*, Vol. 4, 1974, pp. 79–107.

Boyd, Monica, 'Family and personal networks in international migration: recent developments and new agendas', *IMR*, Vol. 23, 1989, pp. 638–70.

Finer, S. E., 'State-building, state boundaries and border control', *Social Science Information*, Vol. 13, 1974, pp. 79–126.

Griffin, Keith, 'On the emigration of the peasantry', *World Development*, Vol. 4, 1976, pp. 353–61.

Harris, J. R. and Todaro, M. P., 'Migration, unemployment and development: a two-sector analysis', *American Economic Review*, Vol. 60, 1970, pp. 126–42.

Hirschman, A. O., *Essays in trespassing: economics to politics and beyond*, Cambridge, 1981.

——*Exit, voice and loyalty: responses to decline in firms, organizations and states*, Cambridge, Mass., 1970.

Holmes, Colin, 'Historians and immigration', in *Migrants, emigrants and immigrants: a social history of migration*, ed. Colin Pooley and Ian Whyte, London, 1991, pp. 191–207.

Jackson, J. A., *Migration*, London, 1986.

——ed., *Migration*, Cambridge, 1969.

Kritz, Mary M., Keely, Charles B., and Tomasi, Silvano M., eds, *Global trends in migration: theory and research on international population movements*, New York, 1981.

Kritz, Mary M., Lim, Lin Lean, and Zlotnik, Hania, eds, *International migration systems: a global approach*, Oxford, 1992.

Kuhnle, Stein, 'Emigration, democratization and the rise of the European welfare states', in *Mobilisation, center-periphery structures and nation-building*, ed. Per Torsvik, Bergen, 1981, pp. 501–23.

Massey, Douglas S., Arango, Joaquín, Hugo, Graeme, Kouaochi, Ali, Pellegrino, Adela and Taylor, J. Edward, 'Theories of international migration: a review and appraisal', *Population and Development Review*, Vol. 19, 1993, pp. 431–66.

Petras, Elizabeth, 'The role of national boundaries in a cross-national labour market', *International Journal of Urban and Regional Research*, Vol. 4, 1980, pp. 157–95.

Ravenstein, E. G., 'The laws of migration', *JRSS*, Vol. 48, 1885, pp. 167–227; Vol. 52, 1889, pp. 214–301.

Stark, Oded, *The migration of labour*, Oxford, 1991.

Todaro, M. P., 'A model of labor migration and urban unemployment in less developed countries', *American Economic Review*, Vol. 59, 1969, pp. 138–48.

Van den Broeck, Julien, ed., *The economics of labour migration*, Cheltenham, 1996.

Zolberg, A. R., 'The next waves: migration theory for a changing world', *IMR*, Vol. 23, 1989, pp. 403–29.

COMPARATIVE STUDIES

Baines, Dudley, *Emigration from Europe, 1815–1930*, London, 1991.

Black, Richard, 'Migration, return and agricultural development in the Serra do Alvão, northern Portugal', *Economic Development and Cultural Change*, Vol. 41, 1993, pp. 563–85.

Brettell, Caroline B., 'Emigrar para voltar: a Portuguese ideology of return migration', *Papers in Anthropology*, Vol. 20, 1979, pp. 1–20.

——*Men who migrate, women who wait: population and history in a Portuguese parish*, Princeton, 1987.

Buechler, Hans Christian and Buechler, Judith-Maria, eds, *Migrants in Europe: the role of family, labor, and politics*, New York, 1987.

Castles, Stephen, Booth, Heather and Wallace, Tina, *Here for good: western Europe's new ethnic minorities*, London, 1984.

Castles, Stephen, and Kosack, Godula, *Immigrant workers and class structure in western Europe*, 2nd edn, Oxford, 1985.

Castles, Stephen and Miller, M. J., *The age of migration: international population movements in the modern world*, 2nd edn, London, 1999.

Cohen, Robin, ed., *The Cambridge survey of world migration*, Cambridge, 1995.

Collinson, Sarah, *Europe and international migration*, London, 1993.

Delia, E. P., 'The determinants of modern Maltese emigration', *International Migration*, Vol. 20, 1982, pp. 11–25.

Entzinger, Han, 'Return migration in western Europe', *International Migration*, Vol. 23, 1985, pp. 263–90.

Ferreira de Paiva, Amadeu, 'Portuguese migration studies', *IMR*, Vol. 17, 1983, pp. 138–47.

Hatton, T. J. and Williamson, J. G., eds, *Migration and the international labour market, 1850–1939*, London, 1994.

Hudson, Ray and Lewis, Jim, eds, *Uneven development in southern Europe*, London, 1985.

Jackson, Marvin R., 'Comparing the Balkan demographic experience, 1860 to 1970', *J. Euro. Econ. Hist.*, Vol. 14, 1985, pp. 223–72.

Jones, Huw, 'Modern migration from Malta', *Trans. Inst. Brit. Geog.*, Vol. 60, 1973, pp. 101–19.

Kindleberger, C. P., *Europe's postwar growth: the role of labour supply*, London, 1967.

King, Russell, 'Population mobility: emigration, return migration and internal migration', in *Southern Europe transformed: political and economic change in Greece, Italy, Portugal and Spain*, ed. Allan Williams, London, 1984, pp. 145–78.

——'Return migration: a review of some case studies from Europe', *Mediterranean Studies*, Vol. 1, 1979, pp. 3–30.

——ed., *Mass migration in Europe: the legacy and the future*, London, 1993.

——ed., *Return migration and regional economic problems*, London, 1986.

——ed., *The new geography of European migrations*, London, 1993.

Krane, Ronald E., ed., *International labour migration in Europe*, New York, 1979.

Kubat, Daniel, ed., *The politics of migration policies*, New York, 1979.

——ed., *The politics of return: international return migration in Europe*, Rome, 1984.

Lewis, J. R. and Williams, A. M., 'Regional uneven development on the European periphery: the case of Portugal', *Tijdschrift voor Economische en Sociale Geografie*, Vol. 72, 1981, pp. 81–98.

Livi Bacci, Massimo, ed., *The demographic and social pattern of emigration from the southern European countries*, Florence, 1972.

MacDonald, J. S., 'Agricultural organisation, migration and labour militancy in rural Italy, 1902–13', *Econ. Hist. Rev.*, 2nd series, Vol. 16, 1963–64, pp. 61–75.

——'Italy's rural social structure and emigration', *Occidente*, Vol. 12, 1956, pp. 437–65.

Martin, Philip, *The unfinished story: Turkish labour migration to western Europe*, Geneva, 1991.

Paine, Suzanne, *Exporting workers: the Turkish case*, Cambridge, 1974.

Pooley, Colin G., 'The role of migration in the development of non-dominant ethnic groups in Europe', in *Ethnic identity in urban Europe: comparative studies on governments and non-dominant ethnic groups in Europe, 1850–1940*, Vol. 8, ed. Max Engman, Aldershot, 1992, pp. 359–73.

Reis, Manuela and Gil Nave, Joaquim, 'Emigrating peasants and returning emigrants: emigration with return in a Portuguese village', *Sociologia Ruralis*, Vol. 26, 1986, pp. 20–34.

Rogers, Rosemary, ed., *Come to stay: the effects of European labour migration on sending and receiving countries*, Boulder, 1986.

Rowland, Robert, 'Demographic patterns and rural society in Portugal', *Sociologia Ruralis*, Vol. 26, 1986, pp. 48–69.

Salt, John and Clout, Hugh, eds, *Migration in postwar Europe: geographical essays*, London, 1976.

Scott, Franklin D., 'The study of the effects of emigration', *Scan. Econ. Hist. Rev.*, Vol. 3, 1960, pp. 161–74.

Williams, Allan, ed., *Southern Europe transformed: political and economic change in Greece, Italy, Portugal and Spain*, London, 1984.

UNPUBLISHED THESES

Burnett, Nicholas R., 'Emigration and modern Ireland', unpub. PhD dissertation, School of Advanced International Studies, The Johns Hopkins University, 1976.

Walter, Bronwen, 'The geography of Irish migration to Britain since 1939 with special reference to Luton and Bolton', unpub. DPhil. thesis, University of Oxford, 1979.

Index

British Nationality Act (1948) 209, 265

Brown, Stephen J. 85

Browne, Michael 135

Browne, Noël 192, 253

Bruce, Steve 85

Canada
  Irish in 29
  see also migration

Cardiff 144

Carlow, county 52, 178, 181

Carr–Saunders, A. M. 88–89

Catholic church
  female migration and 66–68, 134–35, 188–89
  Irish in Britain and 66–69, 141, 258–59, 293
  migration and 4, 64, 65–69, 134–35, 188–89, 191–92, 201–2, 213, 258–59, 293
  position of in Irish Free State 74–76

Catholic emancipation centenary (1929) 74

Catholic Social Welfare Bureau 134

Cavan, county 38, 50, 73, 113, 161, 166, 228, 233, 236–39

censorship
  during Second World War 120, 124, 148

Central Bank of Ireland 260

Central Statistics Office 196–97, 230, 253–54, 262

children's allowances 41

Christus Rex 261

churches
  migration and 1
  see also Baptists; Catholic Church; Church of Ireland; Methodists; Presbyterians; Protestants; religious denomination

Church of Ireland 70, 71, 80, 250, 251, 252
  Commission for Sparsely Populated Areas (1956–64) 251
  General Synod of 83, 251
  see also Protestants; religious denomination

Church of Ireland Gazette 70, 75 *passim*

Church of Scotland
  General Assembly of 85

civil war (1922–23) 38, 42, 70, 73, 96

Clann na Poblachta 190, 191, 202

Clare, county 27, 50, 53, 54, 73, 113, 161, 166, 172, 178, 233, 269, 273

Clynes, J. R. 90

cohort depletion 3, 23, 78, 165, 232, 236, 241, 249, 250

Commins, Patrick 246

Commission for Sparsely Populated Areas (1956–64) *see* Church of Ireland

Commission on Banking, Currency and Credit (1934–38) 199

Commission on Emigration and Other Population Problems (1948–54) 3, 4, 40, 44, 48, 49, 50, 115, 168–69, 174, 175, 180, 189–92, 197–201, 203, 205, 206, 211, 212, 213, 234–35, 243, 247, 294, 296
  see also entries for members: Beddy, J. P.; De Blacam, Aodh; Duncan, G. A; Lucey, Cornelius; Marsh, Arnold; McCarthy, M. D.; Meenan, James; O'Donnell, Peadar

Commission on Higher Education (1960–67) 259

122–24, 126, 127, 150, 172,
196, 203
statistics 253
unionism
southern 74
Ulster 74
University College, Cork 259
University College, Dublin 190, 260
United States
immigration restrictions 43–44
Irish in 29
see also migration

wage levels 51–52, 113, 138, 172,
176, 180–81, 193–94, 198,
212, 238, 241, 246, 257, 290,
295
see also employment; standards of
living; unemployment
Wall Street Crash (1929) 43
Walsh, Brendan M. 165, 227, 229,

230, 232, 234, 248, 249, 250,
272–73
Walsh, Joseph 189, 191
Walshaw, R. S. 45
Walshe, Joseph 67
Walter, Bronwen 84, 270
War Office 149
Waterford, county 52, 131
Watters, Brian 140
Westmeath, county 52, 70, 73, 174
Wexford, county 52, 176, 251
Whitaker, T. K. 205, 227, 255
White, Jack 78
Whyte, J. H. 75
Wicklow, county 52, 131, 141, 166,
233, 253
Williamson, Jeffrey G. 10
Wolverhampton 194

Young Christian Workers'
Association 193